tended to be younger than Marvel's - Stan Lee's firm courted the young adult, college student and even older reader -- but as the seventies sped along DC saw the lettering on the comic panel and wisely followed suit. Much of DC's work wasn't as bad as suggested by "Marvel Maniacs," but it was still operating by silver age standards for quite some time.

Superhuman is a loving tribute to the comics of the seventies and early eighties, detailing all major superhero series, the most memorable issues, talented writers, and skilled artists. This is volume one of a two volume set.

CHAPTER ONE: BATMAN

-- *DETECTIVE COMICS*, MAN-HUNTER, BATGIRL, CATWOMAN

As Batman entered the bronze age, he did so without a partner, as an adult Robin (Dick Grayson) had gone off to college to have his own adventures. In his Bruce Wayne identity, Batman helped form an organization to provide succor to society's many victims. A "new look" - larger panels and more dynamic artwork - had been instituted as well. The Batcave and Wayne Manor had been phased out except for special occasions. Irv Novick was the penciller and his work was often very good, especially when inked by Dick Giordano. A story of a tenement fire in *Batman* 221 features a striking full-page panel of the dark knight flying out of a fiery building with a young boy in his arms. Batman appeared in *Detective Comics*, where his deductive abilities came into play, as well as his own series.

There were murder mysteries in Batman, as well as other kinds of intrigue. In *Batman* 221 a scientist develops a formula to turn normally docile animals into slavering horrors, pits a slew of mutated bats against their namesake, and finally succumbs to the ravenous advances of a snarling little lamb. Frank Robbins' "Dead ... Til Proven Alive" in *Batman* 222 took its cue from the early 1970's obsession on college campuses which had fans listening to Beatles records hoping to find clues to the alleged death of Paul McCartney. In Robbins' story, in which the boy wonder took part, it develops that it was the other three members of an all-male rock band that died while the fourth, who'd hired lookalikes, tried to hide the deception by starting the rumor that he'd been the one to expire. *Batman* 229 introduced a cult of evil "Futurians" who could supposedly see things that others could not, and who became convinced that Batman was not only one of them, but their leader, until he attacked them and brought them to justice.

Batman also had his share of unusual antagonists in the bronze age. "Three-Eyed" Reardon - the third eye was a hollow in his forehead caused by a wound - was a Viet Nam vet and security guard who got in the way of a bomb Batman was trying to snuff, and blamed the detective for his subsequent blindness. A doctor experiments on Reardon, reconnecting his optic nerves to the sensory cells in his fingertips, so he gets five new eyes at the end of each hand and tries to kill the man he irrationally hates above all [*Batman* 226]. In *Batman* 231 Reardon hijacks a plane, insists Batman trade himself for his hostages, and battles him in a booby-trapped jungle in Viet Nam, but still can't defeat him. Reardon next appeared in *Man-Bat* 2.

The Joker finally made his first bronze age appearance in *Batman* 251. The Crown Prince of Crime has escaped from an Institute for the Criminally Insane and is killing off his former gang members. Only one of the men betrayed the Joker, but since he doesn't know which one of them it was he just murders them all in various violent ways. Batman is always one step behind, and some of the gunsels don't even believe his story of the Joker's vengeance and the offer of protective custody and just think he wants to lock them up. The Joker gives one former associate a cigar, and the fellow assumes it must be a gag cigar that will explode in his face. Instead it is full of nitroglycerine and blows the whole room up. "Rest in Pieces," the Joker says. At the climax Batman winds up in chains and is thrown into a huge tank with a hungry shark, but manages to kill the shark, save the last confederate who is in the tank with him, and capture the Joker, who nearly makes his getaway but trips on an oil slick. "To think that you would make me grateful for pollution," Batman tells his nemesis. Beautifully drawn by Neal Adams and with a terrific script by Denny O'Neill, "The Joker's Five-Way Revenge" is a certified classic.

Robin's back-up stories, which later were shifted to *Detective* and then *Batman Family*, and back to *Detective*, were generally written in this period by Mike Friedrich [later Bob Rozakis] and contained topical themes of student unrest and references to the Students for a Democratic Society, agents provocateur, Jesus Freaks, and the shootings at Kent State. *Batman* 235 - 237 had an intelligent three-parter wherein Robin pursues a man who shot a cop to a commune that has its own rules and regulations. The story explores the differing attitudes towards "hippies" during this period, and presents the p.o.v. of both law and order types and long-haired radicals.

The Spook

Batman 434 introduced a brand new Bat-foe in The Spook, who can seemingly walk through walls and spirit convicts out of their prison cells for a price. The Spook has an HQ similar to the Bat Cave where he can keep track of all of his clients, who can call on his services just by tapping the sides of the special eyeglasses he gives them. During his first encounter with Batman, the Spook manages not only to escape with two hoodlums, but inexplicably spirits away the batmobile, which somehow winds up in police custody with the Spook's calling card, a doll of himself, on the seat inside. In the following issue Batman substitutes himself for a recaptured thug in prison in the hopes of getting his hands on the Spook, but when the villain shows up he already knows that the prisoner is Batman in disguise. Worse, the Spook isn't really the Spook but a hypnotized guard with a two-way radio taped over his mouth. Meanwhile, the real prisoner has been spirited away by the Spook.

Batman discovers that the Spook has access to tunnels under the prison, that his HQ is in an abandoned area of the Gotham subway system, and that he stole the batmobile via clever mechanical trickery. He also discovers that the Spook is no ghost when he finally captures him and brings him to Commissioner Gordon, only to learn that the Spook's fingerprints reveal him to be a man who was executed ten years before. In *Batman* 252 the Spook escapes and Batman digs up his grave, to find another one of his dolls even as the real Spook sneaks up behind him and buries him alive. (Batman turns out to be private investigator Jason Bard in disguise, giving the real Batman a helping hand.) The true Batman follows the Spook to his new HQ, an abandoned prison on an island where the criminal supposedly died in the electric chair, and learns that a hypnotized double died in his stead. Batman manages to outwit and defeat his wily foe. Frank Robbins' scripts for these issues were excellent and the Spook a highly memorable creation.

Julius Schwartz brought back a golden and silver age writer named David V. Reed, who'd done many Batman stories in the fifties and sixties, to do scripts for Batman, and he mostly eschewed costumed foes for mysteries with weird but non-super-powered antagonists. Reed used Bruce Wayne more often than other writers, although his characterization was minimal. (Wayne had developed a somewhat sexier appearance as drawn by Ernie Chua and Tex Blaisdell, somewhat reminiscent of Kubert's Hawkman.) He did a Dashiell Hammett homage for *Batman* 269 in which men turn up dead all with the same name card on their persons, and in the following issue scripted another mystery in which future deaths are announced by the appearance of a fiery skull. In *Batman* 272 he introduced an Underworld Olympics, a competition between criminals from many different countries that will take place in Gotham City - it was a good idea, but it was stretched out for four uninteresting issues. He brought back the Spook for one more go-round in *Batman* 276, but this didn't compare favorably with the character's earlier appearances. The Spook also appeared in a somewhat better tale in Batman 304.

Reed was at his best, however, with an excellent three-part

story that appeared in *Batman* 281 - 283, which starts with three agents being murdered in a hit and run, has Batman globe-trotting trying to find out why they were killed, and ends with the Crusader learning that Gotham is to be subjected to nuclear blackmail and that he is being used as a pawn even as he investigates. The story was action-packed and highly suspenseful, yet also intricate, clever, and completely absorbing, and Ernie Chua's art looked better than ever with Chua also doing inks.

Reed also came up with a winner with "The Sign of the Skull" in *Batman* 289 - 290, a tale of Cosmo "Skull" Dugger, a strange man who suffers from anhedonia, the incapacity to experience joy. Dugger uses a special beam from a machine he invented to secretly probe and record the minds of people at their happiest moments - an athlete winning the big game, an actor who's finally won the Oscar, a man who wins the lottery - sucking away their joy and leaving them stone cold dead with the odd marking of a skull on their foreheads. Batman breaks into Dugger's home, discovers his recorder, puts it on, and is subjected to a devastating feedback that causes him to feel anguish and pain whenever he does something that would normally give him pleasure, severely curtailing his heroic abilities. In the second part of the story Batman enlists the unconscious aid of jailed foe Dr. Tzin Tzin to help him regain his sense of joy, and then puts paid to Cosmo Dugger.

After an amusing Mad Hatter story and a series over several issues in which criminals convene a hearing to find out who murdered Batman (who is actually disguised as one of them), Reed also scripted an excellent 34-page tale, "The Last Batman Story" (with art by Simonson and Giordano) for the double-sized *Batman* 300. In a future age when there is much mechanization, as well as such things as hospitals on space stations, a graying Batman and adult, married Robin track down a sinister international organization called Spectrum that is trying to kill a female investigator via assassins who wear different colors of the rainbow. The two leaders of the group use a mes-

merizing drug on their lieutenants, and work out of a spe-
cially-rigged room that explodes if one of them tries to double-
cross or run out on the other. The dynamic duo use much more
technology in their search for the group than usual, and at the
end Batman ponders hanging up his cape, getting married, and
running for governor.

A few issues of *Batman*, such as 304, were instantly dispos-
able; Reed's lead story, in which a blow to the head has Batman
carrying out his night duties while dressed as Bruce Wayne,
and walking around by day in his Batman uniform doing what
Wayne would do, might have worked in the silver age, but it
was a bronze age disaster. Denny O' Neill's back-up - the first in
a series of "unsolved cases" - was equally poor, as it has the Batman (who has always been deeply offended by the crime of
murder) covering up for a murderer because he did good works
later in life even though the man is dead and can't possibly
suffer for his actions in youth.

Len Wein took over as writer with *Batman* 307 and had an
auspicious debut with "Dark Messenger of Death" wherein Batman takes after an unknown man who's mercy-killing the forgotten homeless. John Calnan continued as the main artist; his
work was rarely exciting but inker Dick Giordano often made it
look pretty good. In a few issues Irv Novick came back on as
penciller. Wein added regular supporting characters, such as
Lucius Fox, an African-American man who was Wayne Industries' second-in-command; and Selina Kyle, a purportedly reformed Catwoman, as well as continuing sub-plots pertaining
to them. He brought back Mr. Freeze in an intriguing tale in
Batman 308 but a story with silver age foe the Blockbuster in
the following issue was much less successful, and suffered
from poor Calnan/McLaughlin art. Batman teamed with Batgirl in a story by Steve Englehart for the first time in a decade
in *Batman* 311. Julius Schwartz continued to edit the Superman line of comics, but he left Batman - as well as *Detective* and
The Brave and the Bold - and was replaced by Paul Levitz. Levitz'
plan was to use costumed foes of all kinds in *Batman*, and focus

on mystery-detective tales, appropriately enough, in *Detective*, as well as pay more attention to continuity in the Marvel manner.

Wein scripted an interesting encounter between Batman and Hawkman's old foe, the Gentleman Ghost, and brought back such almost-forgotten baddies as Calender Man and Kite-Man. The Ghost returned in *Batman* 319, and continued to confound Batman as to whether or not he was a true ghost, which Batman simply wouldn't countenance despite his knowledge of supernatural characters such as Deadman. A new foe, Firebug [*Batman* 318], was somewhat similar to Iron Man's foe Firebrand, but has different motivations. He burns down the buildings in which his family members had been killed due to bad construction and other problems. The romance between Bruce and Selina isn't helped when Lucius Fox has the surprisingly poor judgment to tell Selina that Wayne has had her investigated. Lucius has his own problems when his son gets in with a bad crowd.

In some rather unlikely developments Catwoman discovers that she has a fatal illness only rare Egyptian herbs can cure and just happens upon an exhibit featuring urns that may contain exactly what she needs. When the urns are stolen, Catwoman is the logical suspect, but the true culprit turns out to be the silver age Cat-Man, who traps Batman and the now-costumed Catwoman in a deadly web that threatens to tear them apart. Cat-Man and the urns are destroyed in a geyser, but Catwoman's disease goes into remission. She believes it's because Cat-Man's costume, of which she has a piece, was rumored to give him nine lives, but Batman isn't convinced [*Batman* 323 - 324]. Although Bruce has fallen in love with Selina, she leaves him and Gotham in *Batman* 326, citing his lack of trust in her and her need to find herself.

Marv Wolfman briefly took over as scripter with an interesting Two-Face tale in *Batman* 328 - 329. *Batman* 331 introduced the Electrocutioner, a murderous vigilante who literally fries criminals who have eluded justice. He later appeared in *Vigi-*

lante in the copper age. Then there's the problem of Gregorian Falstaff, a corpulent rival of Wayne's who resembles Shakespeare's character in appearance only, and who is out to ruin Wayne and take over his business interests, although he is only the front for a much more dangerous antagonist. "The Lazarus Affair" revealed this villain in a four-part story in *Batman* 332 - 335.

Then Roy Thomas began his tenure with a fine story (plotted by Bob Rozakis) in which the Monarch of Menace takes advantage of Batman's recent adventures abroad during the Lazarus Affair to proclaim that the missing hero is his captive, and all of Gotham's criminals must continue to pay him a percentage of their loot to keep him that way - but then Batman shows up foot-loose and fancy free (*Batman* 336). *Batman* 337 introduced Snowman, who was the son of a human mother and a Yeti, and who flash-freezes anyone who gets in his way. Batman seems more sympathetic to him than he does to his victims, and it is also strange that he appears to be so surprised and perplexed by frozen corpses when he had already fought more than one icy antagonist over the decades. Gerry Conway scripted the tale with a plot assist from Thomas. The same issue introduced a new Robin back-up series in which he joins up with a circus and rediscovers his roots. Dick leaves the circus and makes his way back to Gotham, stopping to deal with a group of Devil worshippers along the way.

There were several sub-plots running through the bat-stories. Poison Ivy uses her special lipstick to hypnotize prominent men, including Bruce Wayne, into signing over their assets; the poison prevents Batman from even telling anyone about it [339]. It wasn't until *Batman* 344 that Batman is finally able to expose the woman's scheme not long after she walks out of the Wayne Industry offices with a massive check. Boss Thorne resurfaces in Gotham City and backs his own mayoral candidate, while Commissioner Gordon is under great strain due to attacks on his competency by another candidate, Hamilton Hill. Batman and Robin are reunited and become a team once again in *Batman* 344. Bruce decides to give up running the Wayne foundation and just continue his activities as Batman so he can get more sleep.

By now continuity between Batman and Detective had been established, with some stories beginning in one title and ending in another.

Detective

Detective 400 introduced a new Bat-character for the Caped Crusader: Museum worker Kirk Langstrom, who injects himself with gland extracts from bats and turns into a hideous Man-Bat. He winds up helping Batman in his battle against a black-out gang who wear special goggles to see in the dark when they rob the museum, and Batman is glad to have a new ally. Unfortunately, Langstrom's grotesque appearance is an unexpected and unwanted side effect, and he is horrified by this development. Although Langstrom is thrilled to be fighting side by side with his idol, Batman isn't certain if Man-Bat will ultimately prove friend or foe. Man-Bat was back two issues later, mutating even further by developing wings, and almost losing his mind with terror at the thought of his mutation becoming permanent, as Batman struggles to cook up an antidote for his condition in the bat cave. Man-Bat, now so crazy that he likes being a "bat-man" even more than the Batman, escapes before Batman can administer the antidote. He returns in *Detective* 407, where Batman pulls off his human mask just as he's about to marry his fiancee, Francine. It develops that Kirk has given the desperately-in-love woman the same bat-glands and now she's become a bat-human hybrid as well. This time Batman manages to give both of them the antidote and things return to normal - for a time.

Man-Bat returned in a wild story appropriately entitled "Man-Bat Madness" in *Detective* 416, both written and drawn by Frank Robbins. Kirk and Francine are happily married but certain influences cause Langstrom to resume experimentation with bats. The couple carry the antidote with them at all times just in case one of them has a "flashback," but when this happens to Kirk at the opera, the soprano's high C smashes the vial and he completely reverts to his old crazy self. Batman pursues Man-Bat into the subways where his actions nearly cause a tragedy until Batman gets through to his humanity and he helps some trapped passengers get to the surface. At the Langstrom's home, Kirk plans to imbibe a formula which will make him a permanent Man-Bat, but Batman manages to substitute the new antidote just in time. While Robbins' somewhat scratchy-looking art was a far cry from Neal Adams' and even Irv Novick's and couldn't exactly be called pretty, it was well-composed and laid out and overall quite effective.

Man-Bat returned in *Detective* 429, which was set in Las Vegas where a huge vampire bat mutation has drained the blood of a man, killing him. Batman suspects Man-Bat, especially when he learns that Kirk Langstrom is experimenting in the area. But the monster turns out to be Francine, who mutated after being bitten by an hitherto unknown species of vampire bat. The two men manage to capture Francine and take her to a hospital for a complete transfusion. A bit of black humor has Kirk offering his own blood for the transfusion, which would probably have turned his wife into a three-headed bat-dragon! Frank Robbins also did both story and art for this flat-out horror story which is creepy and exciting in equal measure. In his next appearance in *Batman* 254 Langstrom has mastered the ability to turn back and forth from Man-Bat to human and decides to try his hand at becoming a super-hero. Man-Bat's next appearance was in *The Brave and the Bold* 119 wherein he and Batman team up to bring a hit man to justice. Then he starred in his own short-lived magazine, more of which later.

Detective 405 introduced the League of Assassins in an exciting story wherein Batman is chosen to protect a shipping magnate on his boat after fifteen other magnates before him have been murdered. It leads to Batman squaring off with a deadly trained assassin on an island after dolphins armed with explosives blow up the boat and the survivors are forced to take refuge. Batman defeats the assassin, but realizes that his boss was hiding on the island and has escaped. In the following issue he is revealed as a sinister if unimpressive figure named Dr. Darrk, who escapes again after bringing another assassin to a castle to kill off a count. In *Detective* 408 the League employs minor silver age foe Dr. Tzin Tzin in an attempt to destroy Batman and Robin but he fails. *Detective* 411 introduced two characters who would become an important part of the Batman mythos, Ra's al Ghul ["The Demon's Head" in Arabic] - who is only referred to in this issue - and his daughter, Talia, who has been kidnapped by Dr. Darrk and who kills him to save Batman's life.

Ra's al Ghul

Ra's al Ghul made his first official appearance in *Batman* 232, where he learns the identity of the caped crusader by figuring who's bought the kind of equipment the Batman would need, and makes his way into the batcave where he confronts the startled hero. He wants Batman's help in saving the lives of both Robin and his daughter, both of whom have been kidnapped by an evil brotherhood. But Batman uncovers the fact that Ghul is actually behind everything and that only Robin was a kidnap victim. Ghul manipulated the whole business simply to take measure of Batman, because Talia has fallen in love with him. When father and daughter reappeared in *Batman* 240 it finally dawns on the hero that "the demon's head" is pretty much a bad guy and had only hoped to enlist his aid in controlling the world.

Beginning with *Batman* 242, Batman decides to wage war on Ghul, enlisting the aid of a Black scientist named Dr. Blaine; one of Ghul's assassins, Ling, whose life Batman saved; and a dead hit man named Matches Malone whom Batman impersonates. Batman also goes so far as to fake Bruce Wayne's death in a plane crash so he can concentrate on his mission, and so that Ghul, who knows his secret i.d., won't know what he's up to in either identity. A champion skier named Molly joins the group in the following issue, in which they penetrate Ghul's mountain HQ only to learn that the demon is deceased. But

Ghul periodically revives himself with a bath in the Lazarus Pit, and he's full of vim and vigor just a few pages later. In *Batman* 244 Ghul and Batman have a duel to the death, which Batman would have lost due to an ill-timed scorpion's bite were it not for the loving interference of Talia. Batman takes Ghul off to jail after he and Talia share one very sexy kiss. While Denny O'Neal's scripts had a few holes in them, the Adams-Giordano artwork was terrific, as it was for *Batman* 245, in which Batman solves the "murder" of Bruce Wayne and brings him back into the fold.

Then Batman and Robin nearly split up when the former agrees to let Talia al Ghul - a criminal, as Robin puts it—stay with them, although it's a bit bizarre that Robin eventually turns to another villainess (however reformed), Catwoman, for advice. Batman had another fight to the death with Ra's al Ghul in *Batman* 332 - 335, "The Lazarus Affair," a four-part story in which it is revealed that the "late" Ra's al Gul is behind all of Bruce Wayne's business troubles and more. Talia turns out to be nearly as old as her father, who gives his daughter treatments to keep her young. Despite that she generally takes Batman's side in his struggles against her father. Ra's al Ghul falls into the Lazarus Pit, which under other conditions would merely keep him young, and turns into a fiery horror that nearly kills the Caped Crusader before expiring. But Ra's al Ghul never stayed dead for long.

A Vow from the Grave

Detective 410 featured one of the best Batman stories ever published in the bronze age or any other period, "A Vow from the Grave," beautifully written by Denny O'Neill and with evocative illustrations by Neal Adams and Dick Giordano, who seemed especially inspired by the violent but poignant story. Batman is pursuing a dangerous death row escapee, Kano Wiggins, when he comes across a stranded troupe of sideshow freaks, including Bones, a living skeleton, Maud, the fat woman, a strongman named Goliath, and a little boy named Flippy who has flippers instead of arms and legs. When Bones is murdered, everyone assumes Wiggins did the foul deed, but Batman makes some deductions, and little Flippy, who is mute, draws certain provocative pictures in the dust. Goliath wanted Maud for himself and tries to kill Flippy, who saw him commit the murder, but Batman intervenes and saves the boy even as Goliath and Wiggins try to smash him. The art imbues each face with palpable emotion, and there is an especially expressive panel showing Goliath holding up the frail little boy whom life has treated so unfairly and telling him why he has to kill him. Human interest stories of this type - although there was a mystery and plenty of action as well - didn't always work for Batman, but this very memorable story certainly did.

Meanwhile Batgirl had a back-up series in *Detective* that ran for a few issues. There had been an earlier Bat-Girl who appeared in comics in the silver age, then the new Batgirl was created for the *Batman* TV show and carried over to the comics. In a two-part story in *Detective* 396 - 397 she joins a dating service to find out which man is murdering red-headed women and learns that the killer is not one of her homely dates but rather a handsome devil who wears various ugly masks. Gil Kane and Vince Colletta provided some nice art for the earlier stories, then Don Heck did the same for the rest. *Detective* 410 - 411 featured a lively story in which Batgirl winds up tied to a pattern-cutting machine that nearly dismembers her and then saves the life of "the world's best-dressed woman" who is targeted for murder simply because she makes the wrong fashion decision. *Detective* 412 - 413 featured an excellent tale by Frank Robbins in which Batgirl goes up against a male-female pair of evil criminals with a unique and sick plot; they are wig-makers whose wigs for wealthy women contain a special mesh that can literally squeeze and crack a woman's head via remote control if she doesn't agree to pay their extortion demands.

During a two-part story in *Detective* 416 - 417, when a phony Batgirl tries to get Commissioner Gordon to finger the wrong suspect in a cop-killing, Gordon realizes that his daughter is the "dominoed dare-doll," as she was occasionally referred to, though whether it's because Barbara's breathing is too fast for someone who was supposed to have been home sleeping all night or because she slips and calls him "dad" while in costume, or both, isn't quite certain. In any case, she reveals her identity to him in *Detective* 422 when she decides to run for Congress, deciding that she can ultimately do more to fight crime that way than just by arresting people as Batgirl. *Detective* 424 presented "Batgirl's Last Case" as Barbara Gordon - after some difficulties - wins the election and flies away from Gotham and to Washington DC at the end of the story. The next issue of *Detective* had a back-up series devoted to her boyfriend, criminologist Jason Bard. This wasn't the end of Batgirl, however. She was an ill-conceived, one-dimensional and rather lifeless character who should have stayed back in the sixties, but as we shall see, she had some staying power.

"The Master Crime File of Jason Bard" debuted in the back of *Detective* 425. Bard was a lanky Viet Nam vet who used a cane and opened up shop as a private investigator. In his first solo adventure he figures out that a psychiatrist was not killed by one of his patients, a mentally-disturbed veteran, but by his secretary, who was using the shrink's files to blackmail his patients. "Case of the Dead-On Target" in *Detective* 435 presented the mystery of a daredevil parachute jumper who falls to his death, but lands with a knife in his back, as Jason has to figure out which of his fellow jumpers murdered him in mid-air. Jason Bard's stories alternated with adventures of the Elongated Man, Hawkman, and the Atom, always centering on one kind of mystery or another.

Manhunter

Archie Goodwin took over as editor from Julie Schwartz with *Detective* 437 because slipping sales dictated that a fresh vision might be advisable. Schwartz, with Bob Rozakis and E. Nelson Bridwell as his assistants, continued as the official editor on *Batman*, which entered an especially uninspired period at about the same time, although old villains like Catwoman and the Penguin were brought back (and may have been part of the problem). In the meantime Goodwin hired Jim Aparo to draw the lead Batman story and Walt Simsonson to do the Manhunter back-up, and wrote the scripts for both features himself; he also brought back the original logo. In his first story Goodwin had Batman deciding to make Bruce Wayne act like a coward, an idea that didn't please the fans and was immediately dropped. Both *Batman* and *Detective* became 100 page giants with extra reprint material. Jim Aparo's tenure on the title was only about two issues.

The Manhunter strip was a variation of the old Simon and Kirby character, Paul Kirk. In the first installment an Interpol agent named Christine St. Clair searches for Kirk in the Himalayas, and speaks to an elderly cloaked man named Haj. She relates the story of how Kirk saved a man from assassins, the strange thing being that all of them had Kirk's face. When she leaves, Haj throws off his cloak - and reveals Manhunter, clad in his blue and red uniform. *Detective* 439 - 440 revealed that this Manhunter was indeed the original Paul Kirk, but that he had been brought back to life after twenty-five years of experimentation and rejuvenation after being killed not long after WW2. This was done by a group of scientists headed by a man that Kirk had once saved from the Nazis, Dr, Mykros. "The Council," as it is called, wants to "save the human race from itself" but to keep the peace they have a group of enforcers, all of whom were cloned from the cells of Paul's body. Unfortunately, the members of the council have become corrupt and egomaniacal, and order Kirk to murder an Interpol agent, Christine's boss, Nostrand. Kirk instead warns the man, who turns out already to be working for the council; Kirk's mission was a test. Before dying during an attempt to kill Manhunter, Nostrand puts him and Christine on the Most Wanted list. Now the two of them are pursued by Interpol as well as a legion of Paul Kirk lookalikes!

In a clever installment in *Detective* 441 Manhunter and Christine's spying on a gathering of the council in a cathedral in Istanbul is intercut with a couple of tourists and their little boy exploring said cathedral without a clue as to what's really going on. In later developments Christine learns that her own father is a member of the council, but she and Kirk gain an ally in Asano Nitobe, who trained Kirk and who was loyal to the council until he learns they murdered his patron. Walt Simonson's unusual art got better with each installment, although it still lacked a certain polish that an experienced inker might have provided. The short-lived Manhunter series had perhaps too wild a premise, and with only eight pages to each installment there was little room for any characterization. The series was wrapped up in a twenty-page tale in *Detective* 443 in which Batman enters the fray when his (hitherto unmentioned) best friend, a private detective, is murdered by members of the council. Only it turns out the friend had joined the council and his dead body is only a clone. Batman joins Kirk and the others in storming the hidden HQ of the group, wherein Kirk sacrifices his life to bomb the whole complex and everyone in it out of existence. (Decades later one of Kirk's clones would become a good guy and a member of The Power Company.)

Night of the Stalker

Detective 443 was Goodwin's last issue as editor; sales had not improved and Julius Schwartz was brought back. Goodwin never had much of a feel for the Gotham Crusader, and did much better with Iron Man over at Marvel. None of the Batman stories during his tenure were memorable aside from "Night of the Stalker" [*Detective* 439], which reminded the readers of just why Batman began his intense and exacting crusade for justice. When a young boy sees his parents shot and killed by bank robbers in front of his eyes, Batman relentlessly pursues the gang members into the country, tracking and subduing each one of them in complete and utter silence, no taunts, no words, just a quiet steely quest for absolute justice for the orphaned boy and his dead parents that completely unnerves the once-arrogant criminals. The story was scripted by Steve Englehart with excellent art by Vin and Sal Amendola, who also plotted, and Dick Giordano. One great panel shows an angry Batman pulling one adversary, who thinks he's drowned him, into the water with him, his face intensely growling while the other man can only look back in terror. The story ends with Bruce thinking of the young boy who just lost both his mother and father in such a cruel, random way and succumbing to tears as he thinks of his own dead parents. The story had originally been submitted to Julius Schwartz, who hated the idea of Batman crying, but Goodwin picked it up as a fill-in, the irony being that it was much, much better than the stories he himself wrote for the comic.

Schwartz brought back artist Jim Aparo and assigned Len Wein to scripts. *Detective* 444 began a new storyline in which Batman is accused of cold-blooded murder when he shoots a fleeing Talia al Ghul in the back after she holds up a theater with some confederates. Talia actually threw the gun at Batman, who caught it, and he claims he never pulled the trigger, although Commissioner Gordon informs him that it's just an ordinary gun with no gimmicks to it. Although Batman never carries a gun and has never shot anybody, Gordon feels it may have been a crime of passion given the identity of the beautiful victim, although it could be argued that Batman has a right to shoot a fleeing criminal who refuses to halt. Whatever the case, this gave *Detective* the shot in the arm it needed. Robin and the Elongated man alternated back-ups.

In the following issue Batman breaks into prison to talk to Ra's al Ghul, who admits he engineered his own daughter's death, and then commits suicide, framing Batman for not one murder but two as guards come to investigate the noise and see Batman outside the dead man's cell. In subsequent issues Batman digs up Ghul's grave and finds an empty casket, but when cops come after him they see Ghul's corpse in the coffin, making even Batman think he's going crazy. The story was wrapped up in *Detective* 448, in which Batman follows a clue to a circus where both Talia and Ra's al Ghul are in disguise, the latter as a circus midget (engineered by an hallucinogenic gas). Ghul admits that the entire plot was to force Batman to join his

League of Assassins and become his second-in-command. This was the first time Ghul was ever connected to the League, which had been headed by the late Dr. Darrk. Either Julius Schwartz forgot that or it was decided there was no reason Ghul couldn't have been the true power behind Darrk.

Batman outwitted and outfought both Ghul and his assassins, and later explained to Gordon all the tricks his wily antagonist used to enact his diabolical plot. Although it began well, the "Bat-Murderer" storyline was nearly undone by awkward plotting, the unnecessary use of the loser character the Creeper at the climax, and the switch from Jim Aparo to Ernie Chua as artist. Talia and Ghul next appeared in the 1978 *Batman Spectacular* wherein Batman winds up shanghaied and wakes up to find himself married to the woman, although not legally as far as the U.S. is concerned. Decades later it would turn out that the two had a child together, Damian Wayne.

The logo for the comic was re-done as "Batman's Detective Comics" and there was a group of rotating writers and artists, including Elliot Maggin, Martin Pasko, Gerry Conway, Len Wein, Bob Rozakis, Michael Uslan, and David V. Reed on scripts, and Mike Grell, Ernie Chau and Walt Simonson on art. Batman encountered an actual dead vampire, was nearly killed by a kiss from a gal wearing poison lipstick, and went back to the alley where his parents were slain to have his annual rendezvous with a woman who was kind to him right after the murders. Minor bat-foe Captain Stingaree thought Batman was actually a well-known group of triplets and tries to murder them all, then turned out to be their brother, the fourth in a set of quadruplets. The Black Spider was an ex-con who had killed his own father while committing robbery for drug money, so he declares war on drug dealers when he gets out; unfortunately, he doesn't care if innocents get caught in the crossfire and comes afoul of Batman. The silver age foe Signalman returned in *Detective* 466, a story distinguished only by the scene in which the villain tries to have Batman incinerated by placing him inside the Bat-signal and hoping the cops will turn it on.

Private eye Tim Trench got a back-up series beginning with *Detective* 460 but reader reaction to this cliched character was so negative that he lasted only two issues. Trench had been introduced in the silver age in Wonder Woman during the period when she'd lost her powers, and was shown to be an immoral sleaze, so casting him as a hero didn't work. (He also had a back-up story in *Batman* in which he was depicted as a nice guy investigating arson for a pretty divorcee.) Instead new back-ups featured a variety of super-heroes battling a baddie named the Calculator, who was captured at the end of each story but escaped in time for the next installment. It all culminated in *Detective* 468 wherein he finally tackled Batman, and came up against the one foe he couldn't outwit. After that the comic presented only full-length Batman stories aside from the origin of his deadly new Foe, Dr. Phosphorus, in a back-up in *Detective* 469. Steve Englehart became the regular writer with Marshall Rogers and Terry Austin on art.

Hugo Strange

Dr. Phosphorus was a doctor who is caught in an explosion of radioactive sand from a reactor core in a nuclear power plant and turns into a maniacal glowing skeleton with a radioactive touch. First he poisons Gotham's water supply, causing a temporary plague, then unleashes a deadly gas at an arena, apparently killing hundreds of people. The storyline also served to introduce two new members of the supporting cast, the beautiful Silver St. Cloud, and city council chairman, Boss Rupert Thorne, who decides to declare war on Batman. In another development, Batman moves all of his trophies from the original Batcave to a new one located in an abandoned subway tunnel directly underneath the Wayne Industries skyscraper. As for Dr. Phosphorus, he returned in *Batman* 211.

Englehart then reintroduced a foe who hadn't been seen since the golden age, mad doctor Hugo Strange, in *Detective* 471. Strange had giant, hulking bodyguards and was now operating a clinic in which he took over the minds of wealthy and influential patients, which includes Bruce Wayne, who comes to be treated for radiation burns he got during his battle with Dr. Phosphorus. Strange discovers that Wayne is his nemesis, Batman, drugs him, and takes over his life as Bruce Wayne. Strange makes the mistake of trying to sell the secret of Batman's identity; one of the bidders is Boss Thorne, who has his men beat Stranger mercilessly so that he'll give up the information. Instead, he stays silent, and dies.

Reintroducing Strange was officially part of a concerted effort to give *Detective* kind of a modern "golden age" veneer, making it distinct from *Batman*. But it was also a conscious attempt to produce *Batman* in the Marvel style, with increased emphasis on characterization, supporting cast, and stories and sub-plots that flowed from one issue to the next. For instance, Silver St. Cloud and Bruce begin a protracted affair, which presents a problem. Bruce had always kept his relationships with women on the brief side, but he's fallen in love with Silver, and vice versa, and during her many nights in his arms she's gotten to know the man so well that she recognizes Bruce when she meets the Batman.

The Joker returned in one of his best appearances in "The Laughing Fish" in *Detective* 475 - 476. The clown prince has put a chemical in the water that gives fish his distinctive wide grin and red lips, and insists that he wants to therefore copyright the fish and get a cut of every fish sale in the country. Unfortunately, he is told that fish are a natural resource and can't be copyrighted by anyone. Therefore he begins killing one bureaucrat after another until they comply with his demands, even though Batman and Gordon do their best to protect each victim. If there's any problem with the story it is that in the second part the much less interesting sub-plot regarding the relationship between Silver and Batman nearly overpowers the main storyline with the Joker. Then Steve Englehart went off to write a novel - and Silver, who hates the idea of worrying every night if her lover will come home or not, goes off as well, leaving Bruce to brood about her for a few issues.

Len Wein did the scripts for *Detective* 479 - 480, which introduced a new Clayface, a disfigured scientist who uses some of the original Clayface's blood to fashion a formula to remold his features. Unfortunately the cure doesn't take, and he reduces people to protoplasmic blobs with a mere touch whenever the fever comes upon him, until Batman intervenes. It was then decided to merge *Detective* with *Batman Family* and the new *Detective* became an 80 page Dollar Comic starring the whole "Batman Family" beginning with issue 481. Paul Levitz took over as editor as he did with *Batman*. Batgirl, Robin, and Man-Bat were featured in back-up stories, and all of these were pretty forgettable in the debut dollar issue. All the stops were pulled out for the Batman stories, however, which were two of his best. Later back-ups included The Demon and Christopher Chance, the Human Target, who disguises himself as people who desperately need bodyguards. Written and created by Len Wein, the Human Target's most memorable story was in *Detective* 486, in which he finds out who tried to murder a man seeking underwater treasure and locates a missing friend (with very nice art by Dick Giordano). The Human Target would also appear in *Action*.

The first Batman story in 481, "Ticket to Tragedy," [O'Neil; Rogers] has Batman in a desperate race on a runaway train as he tries to stop a murderer whose escape might mean death for untold millions in the future; while the second, "Murder in the Night" [Starlin; Russell] pits Batman against a vengeful 90-year-old who has stolen the ability to put the electrical impulses of his brain - in essence, his consciousness - into another body. He has figured out that Batman is Bruce Wayne, and decides to try and inhabit the younger man's body on a permanent basis, trapping him and coming after him in the body of a great white ape he's already used to tear some of his enemies literally to pieces. The conclusion in the following issue features an epic battle between man and ape that was beautifully delineated by some impressive Jim Starlin-Craig Russell graphics; Starlin also wrote the script.

Batwoman/Kathy Kane, who appeared in *Batman Family*,

was murdered by killers employed by the Sensei, the leader of the League of Assassins, in *Detective* 485. Going after her murderers brought Batman into conflict with Ben Turner, the Bronze Tiger, who had once fought side by side with Richard Dragon, Kung-Fu Fighter (see chapter twelve). Batman next encounters the League of Assassins in *Detective* 487, wherein the Sensei employs the recently paroled Granny Goodness-like Ma Murder and her gang to kill off a writer they think has incriminating information about them. In *Detective* 488 Batman again encounters the Spook, who is hired by one of a group of publishing executives to spring a murderer out of the pen. The convict, Simon Thatcher, who was due to be executed, has penned a best-selling book and a sequel might earn even bigger bucks. In the clever story by Cary Burkett, the Spook uses a hypnotic gas to make everyone think the Batman is Thatcher and that the Spook is Batman; his plan is to have Batman die in the electric chair in Thatcher's stead. *Detective* also presented a number of stories dealing with portly criminal Maxie Zeus, who seems to think he is a Greek God, and models himself and henchmen on the same; he was never that memorable an antagonist.

Detective 489 presented a bizarre, vaguely homoerotic tale of world-famous magician Moon the Mystic and his loyal servant and companion, Ivorn, who encounter Batman when he's on the trail of a vampire-like killer of women in Gotham. Moon has also been pursuing this vampire from city to city, but the killer turns out to be Moon himself, wearing fake fangs and using stage magic to fool his victims. Ivorn, however, turns out to be an actual vampire, who tells Batman that Moon went insane after he realized the truth about his friend. Wracked with grief and guilt, Ivorn then flies into the sunlight and dies. Although Batman had already encountered a real vampire in a previous story, he tells himself that Ivorn actually used hypnotism and couldn't have really changed into a bat.

Detective 490 at last continued the story begun with the murder of Kathy Kane, as the Sensei and his league attempt to cause an earthquake that will bring down the house where several religious figures are attending a peace conference. One reverend simply refuses to leave when Batman orders everyone out of the house that's about to be destroyed, so the caped crusader - who went through Hell to protect these men and was nearly killed in the process - throws up his hands, tells him he won't force him, and if the man wants to be a martyr, so be it. The foolish reverend does die, but apparently so does the Sensei. We never do learn why he found it necessary to murder the original Batwoman, however, as she had nothing to do with the peace conference. Then while chasing the Riddler in Houston in *Detective* 493 Batman meets Texas hero, the Swashbuckler, who is the nephew of Greg Sanders, the golden age hero Vigilante; the Swashbuckler was never seen again.

Detective 494 - 495 introduced a splendid new foe for Batman, courtesy of writer Michael Fleischer, Dr. Bradford Thorne (not to be confused with Boss Thorne), who is also known as the Crime Doctor. Thorne not only aids criminals in their efforts for a portion of the take, but has a headquarters under his building where he can treat them if they are wounded in a fight with the police. If he has to be called in to help out on a caper for which he was not consulted beforehand, he charges extra. He uses the money not for his own purposes but to fund medical care for the poor. He refuses to betray his Hippocratic oath and harm anyone, including Batman. When the Dark Knight is injured fighting some thugs, he can't go to his usual doctor - who is aware of his dual identity - because he's out of town, but his temporary replacement is - Bradford Thorne! Thorne bandages up Bruce Wayne, but when the wound is exposed during a battle with Batman, Thorne recognizes his style of bandaging - as well as the position of the wound - and realizes the true identity of his adversary.

The Crime Doctor could have made a fascinating recurring foe for Batman, but his story was wrapped up quickly. Just as Thorne figured out Batman's identity, Batman figures out his, so Thorne goes on the run in a disguise. When an elderly woman collapses, however, he can't ignore a medical emergency and thereby gives himself away. But it is neither the police nor Batman who catch up with the doctor, but Silversmith, a minor Batman foe and crime boss who has learned that Thorne knows Batman's I.D. and kidnaps him to get it. Thorne refuses to divulge anything, so Silversmith poisons him. Batman gets him to the emergency room in time to save his life, but the good/bad doctor has lost his mind and his memory, an unfortunate fate for a character that could have been turned into an unusual and major antagonist for Batman. Don Newton and Dan Adkins were the regular artists for the Batman tales in *Detective* and their work was effective without being especially memorable.

Batgirl

As for the back-up strips in the giant Dollar *Detectives*: Robin's girlfriend takes up with another guy, a football hero, who turns out to be the Raven, a costumed operative of a crime organization; then the teen wonder tackles the Scarecrow on his lonesome in *Detective* 486. Dick Grayson gets a new girlfriend, Jennifer, when she is one of several college co-eds kidnapped by another student who is desperate for cash. A continuing sub-plot deals with a mysterious man in a black suit who keeps following Robin and some of the teen wonder's associates. He turns out to be a bodyguard hired by Bruce's lawyer to safeguard his sole heir, Dick Grayson. Jack C. Harris did the Robin scripts.

Batgirl finally discovers her brother Tony is alive (see chapter two) while on assignment in Japan, but only moments later he is apparently killed in an explosion. She runs for re-election against Bella Abzug clone Della Zigler [487], who thinks the answer to criminal behavior is social reform while Barbara thinks the emphasis should be on wiping out organized crime. Her duties as Batgirl keep her so busy that she fails to mount a strong campaign and loses her seat to Zigler. Batgirl and Robin team up in *Detective* 489 to catch some drug dealers, and Barbara loses her memory due to the machinations of a scientist who wants revenge upon Commissioner Gordon. Robin helps her remember who she is by having her put on her Batgirl costume, but when - to get all of her memories back - she reviews tapes of interviews she made, Robin asks her not to play the tape which reveals his and Batman's real identities, and she complies. Meanwhile, he continues to know her secret.

Cary Burkett and Jose Delbo took over the Batgirl strip in *Detective* 491, wherein she gets a new job at a research firm and is targeted by a crime figure named General Scarr. Scarr hires an assassin, Cormorant, to kill the dominoed daredoll and he threatens a scared little girl with a gun to get Batgirl out in the open. Batgirl is riddled with bullets and seemingly falls to her death, but has actually managed to fake her demise. In the following issue, Batgirl is so shaken by the ordeal that she wants to give up her role of super-heroine. This is an unlikely scenario, as Batgirl had survived hairier situations than this, but after Batman gets captured by Scarr in the first chapter, Batgirl regains her courage and takes after the bad guy herself, managing to capture the cowardly Cormorant and even rescue Batman in the process. In *Detective* 493 Batgirl rescues the same little girl Cormorant used as a hostage when the child's apartment house catches fire, a nice if coincidental bit of continuity. At Barbara's new job there is a hostile associate named Robert Barton and a nicer one named Richard Bender. Both the Robin and Batgirl back-ups continued when *Detective* went back to its regular size.

The Dollar *Detective* also ran an occasional back-up called "Tales of Gotham City," the best of which was probably Bob Haney's "Fifty Million Tons of Soul" about highly dramatic events on the Gotham Memorial Bridge, with a superior art job by Bob Oskner and Bob Smith [*Detective* 492]. Last and least was the clownishly-garbed crime fighter Odd Man, who was really Clay Stoner, private eye. Written and drawn by Steve Ditko, the character appeared once [*Detective* 487] and was never seen again.

The series went back to normal size beginning with *Detective*

496 with Gerry Conway and Don Newton as the creative team. Batman's old foe, the Blockbuster, found a new life with a mining family and buried the hatchet with Batman. In *Detective's* special 500th issue, the lead story had Batman and Robin entering a parallel world - thanks to the influence of the Phantom Stranger - where the Waynes are going to be murdered in a few days, and the dynamic duo race to save their lives and save Bruce's younger counterpart from years of anguish. Another bizarre story has Batman poisoned and in a coma, but still able to use morse code by signaling through his life monitor; Deadman helps Batman come back to life. The Elongated Man was featured in an interesting story about the last days of Edgar Allan Poe, and a Hawkman story, beautifully illustrated by Joe Kubert, had the winged warrior and Hawkgirl discovering what really happened to Professor Erdman, the scientist who brought the Martian Manhunter to earth. Slam Bradly, who'd appeared in the very first issue of *Detective* back in the golden age and appeared for many subsequent issues, starred in one story with a supporting cast of other sleuths who'd appeared in the comic over the years.

Detective 501 - 502 featured an interesting tale in which Alfred Pennysworth and Lucius Fox are the two main suspects in the murder of Mlle. Marie, a French resistance fighter who worked with both men on separate occasions and whose adventures appeared in *Star Spangled War Stories*. The story reveals that Alfred had a daughter, Julia, with Marie, but for inexplicable reasons doesn't tell her who he is. The actual fate of Marie is left hanging, however. (Alfred reunited with his daughter, Julia, in *Detective* 532.) Other Conway stories featured Cat-Man, who comes back from the dead; the Joker, who assembles a deadly rumpus room for Batman to die in; Catwoman, who loves Bruce but goes off to reconcile herself with her criminal past; the original Mad Hatter; Mannikan, a disfigured model who murders fashion designers; and Anthony Lupus, a wolfman who had appeared previously, among others. These were all entertaining if unspectacular bat-tales.

Don Newton's work was not terrible by any means, but when Gene Colan subbed on a few stories the art was significantly improved, as Colan just seemed to have a natural feel for the character.

As noted, by now continuity had been established between *Batman* and *Detective*. *Batman* 345 began the story of Dr. Death blackmailing Gotham with a deadly dust that could wipe out millions; *Detective* 512 had the conclusion - and so on. In continuing sub-plots Boss Thorne engineers the election of a new mayor, Hamilton Hill, who asks for Commissioner Gordon's resignation and gets it. Photographer Vicki Vale returns to town, resumes a romance with Bruce Wayne, and pieces together Batman's true identity. Another crossover brings back Two-Face, who divides his HQ into two halves as well as his gunsels - half of them being gentlemen crooks and the other half being thugs. In this story Batman is imprisoned by Two-Face for seven days, which seems highly unlikely for such an experienced escape artist as Batman, unless he's comatose.

Bruce and Dick move back to Wayne Manor and the batcave in *Batman* 348. Batman goes to LA to tackle an Academy of Crime run by a Headmaster who resembles Sidney Greenstreet from *The Maltese Falcon* while Robin, back in college after a brief sabbatical, discovers that a woman he fell for, Dala, is actually a vampire. This led to an unconvincing story arc in which both Batman and Robin are briefly transformed into bloodsucking "vampiri." In another development, private investigator Jason Bard asks the unemployed James Gordon to become his partner, while Alfred tries to head off Vicki's investigation by hiring Christopher Chance, the Human Target, to masquerade as Bruce, a ploy that works beautifully. Batman finally succeeds in bringing down Boss Thorne, who murdered Hugo Strange and was seemingly haunted by him, but then Strange turns out to be alive. In *Batman* 356 Strange tries to take Batman's place in a highly elaborate revenge plot, but as usual the caped crusader gets the better of him. Then Catwoman goes a little crazy out of jealousy over Bruce's relationship with the rather unappealing Vicki Vale, and nearly kills the both of them.

Killer Croc

One of Batman's nastiest foes, Killer Croc, was first seen in the shadows in *Detective* 523, then revealed in all his hideous glory in *Batman* 358. Croc was a mutant with tough crocodile-like skin and a mottled, green, bumpy face who can practically break alligators in half. He is furious when Batman manages to track him down to his home in the deserted slums of Gotham's Hell's Point. (This had a nice art job by an artist more associated with Superman, Curt Swan, with a more than able assist from Robin Rodriquez.) An even more important character in the Batman mythos was Jason Todd. Jason and his parents, aside from a long shot of their high-wire act in an earlier issue, first appeared in *Batman* 357, the same issue in which Trina Todd (in a slightly ridiculous development) walks in on Bruce being bandaged and sees his Batman outfit, putting two and two together.

The Croc-Jason storylines converged in the triple-sized *Detective* 526, which commemorated Batman's 500th appearance in the comic. In this outstanding story by Gerry Conway, Don Newton, and Alfredo Alcala, the Joker convenes a conference of Bat-baddies because he's afraid Croc will kill their hated enemy before he has a chance to. Croc was running a protection racket at the circus where the Todd family is employed as aerialists and they agree to help investigate. Unfortunately, Jason's parents wind up being fed to alligators when they dig too deep. Batman teams up with Talia and Catwoman - who were both invited to the Joker's soiree and at first think the other plans to kill Batman - while Robin and Batgirl handle things at their end. Jason discovers the batcave while poking around, and digs up one of Robin's old costumes, unaware that his parents are dead, and that he will play a role in defeating their murderer. In a final confrontation between Batman and Croc, Jason makes a crucial difference. At the end Batman decides to make Jason his new ward. With a strong storyline, intriguing developments, a huge cast of guest-stars and a host of villains, interesting inter-play between the varying characters, plus the inevitable poign-ancy of the fate of the Todds, so similar to Dick Grayson's, this was one of the very best Batman stories published in the Bronze age.

By this time Len Wein was the new editor, and Doug Moench became the new *Batman* scribe. The newly re-instated Com-missioner Gordon is given a gross assistant, the repulsive Har-vey Bullock, a disgraced cop, because the corrupt Mayor Hill hopes he can pressure Gordon into resigning again, but instead he has a stroke. A new villainess, a beautiful albino named Na-tasha Knight, or Nocturna, turns up, but despite Moench's at-tempts to make the character interesting, she got lost in a sea of pretension. Jason, wanting to participate in Batman's cases, is rebuffed and runs back to the circus, but Batman thinks ser-iously about making the boy his partner when he helps solve the case of the Chimera, who can look like anyone he wants to and has been committing robberies.

Feeling neglected by Bruce, Vicki Vale takes an assignment overseas in Guatamala and winds up encountering the Joker, who wants to turn the whole country into a big demented fun land. In the three-part story's most exciting sequence, a con-strained Batman manages to get free from his ropes and leap off the Joker's train to rescue Vicki, also tied up, just before the train can run her over. In the third part in *Batman* 366, Batman and Robin are reunited, but it's actually Jason in Dick's outfit and with dyed black hair. Despite the fact that the two work to-gether splendidly as a team, Bruce is angry that Jason is steal-ing another man's identity. In the copper age Jason would take over as the new Robin.

Arguably the greatest bronze age Batman story appeared in *Batman Annual* 8 in 1982. In this exciting and suspenseful tale by Mike W. Barr, with one of Trever von Eeden's very best art jobs, the inhabitants of a small farming community are killed, literally reduced to skeletons, by a ray from the sky that com-bines with a liquid inside their bodies to cause their destruction. Batman discovers that there are only two survivors and tries to find out why they alone should have lived, while he also hunts down "The Messiah of the Crimson Sun," leader of a cult called the Children of Adam. This Messiah is going to lay waste to Gotham city as he did the farming community unless Batman can stop him. The Messiah turns out to be Ra's al Ghul, reconstituted after dissolving in the lazarus pit, and Batman, Robin, and Talia fly to her father's orbiting HQ to put a stop to his plans. Ra's al Ghul dies a very satisfying death - or does he? Von Eeeden's art is very stylized, not to all tastes, but undeniably effective, and Barr's story is top-notch.

Catwoman

Meanwhile in the Batgirl back-up series, Barbara Gordon is charged with murder until her costumed alter ego proves who really committed the deed. Then she has a run-in with Dr. Voodoo, whose drug gives Batgirl heightened emotions that threaten to derail her [501 - 502]. Most of Batgirl's villains - a motorcycle gang, a mutated guy with a big head named Annihilus - were pretty lame, although Lady Viper, who appeared in *Detective* 514 - 517, was slightly more interesting. Lady Viper has a love of snakes, like Marvel's Princess Python, but she can also transform into a giant snake as well. In the rather comical finale, the viper's bite turns Barbara Gordon into another fanged snake-woman and the two ladies have a battle until an antidote reverts Batgirl to normal and Lady Viper completely metamorphoses into a mindless snake. Beginning with *Detective* 518 Batgirl's adventures were penned by Barbara Randall and drawn by Trevor von Eeden. Her first opponent was a spoiled, nasty female computer thief named the Velvet Tiger. Then the Batgirl strip was discontinued for "revamping."

Catwoman was featured in occasional back-ups beginning with *Batman* 345. Selina Kyle really didn't work that well as a heroine, but at least she was an edgier character than the dull Batgirl. In her adventures she investigated the disappearances of entire trains, and played bodyguard to a politician whose wife is plotting against him. In another story [*Batman* 350 -

351] she investigates the murder of a lookalike and winds up going on stage as a stripper before catching up with the killer (one can't imagine Babs Gordon impersonating a stripper even for a second).

Other notable Bat-adventures include: "Secret of the Waiting Graves" [*Detective* 395]; "Forecast for Tonight - Murder" [*Detective* 420]; "A Small Case of Murder" [*Detective* 427]; and "How Many Ways Can a Robin Die?" [*Batman* 246].

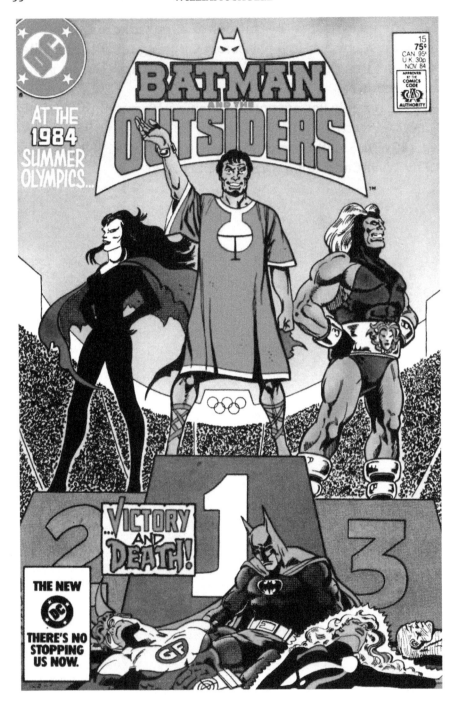

CHAPTER TWO: BATMAN'S SUPPORTING PLAYERS

-- *BATMAN FAMILY, MAN-BAT, THE JOKER, THE BRAVE AND THE BOLD, BATMAN AND THE OUTSIDERS*, NEMESIS

Debuting in 1975, *Batman Family* was a double-sized comic headlining the team of Batgirl and Robin. Barbara Gordon is a congresswoman in Washington DC and Dick Grayson is one of her student aides; they are unaware of each other's secret identity. In their first team-up in *Batman Family* 1, execrably plotted by Eliott S. Maggin, they combine forces when the actual spirit of Benedict Arnold tries to take over the government with the aid of ghostly troops. Satan appears at the end of the tale to deride the traitor for his failure. Although occasionally a Batman story might have a supernatural slant, this was so blatant and ridiculous that it almost sank the comic from the get-go. At the end Robin suggests that Batgirl hang up her costume and do whatever it is she does during the daytime. Having worked with Wonder Girl in the Teen Titans for years, it is unlikely Robin would ever say such a thing. Batgirl retaliates by smooching Robin!? (One letter col writer reminded the editor that Barbara Gordon was a grown woman and Robin still a boy, although as a college student he would probably be 18, while another joked, "what would Bruce Wayne say if he saw his ward covered in Bat-lipstick?") It is bad, really stupid comics scripting that Julius Schwartz never should have approved. Mike Grell's art is the story's only saving grace. The rest of the issue consisted of reprints. *Batman Family* 2 was nothing but reprints, including a story in which Robin supposedly decides to team up with Batgirl instead of Batman.

Batman Family

Robin and Batgirl team up again in *Batman Family* 3, in which they each figure out the other's identity without telling how. In the next issue they have separate stories - Batgirl tackles a hitwoman hired to kill an exonerated ex-con, and Robin smashes the plans of a criminal dressed as Santa Claus - then re-team for BF 5. In BF 6 Robin encounters a gal who calls herself the Joker's Daughter, and uses gimmicks like special powder puffs and lipstick bullets with which she can kiss Robin from a distance, as she puts it. This young lady disguises herself as Catgirl, supposedly Catwoman's daughter in BF 8, Robin's first full-length story, then shows up as the daughters of the Scarecrow, the Riddler, and the Penguin in an idiotic tale by Bob Rozakis in BF 9. Joker's Daughter somehow figures out that Robin is Dick Grayson even as he uncovers her true identity: Duela Dent, the daughter of Two-Face. Duela's motive for causing all of her malicious mischief is that she wants to be a hero [!] to offset her father's criminal behavior, and figures Robin can get her into the Teen Titans. Robin obliges, but he should have spanked her bottom and deposited her in the nearest nuthouse.

Batman Family 7 finally gave the bat-duo some interesting

antagonists in the Earth-1 versions of Mr. and Mrs. Menace, the Sportsmaster and the Huntress, who kidnap the heroes so they can snatch a jewel for them out of a trap, but this was also mediocre. Batgirl had her first full-length story in BF 10, in which a fan suggests that she change her name to Batwoman now that she's older. Of course, Barbara Gordon runs into a woman named Kathy Kane, who owns a carnival near Provincetown, and discovers that she's the original Batwoman. The two bat-gals team up to tackle old Batman foes the Gypsy Moth and the Cavalier. Although Kathy admits that she's not going to come out of retirement, Batgirl decides not to change her name as she feels Kathy is the one and only "Batwoman." Batwoman showed up again in BF 14 where she appears to disintegrate inside her costume but is reconstituted at the end. She was later killed off (see chapter one).

Batman Family began running all-new material beginning with the 11th issue, including back-ups featuring Man-Bat. BF 12 briefly brought back a character who hadn't been seen since 1951 (in comic book time), Barbara's brother, Tony, who was believed dead but who had been placed in another identity for various reasons by the government; although he watched her exploits as Batgirl with pride and amazement, he and Barbara never actually met until, as noted, a story in *Detective*. BF 13 teamed up Robin, Batgirl and Man-Bat in a full-length story in which they tackle the Outsider, the weird evil being that Alfred Pennysworth was transformed into after his "death" in the silver age. Fairly ridiculous, it was probably the best story in the comic so far, which admittedly wasn't saying much. Although Robin has a pretty, devoted and likable, girlfriend, Lori Elkin, at college, he sort of confesses his love to Batgirl only to discover that she's asleep.

Al Milgrom took over the editorship with *Batman Family* 17, which became an 80-page dollar comic for its final four issues. Gerry Conway wrote the lead story, starring Batman and Robin, and Jim Aparo supplied the best art seen in *Batman Family*, for which a wide variety of artists often seemed to turn in rushed and unattractive art jobs. In the story Lori Elkin's old boyfriend returns and turns out to be kidnapping and disfiguring attractive people because his face had supposedly been ruined by a football accident. But when Batman pulls off his fright mask, he discovers the deranged man only has a very tiny scar on his upper cheek. In the same story the Huntress, the daughter of the Earth-2 Batman and Catwoman, travels to Earth-1 via the JLA teleporter and asks Batman for help with her training. He turns her over to Kathy Kane, who suggests Batgirl would make a better coach. In the back-up story, Batgirl battles Poison Ivy, The Huntress takes on Catwoman (and is disconcerted by the fact that this is the Earth-1 version of her own mother), and the duo join forces with Batwoman to deal with those two villainesses plus the mysterious Madame Zodiac, who aided them in their crimes. The Huntress was given her own back-up series in BF 18 which lasted for three issues and pits her against a politician who is setting tenement fires for his own evil ends.

Batman Family lasted twenty issues but that wasn't the end, as it was incorporated into *Detective* beginning with issue 481. The idea of teaming Robin with Batgirl was a good one, but the stories and art tended to be mediocre, and not enough was made of the sexual tension in their relationship (true, a 25-year-old congresswoman having a fling with an 18-year-old college student might have been deemed inappropriate). Batgirl was as hopelessly one-dimensional and bland as ever, although there was some minor attempt to make Dick Grayson into a real person. Writer Bob Rozakis seemed so enamored of the silver age DC style that his scripting often seemed comically dated; it was as if he'd never read a more sophisticated Marvel comic book and probably never had. The coincidences and silliness of many of his tales were either quaint and charming or utterly ludicrous, depending on how you looked at it.

Man-Bat

Man-Bat's very short-lived comic appeared in 1975. In the

first issue, written and edited by Gerry Conway and drawn by Steve Ditko and Al Milgrom, Francine Langstrom is hypnotized by the sinister Baron Tyme into converting to the monster vampire bat-form she had taken in one story in *Detective* and killing off people he wishes to sacrifice to dark gods. Thinking the attacker is Kirk, the Man-Bat, Batman goes after him, but when he learns the truth, allows Langstrom to take care of Tyme and rescue his wife on his own, as he wishes. There was a completely different creative team for the second (and final) issue - never a good sign - with Martin Pasko doing the script while Pablo Marcos and R. Villamonte did the art chores; Conway remained as editor. Kirk has decided to take Francine back to his home town of Chicago where she can finally get treatment (one imagines she'll also need psychiatric help when she realizes how many people she's killed). Langstrom has barely arrived when he is attacked by Batman's foe, Phil Reardon, the Ten-Eyed Man, who is working for a twisted crusader who wants to capture one of the winged "bat-monsters" that he thinks are threatening the city. Kirk's sister, her fiance, and his old friends all think his behavior is very odd. The Ten-Eyed Man, now wearing a spiffy costume with an eye motif, is killed at the end of the story.

DC Comics felt that the horror trend that was very popular in comics in the seventies was on the wane, so they decided to cancel Man-Bat's comic and make him one of the back-up features in their new series, *Batman Family,* beginning with the 11th issue. Before that the story of Kirk and Francine was continued in *Detective* 458 - 459, in which Kirk's sister learns of their transformations. In *Batman Family* Kirk and Francine are now living in Manhattan and expecting a baby. Kirk goes out on nightly patrol and keeps whatever meager reward money he may be offered for solving crimes and saving people from muggers. He has developed the ability to pick up brain waves emitted by persons determined to commit a crime. Man-Bat faces a gang that uses jaguars, as well as a special light that temporarily turns him into a were-jaguar, then deals with a crazed film freak who wants to exorcize him.

The series only became interesting with the installment in BF 15 in which private eye Jason Bard comes to New York and tells Francine that a number of her ex-boyfriends have been killed by a mysterious sniper. While Man-Bat and Bard both suspect the other is the sniper, they team up in the following issue to get the real killer. Such artists as Marshall Rogers and Howard Chaykin had drawn the feature, but Michael Golden seemed the perfect artist for the strip. Bob Rozakis' early scripts for the series were unmemorable, but he began to hit his stride with this two-parter.

In *Batman Family* 17 Man-Bat starred in a full-length tale in which he and Jason Blood, aka the Demon Etrigan, take on Morgaine LeFay, who is hoping to discover a demon child among the infants being born in the hospital where a pregnant Francine is in the delivery room. Rozakis' plotting took a quantum leap forward. One cop observes the goings-on, takes one look at Man-Bat and the Demon, and asks "Whatever happened to heroes who look like heroes? Those two are the ugliest suckers I've ever seen!" Man-Bat decides to give up being a hero in the following issue and get a real job, but he is confused by reports of Man-Bat being seen on parole at night. At first he thinks he must be sleep-walking, until he notices Francine's side of the bed is empty: her subconscious sent her out as Woman-Bat while Kirk slept. In BF 20, Kirk asks private eye Jason Bard if he could be his partner, but Bard only accepts the offer after Kirk uses his skills as Man-Bat to help him with a case. Michael Golden and Josef Rubinstein's art for this installment was especially good. Man-Bat also appeared in *DC Comics Presents* 35 with Superman.

Batman Family was incorporated into *Detective* and Man-Bat's adventures continued. In *Detective* 492 Man-Bat flies into the subway to look for a missing train that his wife and child are on, and runs into one humongous rat; Rozakis, Tanghal and Colletta were the creative team.

Man-Bat went back to being a tormented and dangerous creature in *Batman* 341 - 342. Kirk wrongfully thinks that his daughter is dead and Batman is to blame. His mind is unhinged by hatred, and the antidote that Batman gives him no longer works. In *Batman* 348 another dose of the serum turns Man-Bat back into Kirk Langstrom, but it is clear that his nearly being responsible for the death of his little daughter also helped bring about his conversion.

Unfortunately Kirk went nutso again in *Detective* 527, infuriating Batman when he flies off with his new ward, Jason Todd, because he's still under the delusion that his little girl is deceased. In the conclusion in *Batman* 361, Batman again manages to give Kirk that antidote and save the day, but this provided absolutely no advancement for the character.

The Joker

The Joker was given his own comic in 1975 with Denny O'Neil on scripts and Irv Novick and Dick Giordano on art. In the first story the Clown Prince of Crime is outraged when a man named Alvarez helps Two-Face escape from Arkham Asylum, but refuses to do the same for the Joker because he only needs a "master criminal" - like Two-Face. The Joker manages to escape on his own, throws acid in Alvarez' face, and wages a battle with Harvey Dent, who tries to cut Joker into two parts with a buzz saw. In their climactic battle they knock themselves out. The entertaining story was fast-paced and amusing without being overly campy, and the reader didn't notice that The Batman was nowhere in evidence. The Joker helped out a criminal crybaby named Willie the Weeper in *Joker* 2 and fought with the Creeper in the third issue. The book had revolving writers and artists, including Martin Pasko, but most of the later scripts were done by Elliott S. Maggin, including a fairly serious tale in *Joker* 4, in which the villain kidnaps Dinah Lance, on whom he's developed a distracting crush, and engages Black Canary and Green Arrow in battle high atop a bridge; he plans to murder the drivers and cause a traffic jam so the police will be kept busy while he loots a museum.

One of the best Joker tales appeared in *Joker* 5, written by

Martin Pasko. In this the Joker pretends to be Arthur Wilde, grandson of an eccentric painter, and he's out to steal some paintings, but has to contend with the equally felonious Royal Flush Gang, who first appeared in *Justice League* in the silver age, and are themselves determined to snatch the valuable art work. In *Joker* 6 the villain matches wits with an actor who imagines himself to be Sherlock Holmes. In the following issue, the personalities of the Joker and Lex Luthor are exchanged by a mechanical accident during an attempt to steal Green Lantern's powers (GL himself only appears in one panel as Hal Jordan). In the last two issues of the series the Joker squares off with the Scarecrow and then Catwoman in an entertaining romp in which a famous movie comic impersonates the villain. The Joker was supposed to take on the entire Justice League in the next issue, but the series was canceled before it could be published. *The Joker* was a darkly amusing, albeit short-lived, series, but perhaps it was best that his appearances were reserved for special stories in *Batman* and *Detective* (which seemed to have no real relation to the Joker's own book). Perhaps it was too much of a good thing.

The Brave and the Bold

As in the silver age, *The Brave & the Bold* presented team-up tales with the Batman and one or more special guest-stars. Writer Nick Haney and editor Murray Boltinoff did not care about continuity with other DC mags, including the ones in which Batman appeared. Hence in one issue teaming Batman with Green Arrow, the latter - who went broke in his Oliver Queen identity some time before and took up the cause of the downtrodden - inherits ten million dollars. Readers wrote in wondering if this meant that Queen was no longer poor. Boltinoff explained that stories in B&B did not necessarily occur in chronological order - implying the story occurred before Queen lost his fortune - but the trouble with that was that Green Arrow only switched to his new uniform and hip, bearded look - which he wore in the story - after losing his money. When Paul Levitz took over as editor from Boltinoff,

B&B's continuity was more in sync with Batman stories published elsewhere, and even more so when Dick Giordano became editor.

During the first half of the bronze age, most of the stories were written by Bob Haney and drawn quite nicely by Jim Aparo. There were a few memorable issues along the way. B&B 117 has Batman helping out Sergeant Rock when he's court-martialed for executing a traitor during WW2, although the alleged traitor turns out to be alive. The following issue, guest-starring Wildcat, presents a riotous escapade in which the Joker tries to kill a cute little dog carrying antibodies that can save the life of a convict that the Joker wants dead because he knows too much. B&B 150 teams Batman with a mystery guest-star and has him up against a hulking, massively strong enforcer for a kidnaper-terrorist. This enforcer - and the guest-star - turns out to be Superman playing an undercover role to rescue his pal, Jimmy Olsen. Batman teams up with his enemy Ra's al Ghul in B&B 159, as they both pursue a scientist who has invented a formula that can turn anything or anyone into crystal, including the Earth itself if the formula is released into the sea. Ironically, Ghul winds up saving the world by using silicone to stop the spread of the formula after its creator pours it into the ocean. This excellent story was crafted by writer Denny O'Neill and artist Jim Aparo.

In B&B 178 Batman teams with the Creeper against an odd creature made of paper that appears out of nowhere and targets minorities and others. Working together, the two heroes discover that the creature was brought to life by the subconscious mind and hatreds of a conservative television commentator. The Creeper, AKA Jack Ryder - a former TV personality turned security person - goes on the air to express his own point of view. "Democracy doesn't mean freedom for a majority of people, but for all people. Democracy isn't forcing your idea of what's right on everyone - it's having the freedom to practice your own morality and the courage to allow others to practice theirs." Batman objects when the Creeper calls him

"Bats," but when he calls him "B.M." the Gotham knight says "Go back to 'Bats!'" The excellent script was by Alan Brennert with the usual slick Aparo artwork.

Brennert also wrote a fine, well-received story teaming Batman with the defunct sixties battling brother combo, Hawk and Dove, for B&B 181, and an even better one for the following issue. In this Batman winds up on Earth-2, where the original Batman has died, Robin is the same age he is, and Batwoman - who died on Earth-1 - is still alive and much older. The three of them take on old foe Hugo Strange, who threatens to destroy Gotham but who is secretly hoping that his old enemies will kill him and end his miserable, tormented existence. While the affecting story had plenty of action, the intelligent psychological insights into the characters give it an added resonance. Robin resents the presence of another Batman, who at times treats him like a kid partner; Batwoman hopes Batman will go back to Earth-1 before she finds herself falling in love with Bruce Wayne all over again (and this time he's a much younger man); and Batman is a bit freaked out at not only seeing Kathy Kane (Batwoman) alive again, remembering how much he'd once cared for the deceased Batwoman of his own world, but the fact that his counterpart has died, forcing him to face the reality of his own mortality. As one fan noted, it made the more horrible aspects of the whole Earth 1/Earth-2 situation come alive.

Don Krarr was the writer for a suspenseful story in B&B 183 in which Batman is challenged to a contest in which he must find a kidnaped mystery writer by following clues and surviving death traps. Although Batman at first suspects that the Riddler, who recently escaped from prison, is behind the kidnaping and the deadly game, it turns out that he has been turned into Batman's partner by another unseen foe. It all ends with Batman confronting the mastermind and nearly dying in a fiery conflagration until the Riddler, of all people, comes to his rescue.

B&B 199 presented a team-up between Batman and the

supernatural hero Spectre that was memorable for no other reason than the diabolical curse placed on the two nominal villains. 200 years ago a young woman named Kalinda had been forced to marry the brutish mage Vantos because he saved the life of her father, but she fell in love - and vice versa - with Vantos' apprentice Stephos. When Vantos discovered this, he killed Stephos and made Kalinda immortal, always aware of her lover's spirit but ever unable to join with him. The couple use subterfuge to get the Spectre out of his host body, Jim Corrigan, which Stephos hopes to inhabit. It turns out that Vantos had planned for the eventuality that Stephos would find a host body, and Kalinda, who had remained youthful down through the decades, now reverts to a centuries-old immortal crone. However, the Spectre removes the curse, and Kalinda dies, to finally join with Stephos in the supernatural plain of the dead. The story was by Mike Barr.

Other memorable issues of B&B include: 173 - 174 (Batman, GL and the Guardians vs Sinestro, in disguise as one of the little blue men); 179 (Batman and the Legion of Super-Heroes vs. Universo); 188 - 189 (Batman and the Thorn versus Nazis who have a canister of a super-deadly chemical); 192 (Batman and Superboy, whom the Gotham knight helps guide as to the proper use of his powers); 194 (Batman and Flash against pretty Prof. Wye, who teaches motivational therapy to three-time losers such as Rainbow Raider and Dr. Double-X); 195 (Batman and "I, Vampire" from *House of Mystery* in a bloody good tale); and 200 (Brimstone, an Earth-2 villain, awakens from a coma to discover his nemesis, Batman, is dead, so he possesses his law-abiding Earth-1 counterpart in an attempt to kill Earth-1's Batman).

Batman and the Outsiders

Although Batman had been made the long-time star of *The Brave and the Bold* for sales reasons, the magazine did not sell as well as Batman's regular series or *Detective*, so it was decided to discontinue it with the 200th issue, which also contained a preview of its replacement: *Batman and the Outsiders*, a new super-hero group. In 16 action-packed pages we met the new team - Metamorpho, Halo, Katana, Black Lightning, and Geo-Force, all under the direction of Batman - as they work like clockwork to prevent a group of fanatics from freeing a terrorist who is confined to a hospital bed. The writer and artist team of Mike W. Barr and Jim Aparo were the series' co-creators.

In *Batman and the Outsiders* 1 [1983], which had the same creative team, Batman learns that his trusted employee Lucius Fox is being held captive in the nation of Markovia, where he has gone on Wayne Enterprises business, and where the political situation has erupted in violence. Batman goes to the Justice League satellite where he expects his fellow members to follow him into Markovia on a rescue mission. Unfortunately, Superman has to tell him that the State Department asked them not to intervene in the Markovian business and possibly aggravate a delicate political situation. Batman then decides to quit the Justice League in disgust and go by himself. He does, however, take non-JLA member Black Lightning with him so that the latter can pose as Fox's brother, as both men are black. In the meantime, the Markovian king expires, leaving two sons, Gregor and Brion, the first of whom becomes the new king.

Coincidentally wandering around the small country in Eastern Europe are Metamorpho, who hopes a Markovian lady scientist named Dr. Jace can cure him, and Katana, an extremely skilled swordswoman who gets bloody revenge on a Markovian general. There is also a strange teen female amnesiac with light powers whom Batman christens Halo. Finally Prince Brion is given special powers to fight the country's would-be conquerors by the aforementioned Dr. Jace. Shot by the invaders, he is thrown into a shallow grave, but re-emerges with powers over the earth and the new name of Geo-Force. All of these, along with Batman and Black Lightning, face off against the villain of the piece, Baron Bedlam, in BATO 2.

Batman approves when Geo-Force throws a defeated Bedlam off of the castle roof down to the crowd waiting below with pitchforks and axes; an unlikely reaction, but BATO as a comic was full of unlikely events, such as Batman deciding to turn all of these disparate heroes into a new team to help him fight crime in Gotham. Even more incredible is that he takes them to the Batcave, introduces them to Alfred, and puts them all up in his mansion (Halo and Katano go into the Wayne penthouse), revealing a connection between Batman and Bruce Wayne, who takes Halo - who chooses the name Gabrielle Doe for herself - shopping for clothing the following day. (Geo-Force bought his own home the following issue and Black Lightning got a new apartment.) It was as if Barr created a Batman from yet another alternate universe. Jim Aparo's art was splendid, however.

BATO 3 had the group squaring off with Agent Orange, supposedly an embittered and disfigured Viet Nam vet who gets other disaffected veterans to fight for him; Batman unmasks him as a phony. In BATO 4, the villain is Meltdown, who'd fought Batman in the silver age and Black Lightning in his own magazine (see chapter 17). The 5th issue was the second part of a teaming between the Outsiders and the New Teen Titans (see chapter 8). Batman and the Outsiders continued well into the copper age. When Batman separated from his colleagues the magazine continued as *The Outsiders*.

Nemesis

A series starring undercover man Nemesis by Cary Burkett and Dan Spiegle began in *The Brave & the Bold* 166. Nemesis was actually Tom Tresser, who - along with his brother, Craig - is befriended by FBI man Ben Marshall and his wife after the death of their father. Both Tom and Craig decide to join the FBI, but while Craig is made an agent, Tom is assigned to the scientific inventions division, where he excels. On the day that Marshall is promoted to FBI chief, Craig - who claims the older man is getting credit for his own work - shockingly assassinates him and is shot and killed in turn. Tom finds himself turned into a pariah, as no one wants to associate with the brother of someone who could murder anyone as beloved as Marshall.

Tom decides to become Nemesis, and balance the scales by becoming a force for good. A master of disguise, he wears a device on his neck that can instantly dissolve whatever thin mask he is wearing, and he carries a gun that freezes opponents in their tracks without killing them. Along the way he discovers that his brother was actually brainwashed by a sinister criminal organization called the Council - run by someone known only as the Head - into murdering Marshall. Nemesis then sets out to get the goods on the people who destroyed his brother's and Ben Marshall's lives, and, in a sense, his own as well. Nemesis teamed with Batman in B&B 170 wherein they discover that the Head, a bad guy shot by Ben Marshall, runs his organization from an iron lung; he is murdered by an associate at the end of the story.

In subsequent issues Nemesis took after the rest of the members of the Council, including a crooked casino owner named Curtis. During this adventure a woman named Valerie Foxworth enters the casino wearing a bomb, planning to kill Curtis because her father's gambling losses drove him to suicide. Nemesis removes the bomb from her person and throws it into a vacant corner of the room, but later asks Valerie why she would have wanted dozens of innocent people to die along with herself and Curtis. The answer, obviously, is that Valerie isn't too tightly wrapped, but nevertheless Nemesis makes her his partner instead of turning her over to a mental health professional or the police. "She's as independent as a cat and as stubborn as a mule," thinks Nemesis, "but she does catch on quickly." As members of the Council still desire Valerie's death, Nemesis gives her a new identity.

Beginning with B&B 178 Nemesis finds himself in an especially harrowing situation as Solomon, a member of the Council, puts a device on his chest that at the touch of a remote button will speed up his heart rate uncontrollably until he dies. The device is affixed to his body with a super-glue that is impossible to remove. Nemesis temporarily fools his opponent into thinking he's dead, then makes his way to the home of the scientific associate who had built the device. So engrossed is he in trying to find a way to get the contraption off his chest, he doesn't notice the scientist sneaking up on him - and pressing a button on the remote. Reeling from the pain, Nemesis nevertheless manages to subdue the scientist, then makes his way to Solomon's home where he finally manages to get the deadly device off of his chest by various clever ruses and subterfuge.

In B&B 183 - 184 Ms. Irene Scarfield, the only female member of the Council, hires an infamous hit man known as Greyfox to assassinate Nemesis, but in a very satisfying story, Nemesis turns the tables on him and Greyfox dies in a fiery conflagration. In B&B 188 Council member Jay Kingston puts Nemesis through a gauntlet of hidden traps and murderous opponents in his lion-surrounded estate that would have given Batman pause - to no avail. In B&B 193 Nemesis teams up with Batman in another full-length story where they try to stop a plot by Ms. Scarfield to kill a politician sponsoring an anti-crime bill - which would adversely affect the Council's activities - by using known terrorists as a cover-up. Nemesis gives up his life to stop the plot and kill Scarfield and others connected with the Council. So the Nemesis series, which was very well-written by Burkett and featured some excellent Spiegel artwork, bit the dust despite the fact that it still had much unrealized potential.

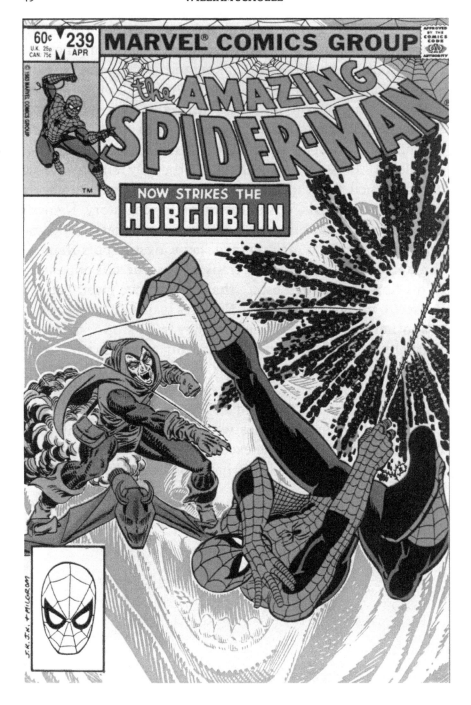

CHAPTER THREE: SPIDEY

Spider-Man aka Peter Parker entered the bronze age with co-creator Stan Lee still handling the scripts and John Buscema and John Romita handling the art chores. Peter still worried about his finances, about being exposed as Spider-Man, whether or not he should tell his girlfriend, Gwen Stacy, about his heroic secret identity, and mostly about his frail Aunt May, who fussed over him like a mother hen. In *Amazing Spider-Man* 80 Peter resolves a conflict with Gwen and Flash Thompson, high school enemy turned soldier, and helps her father, a retired cop, when he's accused of stealing the very paintings he was supposed to provide security for. The real culprit is the Chameleon, a master of disguise who hadn't been seen since *Amazing Spider-Man* 2. Spider-Man is able to figure out who the Chameleon is at his next caper because the villain disguises himself as - Peter Parker!

A three-part story in *Amazing Spider-Man* 83 - 85 brought back the Kingpin and a new challenger to his criminal empire, the Schemer. The bald and corpulent Kingpin has been laying low with his rather attractive wife, Vanessa, neither wishing to face the fact that their son, Richard, probably committed suicide in the Alps after news of his father's exploits hit the papers, causing him much shame and distress. Faced with attacks by the Schemer, who drives about in a fancy tricked-up car and has his own henchmen, the Kingpin breaks his vow to go straight and launches a counter-attack, part of which is offering an anonymous reward for the Schemer's capture. Spider-Man goes after the reward but instead winds up trapped in the Kingpin's building, wherein the Schemer takes off the mask that makes him look middle-aged and reveals himself to be - Richard; he wanted to topple the empire built by tainted money and created a new identity to do so. The shock of realizing who his enemy is puts the Kingpin in a trance-like state, but he is not down for the count by any means.

Dr. Octopus, Spidey's arch-enemy, returned in another three-parter in *Amazing Spider-Man* 88 - 90. After being reunited with the four mechanical arms that give him his name and which he can call forth from a distance, the Doc hijacks a plane in an attempt to get a ransom for an Asian official. When that fails he tries to black out Manhattan, and nearly succeeds in dashing Spider-Man to the ground. Peter invents a special web fluid that makes the doc's arms go haywire, but they knock over a chimney and send it hurtling to the street below. Captain Stacey, seeing that the bricks will hit a frightened little boy, pushes the child away and is smashed by the chimney in his stead. As he dies in Spider-Man's arms, he calls him "Peter" and tells him to take care of his daughter. Stacey may not have been too swift in some areas - saying more than once that all females think with their hearts and old-fashioned stuff like that - but he was wise enough to figure out Spider-Man's true identity. (Of course it didn't hurt that Peter told everyone his secret in a previous issue when he had a raging fever and later blamed it on the flu!) The trilogy also introduced Green Lantern artist Gil Kane as the new penciller and he proved a very good fit for Web-Head.

Unfortunately for Peter, Gwen blames Spider-Man for her father's death, and a corrupt law and order candidate for DA named Bullitt stirs the pot. With the help of Iceman of the X-Man, Spidey exposes Bullitt [AS 92], but Gwen still despises the hero and can't understand why her boyfriend Peter isn't spending all of his time with her during her grief. Peter tries to propose, but the secret of his dual identity holds him back, and

Gwen takes off to London to live with her aunt and uncle. A battle with the Beetle, who nearly kills Aunt May when she gets in the way of his trying to rob a vault, takes Peter's mind off his problems and he makes short work of his antagonist [94]. Gwen eventually comes back and the two are reunited.

Amazing Spider-Man 96 - 98 [May 1971] brought back major Spider-Man foe, the Green Goblin, who was Norman Osborn, the father of Pete's roommate, Harry. Norman had a split personality, and when he was dressed in his maniacal Goblin costume complete with pumpkin bombs, knew Peter's secret identity - and vice versa. The Goblin is prevented from destroying his hated foe by a crisis in his son's life; the insecure Harry, told by his alleged girlfriend, Mary Jane Watson, that she belongs to "no one" and having to watch as she flirts with Peter, takes too many pills that he gets from a pusher and winds up in the hospital. (These issues admirably if superficially dealt with the drug problem affecting many of America's young people but they did not carry the Comics Code Authority's seal of approval because mention of drugs was still verboten in comics. Just a couple of months later, however, the seal was used on an issue of *Green Lantern* that dealt with heroin addiction, *Spider-Man* having broken the ice, so to speak.) Stan Lee followed this up with a superficial polemic for prison reform in AS 99 that was strident and much less interesting.

A startling change came over Spider-Man in his 100th issue when he takes a formula that he hopes will eliminate his powers for good. Whereas once he enjoyed swinging through the city and having an unconventional life, he now feels that he is only watching everyone else live their lives while he's on the sidelines. He wants to marry Gwen and have a more or less normal existence, something he might have not seriously considered had he not been loopy in love. Unfortunately, the formula gives him six arms and makes him seem even more like a spider. He goes to the isolated Long Island home of scientist Curt Connors to try to fix his condition, and winds up in the middle of a battle between Connors' alter ego, the man-hating

Lizard, and Spidey's new foe, the living vampire, Morbius [101 - 102].

Michael Morbius was a Nobel-prize winning scientist with a rare blood disease. Seeking a cure, Morbius inadvertently turned himself into a blood-drinking vampire who is so unable to control his impulses that his first victim is his best friend. Conners and Peter figure out that an enzyme in Morbius' blood will rid Peter of his extra arms, but in a development that plays like black comedy Peter also has to deal with the fact that Connors has transformed into the Lizard, this time with his human brain in control, but the evil Lizard's consciousness keeps breaking out from time to time threatening to make everything go blooey. Peter's sympathy for Morbius, who has already killed many people, is overdone, and there is an unintentional laugh-out-loud moment in temporary scribe Roy Thomas' script when Peter, whose webbing has managed to grab the tube with the enzyme but not a supposedly drowning Morbius, thinks "Things. Somehow we always manage to hold on to things, while men sink, doomed, around us." Oy vey!

The restrictions of the comics code from the silver age had been lifted enough for Marvel and other companies to use horror characters in their comics and even star them in their own books, such as Marvel's *Werewolf By Night* and *Tomb of Dracula* [see *The Horror Comics* by Schoell]. Hence a vampire could now appear in Spider-Man (who would eventually even meet Dracula - sort of). Morbius got his own brief series in a black and white magazine, and made frequent appearances in the comics. In years to come some stories in *Amazing Spider-Man* would have an out and out horrific and even gruesome tone to them.

In another development, Peter Parker's high school nemesis, the bully Flash Thompson, becomes a soldier and goes off to Vietnam. Stan Lee basically sidestepped any commentary on the war by embroiling Flash in a different kind of intrigue when religious fanatics accuse him of leading bombers to destroy a sacred temple he had earlier chanced upon after being separated from his platoon; in reality Flash is trying to warn the priest and others inside the temple after he fails to convince his superiors of its existence. Back in the states, Flash is pursued by assassins and protected by both Spider-Man, Dr. Strange and MP's. The priest, who'd been presumed to be dead, turns out to have only been in a trance and Flash bonds with his lovely daughter, Sha Shan [108 - 109].

John Romita returned to the series as artist and Stan Lee handed the writing reins to Gerry Conway, who brought back Kraven the Hunter and had him use a homely tormented youth with acrobatic powers named Martin Blank as an attempted method of revenge against Spider-Man. Dressed as the Gibbon, the sympathetic - and pathetic - Martin attacks Spidey under the influence of Kraven's drugs but is easily defeated [110 - 111]. Not so easy to defeat was Dr. Octopus, who figured in the next story arc in which the many-tentacled adversary is involved in a gang war with a new foe named Hammerhead. Hammerhead was operated on and has a head made of steel alloy, making him impervious to virtually any blow to the skull.

During this Peter has to contend with the fact that his Aunt May, disturbed by remarks Gwen made about how she fusses too much over Peter, leaves a note and takes off for parts unknown. She has actually become housekeeper for Otto Octavius (Doc Ock), who was one of her boarders during the silver age. During Spider-Man's battle with the "kind" Dr. Octopus, the old lady actually threatens to shoot the web-slinger, whom she has always seen as a menace. Unable to see that the charming Otto is really a deadly and deranged villain, May decides to keep her job even after the dear man is led away in handcuffs and Hammerhead escapes scot free [112 - 115]. Considering all the stress he's under, Peter isn't too surprised to learn that the weakness he's been feeling is caused by a serious ulcer.

The Death of Gwen

His medical problems become the least of his worries when Spider-Man loses the love of his life, Gwen Stacy, at the hands of one of his greatest adversaries, the Green Goblin. Harry Osborn's bad trip on LSD and some serious business reversals bring out the latent fear and hatred inside Norman Osborn, turning him back into the Goblin. Kidnapping Gwen from her apartment, he engages Spidey in a battle at the George Washington Bridge, whereupon he flings the young lady to her death [121]. In the following issue Spider-Man tracks down the villain, beats him within an inch of his life, and watches his foe get accidentally impaled on his jet-flyer, a fate the Goblin had in mind for his angry opponent. Spider-Man is accused of Norman Osborn's murder, mostly by J. Jonah Jameson. When flighty Mary Jane Watson offers Peter condolences, he tells her off, and he walks out on his delirious, desperate roommate, Harry, in order to take down his murderous father. These issues had especially good art by Gil Kane, John Romita and Tony Mortellaro. Ross Andru, a solid professional and veteran of the silver age, then became the new penciller.

Amazing Spider-Man 129 introduced a character who would become quite popular in his own right, The Punisher, who fought a one-man war on crime. A costumed creep who calls himself the Jackal and wants to become crime boss of New York somehow manages to inveigle the Punisher into teaming up with him and going after Spider-Man for the murder of Norman Osborn. But before the story is over Spider-Man manages to convince the Punisher that the one he should really worry about is his duplicitous partner. In the following issue Peter discovers that Aunt May has accepted a proposal from Dr. Octopus and he arrives at his enemy's Westchester abode just in time to see the wedding begin. Otto has discovered that May Parker has inherited a Canadian island rich with uranium as well as the company that owns the nuclear reactor located on the property, the only thing he's interested in. But before the nuptials can reach their conclusion, Doc Ock's old adversary Hammerhead bursts in and causes a huge explosion, of which Spidey and May seem to be the only survivors [130 - 131]. Whether May and Otto managed to get married or not was open to question. Doc Ock and Hammerhead both returned in a three-parter in AS 157 - 159.

May's reaction to the death of the man she loved and wanted to marry (making one wonder if May was suffering from senile dementia or Alzheimer's disease) was simply shunted aside by writer Gerry Conway; we never even learned if Spider-Man had convinced her that her Otto was a bad guy. It was as if the wedding had never taken place, and even the editors didn't seem to know if the old lady was now May Parker or May Octavius. Her nephew keeps busy battling new foe the Tarantula - a vicious South American former revolutionary who went to work for the oppressive government until even they had no more use for him, and who has razor sharp spikes on his toes - while Harry Osborn figures out his roommate's secret identity [134 - 135] and even Mary Jane and Flash Thompson grow suspicious. Harry, now thoroughly deranged, and convinced his roommate murdered his fine, upstanding father, puts on daddy's suit and becomes the new Green Goblin. He tries to kill Spidey's aunt and other friends before being subdued, after which he blurts out Pete's secret identity and says that as the Goblin, he ought to know. But no one believes he's the Goblin, who had been around for some years, or that Peter is a superhero [136 - 137].

Around this time, Marvel instituted some double-sized editions of their most popular comics, and *Giant-Size Spider-Man* was born. Our hero sort of encounters Dracula in the first issue (the two never actually meet), and has a dual time-crossed adventure with pulp hero Doc Savage, whose adventures Marvel was now publishing, in GSSM 3. In GSSM 2 Spidey foils a dastardly plot by Fu Manchu when he first fights and then teams up with Fu's son, Shang-Chi from the *Master of Kung Fu* comic book (see chapter 12). In GSSM 4 Spider-Man teams up with the Punisher to take down Moses Magnum, an Ethiopian weapons manufacturer who had joined Mussolini against his own country and is now kidnapping people on which to test an acidic poison gas. Although Magnum supposedly becomes a victim of this same flesh-eating gas at the end of the story, he actually went on to become a major Marvel villain. GSSM 5 had Spidey caught in the middle of a conflict between the swamp creature the Man-Thing and his old antagonist the Lizard. Gerry Conway wrote the stories and Ross Andru remained on art with an assist by long-time collaborator Mike Esposito. The "giant" issues only lasted about a year, and were ditched in favor of annuals with new material.

In the regular magazine Spidey's next foe was the Grizzly, who is nine feet tall in his super-charged bear suit, has a grudge against J. Jonah Jameson, and makes the mistake of teaming up temporarily with the Jackal [139 - 140]. Then there was an adventure in Paris in which Spidey rescues Jameson from a French kidnapper with tornado powers named Cyclone. Just as Peter finally makes a love connection with Mary Jane - whom he kisses good-bye at the airport, stimulating both his and her hormones - who should appear in his new apartment but - Gwen Stacy [144]! Peter rejects her as an imposter, but then discovers that she has Gwen's fingerprints, and so does the dead woman buried in her grave. Apparently there are two Gwen Stacey's, one alive, one dead.

As they're trying to figure this out, the Tarantula reappears, now working with the Jackal. Peter then gets two new shocks: the first is discovering that the new Gwen is actually a clone of the original, and the second is that his friendly, sympathetic biology teacher, Professor Warren, is actually the Jackal. Warren, who'd cared for Gwen, blamed Spider-Man for her death, and cloned both her and Peter Parker, creating a duplicate Spider-Man [148 - 149]. At the end of the storyline, both Warren and the duplicate Spider-Man are killed, while the Gwen-clone goes off to find herself. In AS 150 Peter asks Curt Connors to run tests to determine if he is the clone or the real deal, but during a battle with the Spider-Slayer he figures out psychologically that he's the true Peter Parker, and tosses out the results of Connors' tests without reading them. (Over twenty years later it would develop that the Parker-clone, now known as Ben Reilly, was still alive, and that Parker himself was actually the clone, but this would turn out to be an untrue manipulation by a very old enemy of Spider-Man's who had also been presumed dead.)

Kingpin and More

Len Wein took over as writer with *Amazing Spider-Man* 151, bringing back silver age foe the Shocker, who attempts to extort money from Manhattan by blacking out sections of the city, and these were the last memorable issues for quite a spell. Ross Andru and Mike Esposito's art seemed slightly rushed and less attractive than before, and Esposito's inks were less effective than John Romita's, at least as far as Spider-Man was concerned. For a few issues Mary Jane was perpetually angry at Peter because his duties as a hero/photographer took him away from parties, and Wein also added more humor to the series, more than was necessary perhaps. He created an unmemorable villain in Mirage, whose costume emitted illusions of where he was actually standing, and brought back, unfortunately, an old villain from AS 2, the Tinkerer, whom Peter had once believed to be an alien but who really wasn't and whose reappearance was more silly than anything else [160]. A bit more interesting was the Fly in *Amazing Spider-Man Annual* 10, a crook and kidnaper who is transformed into a literally bug-eyed menace by weird science.

Amazing Spider-Man 162 introduced an electro-biologist named Dr. Marla Madison. Jameson wanted to team up with the woman to take down Spider-Man -- although Marla wasn't convinced he was the menace he'd been portrayed as, she felt no one could flout the law, and also looked forward to the challenge of capturing the web-spinner. She creates a new Spider-Slayer that is operated by Jameson via cybernetic helmet, but this robot proves no more effective at squashing Spidey than the previous Slayers. A bigger threat is that photos of Spider-Man disposing of the corpse of Peter's clone wind up in Jonah's desk drawer. Confronted by Jonah with the photos, Peter is able to trick the publisher into thinking they are fakes, but he still doesn't know who took them (it turns out to be a hypnotized

Harry).

The Kingpin returned in *Amazing Spider-Man* 163 - 164, which features a rousing battle between the web-spinner and the chubby crime boss, who uses his adversary's energy to bring his dying son, Richard, back to life. The unfortunate result is that Spider-Man now has about six hours to live, but he goes to Curt Connors for help in making a device to help get his life-force back. Thinking his son is dead after the reverse-transference, Kingpin tries once again to smash his hated foe, but only winds up dying himself (or so it seems); Richard's life force has been sufficiently stimulated so that he will recover in time, and he goes off with his mother. *Amazing* 166 brought back Stegron, who uses a device to bring dinosaur skeletons to life and then engages the Lizard in battle. On the personal front, Peter and Mary Jane agree to take one day at a time, while Liz and Harry announce their engagement. Glory Grant, a pretty black lady, gets a job as Jonah's new secretary.

Dr. Barton Hamilton, Harry's therapist, was introduced in *Amazing* 167 along with Will O' the Wisp, a man who can fly and turn immaterial, among other powers, and who is in thrall to Dr. Jonas Harrow. *Amazing* 174 - 175 featured a taut tale in which Jonah is kidnapped by the Hitman, an old friend-foe of the Punisher, who teams up with Spidey to keep the People's Liberation Army terrorist group from blowing up the Statue of Liberty along with Jameson. *Amazing* 176 began an excellent five issue arc in which the Green Goblin reappears after a distraught Harry - whose fiancée, Liz, ran off after her half-brother, the Molten Man, burned to death in front of her eyes - has a physical fight with Dr. Hamilton. Aunt May suffers a heart attack during a Gray Panther demonstration at City Hall, but doctors need Peter to sign a consent form before they can operate. Wouldn't you know that the Goblin attacks just as Peter is on his way to the hospital. (Actually, doctors would not need consent forms during an emergency such as a heart attack.)

The Goblin also wants to finish off the mobster Silvermane

(who'd been turned into an infant in the silver age but has somehow become an adult again) so he can be top crime boss in the city. It winds up with Spidey and the two villains dangling high, high over the seats in Radio City Music Hall as the Goblin's glider fails and Spider-Man's webbing snaps from the strain. Spider-Man manages to save himself and discovers that the Goblin is not Harry, but his power-mad psychiatrist, Bart Hamilton. Liz and Harry are reunited, but when Peter asks Mary Jane to marry him, the fancy-free gal turns him down flat.

Aunt May recovers in the hospital where a doctor mercilessly chides Peter for not being at her side more often, something that it's highly unlikely any medical professional would do outside of Ben Casey. (Later Peter would nearly break the obnoxious doctor's neck.) Peter, who has to fight villains, save lives, and make money still feels guilty, but when his spider-sense flares just outside of May's room, he bursts in dressed as Spider-Man and promptly gives her another seizure [183]! Another personal problem pops up when Peter learns he can't graduate college unless he takes make-up courses at night; presumably he does just that but when he attends graduation his name isn't called because he's missing one credit - he'll have to take "gym" during the summer! (It was somewhat embarrassing as due to a continuity mix-up between editors of *Amazing* and *Spectacular Spider-Man* Peter had to "study" to make up the credit. Who has to "study" gym?)

Marv Wolfman became the new writer/editor with *Amazing* 182. Betty Brant Needs, separated from husband Ned, returns to New York, replaces (the rarely seen) Glory Grant as Jonah's secretary - although Glory would show up now and then sitting at a desk -- and tries to rekindle her relationship with Peter. The D.A. finally clears Spider-Man of charges in the deaths of Gwen's father and Norman Osborne, making him the city's hero as he'd always dreamed of, although it almost becomes a nightmare due to the manipulations of the Chameleon. Keith Pollard replaced Ross Andru as artist, but his pencils did not blend well with Jim Mooney's inks. The art was supposed to be in the style of premiere Spidey artist Steve Ditko, but aside from the occasional panel you would hardly have known it.

Aunt May Packs It In?

Amazing 189 began a story arc in which Jameson's son, John, also known as the Man-Wolf, is kidnaped by Spencer Smythe, who built many spider-slayers for Jonah. Working with the radioactive materials has given him only a short time to live, and he wants to see his enemies suffer before he goes. First, Jameson's son is sort of blinked out of existence, but Jameson, of course, claims that Spider-Man killed him. Then Smythe shackles Jonah and Spider-Man together with a bomb, and in the remarkably exciting and suspenseful *Amazing* 192, Spidey must figure out a way to save both of them while Jonah rants. The story is full of action, but Wolfman's script also manages to get in some interesting characterization as Spider-Man sees himself as a loser about to die, and Jonah recognizes that next to the heroic Spider-Man, he is a mediocrity. (This was somewhat similar to the "relationship" between Superman and Lex Luthor, especially in later years.) If there was any problem with this story it's that Peter, while understandably furious at Jameson, didn't take into account the man's grief over his son, which was only shown briefly.

In the following issues, Peter gets fired by Jameson, dumped by Mary Jane who missed a date, and socked by Ned Leeds before storming off with his wife Betty in tow. Aunt May, now in a nursing home, is threatened by the man who'd murdered Uncle Ben and who wants to find some gangster's booty that was supposedly hidden in her house. Hoping to get Ned and Betty back together, Peter lies and says he'd never cared for her, making everyone think he's a thoughtless heel. The silver-tressed Black Cat makes her debut, with the goal of getting her father out of jail so he can die at home, but winds up dying herself at the end (until an entertaining reappearance in *Amazing* 205 - 206, which reveals that she has an unhealthy obsession with Spider-Man). Then Peter gets a telegram stating that Aunt May has died in the nursing home. *Amazing* 196, showing how Peter deals -- or doesn't deal -- with his grief, being comforted by that fine man "Robbie" Robertson, Jonah's editor, features an excellent script and the best art, courtesy of penciller Al Milgrom, in a long time. Peter and Robbie both leave the Bugle -- Peter goes to work for the Globe -- while Jameson has a literal nervous breakdown. When Robbie takes over as the Bugle's publisher, he nearly becomes as bad as Jonah.

In the following issue the Kingpin returns and tries to kill Spider-Man before a midnight deadline, which is dictated by his wife, Vanessa, but although Spider-Man is bested in battle, his adversary is just a few seconds too late. (Vanessa's ultimatum was that she would leave him unless he gave up his criminal career at twelve on the dot, and Fisk chooses his wife over destroying his hated enemy.) *Amazing* 200 reveals that Aunt May is still alive as part of a contrived plot conceived by Mysterio and that aforementioned burglar who is so convinced Spidey is going to kill him that he drops dead from fright and panic. This is just as well, as Peter had revealed his secret identity to him so he'd realize just why and how much he hated the man. Despite the improbable aspects, this anniversary issue was well-scripted by Wolfman and has some effective Pollard/ Mooney art work.

Peter had juggled two girlfriends for a time, but it was refreshing that Mary Jane and Betty Leeds wasted little time sniping at each other as they would have in the sixties. However in *Amazing* 201 Mary Jane has a verbal girl fight with April Maye, who also works at the Globe and doesn't care for Peter. Of more interest is the fact that the Punisher figures out Peter's secret identity after pictures of the latter's battle, which could only have been taken by Spidey, wind up in the Globe. Peter is able to convince the Punisher that his deduction is wrong. *Amazing* 206 reveals that Jonah and Robbie, who'd been acting strange for awhile, are not really crazy but being affected by long-distance psycho waves sent out by Dr. Jonas Harrow.

More significant is that with this issue Denny O'Neill took over as editor with John Byrne on pencils. Two issues later Al Milgrom was editor and O'Neill was doing scripts with John Romita Jr. doing the art chores. The results, featuring a forgettable villain named Fusion, were awful; the issue also introduced the obnoxious photographer and Peter's rival, Lance Bannon, another thing that was not in its favor. Romita Jr.'s art would greatly improve, ably aided by Joe Sinnott's finishes.

Amazing 210 introduced another bizarre but forgettable character in Madame Web, a weird old blind lady psychic who wears a tight red dress that trails on the floor in front of her like a serpent and who is surrounded by spider-like banks of machinery that keep her alive. More interesting is Hydroman, who could turn into water and flow through any drain pipe, sewer, sink or shower in the city [212]. In a wild follow-up in *Amazing* 217 - 218 Hydroman and Sandman become rivals for the hand of a middle-aged bar fly named Sadie, but they eventually team up, then merge together to form a hulking mindless mass of mud that gets exhibited in a theater a la King Kong.

Amazing 213 - 215 brought back the Wizard and his partners in the Frightful Four, although now they are working with and for a mysterious female who turns out to be Sub-Mariner's hated foe, Llyra (see chapter 16); Subby also gets into the action. In her human form Llyra also turns out to be the babe down the hall who has Peter comparing her to Debra Whitman (whom Peter had met in graduate school) and finding her wanting, leading to him treating her pretty shabbily. By this time the series was back in high gear, with some excellent Denny O'Neill scripts and solid, attractive art by John Romita Jr. and Jim Mooney. *Amazing* 216 was an excellent issue in which an injured Spidey tries to save the life of a man who is supposed to be shot during the New York City marathon, only he doesn't know whom the intended victim is, and must also deal with a surplus of incidents that require his attention along the way.

After a run of stories that seemed like fill-ins, Tom DeFalco became the new editor with *Amazing* 222, in which the villain was the Speed Demon, the new name for the evil Whizzer from the Squadron Sinister. *Amazing* 223 introduced a shy genius and bookworm named Roger Hochberg, whom Peter befriends because he reminds him of the younger and geekier Peter Parker. Peter is furious when some people at a party play a cruel trick on Roger, telling them off in no uncertain terms. When Spider-Man has to battle the Red Ghost and his Super-Apes - always the least interesting of Marvel villains - Roger saves webhead's life by phoning the police. The hokey and unrealistic ending has Roger surrounded by hot babes because of his "heroic" action. However, *Amazing* 224 presented a superior tale in which convict Adrian Toomes meets Aunt May's fiancé Nathan Lubensky in physical therapy, and the latter's positive attitude inspires the depressed and defeated Toomes to new action. Unfortunately, Toomes is the real name of the Vulture, who escapes from the hospital and hides out in May and Nathan's nursing home. Adrian realizes that Peter has recognized him, leading to another lively battle between Spider-Man and the flying septuagenarian from the silver age.

The Black Cat returned in *Amazing* 226 - 227, in which she escapes from a mental institution, claims she was only faking her crazy obsession over "Spider," but still agrees to go straight for his sake. Unfortunately, Felicia Hardy has trouble doing this, and decides it would make more sense if Spider-Man signed up for her team. The Black Cat supposedly drowns - again - at the end of the story, destroying Peter's slightly off-kilter romantic hopes. There were enough differences between the characters to almost disguise the fact that the Black Cat, with her attraction to her adversary, and her on-again off-again criminality, was simply a variation on Batman's Catwoman.

The Will O' the Wisp returned for an exciting story arc in *Amazing* 233 - 236. The Wisp is destroying factories owned by the corrupt Brand Corporation (a subsidiary of Roxxon Oil) because he is a former employee turned into a freak due to an accident. Then he was subjected against his wishes to some further fiddling by his callous supervisor, James Melvin. Trying to create villainous super-agents for Brand, Melvin then sinks the terrorist-for-hire Tarantula into a special solution, and out comes a full-fledged giant tarantula-man, only with the horrified hit man's human brain. By the end of the story Spider-Man has convinced the Wisp not to kill anyone, and the Tarantula, grown even larger, more ferocious, and less human, tries to make a meal out of Melvin. With inkers like Dan Green and Frank Giacoia putting the final touches on Romita Jr.'s pencils, the art took on a new luster, and these issues were especially memorable, particularly a page depicting the Tarantula's messy death plunge in *Amazing* 236. *Amazing* 237 was a change-of-pace story, probably a fill-in, pitting Spider-Man against ten-time loser the Stiltman, who holds his own against web-head until original foe Daredevil enters the scene. After Spider-Man is knocked unconscious saving Stiltman from a weapon run amok, Stiltman decides to save his foe instead of taking advantage of his unconsciousness by killing him.

Hobgoblin

One of Spider-Man's most devious and pernicious antagonists debuted in *Amazing* 238 - 239. An unknown man discovers Norman Osborn's secret caches and discovers many of the secrets of Osborn's deadly alias, the Green Goblin. Changing his costume to make it more fearsome, and employing Osborn's weapons and glider, he takes on the role of the Hobgoblin. In his next encounter with Spider-Man he actually uses a hireling named Lefty Donovan to play the role of Hobgoblin and to test Norman Osborn's formula to increase his strength. The formula explodes, putting Lefty in the hospital for weeks, after which he dresses up as Hobgoblin under the villain's command, battles Spider-Man, and winds up dying in his stead. Spider-Man isn't fooled, however [244 - 245]. The Hobgoblin eventually gained super-strength and bedeviled the web-head throughout the copper age.

Amazing 246 presented another charming change-of-pace and very amusing story in which Peter, the Black Cat, Mary Jane Watson and J. Jonah Jameson all indulge in some very wild daydreaming in which Jonah knocks out Spider-Man with one punch, Mary Jane imagines herself a Broadway star playing herself, the Black Cat unmasks Spidey and discovers Cary Grant, and Peter wins a Pulitzer and creates a cure for everything [Stern/Romita Jr./Green].

Lance Bannon's steady girlfriend Amy Powell makes a play for Peter to get him jealous, with the result that both Lance and new-in-town Mary Jane Watson show up at his apartment to find Peter sporting a lot of Amy's lipstick prints [242 - 243]. Peter somehow manages to ace his graduate school exam, but decides to take a leave of absence from the program anyway because the time it would take for study and lab work would compromise his ability to take photos and make money, which would depend upon his activities as Spider-Man. Aunt May opens a boarding house for the elderly.

Spider-Man's adventures were continued in both *Amazing Spider-Man* and the new series *Peter Parker, the Spectacular Spider-Man*, which is covered in the next chapter.

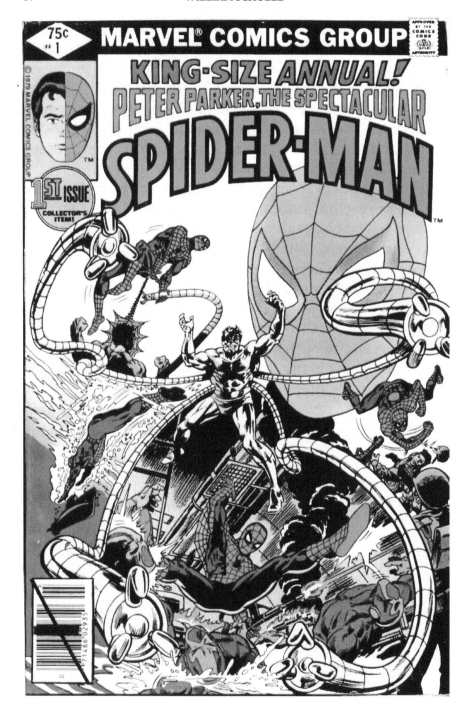

CHAPTER FOUR:
SPECTACULAR
PETER PARKER

-- AND *MARVEL TEAM-UP*

*P*eter Parker, the Spectacular Spider-Man* debuted in 1976 with stories by Gerry Conway and art by Sal Buscema and Mike Esposito; Bill Mantlo, Archie Goodwin, Elliot Maggin and others would do scripts as well. There was not much difference between the two series, which were careful at first to maintain continuity, and it was almost like *Amazing* was published twice a month instead of monthly. In the first issue of PP the nasty, stinging Tarantula returns, kidnapping people for hire, and planning a hit on the mayor which Spidey deflects. Tarantula then teams up with Kraven - the two hate each other and both take orders from a mysterious masked man. This man turns out to be flying, yellow-clad Lightmaster, who is secretly Dr. Lansky, the first kidnap "victim," in an exciting, very well-drawn story in PP 3 scripted by Jim Shooter. The Lightmaster stories also re-introduced the White Tiger, Hector Ayala, a Puerto Rican martial arts specialist who had previously appeared in the magazine *Deadly Hands of Kung Fu*, but his being Hispanic was the only really interesting thing about him. Believing that Hector was Spider-Man, Lightmaster only succeeded in exposing Hector's secret identity.

Peter Parker 12 - 15 brought back the Hate-Monger, who actually turned out to be the Man-Beast in disguise, and introduced a likable if strange hero called Razorback, a good 'ol boy and CB radio enthusiast who decked himself out in a somewhat comical outfit and drove a rig he called Big Pig. Then it was announced that due to changes in editors, *Amazing* and PP would "intertwine only marginally" until the "wrinkles were ironed out" and then there would be an "intricate cross-continuity" which never quite developed. The Scorpion discovers that his costume hasn't adhered to his skin as he imagined, and Electro electrifies himself when a kidnapping scheme goes awry.

Peter Parker 25 began another story arc centering on Carrion, a living ghoul who hates Spider-Man; the Maggia; and the Masked Marauder (who as the leader of the Maggia had been known as "Big M"). The Marauder uses a beam on Spidey that makes him blind, but Daredevil - who'd also fought the Marauder, along with Spidey, in the silver age - comes to his aid when the villain blackmails the city with a mega-bomb. The cadaverous Carrion, hepatitis-yellow and wearing ragged brown clothing with a tattered hood, knew all about Peter and his secret identity and just about everything else. Carrion could levitate, teleport, throw deadly red dust in people's faces, was telepathic, and had the amazing ability to repulse organic matter. He turns out to be the clone of Professor Miles Warren, the Jackal, and is just as crazy, but he is destroyed by a giant spider-amoeba he created to kill off his enemy.

Peter Parker 36 - 37 brought back the bizarre villain, Swarm - a skeleton whose body of bees had the collective mentality of a former Nazi - who'd first appeared in *The Champions* (see chapter 9). Spidey has a harrowing time trying to prevent Swarm from creating a humungous queen bee who will reproduce in fantastic time and whose minions can overcome the earth, the action climaxing inside a gigantic hive where the web-spinner is caught between Swarm and the quickly enlarging insect.

Morbius is finally cured of his vampiric curse in PP 39, although there was no follow-up to explain exactly how this came about, or how Michael Morbius would deal with his guilt over his bloody and evil actions.

It was ultimately decided that *Amazing* and *Spectacular* would maintain separate continuity, each series focusing on different members of the supporting cast; Peter Parker would feature his work as a teaching assistant and the somewhat multi-cultural crew he worked with - black Steve Hopkins; Asian Philip Ching; and two blonds, Marcy Kane, who hates Peter, and Debra Whitman who is crazy about him -- not to mention Dr. Connors, leading into a completely unnecessary story in which Peter turns into Spider-Lizard. Denny O'Neill was editor, with Roger Stern on scripts and Mike Zeck on art. Spider-Man battles the Frightful Four with their new member Electro, and then encounters a mystery villainess named Madame Belladonna who uses a poison spray to rob and get even with her enemies [PP 43].

That same issue introduced stereotypically gay fashion designer Roderick Kingsley, who is shown passed out on the cover with his limp wrist lying on his chest. Spider-Man thinks "even at my spindliest this guy would have made me look like Hercules" while Belladonna calls him a" flaming simp." Several issues later [57] Kingsley was reinvented as a "ladies man" who has a whole coterie of girlfriends, "Kingsley's Kozy Kompanions," as one ex puts it. Kingsley was always depicted as a crook who stole designs and was ruthless in business before he was re-envisioned as one of Spidey's major costumed adversaries decades later. It was also revealed that he had a twin brother who may have been the original "hairdresser."

Although never a fan favorite, Marie Severin turned in a fairly nice penciling job for *Peter Parker* 45, in which Spider-Man and his long-time foe the Vulture engage in a high-rise battle in the middle of Grand Central Station and elsewhere. The art was generally well-composed and flowed cinematically from panel to panel, but it was not well-served by the crude

inking job. The results were a bit more felicitous when Bruce
Patterson did the inks for PP 48, featuring Belladonna, who is
unmasked as a socialite who runs a fashion house with her sister, a business that was destroyed by the manipulations of Rod
Kingsley. PP 50 has Aunt May engaged to Nathan Lubensky
while Mysterio teams up with some phony aliens (who'd first
appeared in the silver age where Spidey thought they were the
real deal).

Peter Parker 49 introduced a brief back-up feature starring
the White Tiger [Stern/Cowan]. In the first installment Hector
Ayala vows vengeance upon whomever murdered his parents
and his sister -- a militaristic bitter maniac named Gideon
Mace. After the White Tiger is shot and nearly dies, Spider-Man
stops Mace from his plans to wipe out all super-heroes in New
York and stage a military coup. When Mace gets shot by his
own men, Peter thinks that he can't find it in himself to hate
Mace, but of course he's not the one who lost his entire family
to Mace's bullets. The White Tiger decides to hang up his uniform and leave town with his girlfriend. Considering how few
Hispanic heroes there were in the comics, it's too bad that the
White Tiger couldn't have been developed more in his own
color comic, but the basic concept for the hero was not that
strong.

Peter Parker 56, which featured the forgettable foe, the Jack
O'Lantern, from *Machine Man,* had an interesting situation resulting from Nathan being held hostage by a terrorist in Bel-
levue along with many others. Aunt May begs Peter to come
home and sit with her as they watch the developments on the
news, but he realizes Spider-Man has to do what he can to rescue his aunt's fiancé. Unfortunately, when Peter finally gets to
his aunt's home, she is disillusioned and hurt by what she sees
as his lack of interest and regard for her. In fact, learning that
it was Spider-Man who affected Nathan's rescue, Peter wonders
if Aunt May has come to have more respect for the man she
once feared and hated than she does for her nephew. It might
have been interesting if the repercussions over this incident

lasted a while longer, but they were resolved the very next issue.

Marcy and Deborah

Around this time there was also resolution to the mystery of why Marcy Kane started always wearing scarves and turbans on her head and was always hiding her blond hair. Many readers may have assumed Marcy was getting chemotherapy and her hair was falling out, but the explanation was only that Marcy had a bad hair cut! Her doctor told her she could no longer dye her tresses blond. While her acceptance of her brunette hair color improved Marcy's disposition, this was one of the most pointless sub-plots in the series. Meanwhile Tom De-Falco took over the editorial reins of all of the Spider-Man titles and promised more cross coordination. Ed Hannigan became the chief penciller, but his work was uninspired; Bill Mantlo's scripting was similarly uneven.

Peter Parker 64 introduced Cloak and Dagger, a white woman who can shoot deadly daggers of light, and a black man who wears a cloak that can envelope anyone in a freezing and endless darkness. The two are murderers, but only of drug dealers who'd used them to test new and hopefully addictive drugs on innocent runaways, causing the teens' deaths. The only two to survive were Cloak and Dagger, who become vengeful furies even as Spider-Man tries to stop their killing sprees on more than one occasion. PP 67 then dealt somewhat heavy-handedly with the issue of gun control as Spider-Man attempts to halt a shipment of illegal handguns while sidebars show statistics and examples of people who have accidentally shot their loved ones or themselves.

Deborah Whitman not only fell in love with Peter but was convinced he was Spider-Man. In especially suspect developments, Deborah turns out to be schizophrenic, and while this never seemed apparent before, has difficulty distinguishing fantasy from reality. Her psychiatrist, Bailey Kuklin, nearly bursts into Peter's apartment asking for his help, betraying a patient's confidence and revealing private information, which is ridiculous even given the suspension of disbelief required for comics. Kuklin goes so far as to ask Peter to dress up as Spider-Man to help Deborah, something even Peter has trouble swallowing. "Real people in real life don't treat serious problems as if they were comic book situations," Peter tells the shrink. Spider-Man decides to reveal his true identity to Deborah so she'll realize she's not crazy, but she only laughs and thanks him for helping snap her back to reality - his secret is still safe. Deborah goes off forever, apparently cured of her schizophrenia and her unrequited love for Peter in one easy stroke [PP 73 - 74].

Of more interest was a three-way battle between the Kingpin, Doc Ock, and Daredevil's old foe, the Owl, which culminated in the excellent double-sized 75th issue, guest-starring the still lovesick Black Cat, and featuring a fine art job by Al Milgrom and Jim Mooney. Just as good was PP 79, which depicts a thrilling "final" and decisive, highly cinematic, battle between Spider-Man and Dr. Octopus as they wage war in a hospital, on the city highways and bridges, and finally in a railroad yard with cars flying about, and a locomotive nearly flattening our hero. While all this is going on, Peter realizes that he has fallen in love with Felicia Hardy, who returns his feelings despite the fact that she'd never seen his face. Not good. In the meantime J. Jonah Jameson is falling in love with his constant companion Marla Madison.

The Punisher had been introduced in *Amazing Spider-Man*, and it was in Peter Parker 81 - 83 that he met what seemed like his final fate. He escapes from prison but his mind has been affected and he begins shooting real bullets at traffic violators and litter bugs. He tries to kill the Kingpin with the help of Cloak and Dagger, but is defeated instead. On trial, his attorney successfully argues that he is criminally insane and although he tries to break free in court, he ends as a beaten man, although the Punisher would return again and again in the future. Meanwhile the Black Cat goes on patrol with Spider-Man but during a battle with the new, improved, super-strong Hobgoblin, finds that she only gets in his way due to her comparative inexperience [85]. Felicia would be a prominent member of Spidey's supporting cast in the copper age.

Marvel Team-Up

Marvel Team-Up debuted in 1972 and was basically Marvel's answer to DC's *The Brave and the Bold*. Instead of heroes teaming with Batman each month, the star was Spider-Man, although there were several issues where the lead character was either the Human Torch or the Hulk. The initial creative team was Gerry Conway and Gil Kane, who were also doing Spider-Man's regular series at the time. Spider-Man's first adventures in MTU had him teaming with the Human Torch. In MTU 2 Spider-Man is hypnotized by the Frightful Four into attacking Johnny Storm in the Baxter building, while the Wizard's fiddling with Reed's machines almost unleashes Annihilus into our universe. Spider-Man teamed with the Thing - who would soon get his own team-up title -- in MTU 5, where they join forces against the duo of the Puppet Master and the Mad Thinker. Ross Andru took over as artist for forgettable team-ups with Thor and Iron Man.

The 9th issue began a multi-part story in which Spider-Man and assorted guest-stars must rescue the Avengers, who have been imprisoned in the future due to a war between future time-masters, Zarko, the Tomorrow Man, and Kang the Conqueror. Zarko has sent back capsules which will cause chronal regression, turning back time until the 20th century becomes the stone age, but Spidey and the Torch stop the scheme even as people and things begin reverting to bygone time-displaced variations in front of their eyes [10].

Len Wein and Jim Mooney became the new creative team for a time, but over the years many, many different writers and artists worked on the series. *Marvel Team-Up* 13 featured an exciting story in which the Gray Gargoyle, working with AIM, intends to create a device that can turn entire cities to stone from space before Spider-Man and Captain America stop his plans. Len Wein's script was ably brought to life by Gil Kane and

Frank Giacoia.

MTU 48 - 51 brought police captain Jean DeWolff, whose unloving and misogynous father, Philip, was once the commissioner, into Spider-Man and Marvel continuity. Philip's successor appoints Jean, but she still has to deal with negative attitudes from some of the men she works with as well as the outright hatred of her father. Her brother, Brian, with whom she had a close and respectful relationship, was also a cop, but he was attacked in an ambush; his body disappeared, but he is presumed dead. Now a masked figure called the Wraith is using model airplanes to cause devastating explosions with much loss of life. A note from the Wraith is in her brother's handwriting. Spider-Man is called in, along with Iron Man and Dr. Strange, to discover who the Wraith is, and it turns out to be catatonic Brian, his mind controlled by an insane Philip DeWolff. Dr. Strange is able to bring Brian back to normal while his father, the true villain, is arrested for the crimes of the Wraith.

Writer Bill Mantlo clearly meant to portray Jean as a positive symbol and a strong officer dominated by men, but it's unfortunate that we are shown her panicking hysterically at one point and fainting at another. True, these are very intense moments for her, but a male cop would probably not have been depicted that way. Also unfortunate is a contrived scene in which Peter refuses to take pictures of the Wraith's trial because it would be "picking the flesh off another person's misery." Photographs or drawings of a trial are fairly common, whatever misery may be occurring in the courtroom, so Peter's outburst is completely unrealistic and even silly, and he doesn't need to change into Spider-Man until later in the story.

Later issues of *Marvel Team-Up* had Spidey interacting with the Guardians of the Galaxy, the Shroud, Devil-Slayer, Kull, and many others; virtually any Marvel character from any genre or time period. (Other issues of MTU will be covered in the sections dealing with Spider-Man's guest-stars.) Writer J. M. DeMatteis had an interesting late run on MTU, and was actually able to take a story guest-starring the dorky wanna-be hero Frog-Man and the weird she-crook the White Rabbit, and make it work due to its plotting and characterization [131]. In MTU 129 - 130 Spider-Man has misadventures with the Vision and the Scarlet Witch, encountering a group of robots imprinted with the personalities of famous people such as Mark Twain. These were created and abandoned by the Mad Thinker.

This story also introduces reporter "Paunch" Pauncholito, who is actually covering a series of gruesome killings committed not by one of the robots but by his old friend, a police chief who's developed emotional issues, to say the least. Paunch figures out that his photographer Peter Parker and Spider-Man are one and the same, but even though unmasking the hero's identity would give the aged reporter one last chance for a great story, in the end he can't betray someone who has been so heroic to so many. In these issues there was also some nice art courtesy of Kerry Gammill and Mike Esposito.

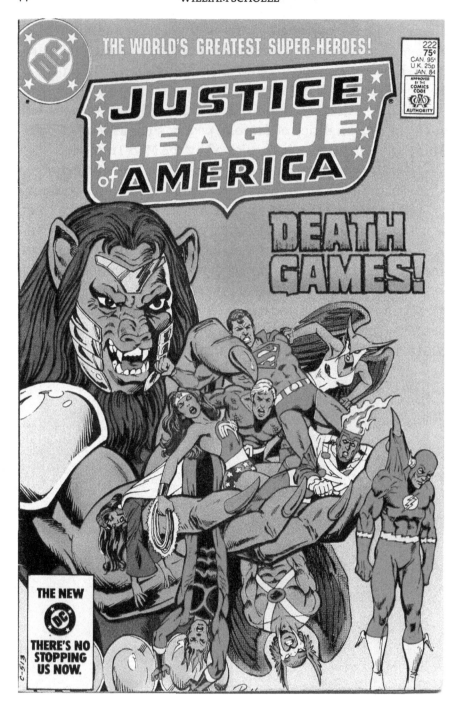

CHAPTER FIVE:
JUSTICE FOR ALL

--JUSTICE LEAGUE OF AMERICA, SECRET SOCIETY OF SUPER-VILLAINS

*J*ustice League of America, which debuted in the silver age, was still going strong at the start of the bronze age. Dick Dillin remained the penciller for many, many issues, and the writers included Denny O'Neill, Robert Kanigher, and Len Wein. The Justice League moved to their new satellite headquarters - positioned in orbit 22,300 miles above the earth - in *Justice League* 78.

This and the following issue, which guest-starred the Vigilante (apparently an Earth-1 version of the character) featured an anti-pollution story - of sorts. Like *Justice League* 90, which had a cover depicting the dumping of "deadly gas" into the ocean, it was "relevant" in name only, the stories actually having more to do with aliens and the like than happenings on Earth. Some of the more entertaining issues made no claim to relevance, such as "Batman -- King of the World," in JLA 87.

In this a robot sent by a distant civilization attacks Batman's mind and makes him turn against the other JLA members. The league then winds ups fighting a band of alien super-heroes who are, amusingly, modeled on Marvel's Avengers; alas the battle itself is much too brief. The story, while a bit disjointed, is nevertheless appealing. There was an attempt to create a triangle between Black Canary, Green Arrow and Batman, but this didn't last too long. Other stories were a little too weird and forgettable: JLA 89 featured writer Mike Friedrich's bizarre homage to fiction writer Harlan Ellison, hereby christened "Harlequin Ellis," who falls for the Black Canary and - like old JLA foe Dr. Destiny - dreams deadly dreams which embroil the JLA members.

The Justice League met one of their mightiest challenges when they took on Starbreaker in *Justice League* 96 - 98. Starbreaker, the Cosmic Vampire, is similar to Galactus in that he absorbs the energy from planets, especially the psychic torment of living human beings. Unlike Galactus, he looks like a modern-day Dracula, complete with sharp teeth and sinister countenance. Starbreaker sells off the energy he acquires (by destroying worlds) to bad guys who need power for their acts of infamy. The JLA first encounters him when he attacks Rann (Adam Strange appears briefly in JLA 96 but does not participate in the action). Three leaguers who are accidentally hit by a zeta beam and transported to Rann battle giant mechanical bugs that Starbreaker uses to make worlds ready for his ravaging.

In *Justice League* 97 Starbreaker, whose energy duplicates are defeated by the members of the league, decides to get even by making Earth his next target. As Starbreaker is the most powerful foe they've ever faced - the real man is much more powerful than the energy duplicates they trounced - the leaguers feel despair (partly generated by Starbreaker) over saving their planet, but Hawkman counteracts this by reminding them of their origin and the spirit that drives the league. Much of the issue consists of a retelling of their origin with a combination of new art and original art from JLA 9 (the two styles did not blend very well). Sargon the Sorcerer then appears saying that he wishes to help the league defeat their enemy.

Sargon needs certain rubies to cast a spell and sends the leaguers out on missions to acquire the gems. Too much time in *Justice League* 98 is spent on these missions, and not enough on the climactic battle with Starbreaker. Sargon's spell imbues the leaguers with "love power" that gives them added strength against a foe who feeds on fear and hatred. While the use of Sargon as a kind of *deus ex machina* is irritating, a clever strategy has the Atom going inside Starbreaker's brain to implant a suggestion (aided by Sargon) that he again split up and attack the leaguers after transferring them to two different time periods; this alone puts a strain on his powers and makes him more vulnerable. Starbreaker is completely defeated and drained of power. He returned in volume three of *Justice League of America* in 2009. Writer Mike Friedrich created a memorable villain, and his touches of characterization throughout the trilogy were welcome. The art by Dick Dillin and Joe Giella was, as usual, alternately flat and striking.

A counterpart to the JLA was introduced in issue 111 when a masked character named Libra organizes the Injustice Gang of the World (modeled after the Injustice Society that had plagued the JSA in the golden age), whose members include such familiar villains as Mirror Master, the Tattooed Man, Chronos, and Poison Ivy. Libra even builds a counterpart to the JLA's satellite HQ, in orbit on the other side of the world. Unfortunately, after some lively battles it is revealed that Libra only started the group so he could use its members in a plot to steal the leaguers' powers, and to absorb half the energy of the Milky Way galaxy into his body. Naturally, this energy proves too much for him to handle and his atoms disperse even as his mind goes loco. Some of the Injustice Gang reappeared in JLA 143 for a disappointingly brief battle in a mediocre story. However, the Gang was given much more to do in JLA 158, where they have the audacity to take over the league's old cavern HQ under the direction of a mysterious leader who turns out to be Flash's old foe Abra Kadabra. The Gang - and the JLA - also had to contend with the ill-advised machinations of Ultraa, a new hero from Earth-Prime, in his second appearance.

More than the Injustice Gang, the Secret Society of Super-Villains were really the JLA's evil counterparts. After their own short-lived series ended its run, the Society guest-starred in a memorable trilogy in JLA 166 - 168. In this the Wizard and his cohorts Blockbuster, Star Sapphire, Plantmaster, and Professor Zoom (the Reverse Flash) switch bodies with, respectively, Superman, Batman, Zatanna, Wonder Woman and Green Lantern. They give themselves away when Green Lantern makes a crude pass at Black Canary and are summarily defeated. (The Society, with many new members from both Earths 1 and 2, returned for a spectacular three part story in JLA 195 - 197, more on which later.)

Adam Strange, the star-spanning archeologist-adventurer who'd had a long-running series in *Mystery in Space* in the silver age, finally married his interplanetary sweetheart, Alanna, in a two-part story in *Justice League of America* 120 - 121. Kanjar Ro, who'd been defeated by both the JLA and Adam, escapes from prison on Rann and creates duplicates of menaces that Adam had fought once before: a cloud creature, the giant ray gun, an ancient gargantuan robot. Adam believes Alanna has been destroyed - and five members of the Justice League as well - but they are happily reunited after the heroes take care of both Kanjar Ro and his recreated menaces. Although Adam proposed to Alanna back in 1965, they didn't reach the altar until ten years later. The cover of JLA 121 depicts this scene, but makes the bodies of Adam and Alanna seem bizarrely thin, almost elongated. Whatever the limited virtues of Cary Bates' story, the uneven art by Dick Dillin and Frank McLaughlin prevented this from becoming a classic.

Writer Martin Pasko reintroduced Dr. Light, who'd first appeared in the classic *Justice League of America* 12 in the sixties, in issue 122. In this the bad doctor is able to infiltrate Superman's Fortress of Solitude, wherein he not only manages to discover the real identities of several JLA members, but makes them so confused that they each imagine they have another member's secret identity: for instance, Green Lantern thinks he's Ray (Atom) Palmer instead of Hal Jordan; The Flash thinks he's Bruce Wayne instead of Barry Allen; and so on. Dr. Light returned in 149 wherein he not only has to contend with the JLA but with ex-mascot Snapper Carr in the guise of the villainous Star-Tsar. Light cooked up a diabolical trap for the JLA members, splitting their bodies into different parts with a light spectrum weapon. Decades later Dr. Light would have a prominent role in the mini-series *Identity Crisis*, with plot threads that reached all the way back to these issues.

Although he had never fought the JLA as a group before, long-time Green Lantern foe Sonar from the silver age unleashed a diabolical plot in JLA 131 - 132. First he uses his super-science to create a deadly insanity-inducing plague that is distributed throughout the US by currency. Then in disguise as a benevolent scientist, he introduces a special new credit card that can replace infected paper money, an attempt to control the minds of everyone in the country. But his plan backfires when emanations from the cards make ordinary animals super-intelligent and especially hostile to humans. Adding to these complications is the return of old foe Queen Bee, who chooses this very time to attack certain cities with swarms of her souped-up bees. Gerry Conway's entertaining two-part story was also bolstered by a guest appearance by Supergirl. But one stupid moment has Aquaman improbably referring to Superman as "cowardly" when a bee gets in the Man of Steel's ear and the magnification of its noise in his auditory canal causes him to react by retreating.

Long-time JLA foe Dr. Destiny, whose face has become a skull due to his inability to dream, returns to bedevil the JLA in *Justice League* 154, giving them sinister nightmares as they sleep in a futuristic hotel of his design. (A clue to his identity is the gravity discs that people can dance on in the hotel's night club; Dr. D's first appearance was in "When Gravity Went Wild" in JLA 5.) When they awake, the heroes discover that their deadly dreams are coming true, but use their quick wits to get out of Dr. D's doom-traps. This was not the first time the evil doctor had used dreams to try and conquer his hated antagonists, but Gerry Conway's story was nevertheless quite exciting.

New Villains

There were new villains as well. JLA 127, written by Gerry Conway, introduced the Anarchist, who is kidnaping world leaders with the aid of super-powered allies. The Anarchist is revealed to be faith-healer Simon Ellis, whose plan is for the people to turn to him as a spiritual leader - and eventual dictator - in a time of crisis created by himself and his minions. He derives his power from Green Lantern's ring, but GL finds himself unable to expel all the ring's power - to prevent the villain from tapping into it - before the 24 hour charge is up. This necessitates Superman giving GL a power-packed punch that only his ring enables him to survive, so that the Anarchist loses his power and is easily defeated. Nekron (128 - 129), who feeds on fear, actually has the JLA members so frightened of dying that they decide to disband and retire until returning member Wonder Woman helps them snap out of it and defeat their antagonist.

Manhunter Mark Shaw, a former public defender, first appeared in a tale written and drawn by Jack Kirby for *First Issue Special* 5 [1975]. When the character wasn't picked up for a series, scripter Steve Englehart used him as the basis for a tale in JLA 140 - 141. In this it is revealed that the Guardians, creators of the Green Lantern Corps, had first employed androids - which they call Manhunters - as a galactic police force. When the androids eventually turned against them, the Guardians recruited human agents and formed the Corps. But the Manhunters still exist as brutal galactic bounty hunters who kill witnesses to their acts as well as anyone who learns of their existence. Pretending to be a force for good, they inveigle humans such as Mark Shaw to join their group. Plotting against the Guardians for centuries, they now engineer a scheme in which Hal. Jordan will be blamed for the death of a world and the trust in the Guardians will dissolve throughout the cosmos. The JLA unveil the Manhunters' scheme and Shaw sees the error of his ways. Shaw rechristened himself The Privateer in JLA 143, but 7 issues later it was revealed that it was Shaw, and not Snapper Carr, who was the sinister Star-Tsar; Shaw had not been able to shed off the dark side after all.

The deranged musician Anton Allegro appeared in *Justice League* 163 - 164, using a mystical machine to create weird music and monstrous magical creatures. He particularly hates Green Arrow because one of the Archer's tuning fork arrows accidentally flew too close to his head and deafened the man. He murders many of the people who have wronged him, and creates a mystical orchestra to send his insanity-causing compositions over the airwaves. Proteus, who plagued the group in JLA 187 - 188, was the chief antagonist of the Creeper in his short-lived silver age series. He uses a device called an Identi-Kit to change the looks and memories of several leaguers, then substitutes his own gang - equipped with artificial powers - to rob a store they'd promised to protect. But as soon as the leaguers remember who they really are - and realize their powers are still intact - they make short work of their criminal imitators.

Editor Julie Schwartz was replaced by Ross Andru beginning with *Justice League* 165; Schwartz left to take over the Superman line. (Andru was eventually replaced as editor by Len Wein.) But this didn't signify the end of an era as much as did the death of Dick Dillin, who succumbed to a heart attack on March 1st, 1980. Mostly inked by Frank McLaughlin, Dillin - whose last JLA issue was 183 - was the look of the JLA for even more issues than Mike Sekowksy. Dillin never had the compositional skills of Sekowsky, and often seemed defeated by the many heroes he had to draw (especially in the JSA team-up stories) but at his best his work was exciting, dramatic, and colorful. Dillin was replaced by such artists as George Perez, Don Heck, Rich Buckler and Chuck Patton.

Several new members were added to the JLA in the Bronze age, even as the Martian Manhunter and Hawkman departed (the latter rejoined after there was a plague on Thanagar). The Elongated Man joined in JLA 105, and the Earth-2 Red Tornado in the following issue. The Phantom Stranger was offered membership, but it is unclear as to in which issue he actually accepted, although he did become a part-time member. Hawkgirl finally became a member in JLA 146, although Hawkman and Superman argued over the rule that said there could be no duplication of powers (which kept out Batgirl and Supergirl). Zatanna the lady magician, who had met several leaguers in the silver age when they helped her find her father Zatara (a very popular Golden age hero) joined in JLA 161. Firestorm -- a composite hero consisting of high school student Ronnie Raymond and physicist Martin Stein who were conjoined after an explosion at a nuclear power plant - joined in JLA 179, which also introduced one of the JLA's rare (and quite forgettable) villainesses, a demon-possessed fashion model nicknamed the Satin Satan. Firestorm's induction into the league (after the black ghetto hero Black Lightning turned down an invitation to join) prompted a long-dissatisfied Green Arrow, who felt the league was too powerful to deal with ordinary people in crisis, to resign. GA and Black Canary remained a couple, however, and had their own series in *Adventure Comics.* Green Arrow rejoined the team in JLA 200.

Green Arrow got a lot of play-up in *Justice League.* A rather drab, colorless imitation of Batman in both the golden and silver age, Green Arrow was re-invented as a hip, bearded social activist just before the start of the bronze age. This happened when his alter ago, wealthy Oliver Queen, lost his fortune in a crooked deal. Frankly, one suspected that under his veneer of liberalism, GA was still a fairly conservative, very insecure "macho" type only making liberal noises. He became the voice of social protest, however, when he teamed with Green Lantern in the latter's own comic book for several issues. The Red Tornado also received a lot of play up - perhaps too much - in the JLA during this new era, trying to find a place in the world, bonding with a little orphan girl that he rescues from a war zone, and finding a girlfriend. It all seemed a little too similar to what the android vision went through in *The Avengers* in the silver age. In JLA 192 - 193 it was revealed for the first time that the Red Tornado had always been a living, sentient creature; in fact he was that weird alien being, the Tornado Tyrant (AKA the Tornado Champion) who first bedeviled Adam Strange and then the Justice League in the classic 17th issue of the silver age. RT himself was unaware of his original incarnation. During this period the Flash, who'd lost his wife Iris, tried unsuccessfully to forge a romance with Zatanna, who also got big play up in the comic. Although she and RT got back-up series in other comics, neither was ever popular enough to get their own series.

Justice League 200 was a 72 page super-spectacular which took its inspiration from the league's origin in *Justice League of America* 9. That classic issue dealt with alien invaders who wanted to fight each other for domination with Earth as the battleground. Now their seed clones emerge from the meteors inside which they'd originally come to Earth, and a suggestion implanted in the minds of the original leaguers years ago comes into play. The result is that the seven primary members of the group wind up fighting against the members who came afterwards. (Wonder Woman vs Black Canary; Flash vs. Elongated Man, etc.) An added plus is that chapters are drawn by the artist most associated with each classic character, with Carmine Infantino drawing the battle between Flash and Ralph Dibny, Gil Kane penciling the fight between the Atom and Green Lantern, and so on. George Perez did his usual fine job on the linking pages and Gerry Conway's script was top-notch.

Gerry Conway

Gerry Conway wrote a number of three and four-part stories that were among the best Bronze age JLA adventures. *Justice League* 203 - 205 introduced the new Royal Flush Gang (the original group, headed by Amos Fortune, had bedeviled the Justice League in the silver age on two occasions). The members consist of an alcoholic actress; a bitter lady test pilot who is sick of sexism; a gigolo whose latest victim fell off the balcony of a skyscraper; a hobo with extra-natural powers of persuasion; and the leader, Ace, a black man who turns out to be a robot. The true leader of the group is Green Lantern's old foe Hector Hammond, who has a desperate battle on the psychic plain with Martin Stein, the intellectual, unseen half of Firestorm. With death traps galore, a card-shaped secret HQ, and villains who are even more neurotic than usual - not to mention solid Don Heck artwork - this trilogy was a winner all the way.

In *Justice League* 210 - 212 our heroes learn that the supply of a certain natural "X-element" is running out in the world, bringing subtle changes that will create a string of disasters. In some parts of the world, a lack of friction means that speeding trains can't break to a halt; in other parts no one can light a fire; and so on. The JLA fight a losing battle to compensate for these losses so that people won't freeze, starve, or die in accidents, but salvation comes in the form of aliens called the Treasurers, who agree to replace the X-element in exchange for certain items. The JLA gather up these items - including sand from the Sahara - but are dismayed to learn that the Treasurers also want one specific man named George Arthur Stuart. A meek postal worker, Stuart agrees to go with the Treasurers, anxious to have a chance not to be "nobody." Some of the JLA members surreptitiously follow the Treasurers back to their home planet, and discover they are in league with a hostile reptilian race called the War-Kohn. Worse, the X-element the Treasurers have sprinkled throughout Earth's atmosphere only serves to change much of the population into monstrous and violent variations of the War-Kohn. The Treasurers want Stuart because he was the one person who carried a full genetic pattern of the human race, which can be - and is - used to change the mutated people back from monsters into ordinary human beings. While it may not stand up to close scrutiny in the scientific sense, the story is quite exciting and suspenseful, and features dynamic Rich Buckler pencils.

JLA 213 - 216 features a fantasy-oriented "Into the Microcosmos," wherein several leaguers follow a disturbed, erratic Atom into a sub-molecular universe that's still mostly in the medieval age. Unfortunately, our heroes lose their memory when they land on a particular planet, and the Atom - gigantic as compared to the inhabitants, as he failed to shrink all the way to "normal" size - has been trussed up in a palace courtyard like a latter-day Gulliver. The leaguers find themselves caught up in a war between the ruler Goltha, and his bitchy daughter, Princess Kass'Andre (who wears a jewel in her eye that shoots out painful ray beams) on one hand, and the kingdom's rightful heiress, Krystal Kaa, on the other. Also embroiled in the conflict are a group of women known as the Siren Sisterhood, who live in a vast underground chamber unbeknownst to Goltha. Among the sisterhood's number are Twigg, whose body is made up of wood with elastic properties, and Mother Moon, a healer, as well as their towering male associate, the strong and silent, bestial Mule. In the meantime, Goltha uses his mind-control over the Atom to keep everyone in line by having the now-big guy occasionally go on the rampage. Kass'Andre, who stabs her own father in the back, is a memorable villainess, and Don Heck's renderings of castles, caverns, sewers, monsters and the like are suitably atmospheric.

After five years of writing the series, Gerry Conway announced on the letters page that this was to be his last JLA story, but after a few mediocre issues by other scripters, Conway was back with another memorable trilogy in *Justice League* 221 - 223. In "Beasts" the JLA comes up against a series of animal-human hybrids - such as a gargantuan whale, a rhino, and giant scorpions that talk perfect English - leading gangs of thieves. Reena, who is a cat-human hybrid, tells the JLA that Rex Rogan, her boss and lover at a genetics company facing bankruptcy, convinced his board members and others to undergo experimentation that would turn them into grotesque half-animal monstrosities. Rex, who is turned into a lion-man, also builds an arena in which bored, rich and bloodthirsty people pay plenty to see ordinary human beings hopelessly pitted against his recombinant monsters. This gruesome, fascinating storyline was one of the best of the series, and Rex Maximus (Rogan) and his ani-men made formidable opponents. Chuck Patton (inked by Romeo Tanghal) turned in a nice penciling job, and Conway's script contains some interesting psychological observances.

Enter the Justice Society

The JLA-JSA team-ups continued in the Bronze age, with the new tradition of adding yet a third group of heroes to the mix. The 7 Soldiers of Victory, whose members included the Earth-2 Green Arrow, were briefly revived for a three part story in *Justice League* 100 - 102. The Quality comics heroes entered the DC Universe in 107 - 108, resulting in a new comic entitled *Freedom Fighters*. In 147 - 148 the JSA and JLA were brought to the 30th century by the evil sorcerer Mordru and battled members of the Legion of Super-Heroes at the command of the three demons who first appeared way back in JLA 10 - 11. Despite all the heroes, and action, these issues were, sadly, forgettable.

In *Justice League* 135 - 137 the JLA and JSA combine forces with heroes from the defunct Fawcett comic book line, such as Bulletman, Bulletgirl, Spy Smasher, Ibis the magician, Mr. Scarlet, and his young adopted son, Pinky. Fawcett's biggest sellers were the original Captain Marvel, Mary Marvel, and Captain Marvel Jr., all of whom show up in the third installment to help save mankind from the evil man-beast Kull. Unfortunately a promised battle between Superman and and his one-time comics rival Captain Marvel never really materialized (and did not occur until an issue of *All-Star Squadron* some years later). The story, by E. Nelson Bridwell and Martin Pasko, brought back some memorable Golden age heroes and even employed a few popular villains such as the Joker, but its appeal was nearly defeated by the rushed Dillin/McLaughlin artwork. There were, perhaps, just too many darn heroes to draw.

In JLA 159 - 160 the league and society battle a group of time-lost heroes of the past - Viking Prince, Enemy Ace, Jonah Hex and others - due to the machinations of the Time Lord. The villain has built an organic computer and ordered it to freeze time, then realizes he's made a big mistake -- only he can't shut down the computer. He empowers the time-lost heroes with extra energy so they can defeat the members of the league and society, giving all of them an extra charge of spirit and determination to win their next battle. The Elongated Man, who admits to himself that he was always full of hot air, feels completely out-classed by the others as they race to the future, but when everyone else is defeated he manages to save the day. Gerry Conway's excellent script highlights both the insecurities and sheer indomitability of the Justice League members. By far the worst JLA-JSA team-up occurred in issues 123 - 124 when writers Cary Bates and Elliot Maggin inserted themselves into the storyline and has them visiting Earths 1 and Earth 2, from "our" earth, Earth-Prime, where the Justice League is just a comic book. Not even the appearance of Earth-2's Injustice Society, which turned Bates into a super-villain, could save this stinker.

A new plot device was introduced for the team-up in an excellent, suspenseful story by Gerry Conway in *Justice League* 171 - 172. In this Mr. Terrific comes out of retirement to tell the assembled heroes that he's tracking down one of his old enemies, the Spirit King. After the heroes are almost destroyed by an act of sabotage to the JLA satellite, they discover that Mr. T has been strangled - and one of them has to be the killer. The satellite is sealed off via a combination of mystic force and power ring - courtesy of Dr. Fate and Green Lantern - and Batman and the Huntress (daughter of the Earth-2 Batman, who by this time was deceased) lead the investigation. The killer turns out to be the Flash of Earth-2, but only because the Spirit King took over his body. The Justice Society vows to go after him, free the Flash from his control, and avenge the death of Mr. Terrific.

The JLA - JSA team up in *Justice League* 183 - 185 has them involved with Jack Kirby's creations, Orion and the New Gods, Mister Miracle, and the villainous Darkseid and Granny Goodness. Members of Earth-2's Injustice Society (not to be confused with Earth-1's Injustice Gang) are drafted by the spirit of supposedly dead Darkseid to steal away all of the inhabitants of New Genesis in a scheme to not only bring the granite-faced dictator back to life, but to move his planet Apokolips [sic] into the same space as Earth-2, thereby destroying it. It was interesting to see writer Gerry Conway and artist George Perez' take on Kirby's characters (although Frank McLaughlin's inks may not have been the best fit with Perez' pencils) and to see them interacting with the more familiar heroes of the DC Universe. A particular bit of fun had Granny Goodness trying to whip Wonder Woman, who seemed a midget in comparison to the hulking Big Barda, Mister Miracle's warrior girlfriend.

As noted previously, the Secret Society of Super-Villains figured in one of the best JLA-JSA team ups in *Justice League* 195 - 197. This time the Society's leader was the Ultra-Humanite, who'd been battling Superman since early golden age issues of Action. UH moved his brain from body to body and finally wound up in the form of a huge white gorilla. Although it doesn't make much sense, the Ultra-Humanite has theorized that if five heroes from Earth-1 and five heroes from Earth-2 are captured and put in limbo, all heroes from Earth-2 will simply disappear, leaving him and his colleagues to loot and pillage. However, UH has lied to the Earth-1 villains -- which include Plantmaster, Killer Frost and the Cheetah - and told them that the results could occur in either Earth and he doesn't know which one. The society members manage to defeat the ten chosen heroes, but then - after all of the Earth-2 heroes indeed disappear - it occurs to the Earth-1 villains how UH has deceived them.

Furious at being tricked into helping villains from a completely different Earth with no pay-off for them, they free the heroes trapped in limbo, who in quick succession recapture them, and then their erstwhile allies from Earth-2. As all of the villains pursue the Ultra-Humanite across limbo, where the heroes have imprisoned them, UH sneers: "Bah! Some people simply have no sense of gratitude!" Gerry Conway's story was pure fun and action, well-supported by art by George Perez and

Romeo Tanghal (John Beatty and Keith Pollard also contributed). In the final JLA-JSA team-up of the bronze age [JLA 219 - 220] it was revealed that the Black Canary who had been appearing in so many stories was actually the heretofore unknown daughter of Dinah Lance.

Guest-stars didn't just appear in the JLA-JSA team-up issues. *Justice League* 144 featured the Blackhawks, the Challengers of the Unknown, Robotman (not to be confused with the Doom Patrol member), Congo Bill/Congorilla, Plastic Man, Rip Hunter, Lois Lane, Jimmy Olsen, Robin, and Adam Strange in a story that explained the real story of how the Justice League got together. Writer Steve Englehart revealed that most of the original members -- while tracking down reports of evil Martians along with the heroic guest-stars - actually met some months before the silver age origin story presented in JLA 9. They decided to postpone the official announcement of the group for the sake of J'onn J'onzz, the Martian Manhunter, so that he wouldn't have to endure the prejudicial fall out from the "invading Martian" scare. (No one seemed to remember that the official first meeting and adventure in JLA 9 also had to do with invading aliens, albeit none of them Martian.)

Just as the Crime Syndicate of Earth-3 figured in the most memorable JLA-JSA team-up of the silver age, so too were they integral to the best team-up of the bronze age, a five part "Crisis on Earth-Prime" that began in *Justice League* 207 and continued for two more issues, as well as in *All-Star Squadron* 14 and 15 (see chapter 6). Classic JSA villain Per Degaton is screwing around with the time stream again in his latest attempt to become master of the world. This results in him briefly becoming allies of the Crime Syndicate, whom he rescues from their prison in Limbo and takes back in time to the Cuban Missile Crisis on Earth-Prime (a world that has no super-heroes) to steal away the missiles before the Russians can withdraw them from Cuba; this results in a nuclear war that wipes out Earth-Prime and turns its survivors into mutates.

Meanwhile, during the annual meeting of the JSA and JLA in

the latter's orbiting HQ, the Crime Syndicate - sent spiraling into time by Degaton when they try to sneak up on him - wind up in the JLA transporter in the place of the JSA, who in turn wind up on the desiccated Earth-Prime. When the JLA go to Earth-2 to try and find out what became of the Society members, they discover that the whole world is now under the rule of Degaton and his Nazi-like goose-steppers. The JLA travel back to 1942 to find out what went wrong, and run into the All-Star Squadron, right after their first encounter with Nuclear the Magnetic Marauder. The members of the league and squadron do not recognize each other and briefly battle before calming down and comparing notes.

Teaming up the groups of heroes not only prevents the Syndicate from stealing the missiles but keeps Degaton from using them in the past to secure power for himself. Both Earth-2 and Earth-Prime are put back to normal, the Crime Syndicate wind up back in limbo, and our heroes, who have lost memories of events that, in essence, never took place, have a vague feeling of having survived a "crisis." Gerry Conway did the scripts for the JLA issues while Roy Thomas did the honors for A-SS. Don Heck came up with some very effective pencils for the JLA stories and Adrian Gonzales and Jerry Ordway did the same for A-SS. While the complex story certainly got confusing at times, generally the case in which time paradoxes are key, it was jam-packed with action, and the Crime Syndicate were as thoroughly evil and obnoxious as ever.

Other memorable issues: 145 -- Count Crystal actually manages to kill Superman with magic and offers the JLA members up as a sacrifice to an evil demon; 146 -- in which the JLA battle the third incarnation of the Construct, an evil sentient mind created in the ether from radio waves and the like; 152 -- Major Macabre and deadly alien artifacts; 189 - 190 -- the return of first JLA foe Starro the Conquerer; 191 -- Amazo and the Key team up (sort of); 194 -- Amos Fortune and living tarot cards; 201-- Ultra and Joe Parry; 202 -- an encounter with a spaceship that's been orbiting Earth for 200,000 years.

The Secret Society of Super-Villains

The Secret Society of Super-Villains premiered in mid 1976. The original concept of the comic had Darkseid bringing together a group of baddies - Captain Cold, Star Sapphire, Clayface, Manhunter, Gorilla Grodd - to form a Brotherhood of Crime (a sort of anti-JLA) that he apparently plans on using in his war against the Earth. However, Manhunter and the others decide they don't want to betray their own planet. After stealing a war gas from a plant as a test planned by Darkseid (who turns out to be a robot duplicate of the real thing), the group decide to stay together as "a secret society of the super-villain elite" to both fight Darkseid's ambitions and at the same time pursue their own "extra-legal goals." Written by Gerry Conway, the story would have sort of turned the bad guys into Heroes for the Earth, but it was scrapped because DC publisher Carmine Infantino wanted a somewhat different concept for the super-villain title. (This dumped first issue was later published in black and white in *Amazing World of DC Comics* 11.)

The actual first issue of *The Secret Society of Super-Villains* brought together ten villains, including a new, unknown Star Sapphire, Sinestro, Grodd and so on, but Darkseid was nowhere to be seen - at first. A mysterious unnamed benefactor has already built a HQ for the group - even though none of the ten have yet signed up - in a skyscraper, complete with men's and women's quarters, bar/club room, meeting hall, and so on. Grodd and Copperhead are sent on a test mission to steal a plutonium globe, but botch it. When Copperhead literally drops the ball, Grodd leaves him behind, but his returning to the others empty-handed seems to be glossed over. Gerry Conway was again the writer, and the fluid artwork was by Pablo Marcos and Bob Smith.

By the second issue, however, Darkseid was making his presence known, and is revealed as the unknown benefactor - pretty much the same concept as before. We discover that Manhunter, a clone of the original Manhunter, Paul Kirk, is not evil but on the side of the angels. SSSV 2 also re-introduces a character that hadn't been seen since the end of the golden age: Captain Comet, the mutant hero from *Strange Adventures*, who had been off roaming space and finding himself for the last twenty years. He gets involved with the secret society when he sees Green Lantern pursuing Grodd and Hi-Jack (of the Royal Flush Gang) and thinks GL is a bad guy.

By the 3rd issue Darkseid and his pals Mantis and Kalibak had pretty much taken over the book, which seemed more and more like a continuation of Kirby's Fourth World saga. Even the unwelcome Funky Flashman from *Mr. Miracle* showed up in in SSSV 4. In that same issue Darkseid battles former servant Mantis, who has absorbed power from Green Lantern and gotten big for his britches, even as Kalibak and Grodd tear at each other in San Francisco Bay. While artist Pablo Marcos was no Kirby, his work was serviceable. Garry Conway was gone as both editor and scripter by SSSV 5, and Darkseid was written out in the middle of that same issue. Bob Rozakis came on board as scripter and Rich Buckler as penciler.

About three issues later, however, Gerry Conway came back as scripter. Unfortunately, the irritating Funky Flashman stayed around, too. He did, at least, have the interesting idea of turning the Society into villains-for-hire, but not enough was done with this notion. The art by Buckler and assorted inkers always seemed a little too rushed to be memorable; when Ayers and Abel (of *Freedom Fighters*) took over for SSSV 10, there was a marked improvement. The stories were fairly unexceptional, however.

One of the best Secret Society adventures took place not in the regular magazine but in *Secret Society of Super-Villains Special* 1, which followed upon issue 10, in which Grodd and some new members mercifully send Flashman packing. Angle Man, Poison Ivy, and Bizarro have signed on, and they are going to help Grodd and Sinestro destroy their arch foes. Arvell Jones' pencils were ambitious, if flawed - especially when it came to the human body and the way it moved. Still some of the full-page panels showing the ignominious defeat of such heroes as

Flash, Wonder Woman, and Green Lantern are quite effective. Captain Comet helps defeat the villains and save the lives of the super-heroes. The climactic battle is much too brief, however. Arvell also penciled a good if somewhat zany story that appeared in *Super Team Family* 14 in which Atom and Wonder Woman team up against the Society, specifically Star Sapphire, Jason Woodrue (the Floronic Man) and Gorilla Grodd.

Mike Vosburg happily took over the pencils in SSSV 11, which has The Wizard from Earth-2 regaining a measure of his powers, donning a spiffy new outfit, and taking over the group. Vosburg's work was uneven, but not without merit. Blockbuster, Plant Master and Professor Zoom (aka the Reverse-Flash) were also recruited as members of the Society. In 13 and 14 the Society tried to cross over to Earth-2 but wound up on Earth-3, where three members of the Crime Syndicate (Superwoman, Power Ring, and Johnny Quick), first seen in *Justice League of America* 29 - 30, have escaped from captivity and are running amuck. The Wizard and his cronies manage to crossover to Earth-2 while Captain Comet has his hands full defeating the Crime Syndicate. In the final issue, 15, they begin attacking members of the Justice Society, while back on Earth-1 the Silver Ghost hires members of the Secret Society to bring down the Freedom Fighters once and for all.

SSSV 16 and 17 were scripted and penciled, but never published. They detail the battle between the Secret Society and the Freedom Fighters (see chapter 6). The promised origin of the new Star Sapphire never materialized (not even in these "lost" issues). It was also revealed that Firebrand and the Silver Ghost were somehow acquainted, but the story behind this was never disclosed. *Secret Society of Super-Villains* was more fun and somewhat more successful than *Freedom Fighters*. While the potential of the latter series seemed to elude the various creative teams, *Secret Society* seemed fraught with endless possibilities. As noted, the Society later appeared in a memorable two-parter in *Justice League of America* wherein The Wizard and others switched bodies with several of the

Justice League members.

CHAPTER SIX:
ALL STAR

-- ALL STAR COMICS, ALL-STAR SQUADRON, STEEL, FREEDOM FIGHTERS

T he 58th issue of *All Star Comics* - which ran for 57 issues in the golden age - finally appeared after a decades-long absence in 1978. The stars were, again, the Justice Society of America, although the focus was on a "Super-Squad" comprised of several JSA members: Earth-2 Superman's cousin, Power Girl; the Star-Spangled Kid (from the 7 Soldiers of Victory), now outfitted with Starman's cosmic power rod; and a grown-up Robin. While the Justice Society members have aged naturally, the Star-Spangled Kid went through a warp from the fifties into the seventies, and finds things a little strange because of it.

All Star Comics

Gerry Conway, with art by Ric Estrada and Wally Wood, got things off to a good start with the heroes reacting to menaces created by golden age foe Brainwave. Brainwave first appeared in *All Star* 15, and was a weird psychiatrist named Henry King who could send out dangerous mental images. He reappeared in AS 17, wherein he shrank the JSA members down to six inches but still couldn't defeat them. Twenty issues later Brainwave joined the Injustice Society - in one of the best golden age JSA stories ever published - but even with his comrades-in-crime at his side he came up a loser.

In *All Star* 59 Brainwave uses his power to bring old ally Per Degaton out of a stupor, and then tries to hurl the earth far away from the sun - to no avail. The next issue introduced the menace of fiery Vulcan, an astronaut gone mad, as well as the early penciling of Keith Giffin, who would gain fame for his work on *The Legion of Super-Heroes*. The Flash's wife importunes him to retire, but he still reports for duty in AS 61, in which the ancient Lemurian menace of Zanadu is unleashed. Hourman is appalled by the fighting between Power Girl and the grumpy, chauvinistic Wildcat. Things aren't helped when Superman shows up, and argues with Power Girl himself; she eventually replaces him when he retires [AS 61 - 63].

When Gerry Conway left DC to work for Marvel, Paul Levitz took over as scripter, and soon inker Wally Wood replaced Giffin as penciller. Vandal Savage enacts a plot involving time travel and ancient Camelot in a ploy to regain his immortality in AS 64 - 65, even as Alan Scott/Green Lantern faces losing his company and Hourman wonders if he's a useless has-been. The second part of the story with Savage is particularly exciting as the villain tries to beat a powerless Superman to death, and Wally Wood's art was the best of the series to date.

Unfortunately, Wood was gone with the next issue, and so was the original logo, which now featured "Justice Society of America" in very big letters under "All Star Comics" in small letters, and eliminated the Super-Squad altogether - in the inside pages as well. Joe Staton and Bob Layton were the new art team. The Injustice Society returned in AS 66 but were dispatched relatively quickly - this was frankly inferior to their golden age appearance -- and the Psycho-Pirate made Green Lantern go on a rampage. It also develops that the Psycho-Pirate is behind the strange behavior of Commissioner Bruce Wayne, the retired Batman, who charges the members of the JSA with reckless endangerment and tries to have them taken into custody. This results in a lively battle between the current members and some of the retired ones, such as Starman and

Wonder Woman, a battle ended when Power Girl reveals the truth about what's happening [AS 69].

The Huntress made a brief shadowy appearance in AS 69, but made her true debut in the following issue as she helps the JSA against a bunch of sophisticated criminals termed the Strike Force. The Huntress was the Earth-2 Batman's daughter, Helena Wayne, and she not only appeared in *All Star* but got a back-up series in *Batman Family* and *Wonder Woman*. The Strike Force was a forgettable group but for the fact that its leader turned out to be the nephew of the "long-Lost" Arthur Pendleton - the Star-Spangled Kid - who is using his vanished uncle's fortune to bankroll his activities. AS 72 - 73 featured an exciting story in which the group takes on the murderous golden age villainess the Thorn, and another villainess from the golden age, The Huntress, corners Helena in JSA HQ because she's furious that the latter stole her *nom de plume*.

Joe Giella took over the inking of the strip with *All Star* 74, and it made Staton's pencils look much less cartoonish. The comic was expanded in size, with more pages, and the story - the JSA fighting a cosmic being called the Master Summoner - was divided into chapters with different heroes teaming up as in the old days. The art was still relatively undistinguished, but there was a great half-page panel depicting the heroes flying into battle. Unfortunately, this was the last issue of *All Star*, but the JSA got a strip in *Adventure* instead. Stories that had already been commissioned for *All Star* were at first split in two and put into *Adventure*. The first story in *Adventure* 461 - 462 featured the death of the Earth-2 Batman while battling a convict who had developed incredible energy powers. The last JSA story appeared in *Adventure* 466 and fittingly explained why the group stopped operating in the early fifties for several years: because the House Un-American Activities committee wanted them to reveal their secret identities!

The Justice Society reappeared in *All-Star Squadron*, but before that there were a few comics that related to the *All Star* series. *DC Special* 29 finally told the origin of the JSA which had never been revealed even during the golden age. In the days before the U.S. entered the war, President Roosevelt is told of a pending major invasion of England by Hitler's forces, but his hands are tied unless America herself is attacked. So he calls together the great super-heroes of the nation, and they band together for the first time as they race to England's defense. The heroes are successful in beating back the Nazis, but then have to prevent a squadron of Valkyries from attacking Washington, D.C. Levitz, Staton and Layton were the creative team.

Power Girl was given a three-issue solo try-out series in *Showcase* 97 - 98. Butch and busty, Power Girl seemed like a combination sex symbol and feminist, but while she was right to bristle at sexist remarks, she also had a chip on her shoulder when it came to big cousin Superman and some other men. She could also be obnoxious and a bully, knocking some reporters to the ground because she doesn't want to answer their questions. Meanwhile PG has problems with Brainwave and the symbioship in which she traveled from Krypton, a living spaceship that still wants to bond with its former passenger whether she wants to or not. She is helped by Andrew Vinson, one of the reporters she bullied, who also helps her get a secret identity and a job. Both Power Girl and the Huntress were bronze-age creations who are still around today.

Power Girl and the Earth-1 Superman teamed up in *DC Comics Presents* 56 wherein the two battle an extremely powerful and merciless entity known as Maaldor, the Dark Lord, a formidable foe that the two Kryptonians barely manage to defeat. Maaldor is literally transformed into a new plane of existence, one that is a "cosmic embodiment of madness," which Superman seals off for the sake of the universe. Maaldor would reappear in the copper age and bedevil both Superman and Green Lantern, among others.

All-Star Squadron

The All-Star Squadron first appeared in a special preview in *Justice League of America* 193. Various members of Earth-2's Justice Society are attacked by villains they'd never seen before (but who claimed to have fought the heroes previously) even as President Franklin Delano Roosevelt desperately tries to contact the heroes to form a special squadron to deal with a contemporary crisis. The date: December 7th, 1941. In *All-Star Squadron* 1 [1981] the story picks up with Hawkman discovering non-member Plastic Man (originally a comical hero published by Quality comics), now an FBI liaison, in the JSA HQ, looking for the missing members. Meanwhile, Sir Justin, AKA the Shining Knight of the Law's Legionnaires (later known as the 7 Soldiers of Victory) encounters volcanologist Danielle Reilly on a mysterious island that only recently appeared. The villain Per Degaton appears, claiming to have come back in time from 1947. (Per Degaton first appeared in a harrowing story in *All-Star Comics* 35 in the golden age.)

At the White House, FDR tells an assemblage of heroes that the Japanese have attacked Pearl Harbor, where Danielle's brother, Rod, also the hero known as Firebrand, is wounded. Roosevelt says that he wants all of the "mystery men" - the term that was used before "super-hero" came into vogue - be they members of the JSA or not, to be organized into a kind of "All-Star Squadron" to assist the country against foreign enemies who may come to America's shores. This they did in the issues to come. Per Degaton was defeated (until his next deadly time jaunt), and the captive JSA members were released in A-SS 2- 3. The main "stars" of the Squadron were Johnny Quick, a super-speedster who'd always been the second stringer after the original Flash; Liberty Belle, a minor character who had athletic ability and a little something extra; and Robotman, the former Dr. Bob Crane, who had a human brain encased in a strong and heavy metal body. (The same concept was used for a similarly named character in the silver age's Doom Patrol.) All three characters had originally appeared in the golden age.

Written by Roy Thomas, with very attractive art by Rich Buckler and Jerry Ordway, the basic concept of *All-Star Squadron* was to create situations where all the great "mystery men" and women - plus a few new heroes created specifically for A-

SS - could intermingle in a way they never could have in the past. The Justice Society, which appeared in *All-Star Comics* in the golden age, only had a select group of members, and many of the other heroes of the period were not published by DC but by other companies (DC acquired the rights to them later on). With the WW 2 home front as the background, Thomas could now take any of these heroes he wanted and have them interact in a way that was a comic fan's dream. Adding to the whole mystique was the fact that rarely had these golden age heroes looked quite so good, thanks to the superlative modern-day art job.

A-SS 4 had the heroes taking off after the Japanese fleet from which came the bombers that attacked Pearl Harbor, killing 2000 American soldiers. Roy Thomas thought of an extremely clever way of explaining why the members of the Squadron couldn't simply use their great powers to wipe out the Axis armies and win the war in a matter of days. It turns out that both Hitler and Toho are in possession of certain mystical objects - the Spear of Destiny and the Holy Grail, respectively - that can take over the minds of some of the Squadron's most powerful members, both those whose powers are magical in origin - Dr. Fate, Green Lantern, Wonder Woman - and those who are especially susceptible to magic, such as Superman. The minute they fly too close to enemy territory these powerful heroes turn against America and attack their comrades. The members who are not affected are not in the same league power-wise. Therefore the strongest members of the group have to limit their activities to the home front.

The first few issues of *All-Star Squadron* were very talky, almost choked with word balloons, giving the stories a draggy pace, but that was eventually rectified. In A-SS 5 it was decided to disband the Justice Society for the duration of the war so that the members could join the Army in their civilian identities. Danielle Reilly also discovered that her comatose brother had been the hero Firebrand, and took the name for himself - as well as a variation of his costume - when she develops fiery powers due to a freak accident during the adventure with Per Degaton. Danielle also develops a severe hatred of everyone Japanese until her brother tells her how his life was saved at Pearl Harbor by a fellow soldier who happened to be Japanese-American [A-SS 13].

Adrian Gonzales took over as penciller with issue 6, detailing a lively fight against the Feathered Serpent, a disguised Nazi, in Mexico, whose oil the Axis powers coveted. As Ordway remained on inks, there was still a certain consistency to the art, which had a kind of elegant beauty and even grandeur. Baron Blitzkreig tried to kidnap the visiting Winston Churchill in A-SS 7, and Steel - fresh from the pages of his own short-lived series where he was battling the baron - showed up in the following issue. In A-SS 9 it is revealed that the baron has brainwashed Steel into attempting the murder of both Churchill and FDR at a certain signal, but fortunately the other Squadron members are on hand to prevent this and help return Steel to his normal patriotic self. In A-SS 13 Steel learns that his mentor Dr. Giles is dead and that his former fiancee Gloria Giles has married another man. He tells her that his alter ego Hank Heywood is dead, presumably killed while on assignment overseas.

In A-SS 10 - 12 a new menace to Earth comes in the form of a huge flying ship called the Eye and a man named Aknet, who claims to come from another planet. Aknet tells world leaders that his people have been following the world-wide conflict and have decided it would be best for everyone to surrender to them; they will choose the right leaders. Any country that refuses to acquiesce will be destroyed. It turns out that Aknet is merely an automaton controlled by Hawkman's first foe, Dr. Nestor, who has taken command of a well-meaning project by several world scientists to unite the nations of the Earth together against a common - if fictional - threat. Nestor, of course, co-opted the project for his own purposes. He is roundly trounced by our heroes after some delicate moments. Robotman took center stage in A-SS 17 in a story which is based on one that had appeared in *Star Spangled Comics* in the golden age. Robotman has to prove his essential humanity in a court of law, where Bob Crane's fiancee Joan discovers for the first time that he is still alive and in a metallic body.

All-Star Squadron 18 was a perfect illustration of one of the main things Roy Thomas was trying to do with the series: retroactive continuity. In the golden age, the hero known as Sandman - playboy Wesley Dodds - abruptly switched from one costume to another without explanation. His girlfriend, Dian, completely disappeared from the strip, and he suddenly had a boy partner, Sandy. At the same time another DC hero named Tarantula showed up whose costume was strikingly similar to Sandman's new outfit. Thomas provided an explanation: Both men had known Dian, who had designed the new outfit for her boyfriend. When he decided not to use it, she gave it to mystery writer Jonathan Law, who wore it as the Tarantula. (He was given a spiffy and darker new costume in A-SS 24). Dian herself was killed fighting Nazi spies while clothed in Sandman's original uniform. Even readers who had not been around when the original golden age tales had been published had to be impressed if not fascinated at how Thomas managed to wrap up loose ends and tie everything up in a consistently entertaining fashion. In A-SS *Annual* 1, Thomas took the three men who'd trained, respectively, Wildcat, the Atom, and The Guardian, and convincingly made them all the same person.

Jerry Ordway did the pencils as well as inks for A-SS 19, and the results were felicitous, and he remained as penciller for the series. This issue also brought back the big guns from the Justice Society, especially Green Lantern, who (due to the manipulations of foe Brain-Wave) dreams that he's wiped out virtually the entire nation of Japan - including ordinary citizens and children - and is temporarily suicidal because of it. The members of the JSA realize they can do more for the war effort in their super-hero uniforms than in khaki, so they form a Justice Battalion - all other heroes remain in the All-Star Squadron, which decides to use the abandoned perisphere of the 1939

World's Fair as their new HQ. Just as significantly, Mike Machlan was brought in as inker over Ordway's pencils beginning the very next issue; unfortunately, the art immediately took a dip in quality. It certainly wasn't bad, but never again would it have the almost glossy luxuriousness that it had boasted before.

A long story arc beginning in A-SS 21 brought in Superman villain Ultra (or the Ultra-Humanite), not in the ape form he would employ in the aforementioned modern-day JLA-JSA team up in JLA 195 - 197, but in the form of his kidnap victim, actress Dolores Winters, into whose body he was forced to have his brain transplanted way, way back in a story published in the golden age. Ultra - still at heart a man despite his outward appearance - employs a number of willing and semi-willing super-folk to aid him in his nefarious causes. One of these is Black Olympic champion Will Everett, who returns to the U.S. from winning medals in 1936 and bitterly discovers that even his athletic achievements can only take a "colored" man so far. In A-SS 23 he is transformed into Amazing-Man, who can absorb the property of anything he touches, becoming living wood or stone, like Marvel's villain the Absorbing Man (who battled Thor time and again). He ultimately turns against Ultra and helps the Squadron defeat him.

A-SS 25 introduced Infinity, Inc., a group of apparent villains who are helping Ultra and who think of the all-stars as "fascists." They are actually heroes from the future - 1983, in fact - who were brain-washed by Ultra into fighting the good guys. They also turn out to be the futuristic sons, daughters and wards of various Justice Society members, although the older heroes are unaware of this. In the culmination of the Ultra storyline in A-SS *Annual* 2, Ultra invades a hospital with the idea of having his brain put inside Robotman's body. Ultra and his henchmen, including some members of the Secret Society of Super-Villains who also come back from the future, get into a riotous free-for-all with the Squadron, the Justice Battalion and Infinity Inc. In fact, there were so many heroes and villains that the story was at times as confusing as it was exciting. Infinity Inc. got its own series in the copper age. As for *All-Star Squadron*, it continued into the copper age and had a respectable run of 67 issues. The final bronze age issues of the series concentrated on the mystic heroes, Dr. Fate and the Spectre.

Steel

Steel, the Indestructible Man made his debut in 1978. The series took place in 1939, before the United States' entry into WW 2. Hank Heywood is a brilliant and promising biology student whose fiancee, Gloria, is the daughter of his professor, Gilbert Giles. He accompanies the professor on a trip to Munich where the older man lectures on his biological retardant, which will enable doctors to replace limbs and organs that would formerly have been rejected. Not only are the German scientists dismissive, but Hank is appalled to see Nazi goons trying to beat up an elderly Jewish man.

Back in the states, when he reads of the increased aggression of the Axis powers, he decides to enlist in the Marines, putting his life and career on hold and worrying and angering Gloria. He wonders if she's right that he's just grandstanding, but reassures himself that he truly believes in what he's doing. Attacking some saboteurs at his marine base, Hank is severely injured in an explosion, and importunes Giles to use the retardant they developed to rebuild his body. Metal tubing - steel, in fact - is used to replace his shattered bones, and special motors are installed to help him move the steel. The result is that he develops into a kind of super-human - he has super-strength, invulnerable super-skin, and his artificial lungs enable him to stay underwater for half an hour. Not knowing of this, the marines give Hank a desk job, so he decides to take on saboteurs in the costumed red, white and blue identity of Steel until America wakes up to the Nazi menace. Written and created by Gerry Conway, the series was designed and penciled by Don Heck.

Somewhere between the 1st and 2nd issues, Steel contacts the Army and - without giving away his real identity - offers to give them a demonstration of his abilities. Although he does this in *Steel* 2, they think he's just a glorified stuntman. The villain for the issue is Mineral Master, who has the ability to animate rocks and things, and wants to destroy anyone who favors U.S. intervention in the conflict overseas. New members of the supporting cast were introduced, including newspaper publisher Edward Runyon, and his sometime girlfriend and senator's daughter, Kathy Kulhammer, who in her patronizing way thinks Steel is "cute." Meanwhile Professor Giles has started to suspect Heywood and Steel are one and the same (in reality he probably would have known right off the bat) and is appalled, because he sees Steel as an over-patriotic war hawk. Giles does not agree with Hank about the necessity of the U.S. entering the European conflict.

Steel 3 brought Heywood into lively conflict with a gangster nicknamed Sledgehammer because of his incredible strength, and also introduced a costumed crook called the Gadgeteer, who battles Steel in issue 4. Seriously injured during the fight, Steel sets off in issue 5 to get more of the bio-retardant, which, inexplicably, is only in the possession of a heretofore unmentioned former classmate of his. This led into a weird *What Ever Happened to Baby Jane?* kind of storyline concerning a silent movie star, whose career ended with sound, and his manager-brother, one of whom was in an accident and turned into a hairy, hulking monster. This was the final published issue of the series.

Arguably the best issue of *Steel* was the unpublished 6th issue (although some of it wound up in *All-Star Squadron* 8 and 9). In this Professor Giles tells Hank that he must make a choice: his Steel identity or his daughter. In all good conscience, Hank chooses to remain a super-hero and says good-bye to Gloria. On assignment in London in his regular identity, he has occasion to stop Winston Churchill's assassination as Steel, and it as also as Steel that he is sent behind enemy lines on a mission to assassinate Hitler. This brings him into conflict with the Nazi who will soon be known as Baron Blitzkreig.

Back in the United States Senator Kulhammer is preparing to denounce Steel as a traitor and warmonger even as Steel wakes up to find himself in a Nazi concentration camp, (barely) living proof of the world-threatening menace of the Nazis. As noted, the rest of Steel's story was covered in *All-Star Squadron* 8 and later issues.

Steel was an interesting series with a lot of potential that it was not destined to fulfill. It was good at delineating the way many perfectly good Americans were alarmed at the prospect of the U.S. fighting Germany because of the heavy cost of WW 1, and the fact that things in the country were just beginning to settle down now that the depression was over. There was a very real horror of becoming embroiled in another world war. As Gloria says about her father: "Dad thought of Hank as his son. It must have hurt him so when Hank chose the warriors over the peacemakers." Setting the series two years before Pearl Harbor meant that Steel could have innumerable adventures -- given the fact that comic book time varies greatly from real time -- both on the home front and overseas before the U.S. even entered the conflict. Gerry Conway's scripts offered incisive characterization, even if his villains were on occasion lame. Don Heck's pencils (with various inkers) were solid; Juan Ortiz and Bruce Patterson also did some work on the series. In the copper age Hank Heywood's grandson became the new Steel and briefly became a member of the Justice League of America.

Freedom Fighters

The golden age Quality heroes were brought back in 1973 in *Justice League of America* 107 - 108. During the annual meeting of the Justice League and Justice Society, a transporter malfunction caused by the presence of stowaway Red Tornado sends a mixture of JLA and JSA members to yet another alternate Earth, Earth-X. Here they encounter Uncle Sam, The Human Bomb, Phantom Lady, The Ray, Doll Man, and The Black Condor, who have banded together to form a group called the Freedom Fighters.

On Earth-X, the Nazi's won the war, then quickly turned on their allies, The Japanese. They use mind-control technology to enslave the world. The Freedom Fighters and assorted League and Society members team up to tear down three big machines that are helping to control the populace, but the Red Tornado discovers the main computer is on a satellite in space, overseen by an android Adolf Hitler. Seems the Nazis were thrown out of real power ages ago by the consciousness of the devilish machine. Red Tornado destroys the satellite and Earth-X is free once more.

Len Wein's script and the art by Dick Dillin and Dick Giordano were colorful - although an alternate universe where Germany had won WW2 was not exactly an original idea - but the Freedom Fighters were distinctly one-dimensional and the art, as usual, rather flat. There were, however, a few striking panels, such as one of the intense Batman climbing the Eiffel Tower. At one point the mind-controlled Justice types begin to fight the Freedom Fighters, with Doll Man winding up dangling from the Elongated Man's stretching silly putty nose. Interesting issues, to be certain, but hardly classic.

In 1976 the Freedom Fighters were given their own series. They crossed over to Earth-1 with the aid of an Earth-X scientist because the war with the Nazis was over and they were bored. (What - there was no crime on Earth-X?) Crossing dimensions gave some of them new powers; for instance Phantom Lady could now literally turn into a phantom, and Doll Man and Black Condor eventually developed telekinetic and telepathic powers, respectively. In the first three issues, written by Gerry Conway and Martin Pasko and drawn by various artists, the FF are not exactly welcomed by New York City, although the district attorney sets them up in an abandoned armory. Unfortunately, a villain called the Silver Ghost turns three of the members into statues and forces the others to do his bidding if they want him to turn their pals human again. This leads into a completely unbelievable scene in the *Freedom Fighters* 2 wherein The Human Bomb uses his explosive touch on a subway train packed with men, women, and children. Although one assumes there were no fatalities, passengers on the train are shown flying through the air, so it's likely there were numerous serious injuries. It's hard to believe that the supposedly heroic Bomb would use his powers against innocents, no matter what the provocation.

The Freedom Fighters seem a bit testy with each other at times, and even disrespect Uncle Sam by referring to him as "old man" and old-timer." In the Golden Age stories in which the character appeared, he was not exactly a senior citizen, but now he's more or less perceived by everyone as just that, even with occasional references to "senility." True, if Uncle Sam had been active since WW2 he was hardly a youngster, but the same applies to the other members of the Freedom Fighters.

On the run from police, the FF tries to storm the UN so as to be declared delegates from their universe (with the added advantage of diplomatic immunity) but in *Freedom Fighters* 4 and 5 Wonder Woman is dispatched to bring them in. With these issues Bob Rozakis took over as scripter. FF 6 had our heroes traveling to Rutland, Vermont for the annual Halloween parade where they battle a demon. The essentially mediocre art of Ramona Fradon and Bob Smith was replaced in FF 7 by Dick Ayers and Jack Abel. While there was a noticeable improvement in the artwork, the story - an evil elf in SantaLand tries to turn the Earth on its axis to protest discrimination against "anyone who's different" and take over the world - seemed more of a dopey parody than anything else.

The Freedom Fighters started coming into their own with *Freedom Fighters* 8 and 9. In this two-part story a super-hero group called The Crusaders tries to bring down the Freedom Fighters. Americommando, Barracuda, Fireball, and kid partners Rusty and Sparky were clearly modeled on Marvel's Invaders: Captain America and Bucky, Namor, and the Human Torch and Toro. The Crusaders, who had only been a fictional comic book team on Earth 1 (and apparently Earth-X as well) are actually The Silver Ghost and some comic book fans he somehow transformed into super-heroes. The story had a very Marvel style to it - there were particularly good battle scenes in FF 8 - and very effective art by Ayers and Abel.

Freedom Fighters 11 introduced a team of Native Americans who are magically and mysteriously granted super-powers and become bank robbers to fund their cause. There was no attempt to actually look into the plight of Native Americans or illuminate their lives; in fact, one of the men who can grow to giant-size is called "a heap big injun" by the Human Bomb. In the meantime The Freedom Fighters learn that Doll Man has been arrested for the murder of the D.A. back in New York, but Uncle Sam strangely vetoes a suggestion to get back to Manhattan because "good old American justice will win out." What about lending moral support to a wrongly accused teammate?

Another Quality hero, The Firebrand, turned up; he, too, had crossed dimensions from Earth-X to Earth-1. Still wanted by the police, the FF decide to disguise themselves as circus performers and join Kathy Kane's carnival in *Freedom Fighters* 14. Kane was the original Batwoman. Batgirl, who also appeared in the story, was not the original Bat-Girl, Kane's niece, but rather Barbara Gordon, Commissioner Gordon's daughter. The FF, with the aid of the Bat-ladies, stop an alien invasion in the fifteenth and final issue. Readers of this issue were told on the letters page that the story would be picked up in *Secret Society of Super-Villains* 16, but as that comic was canceled as well, the story was never published.

All in all the potential of the Quality heroes was never fulfilled. Although there were some interesting elements to Bob Rozakis' stories, he didn't really seem to know where to go with the time-and-dimension-lost characters.

CHAPTER SEVEN: SOME OF MARVEL'S SUPER LADIES

-- MS. MARVEL, THE CAT, TIGRA, SHANNA, BLACK WIDOW

Before the seventies, Wonder Woman was virtually the only super-heroine who had her own comic book. Marvel Comics, in particular, introduced such starring characters as Ms. Marvel, The Cat, and Shanna, the She-Devil. None of their comics, alas, lasted for very long, and neither did the Black Widow's strip in *Amazing Adventures.* (The She-Hulk and Spider-Woman are covered in volume two.)

Ms. Marvel

Ms. Marvel 1, written by Gerry Conway, who created the character, and drawn by John Buscema and Joe Sinnott, debuted in 1976. Carol Danvers, who lost her security job due to her failure to capture Captain Marvel in his series, has turned to writing to make a living. J. Jonah Jameson hires Carol to edit a woman's magazine for him but she has no intention of publishing recipes and the like as he would prefer. Carol has blackouts which leave her terribly weak and with gaps in her memory. During these blackouts a new super-heroine named Ms. Marvel appears: she can fly, has super-strength, and a kind of psychic ability, powers which she claims come from the Kree. Her costume is a variation of the one worn by Captain Marvel and its advanced circuitry also adds to her abilities. In the first issue she saves Jameson from being soaked in an acid bath by the Scorpion, who wants revenge against the publisher for his part in turning him into a monster. Neither Carol nor Ms. Marvel are aware of their dual identity.

In *Ms. Marvel* 2 Carol seeks help from a friend-psychiatrist named Mike Barnett, who helps her remember when she received a massive dose of radiation during the final fight between Captain Marvel and his enemy Yon-Rogg - later her powers were also attributed to the influence of a Kree "psyche-magnitron." In the following issue, on an assignment down in Florida near where she acquired her powers, Ms. Marvel finally realizes that she's also Carol Danvers as she engages a Silver Surfer foe called the Doomsday Man. The abilities derived from her costume become absorbed into her body proper.

By the fourth issue there was a completely new creative team, with Chris Claremont handling the scripts and Jim Mooney taking over from John Buscema, who was over-extended and whose work on the series wasn't quite up to his usual par. Carol and Ms. Marvel are separate personalities who are aware of each other's existence; Ms. Marvel can emerge whenever her "seventh sense" tells her that she's needed. Carol fears being completely absorbed by Ms. Marvel, but frankly enjoys the power and excitement of being a super-hero. Carol gets visions of dangerous future events, and seems to be able to unconsciously teleport to another location just before she switches to her alter-ego. Her supporting cast expanded to include photographer Mike Gianelli and reformed alcoholic reporter Theresa "Tracy" Burke, whom Carol hires as her assistant editor.

Ms. Marvel's foes were not too interesting at first - a lame villain called the Destructor, Grotesk from the silver age X-Men series - but finally Modok appeared in all his hideous big-headed glory in *Ms. Marvel* 7. Modok wants to use Ms. Marvel in his plans to snatch back leadership of AIM, which has its New York HQ under a department store in the Bronx. Then *Ms. Marvel* 9 brought the vicious alien female Death-Bird, whose clawed hands could cut through stone and who threw deadly energy javelins. Death-Bird was an agent for Modok, and in the following issue they attack AIM's Bronx HQ just as Carol is doing some reconnoitering there. What follows is a very exciting four-way battle with AIM's agents blasting at Modok as he blasts back, Death-Bird busy trying to skewer Ms. Marvel, and cops and frightened shoppers not certain what to make of the confusing melee. Modok manages to take possession of a missile and launches it just as the two ladies are engaging in savage combat, and Death-Bird is apparently caught in the rocket's fiery exhaust. With fine artwork by Sal Buscema and Tom Palmer this was the best issue of the comic, and the first to exhibit the series' full potential. And also the last.

The mental conflict between the distinct Carol Danvers and Ms. Marvel personalities worsens, with the latter wishing she never had to change back to Ms. Danvers. For her part Carol isn't thrilled that when Ms. Marvel considerately switches back to her alter ago near her office, she forgets that Carol had been in her nightgown before their transformation. Carol's frequent absences at *Woman* magazine cause friction and anger and have Tracy wondering if she'll lose her job or be given Carol's. Things come to a head when Ms. Marvel chooses to help an alien named Hecate fight a group of elementals who threaten the earth instead of going to the rescue of Carol's best friend, astronaut Salia Petrie - what is one life against millions? -- who dies. But during Carol's rather insane attempt to kill Hecate, the latter helps her realize that she and Ms. Marvel are not separate personalities, but the same person - at first Carol simply couldn't cope with becoming a kind of Kree Warrior due to the radiations she absorbed, and temporarily created a new identity, which she now discards [*Ms. Marvel* 13]. The conflict between the two, which threatened to become tedious, was gone, but Carol never deals with the fact that this means it was really she who decided not to rescue her best friend, albeit for the best of reasons.

Carol has a reunion with her mother and father, an unrepentant male chauvinist pig, as well as mostly forgettable battles with the likes of Steeplejack, Tiger Shark, and a man called Centurion who is armed with a stolen disintegrator gun [16 - 18]. This last character is an associate of the mysterious blue-skinned shape-shifter, Raven Darkholme (Mystique), who has infiltrated the pentagon as well as SHIELD in the guise of Nick Fury. Nick Fury's girlfriend, the Contessa, briefly appears in one story, and the reader is struck by the ridiculousness of the Contessa's very sexy outfit (especially as this is in *Ms. Marvel!*), which looks like she's simply wearing a black leather bra on top - just the sort of thing a woman in a male-dominated profession would wear if she wanted to be taken seriously! Our heroine finally reunites with Captain Marvel in *Ms. Marvel* 19 wherein they stop Ronan and Supremor (aka the Supreme Intelligence) from stripping her of her human qualities and turning her into their drone.

Ms. Marvel 20 - 21 unveiled a "new" Ms. Marvel, which was simply the old Ms. Marvel with an attractive, newly designed costume with a red sash, as well as a redesigned logo and pencils by Dave Cockrum (Carmine Infantino had previously penciled a couple of issues.) Unfortunately the story was that ancient chestnut about a group of nuclear-spawned, intelligent lizard people living in caverns below the desert and snatching away any humans who see them so as to keep their existence a secret, a story which had been done much better in *Green Lantern* in the silver age. Ms. Marvel battles a giant cobra, frees all the prisoners, and even thinks of a way to prevent any of them from talking about the lizard folk. And then Cockrum was gone (except for a couple of subsequent covers). So was Carol's job, as Jameson fires her in the next issue.

At least *Ms. Marvel* 22 brought back Death-Bird, who has another savage battle with her nemesis, and yet stops to help our heroine when two innocent people who are trapped in a burning car need rescuing. Once this rescue is affected, Death-Bird drops half of a concrete highway on top of Ms. Marvel, but both women are much harder to kill than the other imagines. In the next issue Carol discovers that Salia Petrie is still alive and is the mind-controlled prisoner of the alien Faceless One - a walking spheroid head atop a robot body - from the short-lived Dr. Doom series in *Astonishing Tales*. This was the final issue of *Ms. Marvel*, although two more issues had been completed, their covers ready. These stories were eventually published in *Marvel Super-Heroes Special Edition* 10 - 11 quite a few years later.

In what would have been *Ms. Marvel* 24, Carol manages to not only hold her own against Sabretooth, but has a decisive victory over him. In her final solo story she investigates the beating death of Mike Barnett, who wanted to marry her, at the hands of her doppleganger - Raven Darkholme in disguise. She vows to get revenge upon her, and the trail she follows involves her in battles with both the Hellfire Club and the Brotherhood of Evil Mutants. Raven wants to destroy Ms. Marvel because her precognitive friend Destiny had a flash that she would somehow destroy Rogue's soul. Extra pages were added to the story when it was published that brought it up to date to the time Rogue stole all of Carol's memories and powers in *Avengers Annual* 10 (see chapter 14).

Ms. Marvel/Carol Danvers was a terrific character and concept but aside from a couple of issues *Ms. Marvel* was not an especially memorable series. Claremont's scripts were often surprisingly perfunctory and mediocre, without the strong subplots and suspense that distinguished, say, the best of *Amazing Spider-Man*. The frequent change in artists didn't help, either. Carol herself was generally treated with respect -- in her own series at least -- but not much like a major Marvel figure. Ms. Marvel's adventures would continue in *The Avengers*, where her generally negative treatment culminated in a notorious story in *Avengers* 200 (see chapter 14). Years later she got another series which lasted fifty issues.

The Cat

The Cat first appeared in 1972. Greer Nelson is a young Chicagoan widow whose husband, a cop, treated her like a child. Greer realizes that she needs to develop independence and a satisfying career, but has trouble finding anything but secretarial work. She goes to work as an assistant to an old female professor of hers, Dr. Tumolo, who is developing research to stimulate the physical and mental growth of women, who are often held back by society. Tumolo's research is funded by a wealthy man with a horror of being touched, Mal Donalbain, who insists that she use a pretty blond girlfriend of his, Shirlee, as a test subject. Tumolo knows Shirlee is completely wrong for her purposes, so in secret she also does her experimentation on Greer, who develops extreme mental acuity and physical prowess. It develops that Donalbain intends to dress Shirlee and many other woman in a kind of cat costume, sap away their will, and turn them into criminal slaves for him to use however he wishes. Shirlee is killed during a test run of the costume, and Tumolo, who has secretly observed this in horror, steals away with one of the costumes. Tumolo is killed by Donalbain's thugs before she can go to the police (wanting her death to look like an "accident," they use dynamite!) but not before she tells Greer everything that has happened. Fearing the police will be too late to stop Donalbain, she puts on the other costume and takes after him and his men as a new heroine, the Cat. Donalbain shoots himself rather than be raked by her claws, and Greer wonders if she had the right to act as a vigilante.

In *The Cat* 2 Greer learns that Dr. Tumolo wasn't killed in the explosion that destroyed her lab, but faces a worse fate at the hands of Daredevil foe, the Owl, who kidnaps Tumolo from the hospital because he wants to add her mind to a scientific brain bank that he will use for his own purposes. Tumolo survives this ordeal, but the light has gone out of her, and Greer faces a bizarre mystery under the waters of Lake Michigan - and battles Sub-Mariner foe Commander Kraken -- in *Cat* 3. She takes on another Daredevil foe, the Man-Bull in her 4th and final issue. Linda Fite's scripts for the brief series weren't bad, and the strip certainly had potential. The art, despite the work of such veterans as Marie Severin, Wally Wood, and Bill Everett -- along with newcomers Paty Greer, Jim Starlin and AlanWeiss, whose work on the book was amateurish - didn't give the series much of a chance.

The most memorable appearance of the Cat, however, wasn't in her own comic but in *Marvel Team-Up* 8. In this the Cat joins up with Spider-Man to take down a maniacally militant feminist known as the Man-Killer. M-K was actually Katrina Luisa Van Horn, who was horribly injured when a sexist male skier she was competing against deliberately sabotaged her. She was given an exo-skeleton that energizes her weakened muscles and gives her super-strength. Man-Killer tries to blow up a power plant in Harlem, and steals a radioactive device, but is brought down by the two heroes working together. M-K seems to go mad when she finds out her exo-skeleton was funded not by a feminist group but by the male scientists of A.I.M. The entertaining story with its striking villainess was scripted by Gerry Conway and featured a very nice art job by Jim Mooney. The Cat was later reinvented as Tigra, the Were-Woman, and the cat costume was worn by Patsy Walker when she became the Hellcat in *The Avengers.*

Tigra, the Werewoman

As for "Tigra," she first appeared in her new incarnation in a "Werewolf-By-Night" story in *Giant-Size Creatures* 1. Greer Nelson tries to stop the kidnapping of Dr. Tumolo by forces of Hydra, but she is shot by a weapon that causes radiation poisoning. Dr. Tumolo, who has been faking her coma all along, tells Greer that she belongs to a secret race of cat people, and that the only way Greer can survive is if she is transformed into one of her race. Greer agrees, and is transformed into the furry, clawed, cat-like Tigra. She can briefly turn back to her normal self by using a special ring, but by the end of that story she can no longer revert. There is no explanation for why Dr. Tumolo is normal in appearance. Tigra, with the perhaps unwitting help of the werewolf, frees Tumolo and puts a stop to Hydra's dastardly plans for a secret weapon developed by the Cat People, which turns out to be the Black Plague [Isabella/Perlin/Colletta]. To say the whole story, concept and character added up to Marvel Schlock is an understatement, but Tigra - who should have had a one-shot and nothing else - continued to exist.

Tigra next appeared in the 10th issue of the black and white magazine *Monsters Unleashed,* battling an ancient witch who has a symbiotic relationship with a rat-like creature that sucks away men's lives and energies just when they are feeling serene [Claremont/DeZuniga]. Then she got her own series beginning with *Marvel Chillers* 3 with the creative team of Tony Isabella, Will Meugniot, and Vince Collettta. Tigra's foes included Joshua Plague and his Rat Pack; Kraven (in an interesting tale by Chris Claremont, Frank Robbins, and Vince Colletta); and Madame Menace, a former crime queen and member of the Rat Pack. Red Wolf from *The Avengers* teams up with Tigra only to learn that Joshua Plague is actually the Super-Skrull in disguise. *Marvel Chillers* 7 was the final issue of Tigra's strip and of the series itself, and it was a more-than-decent tale of Red Wolf and Tigra trying to survive an attack by an alien who has all of the powers of the Fantastic Four. Jules Bannion, a supposed friend of Dr. Tumolo and the cat people is revealed to be a traitor, but only to the reader. Tigra and Red Wolf defeat the Skrull, but are accused of murdering a police chief who was actually slaughtered by the alien. Jim Shooter, John Byrne, and George Tuska also worked on the series.

Despite the poor sales of *Marvel Chillers,* Tigra returned yet again in *Marvel Premiere* 42. Dr. Tumolo sends out an image of herself to warn Tigra of a terrible danger to the cat people, and the expenditure costs her her life. Tumolo had learned that Tabur, a genetically advanced cat who had once been a member of the High Evolutionary's "new people" (from *Thor*) and who joined the cat people after being abandoned on earth, wants to take over the world with the aid of a special ray. The ray could have been used to make Greer human again - "what makes you think I want to be human again?" asks Tigra - but instead uses it to devolve modern-day animals into monsters that terrorize New Orleans. Tabur makes the mistake of turning some of the cat people into sabretooth tigers, but they retain their memories and attack him, while the ray eventually turns him into a cute little tabby. The cat people have at last made their presence known on earth. Ed Hannigan's script wasn't bad, and there was a nice art job from Mike Vosberg and Ernie Chan, but Tigra was not awarded her own series.

When Tigra wound up in the Avengers and later the Fantastic Four, she was reconceived as a somewhat slinky and not very serious airhead and jokester, a far cry from the more serious woman who had once been Greer Nelson. Tigra's characterization was eventually deepened and became a little more interesting in *The Avengers*. The cat people were not really heard from again, except for a schlocky story in *Marvel Two-In-One* 19 in which Tigra and the Thing team up to stop yet another renegade cat-person, the Cougar.

One rather yucky aspect of Tigra -- as with the Beast -- is the alleged "sex appeal" of the character: considering she is part cat, there's the gross taint of bestiality. True, Tigra has a great figure and pretty enough face, but she's still rather weird-looking. An attraction to her makes slightly more sense than an attraction to the Beast, who is even more like an actual non-human than Tigra is.

Shanna, the She-Devil

Shanna O'Hara, a fiery redhead, was raised in Africa where her mother's pet leopard ran amok. Her father, fearing for the lives of the animals as well as his family, fired at what he thought was the leopard but turned out to be his wife, turning him into a drunk. Years later Shanna is an ecologist at a zoo in Manhattan, when the felines she ministers to are all slaughtered with a high-powered rifle, except for one, the leopard Julani, who is shot by an over-zealous guard who thinks Shanna is in danger. Disgusted with man's inhumanity - even animals don't seem to be safe - Shanna decides to get away from the city and return to Africa. Her boss at the zoo suggests she return with Julani's cubs, Ina and Biri, to the Dahomey Reserve.

Shanna, who had trained for the Olympics and is in excellent shape, and who is independently wealthy due to her father's mining investments, fashions a revealing costume from Julani's pelt [!] to create a bond with her cubs, who when grown help her fight poachers and the like. Game warden Patrick McShane has a crush on Shanna, who would rather spend time with the animals. The first unexceptional issue of *Shanna, the She-Devil* [1972] was written by Carol Seuling and Steve Gerber, with art by George Tuska and Vince Colletta. Ross Andru took over the penciling beginning with the second issue.

In *Shanna* 2, the she-devil, who can act as ruthless and savage as any barbarian at times, goes on assignment for SHIELD to stop an obese mid-eastern drug dealer, slave trader and would-be moon rocket purloiner named El Montano. A lost civilization that originated in ancient Crete and worships huge mutated fear-bulls figures in *Shanna* 3. In the following issue Shanna has an intriguing foe in the form of the mutant Mandrill, whose head looks like an animal's and who has a small army of tattooed female warriors to do his fighting as he has hypnotic power over women. He wants to take over several African nations, make himself ruler, and demands Shanna help him in his efforts, which she refuses. (When the Mandrill is nearly torn apart by some real Mandrills, her "respect for human life" causes her to save him even though in a previous issue she encouraged her pet leopards to literally claw another bad guy to pieces.)

Mandrill's partner, another mutant, is revealed in the 5th and final issue of *Shanna*: the priestess Nekra, who preaches hate, wants to kill Shanna for her role in jailing the Mandrill, and also has super-strength. Nekra has a very striking appearance with fangs, cape, and sickly-colored skin, and is of indeterminate race. (Later we learned she was a black woman with white skin just as Mandrill was a Caucasian with black skin and hair. Her fascinating storyline was continued in *Daredevil* 109 - 112, in which Shanna guest-stars). Steve Gerber's script has Shanna, who'd had a fabulous and chic tree-house built for herself in the reserve, wondering if that was the appropriate way to commune with nature, and wondering, as many readers did (or rather few readers, given the poor sales) what exactly was up with her. Shanna next appeared in *Ka-Zar* 1 - 2, and we learned in *Daredevil* that Mandrill and Nekra killed her father, whom we never saw except in flashbacks, and Patrick McShane. Shanna's uncle turned out to be a police commissioner that Matt Murdock knew in San Francisco.

When Marvel decided to respond to calls to do books on female heroes, it is almost comical that they choose that hoary old -- and rather racist -- cliché of the white jungle goddess. At least Tarzan knock-off Ka-Zar operated in a prehistoric "Savage Land" that had nothing to do with Africa. Jungle queens (such as Sheena, whose comic became a TV show in the fifties) were rife in the golden age, but they seemed very out-of-date in the 1970's. A Caucasian jungle queen swinging through the vines was just as fanciful as a group consisting of super-powered mutants. Despite this, Shanna had a life that lasted past her short and unlamented comic book series.

Black Widow

As they did in the silver age, Marvel decided to issue split comic books that would run two separate strips: *Amazing Adventures* and *Astonishing Tales* (as in the silver age, one strip would eventually edge out the other). The latter featured the adventures of Ka-Zar of the Savage Land, and the misadventures of the classic FF foe, Dr. Doom, while in the former the Black Widow shared billing with the Inhumans. Nastasha Romanoff had originally been a silver age foe of Iron Man, and teamed up with Hawkeye before he, too, repented of his evil ways. The Black Widow strip had excellent John Buscema-John Verpoorten art and a script by Gary Friedrich in which bored, rich Natasha puts on her black form-fitting maskless outfit to deal with some gamblers who are threatening her maid's young son, Carlos. Carlos gets her involved in his Puerto Rican militant group, the Young Warriors, who have simply taken over a public building to use for a free breakfast program. Although Natasha believes they should opt for a legal building, she defends them when more thugs come to shoot them out of the center, and is denounced as a radical by the papers.

Roy Thomas then took over the strip, with art by Gene Colan and Bill Everett, who gave the Widow's moves grace and elegance and made her even more beautiful than before, such as in a shower sequence in AA 5. Thomas' first storyline introduced a villain called the Astrologer, who uses homeless young people to commit crimes. When he decides to rob a blood bank of its entire type O supply, one of the young men objects, pointing out that people could die without the blood, and tries to kill himself before being rescued by the Widow's chauffeur and confidante, the brooding Ivan. The Widow determines to help the youth, but when the Astrologer's men attack her penthouse, the boy is killed coming to her rescue, falling 22 stories to his death.

Gerry Conway and Don Heck finished the storyline, in which the Widow, still disturbed by the tragic death of the youth whose name she didn't even know, tries to halt the Astrologer's new plans and fails. A spurious sub-plot has her going off her game at times because she thinks she's developed a black widow curse or something because everyone around her dies, a feeling that's increased when the Astrologer is killed, and her next foe, a loser called the Watchlord, bites the dust as well. The Black Widow strip ended with *Amazing Adventures* 8, and soon after she became a regular in *Daredevil*. She also became a member of the Champions in its short-lived series, and had already worked with the Avengers in the silver age and afterward.

Black Widow appeared in other comics in the bronze age. In *Marvel Two-in-One* 10 she joins forces with the Thing to stop a dastardly plot to cause radioactive tidal waves that will swamp

America due to the undersea explosion of a Thermo-nuclear device. The villain is a mad Russian and ex-boyfriend of Natasha's named Andrei Rostov, aka Agamemnon, and he heads a terrorist group called the Sword of Judgment [Claremont/ Brown/Janson]. The Widow teamed up with Spider-Man several times, battling the Silver Samurai in MTU 57 and Daredevil foe, The Owl, in MTU 98 wherein he plans a major looting spree during a black out.

One of the most interesting Black Widow stories began in *Marvel Team-Up* 82 and continued for several issues. Spider-Man saves a woman from muggers, and the near-victim turns out to be the Black Widow, only she insists that she's not a super-heroine but a simple school teacher from upstate named Nancy Rushman. Other than that she has no memory. Spider-Man tries to help "Nancy," whom he finds attractive and sympathetic in a way he did not find Natasha Romanoff, but they are attacked by an all-female assault squad from SHIELD. Still believing herself to be a schoolteacher, Nancy nevertheless fights back, until Nick Fury steps out of the shadows and shoots both her and Spider-Man! Luckily he used anesthetic bullets instead of the real thing, but Spidey wakes up to find Natasha/Nancy missing. He rescues her from SHIELD HQ, where a confused Nick Fury has been trying to determine if Natasha has turned roque or not, as well as why some people in the organization are trying to kill her.

In MTU 83 - 85 Peter and "Nancy" are attacked again, this time by the Silver Samurai and Boomerang, and Natasha's memory seems to be returning: she vaguely remembers being tortured by Viper, the former Madame Hydra. To protect herself, Natasha's mind had retreated into the persona of Nancy Cushman. Shang-Chi, the Master of Kung Fu, helps Fury and the others fight Viper, who wants to wipe out the President and the Joint Chiefs of Staff in one fell swoop. Peter and "Nancy" are drawn to one another, going so far as to briefly make out during an inopportune moment, but when Nancy fully becomes Natasha, the romance is over. The Black Widow and Viper have a major battle atop the SHIELD heli-carrier as it heads toward the White House, with the former having a decisive victory. Although Natasha tries to save Viper's life, she is sucked away into the wind [Claremont/Buscema]. But that was not the end of Viper.

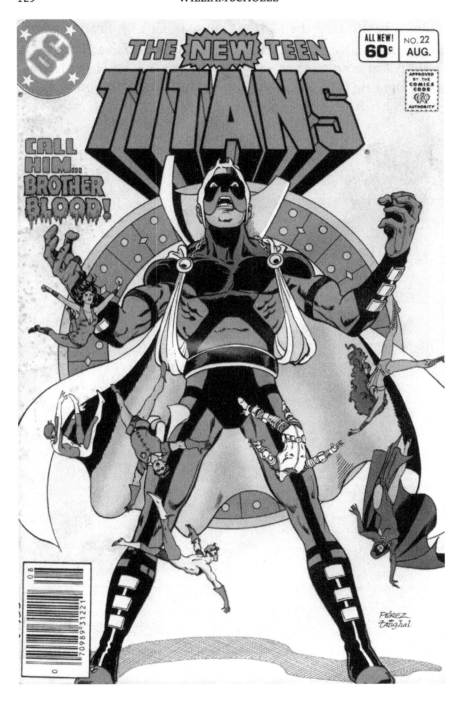

CHAPTER EIGHT: TITANS OLD AND NEW

*T**een Titans* 25 started the group of former sidekicks on a new direction, typical of DC in the bronze age when it came to comics whose sales were less than stellar. When a fight breaks out at a peace rally the group intercedes (along with the brother duo Hawk and Dove), but after a famous peace ambassador is killed during the melee the adult Justice League members accuse them (in rather contrived fashion) of using their abilities irresponsibly. Chastened and guilt-wracked, they agree to stop using their powers and join an organization run by a mysterious Mr. Jupiter. Robin has other plans, and refuses to give up his costume as he quits the group. A new member is a psychic go-go girl named Lilith whom they met a few days before. Kid Flash, Wonder Girl and Speedy are also joined by Hawk and Dove.

Teen Titans

In the following issue the young heroes are subjected to a battery of tests, then given matching uniforms and a penny each and told to go to the toughest area in the city, Hell's Corner, and get jobs. There they meet a black teen named Mal, whose little sister has been menaced by gang members, and indoctrinate the brave youth into Jupiter's group. After receiving what seems like a few hours of training, Mal decides to sneak onto an unmanned space probe to take off on a one-way journey so he can submit human reactions along with other data, his ill-advised way of becoming a ghetto hero. This unnecessary self-sacrifice makes Mal seem more stupid than heroic. In the next issue the Titans fly to the moon and affect a successful rescue. Mal was never developed beyond the bitter black youth with the chip on his shoulder.

Steve Skeates took over from Robert Kanigher as scripter with *Teen Titans* 28 while Nick Cardy remained as penciller. Aqualad returns to embroil the TTs in a battle with Aquaman's foe, the Ocean Master, who has allied himself with some aliens bent on world conquest; the ever-bickering Hawk and Dove take center stage when they take the battle to O-M's HQ in the following issue. TT 33 introduced a cro-magnon teen named Gnarkk that the young heroes accidentally bring back with them after a time-traveling adventure. Since he can't be returned to his own time, the heroes - aided by Lilith's mental powers - educate and partially civilize the brutish youth; he and Lilith develop special feelings for one another. A few issues later Gnarkk is speaking as if he were educated at Oxford.

Teen Titans continued with Murray Boltinoff as editor and Bob Haney on scripts. Haney did try to come up with stories that were different from the usual super-hero fare: Wonder Girl reads for an elderly lady on an isolated island who turns out to be a witch who's trying to possess her; Lilith imagine she's the reincarnation of Shakespeare's Juliet and meets a modern-day Romeo in Verona; the group go to war- torn Ramistan to rescue a photographer friend and encounter the Four Horsemen of the Apocalypse. In TT 42 Wonder Girl is given a golden beetle brooch which talks to her and tells her he is actually a handsome prince imprisoned in this tiny form and she can free him if she travels to his home in the Yucatan. Said home turns out to be a huge forbidding skull rising out of a river wherein the brooch turns not into a handsome prince but a giant ugly bug that wraps the other titans into cocoons so he can feed on them. In TT 43 they try to save a little boy from demons that bedevil him and his grandfather, but discover that the boy is actually a changeling and the demons are under his control. Back-up stories featured Lilith, who had been adopted, on a search for her real parents and meeting one dead end after another.

The lack of traditional super-villains in the series in the bronze age may have contributed to its demise with the 43rd issue in 1973. Also, the characterization was minimal and the whole business with Mr. Jupiter never jelled and seemed pointless. Three years later the series was revived and more emphasis was placed on super-powered antagonists. In the meantime the Titans teamed up with Superman in *World's Finest* 205 when an alien machine in a small town turns the former into racists and chauvinists, and with Batman in *The Brave and the Bold* 102, a fair-to-middling urban renewal storyline with excellent art by Jim Aparo and Neal Adams (working on separate halves of the story).

Teen Titans Redux

In *Teen Titans* 44, the first issue of the revival, Mal has been looking after the equipment given to the Titans by the departed Mr. Jupiter and is angry that hardly anyone ever gets in touch with him. Now Wonder Girl, Kid Flash, Robin, and Speedy have come to the old HQ to answer an emergency summons, only Mal didn't send it. It turns out that this is a trick of Dr Light to capture some of the Titans so he can learn whatever secrets of the Justice League satellite the sidekicks may know. Ignored by Light and dismissed as the "custodian," Mal puts on an exo-suit which gives him super-strength, dons the Guardian's old costume, and adapts the golden age hero's name for himself. Before Dr. Light can obliterate the JLA satellite Mal helps rescue the teens and they wipe out Dr. Light and his plans. The script was by Paul Levitz and Bob Rozakis. Pablo Marcos' pencils were not well served by Bob Smith's inks, but the comic had frequent changes in artists, who included Bob Brown, Jose Delbo, and Don Heck.

Julius Schwartz replaced Joe Orlando as editor for the next issue, which was scripted by Bob Rozakis and drawn by Novick and Coletta. In this Mal is nearly killed in an explosion and sees a vision of Azreal, the Angel of Death, who tells him he'll live if he can defeat him in battle. Mal somehow manages to do so, and "Gabriel" gives him his horn to use in case of trouble. Mal uses his horn to teleport the other titans, including Aqualad, to his side, to help him against a gang called the Wreckers, but none of the young heroes ask him how he managed this feat. The promise of TT 44 was almost completely erased by the ludicrous developments of this issue.

A character named Duela Dent, the daughter of Two-Face, who nonetheless called herself The Joker's Daughter and who first appeared in *Batman Family*, joined the group in the following issue; she later darned clown-like garb and rechristened herself the Harlequin. In TT 46 the group move into new headquarters in Farmingdale, Long Island, a discotheque called Gabriel's Horn, and in the next issue Mal's girlfriend, Karen Beecher, dresses up in a super-powered costume and calls herself the Bumblebee. The series started to show some potential in this story of the Titans stopping Two-Face's dual threats to blow up both Gotham City and New York. However, TT 49, in which some losers calling themselves the Rocket Racers attack the disco, was mediocre. Karen makes Mal a new costume and calls him the Hornblower, but he switches back to the Guardian outfit he hadn't worn since TT 44 when his horn is stolen.

Teen Titans 50 - 52 introduced the west coast edition of the Titans, which consists of Lilith and Gnarrk (who are now engaged), Hawk and Dove, the original Bat-Girl (Betty Kane instead of Barbara Gordon), Beast-Boy from the silver age Doom Patrol, and Golden Eagle, a Hawkman-like lad who'd appeared in one issue of *Justice League of America*. Each team is dealing with bizarre catastrophes - such as a train or skyscraper rising into the air, or an airliner winding its way deep into the ground without crashing - engineered by Captain Calamity and Mr. Esper, who turn out to be the same person. In TT 52 the two teams meet and briefly engage in a stupid battle before going off to stop the villain[s] and preventing him from inexplicably pulling all of Long Island out to sea.

Jack C. Harris took over as editor during the Titan West storyline but the comic only lasted one more issue (1978); this recounted the secret origin of the Teen Titans, who band together when an alien being uses mental powers to turn their mentors, such as Batman and Wonder Woman, into crooks. At the end of the story the Titans decide to disband, as they feel it is time for each member to reach individual goals and prepare to take over from the Justice League some day. Of course they were back together as the revitalized New Teen Titans two years later. The characterization for the series was not its strong point, consisting mostly of Kid Flash's unrequited feelings for Wonder Girl, Speedy's continual tactlessness, Aqualad's inferiority complex, and Harlequin's fear that she'd never be accepted because her father was a bad guy.

New Teen Titans

The Teen Titans appeared again with Batman in *The Brave and the Bold* 119 in 1979, in which they joined a teenage crime gang consisting of runaways, then the following year The New Teen Titans, co-created by Wolfman and Perez, had their first appearance in *DC Presents* 26. In a special preview insert Robin has a prescient dream in which he is one member of a new group fighting an alien monstrosity that escaped from a laboratory. In *New Teen Titans* 1 he meets the woman responsible for the dream, Raven, who has a dark astral being inside her known as her soul-self; and his other new teammates: a buxom flame-haired alien she-warrior named Koriand'r or Starfire; Changeling, formerly Beastboy of the old Doom Patrol; Kid Flash; and Wonder Girl. The only thing memorable about this inauspicious debut, in which the group fight aliens who wish to recapture Starfire, was the George Perez/Romeo Tanghal artwork, but Marv Wolfman's plots would steadily improve.

The improvement was immediate with *New Teen Titans* 2, which introduced an enduring DC villain, Deathstroke, the Terminator, a killer-for-hire who uses 90% of his brain power instead of the usual 10 %. A group called H.I.V. E. (Hierarchy of International Vengeance and Eliminations), made up of scientists who'd come afoul of super-heroes, wants to hire him to kill the Titans, but he walks out on them after they refuse to pay him in advance. After failing to kill Deathstroke, HIVE decides to turn his son, Grant, into a new assassin, the Ravager. But his new powers soon burn him out and he dies, for which Deathstroke blames not the HIVE but the Titans.

Starfire's back story was revealed in NTT 3, in which we learn that she comes from the world Tamaran, which would have been destroyed by a race known as the Citadel if her father, the king, had not turned her over to them, whereupon she became a slave. This issue also introduced the Fearsome Five, a group led by old Justice League of America foe Dr. Light, and comprised of the mind-controlling Psimon with his see-through brain; the diminutive tinkerer, Gizmo; the decorative transmuter, Shimmer; and her brother, the brutish Mammoth. Psimon was originally physicist Simon Jones, who pierced dimensional barriers, and was transformed by an evil being known as Trigon. After the Five defeat the Titans, Psimon erases their memories and puts them on a collision course with the Justice League for his own purposes. (The Fearsome Five also figure in a story in NTT 7, in which it is revealed that the Titans' new HQ, "Titans Tower," was secretly built for them by Cyborg's estranged father, Dr. Stone.)

Trigon, it was revealed the following month, was the issue of a Satanic being and alien female, and resembles the earthly devil in appearance. A group of sorcerers attempt to block his entry into Earth's dimension, but the heroes of the Justice League misunderstand their motives and oppose them. The Titans and the League have a desperate battle in NTT 4 - the Perez/ Tanghal artwork was really looking great by this time - and Raven explains how she is the daughter of Trigon and the earth woman Arella, who now resides in Azarath, a land that lies between dimensions. Arella and her fellow cultists are pacifists and refuse to help Raven and the other Titans retard

Trigon's invasion, although they use their powers to safeguard their own temple. The Justice League had refused to help Raven (which is why she formed the new Titans) because sorceress Zatanna sensed Trigon's evil inside his daughter. Raven offers her father a deal - she will go off and rule with him if he will leave the earth alone, and he agrees [NTT 5]. (It is suggested in Raven's origin in *Tales of the New Teen Titans* 2 that Trigon's father may have been the composite energy of the evil selves of the residents of Azarath that they shed when they left the earth.)

Back in Trigon's world, Raven witnesses first-hand her father's pettiness and cruelty, as he turns a child who innocently calls him a "monster" into a pile of ashes in front of her mother. Trigon demands sacrifices from all the other worlds in his universe, and thinks of his subjects as less than nothing, whose only existence is to serve him. He tells Raven that he lied to her when he promised to leave the earth alone. The Titans importune Arella to lead them to Trigon's world, where their rescue of Raven seems doomed when Trigon floors all of them upon their first encounter. However, Arella has hidden powers of her own, which she uses to save her daughter's life, and she and the Titans are able to force Trigon, on the verge of attacking the earth, through a dimensional rift. Unfortunately, Arella must banish herself along with Trigon to prevent him from returning [NTT 6].

Wolfman and Perez became "co-creators," with the latter contributing plots and story ideas along with Wolfman. Kory (Koraind'r) becomes a golden-hued model; Raven attends college and tries without much success to fit in; Changeling (Garfield Logan) resists taking over Dayton industries in lieu of his missing stepfather, Steve Dayton (aka Mento). Cyborg (Victor Stone) discovers that his girlfriend, Marcy, can't deal with his half-cybernetic state (Dr. Stone used technology to fill in the missing parts when Victor was mutilated by an alien blob), but meets a lovely woman named Sarah Simms who works with children with prosthetics, all of whom look up to Cyborg. Wonder Girl (Donna Troy), who'd been raised on Paradise Island but was not a true amazon despite her powers, wonders who her real parents are, works as a photographer, and keeps company with boyfriend Terry Long. Kid Flash (Wally West) ponders if he really wants to be a super-hero and if he'll get over the romantic feelings for Raven that she'd instilled in him to get him to join the team. On the action front, the Terminator, Slade Wilson, returned with a two-way plot to get millions for a fake Promethean bomb, and to finally obliterate the Titans (NTT 10), and during a trip to Paradise Island to give an injured Changeling a dose of the amazons' healing ray the group met the Titans of mythology, the latter busy waging war with the younger gods who'd imprisoned them eons before (NTT 11 - 12).

A major story arc began in *New Teen Titans* 13 that wrapped up events begun in the silver age Doom Patrol series in which Changeling, then known as Beast Boy, was first introduced. The Titans join Steve Dayton in Africa, where he is searching for the murderers of the DP, General Zahl and Madame Rouge. This duo have hired an Army and use it to attack the island nation of Zandia - which is a haven for criminals of all sorts - from their huge floating HQ. Another factor is the re-emergence of the DP's old enemies, the disembodied Brain and his Brotherhood of Evil, with the genius ape, Mssr. Mallah, and new members Warp, who can manipulate space; Plasmus, who can turn anything into a protoplasmic blob like himself; Houngan, who can employ sinister fetishes with aplomb; and Phobia, a woman who can control emotions. Despite some of Wolfman's awkward if well-meaning dialogue, these issues were the best published to that date. The series became DC Comics' best-selling title.

More good stories followed. Francis Kane seems possessed by an evil magnetic force, but is actually being used as a conduit for Green Lantern foe, Dr. Polaris, to pull himself out of an alternate dimension. All manner of metal objects rain down on Titans Tower, including - in one startling panel - an ocean liner that slams into Changeling when he's in the form of a Godzilla-like dinosaur. The Titans never learn that Dr. P was behind it all and he remains imprisoned in the strange dimension where Green Lantern deposited him [NTT 17]. Russian hero Starfire (not to be confused with Koriand'r), who'd appeared in the silver age *Teen Titans* series, reappears in "A Pretty Girl is Like a - Maladi" in NTT 18. A Russian scientist hates Americans because he blames them for the deaths of his wife and son so he infects his pretty secretary, Maladi, who is about to get married, with plague and sends her off on a phony mission to the U.S. Starfire follows, wishing to end the dying woman's torment and prevent her from infecting hundreds of innocents. The Titans learn that he wants to kill Maladi and therefore oppose him, but he insists that he only wants to end Maladi's suffering. The young lady dies in a hospital, after which Starfire reveals that he was her fiancé and that day was supposed to have been their wedding day. Although the Russian Starfire was perhaps made to appear colder than he would have been in such circumstances to avoid giving away the ending, the story still packs a wallop.

Brother Blood vs the Brain

A major new foe was introduced for the Titans in *New Teen Titans* 21 - 22, which dealt in colorful fashion with the problem of cults run by unscrupulous people who victimize their followers. Brother Blood, a striking figure in a red and white costume with cape and skull-like helmet, already had established his church in Zandia but has come to the United States to expand his regime. Anyone who tries to leave his church, including Cyborg's former girlfriend Marcy, is ruthlessly eliminated. Blood feeds some of his enemies to a gigantic and ravenous giant spider that he keeps in slimy caverns below his church near Buzzard's Bay, Massachusetts. Blood captures some of the Titans and has Robin electronically tortured by the masked Confessor to find out what he knows. When the rest of the heroes come to rescue their companions, Blood arranges, with the help of a confederate, reporter Bethany Snow, to make it look as if their church is being attacked by bigots. He then fakes his own death. These were arguably the best issues in the series so far, with a despicable and evil villain who had unlimited potential.

A new story arc began with *New Teen Titans* 23 which had the group traveling into space in order to rescue Starfire, who has been kidnaped by her own evil sister, Komamd'r, who has taken the name "Blackfire" to mock her captive. Embroiled in this sibling rivalry are the lizard-like Gordonians, Blackfire's uneasy allies; a group of rebel heroes known as the Omega Men (whose member, Demonia, is secretly working for her own interests); the living goddess X'Hal and her son, Auron; and Lord Damyn, the head of the conquering Citadel, and who with his jet-black skin and barbaric attitude greatly resembles African dictator Idi Amin, intentionally. Blackfire murders Lord Damyn with a power blast, and in *New Teen Titans Annual* 1 she and her sister have a duel to the death. The stories were fun, but the Titans weren't really a good fit with far-flung outer space action and star-spawning races, and X'Hal, who was supposed to be her races' finest and most ferocious warrior, looked more like one of the Rockettes. Koriand'r defeats her sister and is temporarily reunited with her family, but must return to earth or endanger the pact that had resulted in her banishment. The Omega Men were eventually given their own series.

"Runaways" in *New Teen Titans* 26 - 27 dealt intelligently with the problem of children who leave often horrible home situations and wind up taken advantage of by adults who turn them into prostitutes or drug dealers. These stories also introduced Terra, who had control over the earth, and who would play a major role in the series in the near-future, and utilized D.A. Adrian Chase, who would metamorphose into a more dramatic personage before too long. Roy Harper, better-known as Green Arrow's ward and partner, Speedy, an original member of the TTs, also showed up as a drug counselor (having overcome the drug issues he revealed in *Green Lantern/Green Arrow*) and stayed for a few issues in costume.

The Brain and his Brotherhood of Evil knew that Brother Blood had been able to step right through Raven's soul-self and were determined to kidnap her to see what secrets she might know of the cult leader, their rival for power in Zandia. Terra, who claims that she was being held captive by terrorists who murdered her parents, is inducted into the Titans, but Raven doesn't trust her. The Brotherhood manages to spirit Raven away from the crowds in Time Square despite the best efforts of the Titans and a visiting Frances Kane even as Terry Long proposes to Donna at a New Year's Eve fete. The Titans pursue the Brotherhood to Zandia where the Brain's probing of Raven's mind almost unleashes Trigon, whose essence resides deep inside her. Wonder Girl is able to help Raven suppress her father's evil before she can destroy everyone [NTT 28 - 31]. These were exceptional issues in the series.

The Titans then tackled the problem of the confused offspring of American soldiers/scientists and Asian women in Viet Nam with the characters of Thunder and Lightning, two former Siamese twins born with genetic powers and searching for their father. [32 and 36]. Said father turns out to be an alien held prisoner by the HIVE. Terra takes on the Terminator by herself in NTT 34 and nearly defeats him, but this issue also reveals that she is secretly in league with the man and that their battle was all an act. Adrian Chase's family is killed in *New Teen Titans Annual* 2, turning him into the costumed Vigilante. A group of costumed hit men, including sexy assassin Cheshire/Jade (the only one of the group to reappear) with poison on her fingernails, tries to off the Titans, but the Vigilante kills many of the bad guys behind the scenes. He was given his own series in the copper age.

The Titans rounded out the bronze age with a crossover with *Batman and the Outsiders*, in which Robin's issues with Batman are finally resolved, with Batman accepting that his ward is not only his own person but a fine leader in his own right. The two teams initially come to blows but ultimately team up to take on Dr. Light and the Fearsome Five, who first turn derelicts into dangerous mud-men [NTT 37] and then try to mind-control all of Manhattan. Terra turns out to be the younger sister of Geo-Force of the Outsiders; he also had earth-based powers. Jim Aparo did the excellent art for the second installment of the series in *Batman and the Outsiders 5*.

As part of the White House's Drug Awareness Program the Titans appeared in two special comic book giveaways that has them fighting drug dealers and trying to help various children who have become addicted to drugs. These raw, hard-hitting books had excellent scripts by Wolfman, with art by Perez and Ross Andru. In both comics the Titans were joined by a masked hero called the Protector. There was also a four-part *Tales of the Teen Titans* mini-series which told the back stories of Raven, Cyborg, Changeling and Starfire in more detail. Of these the most arresting was Starfire's tale of being sold into slavery by her own supremely wicked sister, Blackfire.

DC and Marvel also decided to capitalize on the popularity of their two young teams, New Teen Titans and X-Men, by co-producing a special comic in which the groups meet in some alternate universe (apparently this story was not part of either series' regular continuity). "Apocalypse ... Now" had Darkseid resuscitating the essence of the Phoenix (see chapter 9) and using her in his attempt to recreate his own dark world on earth by forming numerous Hell Pits. The noteworthy book was written by Christopher Claremont and drawn by Walt Simonson and Terry Austin, who provided such striking scenes as Changeling carrying all of the members of both teams on his back while flying over Manhattan in the huge form of a winged green dinosaur, and Phoenix carrying off a defeated Darkseid, whom she turns against in the end, in an sizzling energy claw. The book also features a couple of too-brief skirmishes between Wolverine and Deathstroke, the Teminator. A second team-up one-shot, to be written by Wolfman, drawn by Perez, and featuring the villainy of Brother Blood and the Hellfire Club -- an inspired combination -- was announced, but never materialized, a major disappointment for fans.

CHAPTER NINE: THOSE MARVELOUS MUTANTS

-- *X-MEN, NEW MUTANTS*, THE BEAST, *THE CHAMPIONS*

The X-men returned to the Marvel Universe in the bronze age with the appearance of *Giant-Size X-Men* 1 in 1975, written by Len Wein, and drawn by Dave Cockrum, both of whom created the new team: Nightcrawler, an acrobat of demonic cast who can also teleport; savage, clawed and mysterious Wolverine (who'd first appeared in *Hulk* 181); the screaming high-flying Banshee, who'd fought against the X-Men against his will in the silver age; Storm, or Ororo, an African "goddess" who can manipulate the weather; Sunfire, another silver age foe who needs training and guidance; Peter Rasputin, or Colossus, a Russian youth who can transform into a powerful armored form; and embittered Apache John Proudstar, aka Thunderbird.

The X-Men

Professor Xavier gathers together these new mutants in Westchester because, as Cyclops tells the assemblage, the original members of the X-Men - Marvel Girl, Iceman, Angel, Lorna Dane and Havok -- have vanished. They were sent to investigate huge mutant power readings on the island of Krakoa and never came back. Cyclops and the new team fly to Krokoa and battle all manner of malevolent flora and fauna, including giant crabs and strangling creepers, until they discover the first expedition trapped inside a temple where some vines seem to be feeding upon them. It develops that the mutant is Krakoa itself, a living, sentient island (created by atomic testing, of course) that used its formidable mental control to force Processor X to assemble new mutants whose energies it could feed upon. Working together the two teams manage to blast Krokoa into space. It was an interesting, colorful and entertaining debut for the new X-Men.

The Uncanny X-Men had been running reprints since its cancellation but the new X-Men took over with new stories beginning with *X-Men* 94. Prickly Sunfire takes off, and so do all of the original X-Men with the exception of Cyclops. In a two-part story they battle old foe Count Nefaria and his Ani-Men who have taken over Valhalla, the HQ for the North American Air Defense Command, and commandeered all of its missiles. Striving to prove himself, Thunderbird is blown up when the escaping Nefaria's plane is destroyed, the first casualty of the X-Men, new or old. Although Len Wein plotted and edited, he turned over the scripting reins to Christopher Claremont, who would eventually become the writer most closely associated with the team. Claremont was an excellent scripter, although he tended to have characters say "I am - Power" about a dozen times too often, and some felt the X-Men veered dangerously close to soap opera territory at times.

X-Men 96 introduced "housekeeper" Moira MacTaggert and Steven Lang, a mutant-hating scientist, as well as a horrific demon named Kierrok - the story was minor but enlivened by the Cockrum-Sam Grainger art and Phil Rachelson's coloring -- but the series really began to realize its potential with the following issue. In this Scott's brother Alex, or Havoc, and his girlfriend Lorna, or Polaris, show up again but are being mind-controlled by a character named Erik the Red, which was merely a role that Scott briefly assumed in the silver age. This

Eric, true identity unknown, along with Havok and Polaris, tries to kill Professor X as his plane leaves for a vacation, but their homicidal plans are stymied by the actions of their former colleagues. A particularly good scene has a furious Storm squaring off against Polaris and blasting her into the middle of next week. The Buckler-Cockrum cover for this issue, showing the two brothers striking out at each other in the foreground, is especially effective.

Steven Lang employs the next generation of mutant-hunting Sentinel robots in *X-Men* 98 - 100, as well as utilizing special X-sentinels who resemble some of the X-Men and have all of their powers; hence *X-Men* 100 features an alleged battle between new and old X-Men on an abandoned space station. Using her special powers to pilot a ship back to earth, Jean is nearly destroyed but is reborn as Phoenix, rising from the sea imperiously to talk portentously - or pretentiously - about how she's changed: "No longer am I the woman you knew. I am fire. I am Life Incarnate. Now and Forever - I am Phoenix!" While she recuperates, some of the others travel to Ireland with Banshee, where they encounter his cousin, Black Tom Cassidy and silver age foe, the Juggernaut, Professor Xavier's nasty half-brother.

In *X-Men* 102 we meet Jean's roommate, Misty Knight, and learn Storm's origin. She was the daughter of a photojournalist and an African princess, both of whom were killed when the French bombed Cairo. Young Ororo lay in the rubble for a long time, giving her a bad case of life-long, crippling claustrophobia. The same issue features an especially striking panel of Colossus delivering a massive blow that nearly topples Juggernaut [Cockrum/Granger]. Professor X and Cyclops nearly come to blows when the latter refuses a direct order to go to Ireland to help his teammates, with Cyclops not only insisting he stay with Jean until she's fully recovered, but arguing that he would get there too late to do much good anyway; the new team has to fight on its own for once. The fight is interrupted when Xavier has another vision of an intergalactic visitor that he has been seeing in his dreams for several issues. The new team manages to defeat Black Tom and the Juggernaut in the following issue.

The cover of *X-Men* 104, which reintroduced arch-foe Magneto into the bronze age, was a homage to the very first issue of X-Men in the sixties. Magneto had been turned into a baby in *Defenders* 16, but the new Eric the Red and his allies Polaris and Havok break into his cell and use a ray to turn him back into a grown-up. Said cell is on Muir island, where Moira McTaggert keeps her Mutant Research Center, which mutant Jaime Maddrox (introduced not in *X-Men* but *Giant-Size Fantastic Four* 4) was looking after while Moira was away; Cyclops is not pleased that he had been kept in the dark about Moira and her true connection to Xavier. The new team has a tough time dealing with Magneto in a lively battle, and are urged back to the mansion in Westchester by Cyclops, who fears they are being distracted so that Eric can finish off the professor. Wolverine accuses him of making them look like cowards.

In *X-Men* 105 Eric the Red enlists the aid of former Galactus-herald Firelord to attack the X-Men through subterfuge. The alien that Xavier has dreamed about finally appears: Princess Lilandra, who comes from light-years away to get help against a plot by her brother that endangers the entire universe. "Eric the Red" is Shakari, an agent sent by Lilandra's brother, D'Ken, to either capture her or destroy the mutants whose aid she is seeking. Phoenix and Firelord engage in an explosive battle, but the former uses her powers to follow Eric and Lilandra through a star gate that will take them halfway across the cosmos. The regular story was interrupted by a fill-in issue, *X-Men* 106, in which the new X-Men again battle the old X-Men, but instead of robots these mutants were merely images cast by the evil side of Professor X, unleashed by his discombobulation over the alien visions. This issue almost forecast the emergence of Onslaught, Xavier's evil self, many years later.

In *X-Men* 107 the X-Men arrive on an alien world and demand the return of Lilandra from a group of colorful super-powered beings known as the Imperial Guard, who claim the princess is a traitor and their captive, and refuse to turn her over, leading to battle. The Imperial Guard were based on DC's Legion of Super-Heroes, for which Dave Cockrum had drawn many issues, meaning the X-Men were essentially being pitted against the Legion; there were obvious imitations of Chameleon Boy, Colossal Boy, Timber Wolf, Star Boy and others, while the Mohawk-wearing Gladiator took the place of Superboy. Unfortunately the art was cluttered and messy and did little to make the battle memorable. The tide is turned by the arrival of a heroic group known as the Starjammers, led by the piratical Corsair, who would turn out to be Cyclops' long-missing father. At stake is possession of a crystal which has the ability to wipe out all of existence and all that sort of gobbledygook. Phoenix manages to use her incredible new powers to save the universe in the following issue, which introduced the new art team of John Byrne and Terry Austin. Lilandra stays with the X-Men until things can be settled on her home planet and it is safe to return.

X-Men 109 offered the first look at James Hudson, aka Weapon X (and later, Vindicator), who heads a top-secret Canadian team of super-beings that Wolverine had resigned from but which wants him back whether he wants to go or not. Aided by his teammates, Wolverine successfully drives off Hudson, who vows to return with his entire team. Wolverine is depicted as a crude, touchy, rather unpleasant fellow who feels he is misunderstood but is good to have around in a fight; he is falling for Jean even as Banshee and Moira McTagget grow closer. In the meantime the proud Ororo is treated a bit like a boy toy as she romps around among the clouds in the nude, and can't understand why anyone could object to it. (In this free-spirited, unapologetically sexual aspect, she was similar to Starfire of *The New Teen Titans*).

Magneto

X-Men 111 began a three-parter that is one of the best adventures of the merry mutants ever published. Hank McCoy, aka the Beast, an original member of the group who literally changed into a furry beast-like hybrid and is now a member of the Avengers, is contacted by Professor X, who hasn't heard from his X-Men in quite a while. Investigating, Hank discovers that Scott, Jean, and the new X-Men have been put on display as sideshow exhibits in a circus, and have entirely new personalities from before. The architect of this is silver age foe, Mesmero, who has amazing mind-control powers and wants revenge on them for defeating him years before. Hank and the others are able to break out of their confinement, and Mesmero is himself taken care of by ... Magneto, at the peak of his powers.

Magneto uses his magnetic abilities to send Mesmero's wagon soaring miles into the air, and lowers it and everyone inside into an active volcano that hides one of his bases. There is an exciting skirmish, which Magneto wins, but his aim is not to kill the X-Men but torture them in diabolical fashion by making them helpless prisoners who can think but can't move a muscle, and who are tended to by an annoying robot named "Nanny." Still, the X-Men are eventually able to free themselves, but during the battle between them and Magneto, a massive explosion destroys the complex. Magneto escapes, as do Jean and Hank, who assume the other X-Men are dead. The excellent and attractive art by Byrne and Austin, superbly colored by M. Titus and Glynis Wein, was elevated to a new plateau with these issues, among the best to feature the menace of the master of magnetism.

While Jean and Hank return to Professor Xavier to grieve for the others, Scott and the members of the new team have broken out of the volcano base via a tunnel that leads to the Savage Land, there to encounter Ka-Zar (who first appeared in *X-Men* 10), and silver age foe Sauron, who siphons off mutant energy to become a monster. But the true antagonists are priestess Zaladane and Garrokk, the Petrified Man, who bedeviled Ka-Zar in the pages of his own magazine. Their actions to unite the various tribes of the Savage Land in one enormous city have inadvertently resulted in creating an ice age, a development that the X-Men are instrumental in reversing [*X-Men* 114 - 116]. Scott finds that he is unable to grieve for Jean, that she'd seemed like a different person since her transformation into Phoenix, but even artist John Byrne thought their relationship had seemed solid and Scott's numbness came out of left field.

In *X-Men* 117 Professor X, still mourning the X-Men, thinks back to his early encounter with the gross telepath Amahl Farouk in Cairo, the first evil mutant he fought and defeated. Supposedly Farouk is dead at the end of the story but he survives to become known as the Shadow King. Professor X goes off into space with his lover, Lilandra. His feelings for the alien woman must have been incredibly strong for him to forsake the earth, his fight for mutant acceptance, and his need for Magneto to be brought to justice for murdering the X-Men.

The next issue reunites the X-Men with Sunfire, and introduces his cousin Mariko, who would play a large part in Wolverine's life in the future. Arms dealer Moses Magnum, who now has super-abilities of his own, demands that Japan declare him absolute ruler of the nation or he will use his weaponry to sink the home islands and murder millions of innocents. The X-Men infiltrate his base and manage to stop his plans. By this time the comic had become extremely popular, was published on a monthly basis, and was winning awards and exciting fandom. The teammates, all of whom besides Colossus were loners, were becoming a loving family of good friends.

The run of excellent issues continued with *X-Men* 120 - 121, which introduced the Canadian team called Alpha Flight, which consists of Northstar, his sister Aurora, Sasquatch, Snowbird, and Shaman, not to mention leader James Hudson (now Vindicator), who are assigned to get back "Weapon X" - Wolverine - or else. Shaman casts a spell that creates a blizzard which forces the X-Men's plane down at the airport where Alpha Flight awaits them. Not knowing his own strength, the monstrous Sasquatch not only stops the plane from leaving but throws it across the airport, smashing it, only the X-Men are no longer inside. Wanting to avoid a fight that might level Calgary, the X-Men hide out, but are forced into battle in the Calgary Stampede playground with their foes as Shaman's magically-created storm rages out of control; Ororo uses her abilities to tame it. Wolverine stops the fight between super-teams by agreeing to rejoin Alpha Flight, but at the last minute escapes and catches up with his fellow mutants. The actual free-for-all between the two teams is a bit of a disappointment.

Phoenix and the Hellfire Club

Jean Gray meets Jason Wyngarde, a man who will become important to her future, in *X-Men* 122. (A clue to his true identity can be seen in the fourth panel to show his face.) It also contains the first mention of the sinister Hellfire Club, who would become significant adversaries for our heroes. Storm goes back to the Harlem home she lived in as a very young child and discovers the apartment has become a heroin den. Scott, beginning a romance with Colleen Wing (from *Iron Fist*) asks if he's stuffy, and she replies "like King Tut's tomb," but she still finds him intriguing. Colossus is homesick for his family in Russia. And then Black Tom and Juggernaut hire the diminutive redheaded assassin Arcade to kidnap and murder the X-Men. Chris Claremont had introduced Arcade in *Marvel Team-Up* 65 - 66, in which he tries to kill Spidey and new character Captain Britain in his Murder World, his "Disneyland of Death." In *X-Men* 123 - 124, in which Spider-Man guest-stars, Arcade captures our mutants and tries to kill them off with all of the high-tech equipment and sophisticated robotics at his command. This was followed by *X-Men Annual* 3 in which the mutants deal with the threat of Avengers-foe Arkon, the imperium from a barbarian world who needs Ororo's powers to save his planet from extinction; this was penciled with his usual dramatic flair by George Perez and inked by Terry Austin.

X-Men 125 - 128 presented the "Mutant X" saga, in which Jean discovers that the other X-Men are still alive and vice versa, and she begins to have hallucinations wherein she's living an entirely different 18th century life. In one fantasy she and

Jason Wyngarde run with the hounds hunting a stag, only the "stag" is a man forced to wear antlers and play the role of victim. The main villain in these issues, however, is Moira's son, who has escaped from necessary captivity on Muir Island. "Mutant X," or as he calls himself, Proteus, can suck away the life energy of virtually anyone he encounters, and take on their form. He also has the ability to bend reality to his will, twisting landscapes and causing major vertigo and worse in his opponents. Although Moira manages to get to Edinburgh to warn her estranged husband, a man who could have been prime minister someday, that the son he never knew he had is out to kill him, Proteus takes over the man's body and is further infused with his father's negative life energy.

One of the most deadly opponents the mutants ever faced, Proteus' ability to warp reality even has Wolverine freaking out. In one scene, Proteus takes his mother, bends her body into twisted shapes, then temporarily transforms her into a small elephant-like creature, and then some kind of amoeba. His powers seem literally limitless. Susceptible to metal, he is only destroyed in his host-free energy form when Colossus, in his armored form, attacks and scatters him to the four winds. Jean and Scott reaffirm their love for one another, with Scott recognizing that his inability to grieve was due to his complete non-acceptance of Jean's death. These issues were especially outstanding, but there were still more great stories to come. The Hellfire saga was up next.

X-Men 129 introduced two characters who would become very important parts of the X-Men mythos: 13-year-old Kitty Pryde, who has the ability to phase through walls and the like; and Emma Frost, the White Queen of the Hellfire Club, who has formidable psychic powers. Kitty, along with the psychedelic singer Dazzler (who debuted in the following issue), is one of the new mutants detected by Professor Xavier's machine, Cerebro, mutants that both the X-Men and the Hellfire Club want to enlist. Returning from space to monitor Phoenix's power levels, Xavier criticizes Scott's handling of the team, and goes so far as to give Wolverine "demerits" for stalking out of a training session. Xavier sends one group to Chicago to talk to Kitty's parents, and another to Manhattan, where they find Dazzler in a seedy warehouse disco downtown [X-Men 130]. Although for a time she was part of the Marvel universe and got her own series, Dazzler, who had light powers, was one of Marvel's lamest creations.

The Hellfire Club is a gentlemen's club that has been around for a century and a half and boasts many powerful and famous members. Its inner circle, however, is after a different kind of power, and is run by one Sebastian Shaw, an industrialist who is allied with Wyngarde and Emma. His associates are Donald Pierce, who is a cyborg, and chubby Harry Leland, a mutant who can control mass. Shaw is also a mutant who can absorb kinetic energy and make himself stronger than his opponents. The X-Men manage to fight off an assault by Hellfire forces in New York, preventing Dazzler from being kidnaped, but the White Queen subdues and abducts the other members, including Professor X, in Chicago. The White Queen is no match for Phoenix, however, who defeats her in a psi-battle, but alarms her colleagues by using her powers to manipulate Kitty's parents into letting her attend classes at Xavier's school [X-Men 131].

The X-Men infiltrate the Hellfire Club's Manhattan HQ during a party but are set upon by the members of the inner cabal, including Jason Wyngarde, who is revealed to be the illusion-casting Mastermind, an original member of the silver age Brotherhood of Evil Mutants. Wyngarde/Mastermind takes control of Jean, and turns her into the club's Black Queen, making her believe that she is in the 18th century, that Scott is an enemy, and Ororo, her slave. Of the team, only Wolverine remains free. Mastermind and Cyclops engage in battle on the psychic plain, and the latter is defeated. Unfortunately for Mastermind and his allies, Jean perceives this as the death of the man she loves, and it breaks "Wyngarde's" hold on her. She and the rest of the X-Men engage the Hellfire Club's inner circle in battles and escape, but not before Jean completely shatter's Wyngarde's mind [*X-Men* 132 - 134].

Recognizing the frightening enormity of her abilities as Phoenix, Jean had installed psychic circuit breakers to keep her power from getting out of control. But Mastermind's fiddling has broken those circuit breakers and allowed Jean to give in to the dark side of her nature and the corruption of absolute power. She transforms into Dark Phoenix and attacks her allies, then flies off into space. Nestling within a sun light-years distant, she luxuriates in the energy she gets in destroying it, unconcerned that the destruction of the sun also destroys the five billion souls on the planets in orbit around it. This attracts the attention of Lilandra's people, some of whom are also obliterated by the energy of the Phoenix. When Jean returns to Earth, she nearly destroys the X-Men again, until Professor Xavier is once again able to put back the psychic circuit breakers and return her to her normal, loving self [*X-Men* 135 - 136].

Unfortunately, Lilandra and her people, the Shi'ar, have decided that Phoenix is too dangerous to exist and must be destroyed; they teleport Jean and the other X-Men to their home planet. Although Lilandra is divided by her respect for the heroes and her love for Xavier, she also knows that her duty must be done. (Jean spends no time learning about the races she obliterated.) Xavier suggests that a battle be fought to determine the fate of Phoenix, and Lilandra agrees. This leads into a major rematch on Earth's moon between the X-Men and the Imperial Guard. Seeing Scott struck down, Jean reverts to Dark Phoenix, but allows herself to be attacked, her energy drained, so one of the ancient, hidden weapons on the moon can vaporize her, a sacrifice she makes because she knows what her power is capable of. (The real Jean Gray - as opposed to the Phoenix creature who took her form and memories - turns out to be alive years later.)

Kitty Pryde, aka Sprite, had barely joined the X-Men when she was embroiled in the adventure known as "Days of Future

Past." The story begins in the 21st century, when most mutants have been obliterated by sentinels and a police state rules. Of the X-Men only Kitty, Colossus (her husband), Ororo, and Wolverine are alive, aided by Franklin Richards, son of Reed and Sue of Fantastic Four fame, and his wife, Rachel, a telepath. In an attempt to change the past, Rachel sends the consciousness of older Kitty, Katherine, back in time, to change places with the consciousness of her younger self. Katherine tells her teammates that while she looks like Kitty, she is actually thirty years older and from the future. On this very day the new Brotherhood of Evil Mutants will attack a council on mutants and murder Senator Paul Kelly, Professor X, and Moira MacTaggert, leading into the miserable future that Katherine comes from. While the 21st century X-Men try to survive against attacks by Sentinels, whose actions may lead the world into a devastating nuclear war, the 1980s X-Men engage the Brotherhood, which consists of Mystique (introduced in *Ms. Marvel*); the blind lady psychic Destiny; Avalanche, who can shake the earth; Pyro, who controls flames; and silver age foe, the fat and immovable Blob. Most of the Brotherhood are captured, and Katherine saves Senator Kelly from being murdered by Destiny. In the future most of the X-Men are destroyed by Sentinels, and the reader never learns the ultimate fate of the survivors, but it is indicated that saving the life of Kelly may not have prevented the terrible future from occurring after all. Rachel later reappeared in X-Men and the storyline for these issues was used for the movie "X-Men: Days of Future Past" [*X-Men* 141 - 142].

John Byrne, who had co-plotted many of the stories, left the series to work on other projects and was replaced by original artist Dave Cockrum, whose first assignment was an entertaining three-parter pitting our heroes against both Arcade and Dr. Doom. While one group goes to Arcade's Murderworld to rescue the loved ones he kidnaped, another goes to confront Doom in his upstate castle. Both Doom and Arcade - or rather his assistant Miss Locke, who took over when Doom made the hired killer a "guest" in his castle - conceive of interesting doom-traps for the mutants. Doom imprisons Ororo in a metal shell, turning her into a living statue, which causes her subconscious mind to react to her claustrophobia and create a massive and frightening storm centering on the castle. Escaping their traps, Nightcrawler, Colossus, and Wolverine force Doom to revert Ororo to normal, but for awhile, due to her high power levels, it seems as if a "Dark Storm" will be in ascendance. Fortunately, Ororo is able to reign in both herself and the storm she created. While the Cockrum-Rubinstein art may not have been as attractive as the Byrne-Austin combo, it was not only effective but boasted some especially good panels, such as a shot of a feral and fearsome Wolverine about to attack Doom, and Storm dramatically hurling lightning bolts at the desperately dodging villain [X-Men 145 - 147].

X-Men 150 brought back the Master of Magnetism to have another round with the new X-Men. Magneto has set up HQ on an isolated island in the Bermuda triangle, and issued an edict to the world powers that they must unilaterally give up nuclear weapons. He wisely thinks that money should be spent on, say, feeding the hungry instead of waging war and causing a holocaust that will destroy all mutants as well as ordinary humans. Cyclops points out that despite his lofty sentiments, Magneto is still after total power over mutants and hence the world. When a Russian sub fires missiles on the island, Magneto retaliates by sinking the sub and all aboard, and using a special machine to destroy a small Soviet city, although in the latter case he allows an evacuation. The other X-Men manage to land on the island, but Magneto is employing a field which neutralizes their mutant powers.

In spite of this great handicap the X-Men manage to stymie his plans, so enraging Magneto that he unleashes a lethal charge of electricity through Sprite's body. Magneto is so horrified that he killed a child (she actually survives), a mutant at that, that he stops fighting and flees. This issue added a new dimension to the villain, whose family had been murdered at

Auschwitz, and whose rage and grief had turned him into a fanatic and borderline sociopath. His murder of the men in the submarine would have consequences in the future, but Magneto was never seen as a simplistic, raging, power-mad villain again and would for a time become the X-Men's ally. His telling Cyclops that he grieves for the dead Jean Grey has its comical aspects when you consider he was subjecting her to emotional torture by nanny only a few issues back. *X-Men* 161 relates how Xavier and Magnus, as Magneto was originally known, met years before in Israel where the former helped free the mind of a catatonic concentration camp survivor (Gabrielle Heller, who would figure in X-Men stories many years later) and the latter was a volunteer at a hospital.

The X-Men had a rematch with the Hellfire Club in *X-Men* 151 - 152. Kitty's parents decide she'd be better off being educated with people her own age, so off she goes to the Massachusetts Academy, which happens to be run by Emma Frost, the White Queen. Frost uses a special device to switch minds with Storm, and infiltrates the X-Men in the guise of Ororo. Sebastian Shaw, Harry Leland, and a host of sentinels also attack the Westchester mansion but their scheme is thwarted and Ororo returns to her own body. The good stories were undermined by mediocre work by guest artists. Kitty and Ororo had formed a strong bond, with the latter thinking of Sprite almost as a daughter, and making her jealous of the child's close friendship with Stevie Hunter, her dancing instructor, who played a larger role in *The New Mutants*.

The Brood

The next story arc, heavy with interesting science fiction concepts and space adventure, reintroduced Scott's father, Corsair, and his group the Starjammers, as they are falsely accused of kidnaping Lilandra. Corsair is pursued by Sidrian hunters, who look like mechanical manta rays with sleek black bodies and big red eyes and can come together to form a giant ship that looks just the same as one of the individual Sidri. Ms. Marvel's foe Death-Bird reappears, allied with a group of *Alien*-inspired horrors with big heads, fangs and claws called the Brood; Death-Bird, a Shi'ar herself, hopes to replace her sister, Lilandra, as Empress (That same year *The New Teen Titans* also presented two dueling alien sisters in Starfire and Blackfire). The Brood, who have captured Lilandra and Professor X, operate out of humungous living ships that look like space whales and have had their consciousness obliterated or enslaved by the evil alien race. Meanwhile Admiral Lord Samedar of the Shi'ar, who is actually in league with Death-Bird, is out to vaporize the earth for his own evil purposes. Half of the Imperial Guard have joined his cause, and battle the other loyal-to Lilandra half, as well as the X-Men, while the Starjammers use their ship to block the deadly beam that would shatter planet earth. All is well except that Professor X, alarmed by an evil presence he senses inside of himself, winds up in a coma [*X-Men* 154 - 157].

X-Men 158 had Carol Danvers, the former Ms. Marvel and an ally of the X-Men, wiping out computer records of the group inside the Pentagon, where she and some of the mutants have a violent encounter with Rogue, who stole Carol's powers and memories in *Avengers Annual* 10 (see chapter 14) and has joined the Brotherhood of Evil Mutants, and her surrogate mother, Mystique. In the following issue the X-Men actually battle Dracula, one of several stars of Marvel horror comics who were intermingling with super-heroes, with mixed results, although it was startling to see Ororo, shaking off the influence of the bloodsucker's bite, flying after him after he takes on his winged giant-bat form. Dracula, supposedly killed off in his own series, returned in *X-Men Annual* 6, an exciting story in which his daughter Lilith, who despises him, possesses Kitty in a plot to wipe out her father even as Dracula turns his long-time nemesis Rachel Van Helsing into a vampire. The highlight of the issue is a moving bit when Rachel asks Wolverine to kill her and he lovingly complies. Dracula reverts to a skeleton but the building where the final battle occurs collapses before Wolverine can behead him ...

X-Men 160 had the X-Men trapped in an inter-dimensional limbo ruled over by Ka-Zar foe, Belasco, and his associate, the hideous S'ym. The X-Men encounter warped counterparts of themselves who are actually the real deal - some older, some evil, and so on - as well as the corpse of an aged Colossus. With the help of a much older Storm who has magical powers, they escape, but when Colossus' six-year-old sister, Illyana, who was visiting him, is pulled out of limbo she is thirteen, having spent several years in the horrible place with Belasco. The repercussions of this and its effect on her would resound in *X-Men* and *The New Mutants*.

The horrible members of the Brood with their armor-plated skin, tail stingers full of poison, and razor-like teeth took center stage in the next story arc beginning with *X-Men* 162. After Professor X emerges from his coma, he and the X-Men attend a special Shi'ar ceremony. But the Brood have altered their perceptions - only Wolverine senses the truth - and although they think they are being presented to a dignitary, they are actually being punctured by the hideous Brood Queen, who plants eggs inside their bodies. These eggs eventually take over the host body and turn them into more members of the Brood. The X-Men think they are in a place of safety, but are actually on the Brood's home planet, where the "sleazoids," as Wolverine refers to them, patiently await their transformations. Wolverine can't get the other X-Men to believe him, so he temporarily escapes, only to find they are in a city in a bubble on one of the Brood's space ships, a slowly decaying and gargantuan husk that attracts all sorts of slimy and hungry monster predators. The carcass is so huge that it rises above the planet's breathable atmosphere. Wolverine's healing factor and mutated immune system manage to destroy the brood egg inside of him.

Experimented on by the Brood, who are fascinated by the gene structure created when she became Ms. Marvel, Carol Danvers mutates into a powerful energy being called Binary. The X-Men and Lilandra manage to get off the Brood planet, but as they are pursued by the aliens, Wolverine has to tell them what they are facing. Furious, Binary blasts out of the ship without opening the air lock, nearly destroying her allies, who manage to save themselves. Horrified at what's growing inside of her, Storm takes off in a shuttle craft, nearly turns into a sleazoid, and uses the energy of the stars to destroy the egg, killing herself in the process. But she becomes one with an infant (if enormous) Acanti, one of the huge creatures the Brood use as ships, who heals her shattered form inside its body even as Storm's consciousness controls and maintains it. Peter and Kitty bond as the latter explains how horrified she is at the thought of dying by changing into a Brood, and how scared that she might retain some of her memory and remember who she once was.

The X-Men and Binary decide to have one last battle with the Brood on their home world, an exciting tale told in the double-sized *X-Men* 166. Scott has mentally transformed into a sleazoid without anyone else knowing it and is secretly working against the others. But when he and the others enter a chamber which represents the soul of the Acanti, the Brood-Queen is turned to crystal and the X-Men find the eggs inside of them have been destroyed. Sleazeworld is demolished, the Acanti are freed, and the X-Men head back to earth, where one last egg has been implanted inside Professor X. By this time Cockrum had been replaced by Paul Smith as penciller. Although the stories in X-Men were good enough for the series to be almost artist-proof, Cockrum's work had become rushed-looking and unappealing, and Smith was an improvement, although Bob Wiacek may not have been the best choice for inker.

The X-Men discover that the Brood egg was implanted in Professor Xavier and is already metamorphosing into one of the aliens. What remains of Charles' mind begs the X-Men to kill him before the change is complete, but instead they take him to the Starjammers' ship, where a new body is almost instantly cloned for the professor and the brood egg destroyed. Professor X's legs are no longer crippled, but a psychological block keeps him from walking. The X-Men meet the New Mutants for the first time and nearly come to blows, as they have not yet been introduced.

The Morlocks and Madelyne Pryor

X-Men 169 - 170 introduced the Morlocks, grubby, ugly mutants who live in a gigantic abandoned bomb shelter beneath the city and who are led by the nasty, one-eyed Callisto. Callisto has developed a hankering for the beautiful Angel and kidnapped him to be her groom. The Morlocks capture the X-Men when they go to rescue Angel, and Kitty catches a plague from one of the mutants that might kill her without treatment. Callisto and Storm fight a duel to see who will lead the Morlocks, and Storm wins by stabbing her enemy in the heart. Callisto is eventually healed by one of the other Morlocks, but Nightcrawler worries that Ororo seems to be changing, and not for the better. In the meantime Scott and pilot Madelyn Pryor become good friends and go on a date, and decide to keep seeing each other despite Lynn's (later, Maddy's) resemblance to Jean Grey and Scott's being a mutant. Scott learns that Madelyn was the sole survivor of the crash of a 747 she was piloting the very night that Jean Gray died -- practically at the same moment.

Unable to deal with Ms. Marvel's memories, which she stole from her in *Avengers Annual* 10, Rogue goes to Professor X for help and becomes a probationary member of the team, angering the other X-Men. When Binary, the former Ms. Marvel, finds Rogue inside Xavier's mansion, she literally knocks her through the roof and out into space. Thanks to the professor, Carol has regained many of her memories, but not the emotions that go with them, and she feels crippled because of it. She understands why Xavier accepted Rogue onto the team, but can't forgive her, and flies off [171]. Wolverine has become engaged to Mariko, a lovely Japanese woman whose father, Shingen, was a powerful racketeer. Mariko's half-brother, Harada, also known as the Silver Samurai, is furious that Mariko inherited control of their father's empire while Wolverine worries that she may become corrupted. Wolverine and Rogue successfully fight off the Samurai and his partner, Viper, and at the wedding ceremony Ororo shows up with a brand new look, with a mohawk hairstyle and a black leather outfit that scandalizes Kitty. Lilandra tries to slice up Maddy Pryor, whom she thinks is the Phoenix reborn, and then Mariko calls off the wedding, telling the heartbroken Wolverine that he is "not worthy" and making other unsavory comments, after a meeting with a stranger, an encounter she forgets a moment later [172 - 173].

For some reason Claremont and artist Paul Smith made no effort to hide the fact that a recovered Mastermind was again working behind the scenes, influencing the X-Men and others, just as he had during the Dark Phoenix storyline. On an obvious rebound, even if no one can see it, Cyclops asks Maddy to marry him, then infuriates her when he asks her if she is the Phoenix. As he's picking himself up off the floor, who should appear but the Phoenix in all her glory. The Phoenix shows up at Xavier's mansion and easily fights them off; although Scott is at first convinced that the Phoenix is real, he begins to have his doubts. Later on Jason Wyngard, Mastermind, makes the other X-Men think that Cyclops is really Phoenix, but it is not explained how the Jean Gray who appears earlier, a mere illusion, can throw the mutants around like tenpins. Cyclops helps his former colleagues see through the deception, and Mastermind is trounced. Maddy is discovered alive and well and the wedding eventually takes place [175]. This exciting if unspectacular issue was the 20th anniversary of the X-Men.

The Bronze age of the X-Men ended with John Romita Jr. and Bob Wiacek taking over the art; Callisto vowing vengeance on Ororo and Kitty Pryde; Mariko telling Wolverine that she can't marry him until she clears up issues with her father's empire (it is revealed that she left Wolverine at the altar due to Mastermind's influence); a woman named Valerie Cooper addressing the "mutant problem;" and Cyclops and Maddy being attacked by both a Great White and a giant squid while on their honeymoon.

The New Mutants

The New Mutants, Professor Xavier's second group of X-Men, first appeared in *The New Mutants* graphic novel in 1982. The members include fundamentalist Scots shapeshifter Rahne Sinclair (Wolfsbane); Brazilian Roberto De Costa (Sunspot), who can turn into a dark, powerful energy being; Sam Guthrie (Cannonball), a young miner from Kentucky trying to support his family after his father's death from black lung, who can emit bursts of energy that give him speed and power; Danielle Moonstar (Psyche, then Mirage), a Native American who can cast images, sometimes of the future; and Vietnamese Xi'an Coy Mahn (Karma), who can completely take over the minds and bodies of people while retaining some control of her own.

Donald Pierce, the former Hellfire Club member, has gathered his own force of half-human cyborgs and is out to destroy the new mutants - and all others. Pierce hires Sam, who has no idea of what kind of person he is, to help capture the others, even as Moonstar and Sunspot, whose loved ones were killed by Pierce's men, vow to get even. Professor Xavier, who thinks the original X-Men are all dead in space, has mixed emotions about teaching these youngsters, but agrees, and together they affect his rescue after he is kidnapped, and bring a chastened Sam into the fold. (Professor X has also gathered these mutants together because of the unconscious influence of a brood egg inside him, as the creature hopes to implant an egg in each of the new mutants.) Christopher Claremont's script was good, as was Bob McLeod's art, which was generally attractive, although he was hardly a master of dynamic composition. The best panel shows a saddened and distraught Sam being left behind as the other mutants take off with Professor X, although he is reunited with them by the end.

The New Mutants debuted as a monthly series in 1983, with the same creative team, plus Mike Gustavich on inks. In the first few issues, Henry Peter Gyrich enters into an unholy alliance with the Hellfire Club's Sebastian Shaw, both of whom are secretly working against the other. Gyrich, who wants to confine mutants for study, is unaware that Shaw is himself a mutant and is hoping to turn the New Mutants over to his side. Moria McTaggert learns from Gabreille Haller that she has a mutant son whose father is Professor Xavier. There is an attack by Sentinels, as well as by the Brood Queen egg that is still, at this point, inside Professor X. The third issue has the new mutants in a desperate battle against this brood creature, who can manipulate Danielle's power so that her illusions -- such as an attack by a full-grown member of the Brood -- are real.

Christopher Claremont's characterizations of the new mutants were excellent, and they emerged as sympathetic, sensitive and likable young people the reader could easily care about. In *New Mutants* 4 the teens help out a friend, dancing teacher Stevie Hunter, when she gets threatening phone calls. It develops that the calls are from a boy named Peter who has been so consistently abused by his parents that he loves-hates Stevie, whom he is attracted to, because she doesn't show her love by punishing him. This psychologically astute script made for a compelling story despite the absence of any menace or super-villain. Beginning with this issue McLeod became inker over Sal Buscema's pencils. Unfortunately NM 5 - 6 focused too much on the uninteresting stunt riders Team America, who were mutants and who, like DC's *Forever People*, could combine to form one being, the Dark Rider. (Team America's own series lasted 12 issues.)

The Mutants survive a plane crash at the end of *New Mutants* 6 but Karma is among the missing, perhaps victim of a sinister presence within her mind. Karma had actually been introduced to the Marvel Universe two years earlier in *Marvel Team-Up* 100. In this story she tries to possess Spider-Man so she can use his abilities to rescue her little brother and sister, who have been kidnapped by her crime lord uncle to force her to use her powers to aid his pursuits. Her evil brother Tran has the same possession powers, and nearly has the Fantastic Four responsible for Spider-Man's death when he takes over the minds of each member of the quartet simultaneously. In spite of the fact that Tran seems much more powerful than his sister, Karma is able to defeat her brother and absorb his essence into herself [Claremont/Miller/Wiacek].

As the X-Men search for her, the teens rescue Sunspot's mother, Nina, from Hellfire Club employees, including a massive creep with a Mohawk named Axe. Roberto does not realize that his father, Emmanuel, belongs to the Hellfire Club and hired the kidnappers to prevent his archaeologist-wife from going on an expedition along the Amazon. The Mutants rescue her and they set off on their trip, where they encounter hostile Indian girls and capture one. Under her dark body paint, this captive turns out to be Amara, a self-exiled citizen of Nova Roma, a magnificent city hidden under the clouds in the Andes. (Nearby the Inhuman's Attilan, or Great Refuge, one supposes.) There is civil war brewing in Nova Roma between the Roman descendants, and the Incan descendants, who wish to transform the republic into a monarchy. Amara's father, Aquilla, had sent her out of Nova Roma for her protection until he could discern the identity of a certain dangerous mistress of dark arts, who turns out to be Selene, the wife of Aquilla's rival, Gallio. The male members of the New Mutants are drugged and set against each other in the arena - Wolfsbane enters the fray as well -- but their powers and performances turn them into heroes, with Rahne worshiped as a goddess [NM 7 - 9].

When Selene, who is an ancient mutant who thrives on human sacrifices, throws Amara into a pool of lava, the girl emerges as Magma, a mutant who can burst into flame and control fire. She and the mutants defeat Selene (who would later reappear in X-Men) and Aquilla suggests it would be a good idea if Magma is also trained by Professor X. Back in Rio Sunspot confronts his father over events in the Amazon, and becomes estranged from him, causing the elder Da Costa to join the inner circle of the Hellfire Club. Magma nearly destroys Rio when her powers get out of hand, but the teens help her get things back in control [10 - 12]. That wrapped up the first year of New Mutants, which would run for many years in the copper age.

The New Mutants also appeared in *Marvel Team-Up Annual* 6, one of the better issues of that series. In this Spider-Man and the mutants not only encounter anti-drug heroes Cloak and Dagger, but also a group of drug dealers who are hoping to turn mutants into drug-controlled assassins even more powerful than the original duo. Sunspot and Wolfsbane are injected with the formula and briefly turn into horrific and dangerous new versions of themselves, as does Dagger, until Cloak uses his enveloping and healing darkness to set things right [Mantlo/Frenz/Dzuban].

Various mutants also appeared in other issues of *Marvel Team-Up*. MTU 69 - 70 had Spider-Man assisting Havoc in his battle against the silver age foe, the Living Pharoah, who turns into the Living Monolith after he absorbs Havoc's power, as he did years before. Thor turns up to help deal with this gigantic menace while Spider-Man frees Havoc from his prison, the act of which instantly whittles the Monolith down to size. Claremont wrote the story while Byrne, Villamonde and DeZungia turned in a decent art job, although not quite as "magnificent" as touted on the cover. *Marvel Team-Up* 100 had a back-up which told how Ororo had come to the rescue of T'challa years before in Africa, and in the present day team up again when the bad guy they once defeated tries to get even with them. The end caption suggests that Storm and the Black Panther will only be "friends forever," but many years later they were married, albeit briefly [Claremont/Byrne/McLeod].

The Beast

Amazing Adventures 11[1971] presented the first in a series of adventures of Hank McCoy, otherwise known as the Beast of the X-Men. Marvel had begun publishing several successful horror comics such as *Werewolf By Night* and *Tomb of Dracula* in the bronze age, and it may have seemed a good idea to turn McCoy into a literal hairy beast somewhat similar to a werewolf. This happens when Hank gets a job at the Brand corporation - the other X-Men are hiding out in their Westchester mansion and had no series of their own at this point - where he isolates the chemical cause of mutation and creates a formula that can turn anyone into a mutant for an unspecified period. It develops that there are spies in the Brand corporation and Hank decides to take after them but first he disguises himself by drinking the formula, which turns him into a hairy animal-like creature. (This aspect of the story is very unconvincing, as even Hank himself wonders why he's drinking the formula.) He takes care of the spies, but gets back to his lab too late to take the antidote, and must remain permanently furry. Meanwhile he doesn't realize that his girlfriend and lab assistant, Linda, is also a spy, and a murderous one at that. Gerry Conway scripted the "origin" and Tom Sutton, who did a lot of horror comics, contributed some un-pretty but effective artwork.

Steve Englehart became the new scripter with *Amazing Adventures* 12. Hank manages to make special face and body molds that hide his furry appearance, but when Tony Stark comes to visit Brand's new wonder boy in his lab, a conflict eventually breaks out between the Beast and Iron Man. The Beast thinks he's murdered the golden avenger, but it's all an illusion cast by Mastermind, the former member of the Brotherhood of Evil Mutants, who has been observing the scene with his associates, Unus and the Blob. A confused and partly amnesiac Beast agrees to work with these other mutants, but after helping them steal a diamond, his memory returns and he trounces them. The Beast discovers that if he's shot or injured in any way, his wounds heal almost instantly (this was a couple of years before the introduction of the Wolverine and his healing factor.) Eventually he loses this invulnerability and his fur changes color from gray to black. Meanwhile, Brand's Air Force security liaison Colonel Baxter and his wife Pat show up to investigate the stories of a beast running amuck [AA 13]. Proving that Marvel hardly ever forgets a character, these two people were actually former teen queen Patsy Walker and her boyfriend, "Buzz" Baxter, who appeared in a whole slew of humor-romance comics in the silver age.

After a battle with the living computer Quasimodo, who'd first appeared in the silver age as well, an injured Hank winds up falling into Patsy Baxter's apartment, where she overhears him talking in his sleep and makes a few surmises that will resonate later in *The Avengers*. He then has a reunion with the Angel, as the two fight off the menace of the winged Griffin, who's had claws and a mane grafted onto his body, and who is employed, like Linda, by the sinister group the Secret Empire. In AA 16 the Beast battles the Juggernaut in Rutland, Vermont, where his old girlfriend, Vera Gantor (who'd been trying desperately to catch up with him in previous issues), tells him that the world is in danger and she needs his help as a scientist. Alas, all of these plot threads were left dangling when the series was canceled; AA 17 reprinted the Beast's origin from backup stories in the silver age *X-Men* series.

The Beast was featured in *Marvel Team-Up* 124, in which he sees his parents for the first time since his furry transformation. Mrs. McCoy is at first disgusted by his appearance, and all the changes he's gone through due to his mutant status, but in the end she risks her own life to save Hank when he's endangered by Professor Power. The Griffin returned to battle the Beast and Spider-Man in *Marvel Team-Up* 38.

The Champions

The Champions (1975) was an unusual super-team book created and written by Tony Isabella (and Bill Mantlo) with art by Don Heck, George Tuska and Vince Colletta. Several disparate Marvel characters find themselves on the UCLA campus one afternoon: students Iceman and the Angel (formerly of the X-Men), Hercules and would-be teacher Black Widow (formerly of the Avengers) and relative newcomer and supernatural-based hero Ghost Rider. Their first challenge is the menace of Pluto, who forms an alliance of various leaders of underground realms. Threatening Mount Olympus with a combined attack, Pluto gets Zeus to promise that Venus (a golden age character who worked in an earthly guise at UCLA) will marry Ares, and Hercules will marry Hippolyta, Queen of the Amazons -- figuring since spouses could not oppose one another these two gods could then not prevent Pluto's plans to take over Olympus. The other members of the Champions brave Olympus in *Champions* 3 to stop the marriages from taking place and convince Zeus that he is only being played.

The Champions slowly became an official team, "store-front super-heroes" helping the common people, based in Los Angeles and backed with the considerable Worthington fortune that Warren inherited from his parents. Turning lecture-agent Richard Fenster into their manager and public relations officer, and the Black Widow into their leader, they take up headquarters in a downtown office building. Iceman resents being the "baby" of the team as he was with the X-Men and thinks about leaving. Some of the very insecure men have trouble taking orders from the Widow, who has to remind them that she had been in action longer than they had.

Rampage [*Champions* 5 - 6] was an embittered inventor who lost his company during a recession, robs banks in an Iron Man-like costume, and is roundly trounced by our heroes - after which his lawyer takes over the company, pays off his creditors, and makes a profit while Rampage goes off to the hospital. Originally seen as merely misguided, Rampage proves a more traditional villain when he joins up for money with members of a Soviet task force which includes Darkstar, the Griffin, the Titanium Man, and the new Crimson Dynamo (who was the estranged son of the Widow's companion and father figure, Ivan), all of whom attack the Champions at a press conference announcing their formation - after kidnapping the Widow. By now Bill Mantlo had taken over as scripter while temporary penciller Bob Hall's mediocre art did nothing to bring his stories to life. Darkstar, a woman with special darklight powers, abandoned her Russian team mates to sign up for the Champions, but Ghost Rider never trusted her.

John Byrne took over the art for most of the remaining issues and proved the best choice so far. *Champions* 12 - 13 continued a storyline that had begun in *Black Goliath* 4 (and even earlier in the short-lived *Silver Surfer* mag) with the Stiltman trying to grab a mysterious box from a woman whose boyfriend has stolen it from Stark Industries. This was the Null-bomb, capable of wiping out all life on Earth. The Stranger, who'd first appeared in the silver age *X-Men* 11, tries to stop the bomb from activating but is unsuccessful because the Champions think the big guy is up to no good, but all works out in the end with the aid of a mystical rune staff last seen in the pages of *Thor*.

Champions 14 - 15 brought a new menace in the form of Swarm, an ex-Nazi whose body has been attacked by mutant killer bees who have formed a symbiotic relationship with him. Not only can he employ millions of insects to do his dirty work, but he has a few giant mechanical bees as well. An Interpol agent has stolen the queen bee and imprisoned her, and the Champions now have her in their HQ. A startling half-page panel showing black masses of bees swarming toward Los Angeles appears at the end of *Champions* 14. In the following issue Swarm frees the queen bee from captivity, and she quickly grows to giant size herself. Hercules throws the queen far out to sea and the masses of bees follow, leaving Swarm himself a bee-less -- and fleshless -- skeleton that collapses to the ground.

Champions 16 featured a story originally begun in *Super-Villain Team-Up* 14 with Magneto, of all people, teaming up with the group to free everyone on earth from Dr. Doom's mind-control. Somehow it didn't seem like it was part of normal Marvel continuity. The 17th and final issue of the series featured the return of the Sentinels, but these are guided by old X-Men foe the Vanisher, who is accompanied by the Blob, Unus, and the Savage Land mutate Lorelei, who are easily defeated. *The Champions* was a fun comic of a minor kind, but it never quite hit its stride, despite a few memorable adventures. The Champions teamed up with Iron Man to tackle Modok in the forgettable *Iron Man Annual* 4.

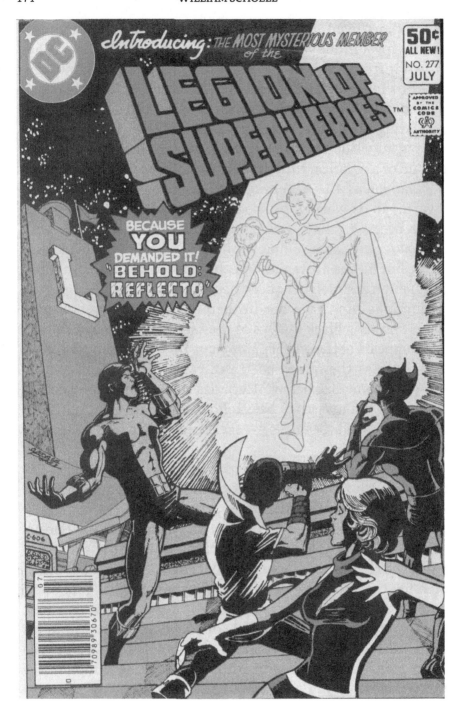

CHAPTER TEN:
SUPERBOY AND
THE LEGION

The first few bronze age issues of *Superboy* featured his adventures in Smallville with Ma and Pa Kent (who had been given a youth formula at the end of the silver age), Lana Lang, and super-dog, Krypto. *Superboy* 168 boasted an evocative Neal Adams cover with a teary Boy of Steel being run out of town, which was appropriate as the two stories in that issue both dealt with Superboy being forced to leave Smallville and his loved ones. In the first story Nazi agents place bombs beneath the town and threaten to destroy it if Superboy doesn't leave forever. Hysterical townspeople, fearing for themselves and their loved ones, turn against Superboy and force him to depart, but he manages to outwit the Nazis anyway. In the second story, a "negative" Superboy - which is actually composed of some of Superboy's excess energy - forces Ma and Pa Kent to pretend that they want the negative Superboy to replace the real one. Fortunately, Superboy is aware of the deception and counteracts it because he knows how much his foster parents love him.

In other stories Superboy deals with a fortune teller who predicts Clark Kent's death but turns out to be Lex Luthor in disguise, meets a trouble-making young cousin named Crusty, and discovers that an extra-intelligent ape had been sent from Krypton before its explosion and now leads a group of gorillas in Africa (not to be confused with the super-gorillas from *The Flash*). He also helps a young Aquaboy deal with oil companies that despoil the seas with leaky tankers in *Superboy* 171, an early ecological tale. Most of the stories were written by Frank Robbins, with art by Bob Brown and Murphy Anderson. Around this time Superboy's adventures were moved from the 1930's to the 1950's to keep up with Superman, who remained 29, as he had been for years, in the 1970's.

Superboy

As for the Legion of Super-Heroes, they got a sporadic back-up spot beginning with *Superboy* 172, in which Lightning Lad and his sister Light Lass take on their evil sibling, Lightning Lord. In *Superboy* 173 evil wizard Mordru creates a duplicate of Cosmic Boy that is indistinguishable from the real thing; Superboy figures out which is which when he throws supposedly metallic objects at both of them and knows the one who couldn't repel them is the real deal because the objects weren't really made of metal - the duplicate's powers come from magic. In another story the Invisible Kid has to come up with a way to defeat a crook who uses the same basic formula that he does; in other words, he has to come up with a way to defeat himself. The clever stories were by E. Nelson Bridwell, while George Tuska did the art.

Leo Dorfman contributed scripts to *Superboy* and they tended to be on the silly side, although he did do a macabre one for *Superboy* 179 in which people melt into gruesome proto-plasmic blobs whenever Superboy comes near them, a rare horror-type story for the comic. David George, a pseudonym for Dorfman, did a silver age-style imaginary story in which baby Kal-El's rocket lands in Africa and the super-baby is raised by apes (not to be confused with the real Kyptonian monkey raised by apes in a previous issue). Other stories dealt with Superboy as a baby having amusing encounters with a little boy witch named Gary who also has special powers; and a little girl named Kathy who develops a super-brain after an accident with an alien space probe. The somewhat schizoid tone of the comic was best illustrated by the grim cover of *Superboy* 189, which has Martha Kent and Superboy opening a door to find the shadow of Jonathan Kent hanging from the ceiling, a supposed suicide, while a banner underneath announced a new "Superbaby" story.

Dorfman wrote a compelling tale, "The Super-Merman of the Sea," for *Superboy* 194, in which an exiled Atlantean scientist transforms an unconscious Superboy into a merman complete with fin and gills. Although the scientist hopes to use the super-merman to get amnesty from his fellow Atlanteans, a despairing Superboy, who feels like a freak and outcast, loses his powers, although he gains telekinetic abilities in their stead. At one point he is chased by sea-wolves - large, deadly sharks - in a suspenseful tale with some effective Bob Brown-Murphy Anderson artwork. [For *The New Adventures of Superboy* see Vol. 2.]

And Now the Legion

After reprinting several old Legion of Super-Heroes stories from *Adventure Comics*, *Superboy* presented a new Legion tale in every other issue, these written by Cary Bates, including one in which Chameleon Kid, under a magical spell cast by Mordru, travels back in time to murder Superboy [*Superboy* 188]. *Superboy* 184 marked the first time Dave Cockrum worked on a Legion story (with Murphy Anderson), although his style didn't really shine through until *Superboy* 190, in which the two candidates for Legion president, Saturn Girl and Mon-El, are kidnapped and nearly killed by Tharok, leader of the Fatal Five. The exciting story has the two legionnaires squaring off against the powerful, hulking Validus, under Tharok's command, but Mon-El manages to save them both by cleverly outwitting Thrarok. The art by Cockrum and Anderson gave the Legion a new luster.

Superboy 195 presented the first appearance of Wildfire, although he was known as Erg-1 at the time and supposedly died at the story's end. Drake Burroughs applies for Legion membership after his body is destroyed by anti-energy and placed inside a containment suit. His powers all seem to mimic other members so he is rejected due to the Legion's pesky by-laws. (You might think they would have taken pity on a boy who lost his humanity in one sense and is seeking a place to belong; at least Phantom Girl shows him some compassion.) Later Erg-1 follows the legionnaires on a mission and unveils his secret power to save the life of Colossal Boy - a blast of energy that completely dissipates his "body." The legion members mourn him, but he was to return some time in the future.

But the first legionnaire to come back from the dead in the bronze age wasn't Erg, but Timber Wolf, in a full-length tale in *Superboy* 197. Thought destroyed in an explosion, the hero returns with no memory of the last six months. It develops that his "rescuer" is a bad guy with bright red skin, a mohawk, and a nasty attitude named Tyr, who only saved his life so he could brainwash him and turn him into an assassin. Beginning with this issue, *Superboy* would present stories of the Boy of Steel's adventures with the 30th century legion every month, with the logo being changed to read "Superboy Starring the Legion of Super-Heroes." Cary Bates and Dave Cockrum were the creative team with Murray Boltinoff as editor. The next issue featured the Fatal Five going back in time to Smallville of the 1950's with a diabolical plot to erase the Legion and all of its members right out of existence.

In *Superboy* 200 Bouncing Boy learns that he is losing his powers and has to resign, but he takes Duo Damsel with him when they get married, but not before they have to deal with silver age foe Starfinger and his plot to create a zillion duplicates of himself. Erg-1 manages to move his energy across the galaxy back to earth by *Superboy* 201 and is inducted into the legion - after saving all of their lives - as "Wildfire" in the following issue. *Superboy* 203 had two surprises for readers: Invisible Kid is killed off during a battle with the hulking, mindless Validus (sans the rest of the Fatal Five) and goes into another plane of existence with a lady ghost he's fallen in love with, and Dave Cockrum left the series.

Editor Boltinoff sounded a touch bitter as he wrote: "Dave Cockrum, who was virtually unknown in the field and gained star-artist stature only after we gave him the opportunity to do the Legion, has departed." Cockrum had gone over to Marvel where he continued his rise in the industry by soon thereafter becoming penciller on their revived *X-Men* series (In fact, Nightcrawler was originally conceived for the Legion). Mike Grell, who'd inked a couple of Legion installments over Cockrum's pencils, became his replacement. Grell had a distinctive and attractive style and after a while became even more associated with the Legion than Cockrum was.

Superboy 204 featured a tale in which Brainiac-5 quits the legion to run off with Supergirl from the 20th century, with whom he's always been infatuated. But in a rather kinky twist this Supergirl turns out to be an android that Brainiac in his loneliness - and lust - cobbled together in his lab at night while walking in his sleep! *Superboy* 208 has the super-heroes squaring off against their counterparts in the Legion of Super-Villains, as the bad guys - who consist of Chameleon Chief, Sun Emperor, Lightning Lord, Radiation Roy, Nemesis Kid and Spider Girl with her living hair (a la Marvel's Madame Medusa) - try to blow up a peace ambassador and most of the legion along with him. Nemesis Kid and Spider Girl had previously applied for legion membership and been rejected.

Jim Shooter, who'd written Legion stories starting at the ripe old age of 13 in the sixties, was brought back to handle the scripting chores with Cary Bates. His first appearance in *Superboy* 209 was a typical Shooter tale in which Princess Projectra contracts an illness that causes nearly unbearable pain - and then death - within six hours. The legionnaires on hand affix equipment that will siphon off her pain into their own bodies, one at a time, for an hour each. *Superboy* 210 has another Shooter tale in which he tweaks Karate Kid's origin a bit and makes him half-Japanese, the son of a notorious criminal known as the Black Dragon and an American mother; Mike Grell modeled him on Bruce Lee. Shortly afterward Karate Kid was given his own short-lived series to take advantage of the then-current craze for the martial arts (see chapter 12). In *Superboy* 212 Shooter dealt with the Legion rules for not accepting heroes whose powers are already duplicated in a member when six applicants from the same home worlds - and with the same powers as six legion members - challenge them and boast of their superiority. The legionnaires defeat them by using team work instead of tackling them one on one, but this sort of defeats the purpose of deciding which of each pair is the more powerful.

Cosmic Boy was given a new outfit in *Superboy* 215 which was somewhat unusual, resembling a kind of tight black bustier - something rock singer Madonna might wear - which left his shoulders and the middle of his chest and back completely uncovered; his black pants could best be described as short-shorts, exposing his legs completely, and he also wore black gloves. In other words, the outfit was pretty sexy for a superhero uniform, but it was also an odd choice for a man to wear, leading some wags to label it a "gay" costume for that reason and because gay men were stereotypically seen as vain and anxious to show off what good shape they were in, which this costume certainly did for Cosmic Boy; in any case, the character was apparently not gay. One letter writer asked what was holding the uniform up, while others thought its appearance overwhelmed the story, but loved it. The tale in which the outfit first appeared concerned Cosmic Boy being unable to use his powers on a day sacred to his people, but managing to save several legionnaires in spite of it.

Now that the Legion had an Asian member in Karate Kid, it was about time for a Black legionnaire, who debuted in *Superboy* 216. Tyroc belonged to an independent but isolated nation, Marzal, that wanted nothing to do with outsiders. According to Tyroc, racial prejudice had finally been eradicated, but he thought the Legion might be behind the times as they were always (coincidentally) somewhere else when there was a crisis in Marzal. Tyroc and the Legion worked out their differences, however. Tyroc had sonic powers, although he was perhaps not in the power range of the Inhumans' Black Bolt. His costume was as skimpy as Cosmic Boy's, but with the chain across his chest it was somewhat more masculine.

Tyroc, who could also produce vocalisms that allowed him to teleport and bend the laws of physics, was officially inducted into the legion two issues later. Tyroc also figured prominently in *Superboy* 222 when he flushed out some criminals by pretending to go rogue. And that was about it, as even on the very few occasions Tyroc was mentioned he was generally home on Marzal attending to unspecified business. In a giant-sized tabloid edition of the Legion, Tyroc was selected by computer to stay behind on monitor duty! He was finally featured in a story over forty issues later, and permanently departed this dimension when it was revealed that Marzal periodically disappeared for 200 years like the mythical Brigadoon. It was rather outrageous that in the 1970's -- as in the silver age -- the Legion still considered itself "integrated" because of Brainiac-5's green skin, and Shadow Lass' purple hue! That there was not a single regularly-appearing black character may not have been conscious racism, but it was certainly racism of an unconscious -- and thoughtless -- kind. It had certainly never been established that 30th century earth was an all-white society. A new Black legionnaire who was somewhat more important would come later.

The entire Fatal Five returned in *Superboy* 219, stealing a variety of objects from different planets and trying to stay out of the way of the Legion. It turns out that all they wanted this time was to build a retreat for themselves where they could relax while plotting their next attempt to take over the universe. Then the Time Trapper returned in a twisty tale in *Superboy* 223. But there were new antagonists as well. *Superboy* 221 introduced two novel opponents, created by Jim Shooter, in Grimbor, who could trap and/or safeguard anything, and his lady love, Charma, who casts a hypnotic spell over men. The two manage to capture about a dozen legionnaires, but

Charma wants to ransom them for a trillion dollars from their wealthy benefactor, R. J. Brande, while Grimbor wants to keep them on display as examples of his handiwork. Shrinking Violet, who manages to escape the pair's clutches, starts whacking on Charma, which so enrages the hypnotically-smitten male legionnaires that they break out of bondage. The whole story has a slightly kinky "s and m" undertone to it. Grimbor tackled the legion again in a lively story in *Superboy* 240 and was thoroughly beaten despite his clever machinations.

An even more formidable antagonist was Pulsar Stargrave, introduced in *Superboy* 224, whose body has been placed by aliens inside a sun because they mistakenly think he's dead. His body is destroyed but he gains the powers of a Pulsar and recreates his physical form. He is almost indescribably powerful, and turns out to be Brainiac-5's father. Stargrave wants the Legion to help him against the deadly sorcerer, Mordru, but after that they will have to do their utmost to prevent Stargrave himself from conquering the universe. Then the Stargrave story was put on hold for a couple of issues.

Denny O'Neill took over as editor with *Superboy* 225. As Cary Bates was busy with *The Flash*, and Jim Shooter had left for Marvel, where he eventually became editor-in-chief, Paul Levitz took over as scripter. His first tale was an inauspicious one in which Superboy acts like a jerk, objecting to Wildfire being named the new leader of the group over him even though he is only a part-time legionnaire, with a contrived last-minute explanation for his behavior. However, the following issue introduced Dawnstar, a lady with wings who can track anyone or anything not only through space but through space *warps*. Mike Grell moved over to *Batman*, so the art was done by James Sherman and Jack Abel, and it was a classy job, giving the series a new luster and attractiveness. Jack Abel's inks also gave added luster to back-up artist Mike Nassar's pencils, as well as Joe Staton's, who penciled the following issue. Meanwhile, Levitz proved the most durable Legion scripter of all, and added a new serious tone to the proceedings, heightening characterization as well.

Paul Levitz decided to tinker a bit with Stargrave, and changed him from Brainiac-5's father to the original android Braniac, who had come to the future. Levitz introduced Deregon, the leader of Australia, who is in league with the sinister silver age group, the Dark Circle, and wants to plunge the world into war. His plan is foiled by the fatal sacrifice of Chemical King, who earlier in the story complains that he feels he isn't pulling his weight as compared to members like Superboy [*Superboy* 228]. The issue also reintroduced the Legion Espionage Squad, headed by Chameleon Boy, who goes undercover to investigate rumors that Deregon is gathering an army. The Legion catch up with and capture Deregon in the following issue, and also have a brief, indecisive skirmish with the Dark Circle on their home planet.

Superboy in *Adventure*

Around this time Superboy appeared in a solo adventure in *DC Super-Stars* 12 to see if there was still any interest in his stories without the Legion. He was given a new solo series in *Adventure*, but it only lasted six issues, until *Adventure* was turned into a dollar comic book. Cary Bates' tale in *DC Super-Stars* has Clark falling in love with an attractive and brainy gal named Misty even as his Kyrptonian robot teacher who'd appeared in the silver age shows up again to give him further tests. These tests include making Superboy think that Misty has been killed, which is bad enough, but it also turns out that he gave Misty her special qualities artificially, and even "borrowed" her from another town for a few days. Superboy is convinced that his experiences with the teacher qualify him to be called Superman from now on, but he hasn't the sharpness to accuse the robot not only of cruelty, but of actual criminal conduct in taking Misty away from a family that had to be horribly worried about her. And this was a teacher!

Adventure 453 had the Boy of Steel dealing with a mischievous young camper who gains super-powers from Mordru's crystal, which Superboy has in his possession. Once the boy of steel realizes what's happened, he throws the crystal into space and the little girl returns to normal. She turns out to be Barbara Gordon, who would grow up to become Batgirl. In the next issue Superboy is in the midst of a real dilemma when all the inhabitants of Smallville turn green from kryptonite rays. He assumes his old foe with the "kryptonite" touch, the Kryptonite Kid, is responsible, but this proves not to be the case. Instead Lex Luthor has used a special satellite to pull a hoax, sapping Superboy's powers and turning the townspeople green. Bob Rozakis was the writer of these stories, while David Micheline came up with a tale about Lester Wallace, a man who campaigns against Superboy as if he were a dangerous alien invader; at the same time parts of Superboy's body become insubstantial. Wallace is actually being manipulated by a phantom zone criminal who is hoping Wallace will send Superboy into the zone using the latter's special projector, and give him, the criminal, a chance to get free [457 - 458]. After this story, Superboy moved to *Superman Family* while *Adventure* went to a dollar format with a variety of features for nine issues.

As for *Superboy*, the title was officially changed to *Superboy and the Legion of Super-Heroes* beginning with the 231st issue, which also signaled a change in format to a giant 60-cent size. The first extra-long story by Levitz was one of the best ever to feature the Fatal Five, who came up with an especially loathsome plot: Tharok arranges for the sun of a planet with a million inhabitants to go nova, because the rays will turn their bodies into the rare and extremely valuable element, energite; with this they hope to fund many projects, such as the Emerald Empress literally buying back the home world over which she used to rule. As the Legion hurriedly try to evacuate every person on the planet, the Fatal Five do their best to stop them, the equally desperate heroes and villains engaging in the most energetic battles of their long and combative association. James Sherman and Jack Abel turned in an especially attractive art job.

Gerry Conway contributed two interesting tales for *Superboy*

232 and 234. In the first, an outbreak of a plague that causes everyone to shrink is wrongly blamed on the inhabitants of Imsk, the home of Shrinking Violet, while in the second tale four legionnaires are accidentally combined during an explosion to become a rampaging composite creature that is hunted by a man named Bounty. Paul Levitz and Mike Grell handled a story in *Superboy* 235 in which Superboy discovers that the legion has been hypnotizing him into forgetting something everytime he returns to the past. Since he has already subjected himself to self-hypnosis to forget whatever he may learn about the future, he's baffled as to why the Legion takes this extra precaution. The legionnaires lie to Superboy and tell him that they are capable of creating artificial life in the 30th century, but don't want this knowledge revealed to anyone in a past era, and Superboy believes them. What they don't tell him is that the actual secret they zealously guard is that people of the 30th century have a greatly extended life, hundreds of years, with their youth literally lasting decades - the legionnaires appear to be teens but are actually older, which explains why those in their twenties are still called "boy" or "kid." The legionnaires are afraid that even Superboy won't be able to resist the temptation to extend the lives of his loved ones, such as Ma and Pa Kent. This was a very clever way of dealing with the fact that the members of the Legion always seemed much more mature than typical teens and were given serious and adult responsibilities.

Paul Levitz and Jim Starlin came up with a very interesting tale in *Superboy* 239 in which Ultra Boy is framed for the murder of an old girlfriend who has become a desperate prostitute. Ultra Boy refuses to be taken into custody so that he can track down the real killer, leading him into dramatic and violent conflict with the rest of the Legion even as Chameleon Boy plays detective and realizes that Wildfire has been replaced by a dangerous robot. But the man behind the whole plot, who wears an executioner's hood, remains unmasked at the story's end and wasn't revealed until nearly a year later in *Superboy*

250.

Earthwar

In the meantime *Superboy* 241 began a multi-part saga, "Earthwar," in which the alien warlords, the Khunds, launch an attack on Earth. This occurs just as some members of the Legion are assigned to help guard a conference between the United Planets and another alien group called the Dominators, with trouble breaking out, such as explosive sabotage, before the Dominators even arrive. This story introduced Weber's World, an artificial planet where the bureaucrats of the United Planets do their work, as well as Ambassador Relnic and the snake-like security chief, Ontiir. We also meet science police officer Shvaughn Erin, who, due to everything going on, is unable to deliver her message that one of the Legion's foes has escaped captivity. Recognizing that the odds are against their repelling the Khund war ships, Superboy and three other legionnaires take the battle directly to the Khund home planet, where they discover that the leader is being mind-controlled from space. Following the beam leads them to Weber's World, where other legionnaires anxiously wait for the Dominators to finally emerge from their ship. There seemed to be a new maturity to the tone of the comic, greatly abetted by the illustrative work of James Sherman and Bob McLeod. (Another change was that Timber Wolf was becoming more and more savage a la the X-Men's popular Wolverine.)

The Earthwar saga became more even more thrilling with *Superboy* 243, in which the Khunds defeat the legionnaires who remain on Earth, as well as the valiant members of the Legion of Substitute Heroes, even as Superboy and the others try to track down the true enemy -- and people began strangely disappearing from Weber's World without a trace. New penciller Joe Staton proved a surprisingly good fit for the Legion with his superlative art job, embellished by Jack Abel, and then Joe Giella, both of whom smoothed out Staton's pencils and eliminated the cartoonish elements that often marred his work. The Dark Circle proved to be behind the Earthwar in

Superboy 244, and Mordru behind the Dark Circle in *Superboy* 245.

Although Mordru never really seemed that much more formidable than other Legion foes, he was considered their most dangerous enemy, and they always seemed to be running away from him before ultimately defeating him, as they do this time. It was decided at this point to amend the Legion constitution so that married couples could remain in the group; Saturn Girl and Lightning Lad return but Bouncing Boy and Duo Damsel decline. (Saturn Girl and Lightning Lad got married in the all-new collector's edition tabloid, which contained the longest Legion story to date as they battle the Time Trapper; it was, unfortunately, a disappointment.)

The Fatal Five returned in *Superboy* 246 - 247, as delegates from the planet Corvan-IV, which seeks entry into the United Planets. Winding up on the planet after escaping from the Legion during their last escapade, the Five actually tender service to the friendly Corvanians, and make life much easier for them. Unfortunately the UP rejects their application because the Legion feels they created too much culture shock on Corvan-IV by introducing major new technology much too quickly. Reverting to type, the Five try to smash Superboy, Element Lad, and Colossal Boy in revenge, but take a powder when even three legionnaires ultimately prove too formidable for them. Some readers argued that the story, however entertaining, trivialized and somewhat diminished these incredibly powerful and resolutely evil characters.

Gerry Conway scripted a two-parter for *Superboy* 248 - 249 in which the Legion battle weird sewer monsters and Brainiac-5 begins acting very oddly. In the next issue he is revealed as the masked stranger behind the plot to frame Ultra-Boy; he has also created a super-powerful being named Omega who threatens to destroy not only the Legion but the entire universe. Omega gets his/its strength from the collected hatred of the world, especially Brainiac-5's, who supposedly wants revenge because he has received no recompense for using his genius to save the world and the legion on so many occasions. In other words, B-5 has succumbed to total madness due to stress, and is, sadly, quite certifiable.

Knowing that Omega wants to use a reality-warping Miracle Machine (introduced in the silver age) that the Legion keeps safely in their possession, to destroy the cosmos, even B-5 is worried, and he instructs Matter- Eater Lad to devour the device, which had resisted all other efforts to destroy it. Unfortunately, absorbing the alien energies of the machine also drives M-E Lad mad. To make matters worste, R. J. Brande, the Legion's benefactor, discovers he is broke and facing bankruptcy. Of course, none of this explained why B-5 murdered a prostitute or framed Ultra Boy for her death in the first place. B-5 was cured of his insanity in *Superboy* 256, and it turns out that the Earth's president had illegally siphoned off Brande's fortune to help rebuild Earth after the war with the Khunds/Mordru. Brande agrees that the lives of millions of people are more important than him being rich. The legionnaires finally realize that Brainiac-5 had been framed for murder by Pulsar Stargrave, the original Brainiac, many issues later [*Legion* 273].

The Legion of Super-Heroes

The title of the comic was changed to *The Legion of Super-Heroes* beginning with issue 259. During the story Superboy learns how Ma and Pa Kent would die, and Saturn Girl uses her telepathic power to give Superboy a command to stay in the past and never return to the 30th century where he would have to constantly deal with his anguish over Ma and Pa Kent's deaths even before it happened in his own timeline. (Superboy was again given his own series, *The New Adventures of Superboy*, detailing his adventures in the sixties when he had just turned sixteen; Cary Bates and Kurt Schaffenberger were the creative team.) New *Legion* editor Jack Harris bemoaned the fact that it was difficult to find a permanent penciller for the top-selling *Legion* because the day's less dedicated freelancers found it too much work to draw so many heroes or couldn't meet deadlines. Jimmy Janes became the new penciller and while his work wasn't exactly exciting, it was professional and effective. Gerry Conway remained the chief scripter.

There were some excellent stories during this period, such as a two-parter in *Legion* 266 - 267 in which Bouncing Boy and Duo Damsel return to the legion after inadvertently freeing an ancient gargantuan alien "genie," Kantuu, from captivity, which incorporates and explains the early legends of djinn and gives the group of heroes a very formidable antagonist. *Legion* 269 - 271 brought back the Fatal Five, who are being manipulated by a mysterious "Dark Man," who turns out to be an even more evil, fully "human" clone of the half-mechanical Tharok. The FF and the legion - along with the large rock-being Blok, one of the Dark Man's former allies - wind up joining forces to defeat the Tharok clone but the implication that the FF allow themselves to be meekly arrested by the legion at the end is improbable to say the least. The reformed Blok became a legion member in *Legion* 272.

Gerry Conway's characterizations of individual legionnaires added a new dimension to the series, such as in a two-part story in *Legion* 274 - 275 in which Ultra Boy is presumed dead after being blasted by Pulsar Stargrave in the previous issue. Ultra Boy survives, but has amnesia, and is rescued from space by a band of pirates with a woman leader who takes a shine to him. Colossal Boy is suffering from feelings of inadequacy after his mother becomes Earth's new president and seems to have especially harsh attitudes towards the legion. Timber Wolf, formerly known as Lone Wolf, feels hemmed in, constricted by, his legion membership and tells his girlfriend, Light Lass, that he only stays because of her. Phantom Girl, who loved "Jo Nah" (Ultra-Boy) is shattered by his death and lashes out at the "ice princess," Saturn Girl, who uses her powers to bring pleasant memories of her romance with the hero to the forefront of her mind.

Saturn Girl is delighted to discover that Jo is alive, but before she can tell Phantom Girl, Jo realizes who he is, turns against the pirate band, and is killed for real this time in another devastating explosion as he sacrifices himself to save the legion. Conway's touch, however, didn't always extend to villains, as the Legion encounter their supposed arch-foe Mordru in *Legion* 276 -- after he takes over a medieval world under a new name -- and he is defeated in only a couple of pages. On the plus side, readers noted that Conway's women were always equal to the men.

Still, Conway was temporarily replaced by Roy Thomas as scripter beginning with *Legion* 277; Mike W. Barr took over as editor. Thomas had an auspicious debut as scripter with a fascinating three-part story in which Grimbor places gigantic energy chains all around the earth, chains which can tighten and cut off the air supply, suffocating the planet's billions of inhabitants. All Grimbor wants to call off the chains is for the members of the legion to become his slaves and ultimate victims. For good measure a new hero named Reflecto saves the life of Light Lass and seems thereafter obsessed with her. The story was nearly as suspenseful and exciting as "Earth War," even if the confusing ending had Reflecto turning out to be Superboy -- who for some reason thought he was Ultra Boy.

Paul Levitz returned as scripter and examined the mystery of Reflecto/Superboy/Ultra Boy (working from Thomas' plots), sending some legionnaires back to 20th century Smallville to seek answers and throwing in the Time Trapper for good measure; it was a horribly contrived mess, far below the level of the Grimbor story, in which Ultra Boy attempts to get out of a weird limbo by taking over the boy of steel's mind, giving him amnesia and turning him into "Reflecto." Levitz' changes to our heroes included Timber Wolf getting cosmetic surgery [*Legion* 284], which made him seem less like Wolverine but also much less distinctive than before; Bouncing Boy and Duo Damsel going back to wedded bliss as legion reservists; Tyroc, lost on Marzal, being given an honorable discharge in absentia; and Princess Projectra becoming queen of her feudal-style planet -- for a couple of hours until a challenger to the throne defeats her and sentences both her and Karate Kid to death. The legion helps defeat the usurper and Projectra becomes the new ruler of Orando. Pat Broderick and Keith Giffen became *Legion* artists and Laurie Sutton the new editor. Eventually the creative team was Levitz and Giffin as writer and artist, as well as coplotters, with Bruce Patterson on inks, then Larry Mahlstedt.

Chameleon Kid had discovered that R. J. Brande was his father in a special *Secrets of the Legion of Super-Heroes* mini-series, but his unease with this development led him to make bad decisions, such as taking a group of legionnaires to the Khund home world to do an unnecessary bit of reconnoitering which nearly gets them all killed. Lightning Lad finds the rigors of being Legion president are too much for him and abruptly resigns in favor of his deputy, Element Lad. Science police officer Shvaughn Eric from the "Earthwar" story becomes official liaison to the legion in their first annual, which also brought back silver age menace Computo and introduced a new Invisible Kid, Jacques Foccart, who is both Black and French.

The Great Darkness Saga

"The Great Darkness Saga" began with a prologue in *Legion* 287 in which Mon-El and Shadow Lass explore a foreboding and barren planet, unaware that a mysterious, powerful figure is coming awake in a dank grotto. Subsequently, beginning with *Legion* 290, the Legion members come up against several "Servants of Darkness," who turn out to be warped and evil clones of the following: Superboy; one of Shadow Lass' ancestors; and a Guardian (of the Green Lantern Corps); among others. While the legion tries to fight off these powerful servants, the dark unknown figure that created and controls them uses his incredible power to take over the world of Daxam (from whence comes Mon-El, who has been put into a coma), transforming the Daxamites into super-powered slaves and switching the entire planet in space with the shattered world upon which he awakened. Then he sends three billion Daxamites out to conquer the universe, which they begin to do by attacking and shattering entire civilizations. Their leader is ultimately revealed to be Darkseid.

In the double-sized conclusion in *Legion* 294 (dedicated to Jack Kirby), new Legion president Dream Girl, learning from Brainiac-5 just whom their legendary opponent is, calls in every super-powered individual who has ever been associated with the group, including the Legion of Substitute Heroes, Dev-Em, and Supergirl. The wizards on the Sorcerer's world cast a spell that brings forth a silent baby who grows to adulthood rapidly and turns into Darkseid's ancient foe, Highfather, who uses his power to aid the White Witch (Dream Girl's sister) in casting powerful spells and turns one of the Servants of Darkness back into Darkseid's son, Orion, who hates him. Only a shadow of his former self, Orion is unable to defeat his father as prophesied, but the legion members, and especially Supergirl, bolstered with power from Highfather, are able to distract Darkseid long enough for him to lose his hold on the Daxamites, who come after him en masse as he makes a hasty retreat. Darkseid then warns the legion of his curse. "The Great Darkness Saga" was probably the best story employing the malicious Kirby character since Kirby left DC.

Darkseid's curse was revealed months later in *Legion of Super-Heroes Annual* 3 when Lightning Lad and Saturn Girl are expecting their first baby. First Lightning Lad stops a new attack by silver age foe Starfinger even as other legionnaires prevent the awakening of Mordru, who has been comatose since Darkseid siphoned off his power to add to his own in the Great Darkness Saga. Darkseid himself appears at the very end, stealing off with one of the twin boys born to Saturn Girl without the couple ever knowing it. He sends this child back in time and transforms him -- in a masterstroke -- into Validus, the first time this member of the Fatal Five was given an origin. Thus the legion fought the couple's child before he was even born. The story was extremely well illustrated by Curt Swan and Romeo Tanghal.

Legion 295, which explains why the Green Lantern Corps is no longer welcome on earth, also reveals that silver age foe Universo may have once been a renegade GL called Vidar. In subsequent issues Brainiac-5 finally manages to cure Matter-Eater Lad of his madness; Chameleon Boy and his father travel to their weird home planet so that the former can regain his lost powers; Dream Girl and her deputy leader Ultra Boy have issues; and Lightning Lad and his psychotic brother Lighting Lord have a battle royal in *Legion* 302. In the following issue the Emerald Empress, sans her partners in the Fatal Five, takes over Weber's World, inserts her own mind into the movable planet's computer system and sets it on a collision course for the United Planets' Main Fleet Base. Security officer Ontiir, who figured in the Earth War, turns out to be aiding the Empress, but his true allegiance is to the Dark Circle. The legion, with Supergirl's help, defeat both of them. This was one of the very best single issue Legion stories of the bronze age (although the Empress first appeared in the previous issue's climax).

Legion Annual 2 featured the wedding of Queen Projectra and Karate Kid, but of more interest was the main storyline in which a legion cruiser is caught in Superboy's backwash as he emerges from the time stream and our heroes wind up in ancient Rome. There they encounter Zeus and the other "gods," who turn out to be shape-shifting Durlans on a visit to earth before the decimation of their own planet. While things work out for Projectra and Val, other legionnaires are not so lucky in love. Timber Wolf is heartsick and discombobulated because Light Lass quits the legion, but he is too attached to the group to go with her. Disembodied Wildfire loves Dawnstar, who goes off to fulfill a ritual of her people and wishes Wildfire had a body she could actually touch; finishing her quest for a soulmate she realizes that Wildfire is the life companion for her and that she'll just have to make do with the lack of physicality in their relationship [*Legion* 311].

Colossal Boy, who has fallen in love with Shrinking Violet, discovers that she's actually an imposter, a shape-shifting Durlan like Chameleon Boy, who infiltrated the legion without realizing her employers were dangerous revolutionaries. The real Shrinking Violet is rescued and Colossal Boy and the imposter, who had been secretly married, confirm their love for one another [*Legion* 304 - 305]. Some readers noted Star Boy's selfishness in hoping that his girlfriend Dream Girl would lose her bid for re-election (Element Lad wins) because he missed "cuddling" with her, feeling he should have quashed his horniness and been more supportive of the woman he was supposed to have been in love with. His feelings may have been understandable, but his lack of guilt over hoping she would lose made him unsympathetic.

Legion 307 - 310 had a confusing four-part story about a character named Prophet who screams about another character named Omen coming to destroy everyone, but the legionnaires can't decide which one to side with, Prophet or Omen. Most of the story takes place on the Khund homeworld, where the war-like natives want the legion to leave even though they are busy fighting off Prophet and Omen. Omen's origin was never revealed, and the surprisingly dull story served chiefly to bring the original Invisible Kid back into the fold - he had not really died but was lost in a very weird dimension he swore was Hell. In *Legion* 311 Brainiac-5 finally manages to separate the consciousness of Computo from the mind of the 2nd Invisible Kid's sister, curing her; turns Computo into a computerized major domo; and as his first task has him build a huge new Legion headquarters after B-5 accidentally destroys the old one. *Legion* 312 - 313 was a suspenseful story in which disguised legionnaires join the science police to figure out who is committing acts of deadly sabotage and threatening the life of the earth's president, Colossal Boy's mother.

This volume of the *Legion* series continued a bit into the copper age. While *The Legion* began a new volume beginning with number one (known as the "baxter" series because of the thicker paper stock it was printed on), the original series was retitled *Tales of the Legion of Super-Heroes*, which would eventually run reprints of the stories from the baxter series. However, there was all new material in *Legion* 314 - 325, written by Paul Levitz and initially drawn by Terry Shoemaker and Karl

Kesel. *Legion* 314 featured the trial of Ontiir, the serpentine security man of Weber's World who is accused of being a double agent for the Dark Circle, who think he's working with the science police and vice versa. The members of the dark circle are seemingly revealed to be alien, tentacled creatures whose main HQ is within their sun, and Ontiir dies without anyone being quite certain whose side he was on, if any.

In the meantime, Lyle Norg, the original Invisible Kid, is morbidly depressed and still thinks of himself as being dead. In *Legion* 317 he is actually revealed to be a dream-demon from another dimension; Norg is still dead. (In truth his "return" was so indifferently handled -- even the legionnaires were never really shown reacting to it -- that this revelation hardly made any difference or had any impact whatsoever.)

The Legion took on the team of the Persuader and Lady Memory, who represent the barbaric, superstitious past of Shadow Lass' world Talok VIII, in *Legion* 318 - 319. Lady Memory brings back all of Mon-el's horrible memories of being a disembodied spirit in the Phantom Zone for a thousand years, temporarily driving him mad, and wages a duel to the death with Shadow Lass, which the latter wins, sparing the villainess' life. In an exciting tale in *Legion* 324 - 325 the Legion finally take care of the Dark Circle, discovering that its vast membership consists solely of clones of the five leaders, one of whom turns out be the original Ontiir. The Circle also cloned Dev-Em, sending out his duplicates to cause mass death and destruction, and nearly kill the real man with kryptonite, but a spell cast by the White Witch causes the clones to merge with the original and ends their threat as well. Dan Jurgens did the pencils for these stories while Mindy Newell scripted from Levitz' plot.

Other memorable Legion tales: Super-thief Benn Pares announces that he's going to steal the alien miracle machine from Legion HQ and has his own headquarters inside the mouth of a huge space dragon [*Superboy* 213]; The League of Super-Assassins (one of whom, Blok, would eventually become a legionnaire) try to kill off six legion members under orders from a mysterious "Dark Man" [S 253 - 254]; the legion investigates mysterious murders at a circus promoting good relations between planets [*Legion of Super-Heroes* 260 - 261]; Wildfire bares his soul to two hopeful legion applicants [L 283].

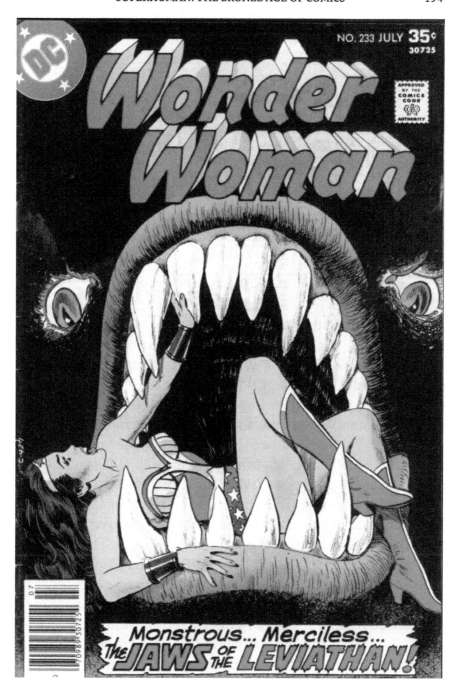

CHAPTER ELEVEN: AMAZON

-- *WONDER WOMAN,* THE HUNTRESS, *KOBRA*

Wonder Woman, the amazin' amazon, began life in the bronze age right where we left her in the silver age -- a powerless adventurer in a white outfit who traveled the world with her elderly Chinese mentor, I-Ching. Not that her heritage was completely forgotten. In *Wonder Woman* 190 she travels back to see her mother on Paradise Island - which has been shifted to another dimension - and winds up in the court of the cruel queen of Chaldonor, who likes to capture people for her arena. Princess Diana (Wonder Woman's true identity) gets her mitts on the queen, gives her a bitch-slap, and says "Not so much fun when you're on the receiving end." Diana and Ranagar, a prince of another nation in this dimension, face a Gnarth - a multi-limbed giant lizard - in the arena and manage to defeat it. When Diana suggests that they escape by jumping off the castle wall into the moat, Ranagar is dubious, so she pushes him. "I'll never understand you men," she says. "Ready to face a hundred soldiers - but afraid to jump a few dozen feet into a moat!" In the following two issues WW participated in an epic battle between Ranagar and his barbarian forces and the defenders of the evil queen's Castle Skull.

Wonder Woman

Writer-artist-editor Mike Sekowsky tried a variety of stories with the new Wonder Woman. She became involved with the residents of the neighborhood where she had a boutique, preventing one man from murdering the person responsible for putting his sister in a coma. She stood in at a wedding ceremony for a lookalike princess who'd been kidnaped. In *Wonder Woman* 195 she and I-Ching wind up in an inn during a storm in which the elderly proprietress and her hulking son turn out to be ghosts who had murdered their customers and are still at it years after their deaths. The following issue she was again a kind of Girl from U.N.C.L.E., repeatedly saving the life of an ambassador who turns out to be an assassin in disguise. Although some readers objected to this new version of a venerable old character, the fact is that the change saved the title from ignominious cancellation and the stories were an improvement over the mostly idiotic tales of the silver age Wonder Woman. As sales began to pick up, earlier stories showing how and why the change occurred, along with the first adventures of the new WW vs Dr. Cyber, were reprinted.

Dennis O'Neill took over as editor/writer with the 199th issue, teaming Diana with private eye Jonny Double. The following issue the two were captured by Diana's greatest nemesis, Dr. Cyber, who, like most villains, has more lives than a cat. Cyber, who blames Diana for her face being disfigured, plans to have her associate, Dr. Moon, transplant her, Cyber's, brain into Wonder Woman's body. But Diana uses yoga to suspend her breathing while she's being put under and manages to escape her fate. Considering everything Cyber has put her through, Diana seems to over-react tremendously when the villainess falls on her own knife. Dick Giordano's art gave the lurid tale a certain classy aura. In *Wonder Woman* 201 the amazon came into conflict with Catwoman from Batman, and the two wound up suspended in harnesses over a pit of fire, each with a sword meant to slash the ropes holding up their opponent. Luckily, Diana came up with a plan to save both of their lives.

New WW scribe Samuel R. Delany, better known as a science fiction writer, developed an interesting "women's lib" story, as it was touted, for *Wonder Woman* 203. Grandee, a department store owner, wants to use Diana to hawk his clothing - "for the liberated woman"- but he pays his sales ladies less than men would get if he hired guys. Diana's younger friend, Kathy, warns her that the man is only out to use her and importunes her to attend a Woman's Lib meeting. Diana protests that not only isn't she a joiner but that in most cases she "doesn't even like women" - what, she hates her fellow Amazons?! -- which has Kathy replying that that must mean Diana doesn't like herself. WW tries to get support from Jonny, but he agrees with Kathy. Diana decides to attend the meeting, takes care of thugs hired by Grandee to disrupt it, and shuts down his whole illegal operation. At the end of the story Diana herself is being picketed - by all the women who lost their jobs when Grandee's was shut down!

With the very next issue Robert Kanigher replaced O'Neill as writer/editor and the strip moved in a new direction with Don Heck at the art helm. In "The Second Life of the Original Wonder Woman," I-Ching is one of several people killed by a sniper, and Diana loses her memory. She makes her way back to Paradise Island - which has somehow come back from the other dimension - and there Queen Hippolyta directs that her daughter be put under the "memory machine." However, she also commands that certain periods in her life be eliminated. In any case, WW gets her memory back just in time to be challenged for the "Wonder Woman" title by the Black Amazon, Nubia of the Floating Island, who gives a good accounting of herself but fails to unseat Diana. Nubia turns out to be Diana's sister, stolen from Hippolyta when she was a baby by Mars, the God of War. Clad in her original uniform, with all of her superpowers once more intact, Diana makes her way back to New York where she gets a job as a translator and acquires two pretty roommates. In the next issue she battles a silly villain named Dr. Domino who wears a ridiculous headpiece shaped like a domino. As Diana Prince, she is once again considered a "plain Jane."

Whereas Delany and O'Neill seemed sincere, one suspected Kanigher was only giving lip service to women's lib in his stories. (Answering one letter he resorted to that hokey cliche "Wonder Woman is a woman ... she's unpredictable.") In any case, beginning with *Wonder Woman* 207 Kanigher -- completely out of touch with comic book tastes of the period -- decided to have artist Ric Estrada (inked by Vince Colletta) do an approximation of the golden age art style of the strip while he wrote the kind of childish scripts that had once predominated the series. In stories that seemed to be set in the past, he even brought back old boyfriend Steve Trevor and Wonder Tot! This experiment had already been tried in the silver age, and didn't work, and it didn't work this time, either, lasting only five mostly miserable issues. Only "The Shrinking Formula" [WW 210], in which WW is shrunk to tiny size and has to fight off a "gargantuan" fly, was even remotely memorable.

Julius Schwartz took over as editor beginning with the 212th issue and thought of a novel way of getting her back into modern-day action. Diana encounters Superman but has no idea what he's referring to when he asks her when she got her powers back. Apparently Hippolyta saw fit not to give her back the memories she lost of her time with I-Ching. Superman and the other JLA members want to immediately reinstate WW, but she's afraid she's unfit due to her memory loss and the emotional crisis it engenders. She decides that if she passes ten trials - like Hercules - supervised by her fellow leaguers, she will then rejoin the team. In this way Schwartz got a different big gun from the JLA to guest star in the next several issues. Although it would have been better to ignore the stories in the five previous issues, or simply remind everyone they were adventures from the past, instead Schwartz has Hippolyta explain that the Steve Trevor of WW's last few adventures was just a figment of Diana's imagination created for Diana's mental stability; Steve Trevor is dead. Diana also got a job with the crisis bureau of the United Nations, and worked for a man named Morgan Tracy.

Aquaman monitored Diana's activities in *Wonder Woman* 215, in which Mars, the God of War, tries to foment a conflict between the Amazons and Atlantis, a concept which decades later became the basis of the *Flashpoint* mini-series. WW 216 answered the question of what exactly would be the dire consequences if a man were ever to set foot upon Paradise Island, although the wealthy Greek shipping magnate who risks fate and the Amazons to find out never learns the truth: the amazons would all fall in love with the man, and descend into barbarism fighting over him. This was due to a spell the goddess Aphrodite cast as punishment for Hippolyta temporarily losing her magic girdle of immortality to Hercules. The story was by Elliott Maggin.

Martin Pasko took over as scripter and did a fun tale in which Atom's old foe, Chronos, manages to throw Manhattan into a panic by making it impossible for anyone to tell what time it is, and throwing some lively doom traps at Wonder Woman as she tries to stymie him and set things right. In the following issue Hawkman narrates how Wonder Woman once again encounters the disfigured Dr. Cyber, who wears a glass mask that could make her look like anyone she chooses, and who tries to slice off Wonder Woman's face before falling to her death. When Atom and Hawkman compare notes they realize that these adventures occurred at the same time, and that there are apparently two Wonder Women. *Wonder Woman* 222 revealed that one of the amazons is actually an inorganic but otherwise perfect duplicate created by a Walt Disney-type who had died and been replaced by another demented duplicate. The story was fairly idiotic but it did serve to finally get Wonder Woman reinstated in the JLA.

Steve Trevor

For reasons that didn't make all that much sense, the spirit of Steve Trevor is used in a masquerade engineered by Hippolyta and Aphrodite in *Wonder Woman* 223 to test Diana as the Justice League had tested her (Hippolyta has a problem with the fact that most of the Leaguers are men). At the end of the story Diana begs Aphrodite to bring Steve back to life, and she complies. Even Hippolyta has to wonder if this is a good idea. Trevor hides the facts of his re-birth (apparently he has zero friends and family) and joins S.O.S., aka Spy-on-Spy, a group that answers directly to the president [WW 225]; he also dyes his hair black and calls himself Steve Howard (after the actor Trevor Howard).The development with SOS went absolutely nowhere and it was never mentioned again.

In a two-part story in *Wonder Woman* 226 - 227 the special guest-star was, of all people, singer-actress Judy Garland, although she was called "Julie Gabriel." Hephaestus, the evil God of fire, seeks to win boons from fellow god, Mars, and to that end is testing a magical fire that is fed not by oxygen but by human emotions. It develops that he has planted devices that will cause the fire in Carnegie Hall where Garland - that is, Gabriel - is giving a concert. (The real Judy Garland did have a well-publicized concert at that venue.) When the fire erupts and Wonder Woman is busy battling Hephaestus, Julie deliberately sings a highly emotional song in her inimitable style and draws all of the fire away from the audience and to herself. She saves the lives of her fans, but is herself immolated. The story seemed to be an excuse to draw a sympathetic portrait of Garland by writer Martin Pasko, but it's never explained why Wonder Woman simply didn't look for and destroy the fire devices before the concert began. Pasko has said that it was the favorite of his Wonder Woman stories because it had "heart."

With *Wonder Woman* 228, the editorial chores were taken over by Joe Orlando - with Denny O'Neill as "story editor" - and the strip was given a completely new direction. Lynda Carter had played Wonder Woman in a couple of TV movies and now the show was becoming a weekly series. Since the telefilms had been set during WW2, it was decided the comic should now feature the exploits of the original Earth-2 Wonder Woman who had come into her own twenty years earlier. To set the stage, the current, Earth-1 Wonder Woman is accidentally sucked back in time and through the dimensional barrier by the Nazi Red Panzer, and she and the original WW have a brief battle before comparing notes. Wonder Woman returns to her own time and dimension, and the original amazing amazon takes over, fighting the Red Panzer during the war.

As both Wonder Womans were utterly one-dimensional, it scarcely made a difference. Steve Trevor, now a brunette on both Earths (because the actor playing him on TV had dark hair), appeared -- now a major who was Diana's boss in Army Intelligence -- along with chubby Etta Candy, an irritating character from the golden age. Martin Pasko continued on scripts with Jose Delbo and Vince Colletta on the art. The Earth-2 Wonder Woman was also given a new series in *World's Finest*, with most of the stories written by Gerry Conway and drawn by Don Heck. A memorable villain, Baron Blitzkrieg, the super-Nazi, battled the amazing amazon in WF 246 - 247.

The Nazi agent Red Panzer returned in the 1978 *Wonder Woman Spectacular*, a 70 page story that features the Baroness Paula Von Gunther and her bevy of slave girls; the ancient Gods such as Mars and Aphrodite; a new hero named the Bombardier who turns out to have a dire secret; Adolf Hitler himself -- as well as Harpies who attack the Amazons -- and still manages to be boring and not very well drawn by a variety of presumably rushed artists. Far superior was the *Superman vs. Wonder Woman* oversized tabloid edition, which came out around the same time and features an excellent 72 page story written by Gerry Conway and beautifully drawn by Jose Luis Garcia Lopez and Dan Adkins. In this the Man of Steel and the Amazing Amazon come to blows because the lady has learned of the Manhattan Project and is afraid of the consequences if the atom bomb is ever used. She subsequently tries to destroy the reactors while Superman attempts to stop her. Complicating matters are the presence of Nazi blowhard Baron Blitzkrieg and the Nipponese samurai known as Sumo. While it was clearly the Earth-2 Wonder Woman, and was supposed to be the Earth-2 Superman, he came off more like the familiar modern version in powers, demeanor and the fact that he worked for Perry White at the *Daily Planet* (as the modern Superman did) instead of George Taylor of the *Daily Star*.

Wonder Woman 230 brought back the golden age Cheetah, a split personality who spends half of her time as socialite Priscilla Rich and the other half robbing people and trying to kill Wonder Woman, something she nearly succeeds at in this exciting story. The following two issues had the amazon in conflict with Osira, an alien who was worshiped as an Egyptian goddess thousands of years before and who wants to use her powers to end WW2. Wonder Woman knows that a forced end to the fighting wouldn't work or last, and stops Osira in her tracks, but not before the woman pits hypnotized members of the Justice Society against her.

Gerry Conway took over as scripter with *Wonder Woman* 233 -234, in which the amazon takes on a Nazi U-boat captain who is able to turn mammoth sea creatures against the allied powers. These saurians include whales and a humongous sea serpent from the deep who tries to swallow our gal, a scene which is beautifully rendered on the cover. WW also has to deal with a masked Nazi named Armageddon, who is head of a group of saboteurs, wears boots that emit vibrations that can shake things to pieces, and turns Steve Trevor into a giant-size mutated monster. As in the silver age, Steve Trevor pined for Wonder Woman, which annoyed Diana because he was so obsessed with the amazon's "glamor" that he ignored her four-eyed alter ego. Conway made Diana more human and emotional (if not fully dimensional), her anger, love for Trevor, and distrust of other men often getting the better of her. She was also understandably upset that she was hardly ever treated as an equal by men - even the Justice Society made her their secretary!

In *Wonder Woman* 237 - 238 our amazon fights an especially action-packed battle against Kung, a Japanese assassin and shape-shifter who is out to murder General MacArthur. The Sandman of the Justice Society is a special guest-star, along with his boy partner, Sandy. During this adventure Wonder Woman gets angry at soldiers for shooting at Kung - her rationale was that she'd seen enough violence - so that the assassin gets away, leading Army officials to wonder if the amazon is more hindrance than help, and if she perhaps might be a traitor. The Duke of Deception comes to Earth and makes Diana see illusions that have her fighting American servicemen because she thinks they're Nazis - she also fights an animated Statue of Liberty for the second time in as many years. This led to the amazon princess being arrested for treason, but the Golden Age Flash helps her out of this jam [WW 240].

Back to the Future

Larry Hama became the new editor with *Wonder Woman* 239, and it was decided to move the amazon back to the seventies because that's what the TV show did. Her last golden age adventure was in WW 243, wherein the Angle Man and his dimension-hopping Angler device cause the two Wonder Women of different Earths and different time periods to meet again in the past. The Earth-1 modern-day Wonder Woman takes the Angler back to prison and took over the book from there. This left a few unanswered questions, such as the identity of Armageddon, and the reason why a handsome if sinister French soldier got engaged to the dumpy Etta Candy (although in subsequent "golden age" issues the soldier disappeared and there was no more mention of a marriage). Jack C. Harris took over the scripting for the new modern-day adventures. The original Wonder Woman was replaced by her younger Earth-1 counterpart in *World's Finest,* as well, such as a melee with Poison Ivy in WF 251.

Diana is bothered that her feelings for Steve and vice versa have altered since his re-birth, and that he no longer seems like the man she had once loved. Before any of this can be resolved, Steve Trevor-Howard is killed off - this time for good - in *Wonder Woman* 248. The following issue reveals a hitherto unknown brother of Steve's named Greg, who works for an unknown organization and turns out to be quite crazy. In *Wonder Woman* 250 an Amazon challenger named Orana insists that Hippolyta hold a new tournament, the same one that determined which of the amazons would become Wonder Woman and travel to Man's World. Diana has no wish to give up her role as super-heroine, but her mother tells her that Orana does have the right to issue the challenge.

One by one the other amazons are eliminated in each contest, until only Diana and Orana are left. While Diana shows skill and compassion in each contest, Orana seems determined to win with brute force come hell or highwater, but Hippolyta picks Diana as the winner. (The last contest takes place in outer space, but the notion that the Amazons, who shun contact with outside races, would have spaceships seems highly improbable.) But then a group of male gods intervene and insist that according to the rules they stipulated long ago, Orana is the true winner of the contest. For some reason Hippolyta obeys the men's edict and Orana is given Wonder Women's costume.

Ross Andru took over as editor with the following issue (DC had the habit of giving veteran artists editorial assignments along with writers young and old) as Diana, still determined to have a life in the U.S. despite losing her title, follows Orana to New York, where Diana has been accepted into NASA's astronaut training program (and this after knocking meteors around with her feet in the previous issue). The hard-hearted and stubborn Orana makes a botch of being Wonder Woman and dies in a hail of bullets from the minions of a ludicrous villain called Warhead who wears a ridiculous missile-like headpiece. Diana returns Orana's body to Paradise Island and once again takes up the mantle of Wonder Woman. Orana's tenure was so brief that the concept of a new Wonder Woman, which had definite possibilities, almost seemed pointless. Jack Harris had some interesting ideas but he was never a good fit for the amazon.

As an astronaut-in-training, Diana has a budding romance with another trainee named Mike Bailey, but new writer Paul Levitz made him a new costumed member of the old Royal Flush Gang from *Justice League*, with whom our amazon tangled in WW 256. Levitz also had Diana drop out of the space program, with her thinking most credibly that as Wonder Woman she had already seen the stars. Then Gerry Conway was in as writer, and he brought Diana into conflict with Hercules and Mars, the latter of whom descends from Olympus to become a gargantuan giant striding through Manhattan. Losing her bracelets of submission, Diana not only runs berserk and is arrested, but she literally throws her Greenwich Village actor-neighbor Lance out of her apartment when he tries to show her some 8 X 10 glossies of himself. This must have been quite traumatic because in the next issue, although Lance still invites Diana to his party and tries to set her up with his roommate, Tod, he metamorphoses from a handsome blonde hunk to a Woody Allen clone. (One suspects that Lance and Tod were meant to be a gay couple but that the powers-that-be lost their nerve.)

In both his Marvel and DC assignments, Gerry Conway was fond of sending a variety of costumed menaces after whichever character he was writing for, all of whom reported back to a sinister, half-seen figure who has mysterious motives for wanting to do away with the hero and others. Wonder Woman was no exception. Conway introduced the Prime Planner, who works out of a huge floating mobile base that is suspended below a pleasure ship called Leviathan. The Planner, who runs an assassin-for-hire group called the Cartel, utilizes the talents of Bushmaster, who'd already appeared in the comic some months earlier. In a sub-plot that develops after Bushmaster attacks the U.N., Diana thinks there will come a day when children will not think it strange to have their purses opened and belongings searched and wonders if people's minds will be probed as well. Perhaps that's why she over-reacts to a UN security man's perfectly understandable questions after he discovers that just about everything in her personnel file is made up. Hating anyone butting into her personal life, Diana tries to get both her own and Wonder Woman's FBI files via the right to privacy act but is stymied by red tape.

Again Steve Trevor

Wonder Woman got yet another editor in Len Wein, as Diana and guest-star Animal-Man take on the Cartel in California, Marseilles, and finally on the Leviathan. The Prime Planner is revealed to be none other than Diana's old boss at the UN, as well as head of security, Morgan Tracy [WW 267 - 268]. The next issue announced a "new beginning" - again! - for the supposedly ALL NEW amazing amazon. What was "new" was that Diana, disheartened by all the violence and tragedy in Man's World, and unable to get over her grief for Steve Trevor, decides to return to Paradise Island for good. Hippolyta begs Aphrodite to cast a spell of forgetfulness over Diana so that she will no longer feel any pain over Steve's death. Then another Air Force jet crash lands off Paradise Island and the pilot turns out to be - Steve Trevor?! Aphrodite explains that this Steve Trevor crashed through from a different dimension, but she has no way of knowing which one it is and therefore can't return him to his true universe. She tells Hippolyta that her daughter and Trevor must be fated to be together, then causes the whole world to forget Trevor's previous deaths. Wonder Woman then returns to civilization bearing Steve in her robot plane; her mother warns her that she thinks some person or force is causing much mayhem in man's world. All this "all-new" *Wonder Woman* proved was that everything old was new again. The Huntress was given a back-up spot in the comic, however, and at least that was something different.

In *Wonder Woman* 271 Diana is a Captain in the Air Force with the Special Assignments Branch, working with Colonel Trevor, and plump Lt. Etta Candy is back in the picture as well; she and Diana become roommates. As usual, Trevor only has eyes for busy Wonder Woman and barely knows Diana is alive (although a General Darnell who works with them is attracted to Diana; in the silver age this character nearly married her). Now that the mysterious Prime Planner is gone, he is replaced by the equally mysterious Holy One, a hooded figure who orders operatives to cause disasters such as plane and bullet-train crashes -- yes, another of Conway's half-seen masters of menace. Diana's first foe in this "all-new" incarnation was the all-old Angle Man. There was a new Cheetah, however - Debbie Domaine, the niece of the dead Priscilla Rich, the original Cheetah, who is turned by persistent super-villain and cult leader Kobra - apparently he was the "Holy One" - into an ecological terrorist in WW 274 - 275.

Kobra vs WW

Wonder Woman realizes that Kobra is not only the person who was really behind Morgan Tracy's Cartel, but is also the evil force her mother had warned her about. She takes after him in WW 276 - 278, chasing him and his minions from Carlsbad Caverns to India to a pyramid in Cairo. Kobra tries to blackmail the world with a stolen Cobalt-93 bomb but WW and Steve Trevor foil his plans in the nick of time. These exciting stories were the best to be seen in the comic for quite awhile, and even Jose Delbo's pencil work, which was attractive and occasionally striking if never entirely satisfactory, took a turn for the better.

Diana next rescued Etta Candy, who'd been traded to a demon who wanted the plump gal for his supper (a rather "tasteless" joke) in exchange for healing a powerful if crippled man's legs. This unholy bargain was set up by Klarian, the Witch Boy, who'd bedeviled Etrigan the Demon in the latter's short-lived series. The Demon and his supporting cast guest-star in this three-part story which takes him and the amazon into the underworld and back again to keep poor Etta out of the soup pot [WW 280 - 282]. In the next three issues Diana and Steve take on the diabolical menace of the Red Dragon, a Chinese villain who uses masked soldiers and a mechanical dragon to wreak havoc on his enemies. It was then announced that a new team would be taking over the comic with *Wonder Woman* 288, so the two remaining issues had different writers.

Wonder Woman 286 had a bizarre if familiar story by Robert Kanigher in which a terminally ill actress gets a role as Wonder Woman in a movie, and survives on pain pills and with the real amazon's help until she can finish the picture; the basic idea came from the film "Miracle of the Bells," which had a similar premise. Marv Wolfman did the much better script for WW 287, which teams the amazon with the New Teen Titans as they take on the menace of Dr. Cyber, even deadlier than usual, who wants to place her brain in Wonder Woman's body, still wrongly blaming the amazon for her facial disfigurement; Don Heck and Romeo Tanghal's fluid art maximized the excitement.

The Spectacular New Wonder Woman

The "Spectacular New Wonder Woman" by Roy Thomas and Gene Colan (with Romeo Tanghal on inks) was unveiled in a back-up preview in *DC Comics Presents* 41, detailing her battle with Hermes and Hercules after they try to take over Paradise Island and enslave the amazons. She also agrees to lend her name to the charitable Wonder Woman Foundation, and wears a modified costume whose halter has a big "W" on it that stands for Women. This "preview" was actually an entirely separate story from the one in *Wonder Woman* 288, which was the debut issue for the new creative team, although it led into it with Diana visiting Steve Trevor in the hospital after he is injured in the preview. In an amusing touch a blurry-eyed Trevor first asks Wonder Woman if she got a certain briefcase away from the spies who attacked him, and *then* asks if Diana Prince is all right.

An exciting, new and beautiful villainess was introduced in the person of Silver Swan, who is transformed from the plain, pimply, embittered dancer Helen Alexandros by Mars, who hears her pleas for revenge against the men who shunned her and wants her to wage war on men with her new powers of flight, strength, and sonics; if she kills Wonder Woman she can remain the Swan permanently instead of just for an hour at a time. Unaware of her other identity, Diana and Etta make Helen their new roomie when the rent goes up. While there were really no major changes to the premise or supporting cast, the attractive art by Colan and Tanghal did give the comic a dynamic new look.

In the following two issues a new version of the golden age villain Dr. Psycho, a mad scientist and homely dwarf who hates the women who shunned him, appears and is able to take on an ectoplasmic identity as Captain Wonder, who has Steve Trevor's looks and Wonder Woman's powers. He and Silver Swan, who are instantly attracted to one another, try to destroy the amazon in tandem, but ultimately prove no match for her. Seeing their true selves, they are as repulsed as everyone else. Certainly there was nothing "new" - or progressive - in the concept of evil and bitter gnomes and ugly women, and Dr. Psycho was an especially ludicrous character.

Wonder Woman 291 - 293 features a three-part story, "Judgment in Infinity," involving a mysterious alien figure called the Adjudicator, a robed silent giant who judges worlds and destroys them if they are, in his eyes, found wanting (this is similar to Marvel's Celestials). He intends to judge all the other-dimensional Earths as well as Earth-1, so Wonder Woman convenes a meeting of the Justice League while Black Canary hops on the teleporter to inform her former Justice Society teammates of the crisis. Oddly The Adjudicator materializes the Four Horsemen of the Apocalypse - an Earthly concept - and sends them out to four more Earths, with Famine causing same in an already starving India on Earth-1, inducing Zatanna and WW to observe that "what most Americans know isn't true hunger, but appetite."

In the next issue, Plague causes an outbreak of disease and battles Power Girl, Black Canary, and the Huntress on Earth-2, while War takes on Supergirl, Madame Xanadu (of the *Doorway to Nightmare* supernatural series) and Phantom Lady on Earth-X, where he has caused allies to wage war upon each other. In WW 293 Wonder Girl and Starfire of the New Teen Titans journey to Earth-I (for Immortality), where death has been largely banished, to deal with Death, whose scythe is figuratively cutting down thousands of inhabitants. In the second half of the story all of the women manage to defeat the Adjudicator, or at least hold him off until his keepers - as he turns out to be quite mad - can come and fetch him. A unique aspect to the story is that for some reason all male heroes seem to be off doing something else, as the battle is fought only by a variety of superheroines. Unfortunately, the stories were not that memorable, and Gene Colan's art was already beginning to wear thin, possibly because Frank McLaughlin's inks didn't work as well as Romeo Tanghal's, whom he replaced.

Dan Mishkin took over from Roy Thomas as scripter only a few issues after Thomas took over the series. Wonder Woman next faced a villain named "General Electric," of all things (from the short-lived bronze age Sandman series), who invents a video game that saps the minds of military personnel and others while in prison [WW 294 - 296]. Nikos Aegeus is a terrorist given access to the famous winged Pegasus as well as Zeus' thunderbolts by the blind mythological figure, Bellerophon, who'd tried to destroy the Amazons before and was punished by Zeus for his temerity in attempting to reach Olympus. Now he hopes the younger Aegeus can finish what he started so long before, but Steve and Wonder Woman are able to stop Aegeus before he can obliterate Paradise Island and its residents with his devastating thunderbolts. The stories were well-scripted by Mishkin.

Wonder Woman 300 featured a terrific 75 page story by Roy and Danette Thomas and drawn by Colan, Ross Andru, and several other notable artists. Plagued by nightmares in which a sinister dark figure attacks her, Diana encounters the new Sandman, who operates out of a dream dimension. She inadvertently winds up on the real Earth-2, where she learns that the older Wonder Woman has revealed her Diana Prince identity to the world and married Steve Trevor, even though he ages twice as fast as she does. Our Diana makes up her mind to marry Trevor, then gets rid of her alter ego Diana Prince at the first opportunity by making it look as if she were blown to bits by a bomb when the situation presents itself. She then dreams that years ago when she won the contest that turned her into Wonder Woman, Hippolyta decided to "retire" to Olympus, and Diana has to take her place as ruler of Paradise Island; another amazon becomes WW and takes Steve Trevor back to America.

Subsequent dreams, all illustrated by varying artists, show what would happen if a criminal type had crash-landed on the island, or Superman, or if WW had ruthlessly tried to take over Man's World. In the real world, at the altar on Paradise Island, Steve backs out of the wedding, citing the fact that he can't stop thinking of ... Diana Prince, whose death -- despite his apparent disregard for her (he even told Diana he never thought of her as a woman!) -- deeply affects him! He and Wonder Woman agree to wait until he's worked out his feelings and is ready for a commitment. (Perhaps Diana should have picked Steve up and simply *thrown* him back to the mainland.) Because Roy Thomas was no longer the regular writer of the series, it took a while for some of the ramifications of this anniversary special to be felt in the following issues, if at all.

By this time Trevor had changed a great deal from the meatheaded silver age character who kept desperately asking Wonder Woman to marry him, and who had to be rescued by her as often as Superman rescued Lois Lane. He was a more forceful, dynamic individual who often got into the thick of the action, and while one couldn't consider him overly sensitive, he still had his share of insecurities - and issues. When Diana Prince, whose death affected him so much, turns up alive, Steve barely acknowledges her existence when she walks into the office. As for the others, Etta Candy, while likable, was never really developed beyond that of the sweet chubby gal who loves food a little too much because there's absolutely no love in her life. General Darwell never comes off like anything more than a horny middle-aged man, and newcomer Major Keith Griggs, although he and Diana eventually develop romantic feelings for one another, is just another good-looking military man with a mustache.

During the Nikos Aegeus storyline, Steve Trevor discovers a skeleton wearing a tiara like Wonder Woman's on the amazon's old home, Themiscrya. This skeleton reappears in *Wonder Woman* 301 - 302 and turns out to be the remains of the original WW, Artemis, sent to Man's World thousands of years before, and who was corrupted by civilization. Artemis comes back to life and the current Wonder Woman manages to defeat the ancient one. She next faces Green Lantern's old foe, Dr. Polaris, and then Circe, the witch fond of turning men into animals, after which Aegeus makes a return appearance. It is not made clear if Circe is the mysterious woman whom Artemis considers her new mistress. Ernie Colon became the new editor, then Alan Gold, with Don Heck replacing Gene Colan, while Dan Miskin remained on stories into the copper age.

There were only a few more issues of volume one of *Wonder Woman* in the copper age. The amazon tries to tell Steve her secret identity, but he doesn't want to know, afraid it might strip her of her glamor; some fans therefore denounced him as superficial. An adventure involving aliens gave Trevor a little companion, Glitch, an invisible gremlin, who appeared in virtually every issue thereafter and added absolutely nothing to the series -- it was as if there were a conscious effort to dumb the series down to silver age childishness. On the other hand, there were a few intriguing storylines.

Diana discovers a lost tribe of Brazilian Amazons, who'd split from Hippolyta years before; and Sofia, a former associate of the terrorist Aegeus, who'd reformed and been taken to Paradise Island, learns that Hippolyta altered her daughters memories regarding the earlier and very dead Steve Trevor. Dr. Cyber impersonates Diana, steals nuclear launch codes, and has her branded a traitor, then tries to tear the flesh off her body with an especially deadly device [WW 319 - 321]. Eros, the God of Love shows up, claiming he and Princess Diana were once lovers - it develops that Aphrodite used her son, Eros', essence to bring Steve Trevor back to life after he was killed by Cyber in the silver age, and the god, although no longer combined with Trevor, still bears vestiges of his love for his "angel." Diana is furious with her mother for removing these memories, no matter how well-intended she may have been.

Wonder Woman 323 features a free-for-all with Dr. Psycho, the Cheetah, Silver Swan and Captain Wonder all fighting our amazon, a conflict that embroils Steve, Etta and her new boyfriend, Henry, who was convinced that she was Wonder Woman. Psycho has a new machine that can transform him into the Captain -- and later, Etta into a version of Wonder Woman -- but it's never explained how Helen Alexandros has managed to become Silver Swan again after Ares stripped her of her powers. Sales for *Wonder Woman* so declined that it was reduced to a bi-monthly schedule, and the response to this was to publish stories like "The Gremlin in the Kremlin," in which the ridiculous Glitch took center stage -- but at least this was his last appearance.

Mindy Newell took over as writer and brought back the giant Mexican deity, Texcatlipoca, who'd first appeared some months previously; had Etta Candy snapping at Diana out of tension; and presented a kind of mutiny on Paradise Island where the Senate first try to throw out Hippolyta in favor of Paula von Gunther, who turns them down, and then offers the throne to the plotting Antiopa, who eagerly accepts it, which has Hippolyta seething. In the penultimate issue of Wonder Woman Newell manages to balance all of this and also gets the Amazons involved in events from the current *Crisis on Infinite Earths* mini-series. Newell also provides a mini-history of General Darwell, who disobeys orders and might go to prison, and introduces the woman he met and, in her opinion, betrayed in Burma during the war, and who wants to destroy him (this sub-plot went unresolved).

Steve, Keith Griggs, and Etta all learn Diana's secret identity when Hermes comes to summon her back to Paradise Island to aid her mother and sisters against an attack by strange Shadow creatures, but not before her office at the Pentagon is invaded by Weaponers from Qward (from *Green Lantern*). Gerry Conway scripted the double-sized final issue in which Hades, the God of Death and Ares join forces with the Anti-Monitor (from Crisis) to attack Olympus even as chaos reigns on earth. Wonder Woman and Steve, as well as the amazons from both Paradise Island and South America, join forces to defeat Ares once and for all. Steve and Princess Diana get married, and awaken the morning after to begin their new life together. It only took 329 issues for Wonder Woman to finally lose her virginity!

Wonder Woman teamed up with Batman and Superman in several issues of *The Brave and the Bold* and *DC Comics Presents*. In the former, she and the Dark Knight take on the Catwoman and her jaguars; a multimillionaire spy who is after secret info and would kill to get it; and, in the best story, a chemist named Flashback who creates realistic visions of the deaths of Steve Trevor and Mr. and Mrs. Wayne to bedevil the heroes as he goes about his criminal business [B & B 158]. Jim Aparo's art was especially good on the last story, and his rendition of Wonder Woman was excellent. Wonder Woman and Superman teamed to defeat a giant being made of ice, and in an especially forgettable story, were forced to fall in love due to the machinations of Eros, in DCP 32.

With frequent changes in creative teams, and no consensus as to how exactly the character should be handled, Wonder Woman was an entertaining but uneven and often frustrating comic series. As well, in general the mythological aspect of the comic was never particularly well-integrated into the superhero side as it was in Marvel's *Thor*. Wonder Woman would make a sterling comeback in a new series written and drawn by George Perez in the 1980's.

The Huntress

As for The Huntress, the back-up strip by Paul Levitz and Joe Staton, she was Helena Wayne from Earth-2. She is a partner in the law firm of Cranston, [Dick] Grayson and Wayne, and is friends with Harry Sims, the D.A. who wants stricter controls on super-hero activity but turns out to be mind-controlled by the Thinker, whom Huntress teams up with Power Girl to defeat. She also battles the old golden age monster Solomon Grundy, and one of her mother, Catwoman's, old teammates, Lionmane, and takes care of the ex-husband who is blackmailing and beating on her African-American secretary, Carol (who is never seen again). Harry figures out Helena's secret ID but this becomes moot when he becomes a victim of the Joker's poison venom, which puts him in a coma. The Earth-2 grown-up Robin masquerades as Batman (who died on Earth-2) to draw the Joker out of hiding, and Huntress manages to bag him. She also gets the better of the vicious Karnage, who hopes to build a rep by killing her. She saves the life of the Earth-2 Alfred (his last name is Beagle instead of Pennysworth) after he's poisoned. Harry survives but isn't sure he can deal with the fact that the woman he loves could be killed at any moment -- his dad was a cop and he remembers the constant worrying over him -- but his love for Helena overrules everything else. As for the art, Joe Staton's pencils were cartoonish, but effective and well-composed - inker Jerry Ordway added some depth to his compositions later on - and the Huntress proved a more interesting, edgier character than the comparatively flat Batgirl.

New writer Joey Cavalieri introduced a black super-hero, Blackwing, who is actually a lawyer named Charlie, who is sick of the revolving door justice system and has always admired the late Batman of Earth-2. He and the Huntress take care of a bad guy with a protection racket, and a penchant for big snakes, known as the Boa [WW 297 - 299]. In *Wonder Woman* 302 - 304 Huntress is suspected of killing a small-time criminal named Pat Pending, but this turns out to be a hoax, leading into a multi-part storyline (with virtually a different artist each issue) wherein Huntress is imprisoned in Arkham Asylum. She next tackles the Earthworm, then a martial artist known as the Nightingale who is supposed to be female but turns out to be a male Kabuki artist. The Huntress sees a shrink when she is afraid she's blacking out and committing crimes like her late mother, the Catwoman, and the woman pulls a gun on her; this lady psychiatrist had been involved in one of the Huntress' previous cases and thinks she's come to arrest her. A number of artists worked on the strip, which ended in WW 304: Tim Burgard, Mark Beacham, and Stan Woch. Dan Spiegle was one of the more notable pencillers, but he only did one installment in WW 312. It was announced that a Huntress mini-series would soon be appearing, but this never materialized, although there was more than one Huntress series many, many years later.

Kobra

As Kobra became a major foe for Wonder Woman in one story arc, and, after Batman, was the first DC hero to fight him, it's worth taking a look at the villain's very short-lived series. *Kobra*, which debuted in 1976, was worked on (and part of the first issue penciled) by Jack Kirby, who left DC before his plans for the comic could reach fruition. The premise had to do with Siamese twins born 23 years ago in New Delhi, who were separated shortly afterward. Jason Burr has always believed his brother died that day, but now he learns that his twin was kidnapped and has become the leader of a fanatical cult; he is now known as Kobra. Kobra wants to kill his brother, but discovers that the two share a special link in that whatever happens to one affects the other; he's forced to keep Jason alive and vice versa. Kobra wears an outfit and has slithering powers that remind one of Thor's foe the Human Cobra. Other members of Kobra's cast include Ricardo Perez, the cop trying to stop Kobra, possibly over Jason's dead body, and Melissa, Jason's girlfriend. Kobra has an HQ in New York under the subways with walls lined with leather, and his head is completely shaved under his hood. His followers are fond of calling him "Najanaja."

With the second issue the creative team was Martin Pasko on

scripts and Chic Stone and Pablo Marcos on art; Keith Giffen took over as penciller the following issue, to be followed by several others. Jason is given an outfit and a code name: Gemini. Kobra attempts to steal a deadly device from a maniac calling himself Solaris, who wants to turn a death ray on an entire city for money. In *Kobra* 3 the two brothers team up against Solaris, and Kobra tells his twin a little more of his origin. Apparently the Kobra cult was merely a weird religious sect when Kobra was abducted into its fold. At 18 during a hospital stay, Kobra met and fell in love with a woman named Natalie, who is later killed (or so he believes) by police for being a thief and murderess. Kobra had left the cult after falling for Natalie, but after her death he is furious at the forces of law and order that killed her, so goes back to the cult to transform it into a ruthless and evil crime cartel. Melissa, Jason's gal pal, is the spitting image of Natalie.

Kobra 4, in which the madman interacts with aliens, brings in Randu Singh, UN delegate from India (introduced earlier in Jack Kirby's *The Demon*), and kills off Perez when Kobra sends his giant robots after him. Singh suggests that Jason could permanently end the menace of Kobra by killing himself, which does not at first sit well with the young man but makes undeniable sense. Melissa resists answering questions about what she knows about Kobra. Private eye Jonny Double joins the cast in *Kobra* 5, in which he inadvertently uncovers a plot by Kobra to decimate San Francisco with an earthquake machine. Melissa has disappeared and Jason is convinced his brother is behind it.

In the following issue we learn that Kobra caused the earthquake so that he could use repair operations to disguise the fact that his agents were tapping the undersea communications cables. In the 7th and final issue of the series Jason manages to get into Kobra's flying arc whereupon he discovers Melissa -- or is it Natalie? -- captive in a stasis cube, and also learns that Kobra now has a "neutralizer" which will negate the symbiotic connection between the two men. Kobra has also developed the ability to resurrect the dead, which he plans to use on the corpses of the Burr boys' parents, who died six years before. A blurb at the end announced that the story would continue next issue when Batman guest-starred, but it was not to be.

What was supposed to be the *Kobra* 8 was reworked and turned into a Batman story in the dollar comic *5 Star Super-Hero Spectacular* in 1978. In this Kobra has taken over an HQ abandoned by Batman's foe Ra's al Ghul that contains the Lazarus Pit which Ghul used for many decades to extend his life. Kobra uses the neutralizer that negates the connection between him and his brother, so that he is finally able to kill Jason by using the mind-controlled corpse of his girlfriend, Melissa, who stabs him and then throws him out of a cable car. Kobra escapes, but Batman - who is briefly his captive - vows vengeance, and swears that the entire Justice League, if necessary, will smash his operations and bring him down. Kobra remained part of the DC universe and bedeviled various heroes, such, as noted, Wonder Woman, in the years to come. *Kobra* was entertaining and well-written by Pasko, with real possibilities, but the rotating and often amateurish artists working on the series didn't help.

CHAPTER TWELVE: KUNG FU FIGHTERS

-- *RICHARD DRAGON, KARATE KID, MASTER OF KUNG FU, IRON FIST*

Martial arts were the "big thing" in the seventies, with high-kicking, karate-chopping characters on television, on the motion picture screen, and of course, in comic books. DC's Richard Dragon never developed into a major character, and the Karate Kid was probably more at home in the Legion of Super-Heroes, but Marvel's Iron Fist, and Shang-Chi, the Master of Kung Fu, had more staying power.

Richard Dragon

Richard Dragon, Kung Fu Fighter made its debut in 1975. The character first appeared in a series of novels written by "Jim Dennis," who was actually Denny O'Neill, who adapted Richard Dragon to comics form. When we're first introduced to the "hero" he's a pretty loathsome young man who attempts to "fillet" an aged Chinese man -- an "O- Sensei" [Great Teacher] -- during a robbery, and is a racist to boot. Incredibly, the aged man senses "goodness" in Dragon and he and his young black assistant, Benjamin Stanley -- who's been called an "ape" and a "refugee from a minstrel show" by our hero -- decide to take him in and teach him the martial arts. If you can get past the unlikelihood of this scenario - in reality the O-Sensei would have called the police and Benjamin would have flattened Dragon for his unconscionable remarks -- you can go forward six years to when both young men have finished their training. Dragon gets extra power in moments of crisis from a jade dragon's claw figurine given to him by the O-Sensei and which he wears around his neck. He and Ben meet Barney Ling, who heads a group called G.O.O.D. Ling importunes them to take on a slave trader, whom they manage to defeat with comparative ease. The pleasant enough art was by Leopoldo Duranova.

Richard Dragon 2 was drawn by Jim Starlin and Alan Weiss (with Al Milgrom on inks) and introduces the sensei's god-daughter, Carolyn Woosan (this had changed to "Wotami" by the third issue), and a bad guy known only as The Swiss, who wants a certain formula and is not above kidnaping Carolyn to get it. The third issue, as Dragon pursues the Swiss and the captive Carolyn, was drawn by no less than Jack Kirby. Hardly one of the King's major efforts, the action-packed art nevertheless imparted a sudden mythic quality to the character that was completely lacking from the writing. Ric Estrada and Wally Wood were the art team for the fourth issue, as the comic continued to play the game of musical artists -- they remained on the book, however. Dragon at last catches up with the Swiss, but unfortunately Carolyn is killed in an accident during the chase.

Richard Dragon 5 introduced Ben's girlfriend, Joy Dillard, and Carolyn's sexy sister, Sandra Woosan (instead of Wotami), who turns out to be a would-be villainess named Lady Shiva. We also meet an evil industrialist with the amazing name of Guano Cravat, who is behind the efforts of the Swiss. Cravat tells Sandra that Dragon was responsible for her sister's death, so she tries to kill Richard in a grudge match - with a deadly laser beam hovering throughout - but when Cravat stupidly blurts out the truth during the battle she and Dragon defeat him and become friends. In RD 6 they team up against the hijacker Slash even as Barney Ling of G.O.O.D. stupidly hides a bomb, which was taken away from terrorists, inside an active volcano. Dragon uses the giant magnet which Slash had used to snatch planes from the sky to retrieve the bomb and to take care of Slash.

Due to injuries - and the introduction of Lady Shiva - Ben Stanley hadn't much to do since the first couple of issues. He was back in action with *Richard Dragon* 10, his last name mysteriously changed to Turner (until the following issue when it is Stanley again), where he discovers both that he's inherited acres of timber land, and that his sister has been murdered, leaving him with a young nephew, Ben Jr. In the following issues Ben learns the hard way that someone has put out a contract on him, but even Barney Ling of G.O.O.D. doesn't know why. In RD 12 Richard, Ben and Shiva encounter Madame Sun, who - like Shiva herself - is the twin of another lady who'd been killed. Madame Sun has a device that projects deadly holograms of people - if the hologram dies, so does the real person whose image it projects. Using this device, Sun has the novel idea of forcing Dragon to fight himself - or rather his own hologram - knowing that if he "killed" the twin, he would also die. He gets around this dilemma by attacking the holographic machine instead of the image. The script was by guest writer David Anthony Kraft.

By *Richard Dragon* 15 we still don't know who's out to get Ben, whose last name was back to Turner (and apparently stayed that way throughout the character's future history). His girlfriend is now known as Jane, and she is murdered in this issue by the Axeman, who turns out to be working for her own father, Lewis (who, naturally, didn't expect his daughter to die at the hands of an associate, although in the next issue he supposedly ordered her death). Dragon and Ben are accused of stealing the sub that was actually stolen by Lewis. In the final two issues of *Richard Dragon, Kung Fu Fighter* [17 and 18] Ben catches up with Lewis and then disappears, resurfacing as a costumed and masked character known as the Bronze Tiger. In this identity he had further life in the DC Universe, especially in *Suicide Squad;* Richard Dragon himself pretty much disappeared. We never learned who had been trying to kill Ben in all those issues.

Other foes for Richard Dragon and his associates include: the Sumo-like strong man Topper; the disfigured South American freak and insect-like Preying Mantis; the axe-wielding lumberjack Hatchett; the silent sword-wielding Samurai; the Viper, chief poisoner of the League of Assassins; Dr. Moon and his associate Sing, a martial arts master who studied under Bruce Lee; and Ojo, who supposedly turned his foes into human magnets and then threw daggers at them.

Richard Dragon, Kung Fu Fighter was a reasonably entertaining if unremarkable series. Richard Dragon and the other characters remained one-dimensional in every issue, and we never learned much of Dragon's background, or what had turned him into a teenaged hoodlum. Lady Shiva was, perhaps, the most interesting character, a cold-blooded lady who craves action and excitement, cut from the same cloth as such women as the Valkyrie, who appeared in the golden age comic *Airboy.* Lady Shiva made it clear that she had no romantic or sexual interest in Richard Dragon. When Ben reminded her that Shiva was not just the goddess of destruction but of reproduction, she was not amused. Her sexual orientation remained unexplored. She was the DC forerunner of the character Katana, another sword-wielding, take-no-prisoners dame who became a member of Batman's team, the Outsiders.

The art in *Richard Dragon, Kung-Fu Fighter* was generally good. Jack Abel took over the inks from Wally Wood, and was equally adept and distinctive. In the final few issues Estrada inked his own pencils and the results were less than felicitous. Richard Dragon both battled and teamed up with Batman in *The Brave and the Bold* 132, with a story by Bob Haney and Jim Aparo artwork. Like the series itself, it was well-drawn and entertaining, but not especially memorable.

Karate Kid

Karate Kid from the Legion of Super-Heroes debuted in his own title in 1976, when karate and kung fu and all manner of martial arts were at the height of their popularity. The Kid, AKA Val Armorr, had always been drawn as a Caucasian (with an Oriental mentor) but now he became half-Asian. He first travels back to the 20th century when he is issued a challenge by Nemesis Kid, who escapes from prison and travels back in time for his own purposes. Members of the Legion follow after Val, but he's so testy with them that they retreat. After tracking down and defeating Nemesis Kid -- and meeting a freckled, red-headed teacher named Iris Jacobs -- Val decides to stay in the 20th century for a while, as he likes being his own person away from the super-powered big guns of the 30th century legion - and for less specious reasons which are hinted at over the following few issues. Paul Levitz was the writer of this first tale, with Ric Estrada and Joe Staton on the art. The art was by no means terrible -- it was often exciting, well laid-out and composed -- but both Estrada and Staton were essentially cartoonists as opposed to illustrators, and the work, as the editor admitted in one letter column, came close to caricature at times. Worse, it was never especially attractive, more suitable for, say, *Binkie's Buddies* than a super-hero comic. Estrada's pencils looked much better when inked by Jack Abel in KK 10.

Barry Jameson replaced Levitz on scripts beginning with the second issue. *Karate Kid* 2 features a lively battle between the Kid and Green Lantern foe Major Disaster, who's been hired to destroy the U.N. building by a terrorist group. Iris is at the Kid's side for much of the story, although at one point he forgets about her and leaves her on top of a roof - a bit of foreshadowing vis a vis their relationship. Val takes on the whip-wielding Revenger who targets businessmen who wronged him in KK 3. In the 4th issue the Kid rescues Iris and her students from a Japanese fanatic named Master Hand, who resents the increasing Westernization of the Orient and threatens blood and disaster; instead of a hook he has a sword in place of one of his missing hands.

The villain for *Karate Kid* 5 and 6 was hawkish Commander Blud, who kidnaps poor Iris to force Val to give him the skinny on the wars in Earth's future, so that he and his army can fight for the losing side and actually change the course of history, something which Val knows is absolutely verboten. KK 7 featured the forgettable villainy of the equally forgettable spinning Gyro-Master (a quick substitute for Flash-foe the Top, who'd just been killed off in the speedster's own mag); a more interesting development is that Val is arrested for the alleged murder of his landlady, who gets temporarily zapped by a TV-like device in Val's apartment. Val tussles with the reluctant hit man, Pulsar, in KK 8 and 9; this family man is forced to murder because of a device surgically inserted inside his heart that can not only stop his heart but even explode it. Princess Projectra, Val's lady love, comes back in time in KK 9 to check up on him only to see him getting bussed by Iris, leading to a childish quarrel between the two women. (Oddly Val didn't even seem to say good-bye to Projectra, the woman he loved, until KK 6.)

Karate Kid 10 finally explained the purpose of the TV-like device - or "monitor" -- in Val's apartment. It is a way for him to stay in touch with the King of Planet Orando, Princess Projectra's father. Apparently the king wants Val to prove that he is worthy of his daughter by exiling himself to the distant past and performing many deeds of derring do. Even after helping to save Orando from the threat of the Black Dragon, the king insists he must return to the 20th century to commit more heroic deeds. Major Disaster - this time teamed with JLA foe the Lord of Time - appeared in the next three issues. In KK 11 he imprisons the Kid in a testing range that is a phony mock-up of Manhattan. In KK 12 - 13 he sends both Val and the Legion of Super-Heroes back in time to Superboy's day, only the Legionnaires come from a time before they'd ever met Val, leading them to see him as an enemy.

Bob Rozakis took over as scripter with *Karate Kid* 12, and there was a new art team consisting of Juan Ortiz on pencils and Bob McLeod on inks. If anything, the art was worse than it had been before, and a change in inkers for the next two issues didn't help. In KK 14 Iris is transformed into the menacing Dia-

mondeth after stupidly volunteering for an experiment involving hydrocarbons to show Val that she can be just as brave
and adventurous as her love rival, Projectra. It turns out that
Major Disaster and the Lord of Time are still manipulating
things behind the scenes. In the utterly abysmal 15th and final
issue of the series, KK takes Iris to the 30th century to cure her,
but winds up in the alternate future world of Kamandi, a
human boy living in a time past the "Great Disaster" when animals such as dogs have human-like intelligence. The story was
continued in *Kamandi* 58 (*Kamandi* was itself canceled with
the following issue) and ended, for KK at least, with him hoping to reach his own 30th century and there affect a cure for
Iris/Diamondeth. (Iris was cured of being Diamondeth in
Superboy and the Legion 246.)

We next saw Iris Jacobs - back in her normal form - in *The
Brave and the Bold* 198. Karate Kid comes back to the 20th century and winds up battling against his old foe Pulsar side by
side with the Batman. Iris assumes that Val has come back to
be with her, but instead he's only come to invite her to his wedding to Princess Projectra. Iris is shattered and hurt by his in-
sensitivity, and accuses him of using her. But the reality is that
Val never really led Iris on, and told her more than once that
she was a "friend," nothing more. Still, you couldn't help feeling sorry for the gal who fell unrequitedly in love with an un-
attainable man from the future.

As for *Karate Kid* the series, it was a modestly entertaining
book that never fulfilled its potential, or perhaps never really
had that much potential to begin with.

Master of Kung Fu

The Sinister Dr. Fu Manchu was created by Sax Rohmer and
first appeared in a series of novels dating back to the early
twentieth century. The first couple of books had an undeniably
racist tone, with talks of the "yellow peril," but as the years
went by this aspect was minimized. Fu Manchu was a bit more
dimensional in the books than in the movies, such as *The Mask
of Fu Manchu* with Boris Karloff, which simply portrayed him

as a sadistic megalomaniac. Fu Manchu could be ruthless and enact horrible punishments on those who transgressed, but he didn't have people tortured because he enjoyed it but because he needed information that was not otherwise forthcoming. His goal was to bring China to the forefront of the world, and he would stop at nothing to achieve that goal. Evil? Perhaps, but a little more complex than he was usually portrayed, such as in *Master of Kung Fu,* which had the brilliant idea of bringing back the Chinese doctor but giving him a heroic Asian son who fought against him.

Shang-Chi, the Master of Kung Fu and son of Fu Manchu, first appeared in *Marvel Special Edition* 15 in 1973. Like Danny Rand (or Iron Fist), Shang-Chi is also 19, but unlike Rand he is Chinese-American. Shang-Chi's mother was chosen by Fu Manchu almost mathematically to give him a perfect son; it was by no means a loving or romantic union. Shang-Chi has been prevented from knowing the truth about his father and thinks he is a beneficent and kindly man. Fu Manchu tells his son that he wants him to kill a man who is the very embodiment of evil, Dr. Petrie. Shang-Chi is surprised that his first assignment for his father is assassination but he doesn't question him. He is even more surprised to discover that his target is an elderly, bed-ridden person who couldn't possibly harm anyone. Shang-Chi hesitates but then delivers a swift, killing stroke.

Before he can leave Petrie's death bed, he is startled by a man in a wheelchair: Sir Dennis Nayland Smith, his father's chief antagonist. Smith tells Shang-Chi the truth about his father; when confronted by his son Fu Manchu does not deny it. He only says that while his original goal was to bring China back to its former glory, he is now opposed to all recognized governments. With his dreaded Si-Fan organization, of which he is head, he wishes to destroy them and anyone else who opposes him - and that includes Shang-Chi. Man and son become bitter enemies. Oddly, Shang-Chi expresses no remorse for his murder of Dr. Petrie, but even stranger is how quickly he accepts what Smith tells him (without any real proof) and turns against his father. This was probably the first time that a comic book hero committed murder, in his first issue no less. The script was by Steve Englehart and the art by Jim Starlin and Al Milgrim, all doing first-rate work.

Marvel Special Edition 16 continues the story, with Shang-Chi wandering through Manhattan, then challenged to a duel by his childhood friend, a disfigured African raised by Fu Manchu who wears a cloak and hood and is known as Midnight. Fu Manchu has ordered Midnight to kill his son - although Shang-Chi is his only friend he is loyal to the last to Fu Manchu. Shang-Chi accepts the challenge, but Midnight is apparently killed in a freak accident during the duel. With the next issue the title was changed to *Master of Kung Fu*.

Nayland Smith's ally, the hulking Black Jack Tarr, who tries to kill S-C in revenge for his murder of Petrie, made his first appearance in *Master of Kung Fu* 17. Tarr always spoke with racist contempt of "Chinamen" and for some reason Shang-Chi lets him. (Later Tarr comes to admire Shangi-Chi.) In this same issue S-C somehow manages to talk Smith into getting out of his wheelchair and walking on his shattered legs, meaning Smith is now in his debt. Smith also decides that S-C was acting under the influence of his father when he murdered Petrie, somewhat absolving him of guilt.

At the direction of Smith, Shang-Chi goes to Florida to stop a plan by his father to mind-control everyone in the USA. In MOKF 20 - 21 a mob boss puts out a hit on S-C in the hopes he might be rewarded by Fu Manchu -- instead the mandarin kills him with the bite from a snake; He will decide when Shang-Chi dies and no one else. *Giant-Size Master of Kung Fu* 1 featured a fast-paced, entertaining story in which Fu Manchu sends out assassins to kill his son on his birthday, and Shang-Chi manages to sneak inside his father's stronghold and masquerade as one of the "Council of Seven" of the Si-Fan. By this time the creative team had switched to Doug Moench on scripts and Paul Gulacy on pencils, although a number of artists would work on subsequent issues.

Shangi-Chi gets caught in a war between Fu Manchu and a crazy Nazi named Bucher who has a particular hatred for Orientals in *Master of Kung Fu* 23 - 24. When the Nazi takes dead aim at Fu, Shangi-Chi, in an interesting turnabout, saves his father's life. "He may deserve to die but not at the hands of a man like Bucher" he says - whom Shangi-Chi knows would kill his father merely because of his race. In MOKF 26 - 27 Shangi-Chi again gets caught between two opposing factions: his father and his sister, Fah Lo Suee. As in Rohmer's novels Fah Lo Suee works for her own ends and is often at odds with her father. In this she hopes to acquire a scarab with ruby eyes that she imagines will give her domination over Fu Manchu.

In the second part of the story Shangi-Chi and his father have a conversation in which Fu Manchu reveals that after living for centuries he has become emotionally numb, and world conquest is the only thing that interests him. Still, he is deeply disheartened by the betrayal of his son, and sees him as the "evil" one. (Yet Fu refers to himself as the "Devil-Doctor," perhaps ironically.) In the meantime the Armies of the Si-Fan have been split with many members now swearing loyalty to Fah Lo Suee. Fu Manchu sees an epic battle between father and daughter with much bloodshed, and he suggests that Shang-Chi can stop it simply by killing him. But this Shang-Chi is unable to do. Doug Moench wrote an especially good script for this issue, and the art by John Buscema and Frank Springer was excellent.

In *Giant-Size Master of Kung Fu* 3 Shang-Chi learns that he didn't kill Dr. Petrie at all, but only an unliving duplicate crafted by the genius of his father. The real Petrie, who is rescued at the end of the story, has been imprisoned by Fu Manchu for months. Still, Shang-Chi has to wrestle with the fact that in his heart and mind he committed the murder of an innocent. Meanwhile the struggle against Fu Manchu is set aside for a time as Shang-Chi becomes an official British agent for MI-6, working for Smith alongside Black Jack Tarr and dapper Clive Reston (and later the lovely Leiko Wu) and takes on such opponents as drug dealer Carlton Velcro [MOKF 29 - 31] and his chief enforcer Razorfist, who has sharp blades where the lower half of his arms should be. It turns out that Velcro is just as eager to take over the world as Fu Manchu is, and uses his heroin operation to fund the stockpiling of weapons in caverns below his headquarters. It was all very reminiscent of the type of stories that appeared in *Nick Fury, Agent of SHIELD* in the 60's; indeed this was true of *Master of Kung Fu* in general.

Shangi-Chi's next opponent was Mordillo [MOKF 33 -35], a mad genius inventor for hire who wants to secure a weapon that will instantly destroy the ozone layer over certain geographical areas and make everyone below subject to flash-frying. Mordillo has an island headquarters full of talking robots and toys he's invented, including his little buddy, the weird and cheerful Brynocki, who looks like something out of a cartoon; there's also his whip-wielding blonde playmate, Pavane. Mordillo is actually a British agent who had been the lover of female spy Leiko Wu after she was finished with Clive Weston. (It was intimated that Weston was related to everyone from Sherlock Holmes to James Bond.)

Love and Leiko

The introduction of Leiko created a lot of tiresome soap opera in the comic, with Weston temporarily turning to drink due to Leiko's rejection of him (even though in the previous issue it sort of looks as if they've gotten back together). Leiko herself doesn't seem too tightly wrapped when she assumes Shang-Chi is in love with her after only knowing her a short time. A new character named Larson - a former agent who's also turned to liquor - blames Leiko for the death of his girlfriend, another agent named Jennifer. All of this didn't create characterization so much as it added a lot of tedious, space-consuming angst, with people arguing about their love lives with one another instead of concentrating on the job at hand.

It is determined that there is a mole among Smith's forces, who turns out to be a brain-washed Dr Petrie. Shock-Wave, Smith's deranged nephew and another former agent, goes around blowing up his former associates. Shang-Chi is disillusioned with Smith and his service by this time, but agrees to help him in this moment of crisis. Ducharme, a "servant" of Fu Manchu's, turns out to have been secretly working for Smith for forty years as she had also been given Fu's immortality serum. (It turned out that she was actually loyal to Fu Manchu.) Fu Manchu -- and Fah Lo Suee -- at last returned in *Master of Kung Fu* 45, beginning a six issue story arc in which Fu Manchu plans to move the moon out of orbit causing world-wide disaster, after which he will rule the earth's mostly Chinese survivors. Fu Manchu also resuscitates the bones of Shaka Kharn, his ancestor who developed the immortality serum and whom Fu now proclaims his one true "son."

For six issues the battle raged between a gigantic, lavish mountain base in the Antarctic - below which there were caverns full of hungry giant scorpions - to an elaborate space ship from whence Fu planned to fire the missiles that would set his plan into motion. Shaka Kharn dies when he has no chance to take the renewal bath that would have kept him alive and Shang-Chi lops off his sinister grinning skull. While Reston sabotages Fu's equipment, Shang-Chi shakes off years of conditioning and shoots his father, who flees in a shuttle craft. Fu's death, of course, is celebrated prematurely. Larson also dies, but as we know little of him and his lost love Jennifer (or exactly under what circumstances she died) it had little impact on the reader.

In truth, the trouble with the series at this point was that there were too many one-dimensional characters filling up its pages. While most stories were narrated in first person by the intense, low-key Shang-Chi, each chapter of this Fu Manchu arc was narrated by one of his associates or by Fu Manchu himself, which only served to make the star of the book seem even more like only one of a half-dozen supporting characters. The characters were defined more by their problems than anything else. Whether he was brain-washed or in his right mind, Petrie never came alive for the reader, and Black Jack Tarr was little more than a blustering stereotype. Leiko was the pretty Asian chick flitting from man to man, and Smith -- like his nemesis -- was another bored old man getting up to mischief for lack of anything better to do.

Most of these characters left MI-6 after the six-part battle with Fu Manchu, although they remained in the magazine. (Artist Paul Gulacy also left, replaced by Mike Zeck.) When a madman named War-Yore comes after them in different historical guises, they erroneously come to the conclusion that an angry Smith is trying to kill them all for defecting. Then followed a completely unnecessary and completely contrived battle with Doctor Doom and a lot of robots [MOKF 59 - 60]. Much better was the "China Seas" story arc [MOKF 61 - 68] in which Shang-Chi and company get embroiled in a battle between two ex-partners, the sleek man known as Cat and the bestial, portly Kogar, who screws different weapons into his artificial hand and has a very elaborate hide-out behind a waterfall. Cat, a martial arts expert, has now hooked up with the nutty whip-woman Pavane, who finally has a major fight with Shang-Chi in MOKF 65. The prize that both Cat and Kogar are after are the plans for the neutron bomb which are on microdots secreted inside crates of hash hish. The action moves swiftly with only an occasional detour into unconvincing soap opera, the characters confusing mere sexual curiosity with love. Juliette, the blonde former lover of Cat, is particularly fickle, moving from one man to another as long as he is Asian. In MOKF 67 Mike Zeck's pencils looked especially attractive under Fred Kida's inks.

For reasons that never made sense, a now thoroughly corrupt MI-6 decides to wipe out Smith, Black Jack, Leiko, Shang-Chi etc., because MI-6 supposedly fears they've been indoctrinated by Fu Manchu, even though there is no evidence to support this. The whole premise seemed dragged in just to create a "shocking" new story line. Various bad guys -- the neurotic Shock-Wave, Zaran, even the apparently sentient robot Brynocki -- are sent after the crew with the usual negative results. In the meantime Shang-Chi -- whose name means "the advancing and rising of a spirit" and who really wants to spend his life in contemplation and study -- wonders if he is fulfilling his destiny with his constant fighting, something he seems completely unable to avoid.

Hints of Fu Manchu's return for months finally materialized in MOKF 83, which began another long story arc [until MOKF 89]. Fu Manchu has managed to plant mind-controlling electrodes in the brains of selected individuals in all of the major powers. At a signal from him, these agents will commit acts of sabotage meant to plunge the world into a chaos that Fu Manchu will use to his ultimate advantage. Fu's daughter Fah Lo Suee is working against him again, only this time she wants to work with Smith and the gang, but there's too much bad blood between her and her former opponents. Karamaneh, the late wife of Dr. Petrie, turns out to be alive, but although she has seen her husband many times, she has never approached him. As she puts it: "[Fu Manchu's] elixir of youth has kissed my lips, but age has spit upon my lover." In other words, she doesn't want to be with an elderly man now that she's a babe - that's love for ya!

Fu hides a bomb in tunnels beneath Manhattan, which Smith and Tarr try to defuse while Shangi-Chi and Leiko battle Fu's forces on top of the World Trade Center. The bomb doesn't go off, and Shang-Chi manages to jump from the roof of the Trade Center to his father's air craft as it rises high ahead. He confronts his father for the final (?) time, explodes the craft, and gets off in safety, although his father is, presumably, not so lucky. Although a bit lackluster at first, this lengthy battle, courtesy of Moench and Mike Zeck, eventually becomes suspenseful and exciting.

Freelance Restorations

Sir Denis and the other characters -- Leiko, Clive Reston , Black Jack, Melissa Greville -- who were ousted by MI-6 become operatives of a new group called Freelance Restorations, Limited, which plans to charge a small amount for its services. The HQ for the group is Stormhaven, a magnificent castle in

Scotland bought with Sir Denis' last penny. The first story arc deals with a man named Samisdat who is head of a cult called Dawning Light, which is actually a front for a KGB operation involving a laser satellite [MOKF 93 - 95].

The 100th issue of *Master of Kung Fu* featured one of the series' best latter-day stories, and it is one in which the tiresomely philosophizing Shang-Chi doesn't even appear (at least in part one). Set in 1932 it details Sir Denis and Dr. Petrie's attempts to foil yet another fiendish plot by Fu Manchu, a ploy which succeeds in large part due to Fah Lo Suee, who is in love with Denis and strikes out at her father to save him. In the second part, a young Shang-Chi witnesses the results of his sister's long-ago betrayal of their father and encounters an old woman he doesn't realize is Fah Lo Suee. deprived of the immortality elixir that keeps both her and Fu Manchu relatively young. In the third part, Leiko tries to stop a Jack the Ripper-type killer who is slaughtering women in Whitechapel, and was once Fah Lo Suee's lover, transformed by Fu Manchu into a maniac years before. Sir Denis is convinced that Fu Manchu knew who the original Jack the Ripper was, knowledge he never shared with anyone else. As for Fah Lo Suee, she goes to work for a new MI-6 after its corrupt operatives are weeded out.

In subsequent issues Shang-Chi re-encounters Juliette and the Cat, then battles two new versions of Razorfist and discovers that his master, Velcro, is still alive. There seemed to be as much anguished talk of love among the characters in these issues as action. A KGB operative known as "Dark Angel" - rechristened Mia Lessing by Sir Denis - defects, and attracts the ire of Zaran, the Weapons Master, simply because his lover, Fah Lo Suee, is devoting all of her attention to debriefing her and coldly dumps him. Even more dangerous is the Ghost Maker, another assassin who is out to drop a cloud of acid rain on the Queen of England when she attends a parade in France, but who winds up skeletonized by his own weapon [MOKF 110 - 111]. Meanwhile Clive Reston and Mia fall instantly in love and Reston breaks up with Melissa Greville, who is not pleased.

Master of Kung Fu 114 presented an interesting story in which Shang-chi helps a Chinese couple who have been stalked by a member of the Si-Fan for forty years because the wife drank of Fu Manchu's immortality elixir. In the following issue Smith learns that he is broke and will lose his castle, and he at least seems to make a deal with Fah Lo Suee to arrange for him keep the castle via forged documents, but only if he has a certain MI-6 agent eliminated. However Smith is only playing along until Shang-Chi discovers the target is actually a double agent named Death-Dealer. This assassin works for an elderly Chinese named Wang Yu-Sen. Shang-Chi engages with Death-Dealer only to be attacked by a giant scorpion, after which he wakes up to find himself Yu-Sen's prisoner. However Yu-Sen drinks an elixir derived from Shang-Chi's blood, and becomes young and vigorous again. And turns into - Fu Manchu [MOKF 116]!

Fu reveals that the efficacy of his immortality formula has waned over the years and he now needs the blood of his off-spring to give him back his youth. He also holds the mortgage on Smith's castle. He made a clone of his son years before, and now the clone is full-grown, a double of Shang-Chi but for a scar, and completely devoted to Fu Manchu's evil teachings. Shang-Chi and company invade Fu Manchu's castle, where our hero frees a captive Fah Lo Suee, whose blood is being drained by her father, and the clone dies in final battle with his "brother." Fu Manchu is last seen desperately licking his son's blood off the floor before an explosion. Like Ra's al Ghul before him, and Brother Blood after him, Fu also bathes in a special solution to extend his youth. The most exciting scene has Shang-Chi nearly eaten by a gigantic and voracious praying mantis. At the end Shang-Chi tells Sir Denis that to all intents and purposes, he is his true father, and that he loves him [MOKF 118].

Master of Kung Fu was more or less over at this point but it muddled on for a few more issues, the best of which was MOKF 122. In this a murderous and insane agent from the past cooks up an elaborate scheme to drive Clive Reston insane, but his colleagues come to his rescue. Then Shanghi-Chi travels to New York to see his mother and fears that she has been kidnaped by agents of the Si-Fan seeking revenge for Fu Manchu's death. Instead it develops that his mother is in league with the Si-Fan, hopes that they will eventually kill him for "murdering" his father, and calls Shang-Chi her "false son." Reeling from this development, Shang-Chi travels to Tibet where he enters a monastery seeking answers, and learns that it was in this very monastery that Fu Manchu was trained and reared. The monks there despise Shang-Chi for murdering a man whose scientific knowledge saved the lives of many of them, and they almost succeed in killing him [MOKF 123 - 124].

In the final and 125th issue of the series, Shang-Chi travels through China, rediscovering his Eastern roots, making peace with his father's death at his burial place - a type of "atonement" for a man he can not respect -- defeating one final opponent sent to slay him by his own mother, and discovering a simple peasant life that is in sharp contrast to the violence and betrayal of his life in the Western world. Although he thinks of Leiko, the supposed love of his life, in one flashback sequence, he basically turns his back on her and decides to stay in China at the end without even saying goodbye to her -- what a nice guy! While Shang-Chi was always uncomfortable in his role as a warrior, his abject abandonment of the woman who loves him is incredibly selfish and cruel, hardly the actions of a man of sensitivity and compassion, as he was portrayed throughout the series; it also makes him seem like a ditz. The creative team for these last three issues was Alan Zelenetz, William Johnson, Alan Kupperberg, and Mike Mignola. Gene Day did the pencils for a great many issues but while they weren't particularly pretty to the eye, his work could be cinematic and well laid out.

Iron Fist

Iron Fist first appeared in *Marvel Premiere* 15 [1974] in a tale written and drawn by his creators, Roy Thomas and Gil Kane, who were inspired in part by certain aspects of Bill Everett's golden age hero Amazing-Man. Iron Fist was 19-year-old Daniel Rand. Ten years earlier his father Wendell had taken him - along with his wife Heather and business partner Harold Meachum - on a journey to the snowy mountains of Asia to search for the fabled city of K'un-Lun. Greedy Meachum, who loved Heather, threw Wendell off a peak and left Heather and the boy to survive on their own when they refused to go with him. Heather sacrificed herself when a pack of wolves attacked her and her son, and Danny was taken in by the residents of K'un-Lun, where he acquired mastery of the martial arts. He was able to focus all of his power into one of his hands, creating the "iron fist." On the day he decides to leave the city to return to civilization and get revenge on Meachum, his mentor, Yu-Ti, finally reveals that he is his uncle. Iron Fist deals with a variety of assassins sent by Meachum - who knows that he is back in New York - and storms his skyscraper HQ, which has been turned into one huge death trap.

In *Marvel Premiere* 18 Danny finally confronts Meachum himself. Danny learns that Meachum had lost his legs in the icy mountains years before, and has spent the last decade in terror, knowing his victim's son would come after him when he was grown. (The city of K'un-Lun only appears once every ten years; people can not leave or enter the city at any other time.) Now finding the object of his hate to be more pitiful than anything, Iron Fist decides not to kill him. But as a desperate Meachum, craving death, tries to shoot Danny, the crippled man is suddenly executed by a sword-wielding ninja assailant who had helped IF a couple of times as he made his way towards Meachum's office; Dannny's life is saved. Meachum's daughter Joy wrongfully assumes that Iron Fist murdered her father and now vows her own revenge upon him. In the following issue, Danny meets Colleen Wing, whose father, Professor Wing, has also been targeted by assassins because of his knowledge regarding K'un-Lun.

Doug Moench, Larry Hama and Dick Giordano were the creative team for most of these stories but that changed with *Marvel Premiere* 20, when Tony Isabella and Arvell Jones replaced them. There followed a convoluted storyline explaining that the aforementioned ninja is the spirit of a samurai held captive in a sacred book found by Professor Wing; the samurai uses the professor's body when he wants to go into action. Colleen and her father are kidnaped by the cult of Kal, bringing an innocent Iron Fist into conflict with Colleen's P.I. partner, Misty Knight (the two have a company called Nightwing Restorations), who thinks he is the culprit - and Iron Fist fights the ninja on a kind of astral plane. None of this was terribly interesting, however, and the blah art didn't help.

Chris Claremont became writer of the series with *Marvel Premiere* 23, with Pat Broderick as artist, and then John Byrne. An action-oriented battle with the psychotic sniper Warhawk was an improvement over previous issues, but MP 24, with Iron Fist fighting a creature called the Monstroid, might as well have been used to wrap fish. MP 25, in which Colleen is kidnaped and IF battles Angar the Screamer, was somewhat better, but was mostly notable as an early penciling job of future comics superstar John Byrne. Iron Fist was then moved into his own monthly title, while *Marvel Premiere* continued to present try-out series. *Iron Fist* 1 [1975] -- with Claremont and Byrne at the creative helm -- has our hero trying to track down Colleen's kidnapers and getting into a violent misunderstanding with the golden Avenger, Iron Man. IF 2 was a silly business with Iron Fist thinking back to a misadventure in a strange land next to K'un-Lun full of sentient, embittered plants.

The series kicked into high gear with *Iron Fist* 3, in which Danny and Misty go to London on the trail of Colleen. The action starts before they even arrive in the city proper, as their plane is brought down by the deadly beams of a terrorist called the Ravager. Danny discovers that Misty has a bionic arm (a former cop, Misty's arm was blown off by a bomb), and is torn between continuing the search for Colleen, or doing his utmost to stop the Ravager before he can kill many more people. Discovering that a little girl he saved on the plane has died on the operating table, he determines to go after the Ravager and end his threat forever. John Byrne's pencils, under the inks of Frank Chiaramonte, exhibited the flair and dynamism that would make him a fan favorite in very short order.

Iron Fist 4 continued the fight with the Ravager aka Radion, and IF 5 brought in the egocentric hit man Scimitar, as well as reformed IRA terrorist Alan Cavanaugh. Danny eventually rescues Colleen from Angar and the rather generic, revenge-motivated villain Master Kahn, who reveals that there were certain secrets back in K'in-Lun concerning his uncle Yu-Ti and his relationship to his parents and their deaths; all was not necessarily sunny in that comic book Shangri-La. On the other hand, Danny learns he has a fortune if only it can be wrested from the Meachums. (This sub-plot didn't really go anywhere, although Danny did appear in later stories to have control of his fortune and some say in the goings-on at Rand-Meachum Industries.)

Although Harold was dead, there was Joy and her nasty Uncle Ward to contend with, as well as the crime lord Chaka, who breaks into the Meachum conference room where Danny, his lawyer Jeryn Hogarth, and Misty Knight are having a financial pow wow with Joy and Ward Meachum. Chaka threatens to kill everyone until Meachum makes good on delivering everything he'd promised in deals he'd made with Chaka's gang. Danny switches to his alter ego by maneuvering to have Chaka hurl him out of the fortieth story window, then hopes he can convince everyone he was rescued by Spider-man just happening by.

The Chaka storyline lasted for three issues [IF 8 - 10]. Chaka feeds Iron Fist a poison and says he will get the antidote if he locates his opponent in Chinatown and manages to subdue both him and his henchmen. Realizing that there probably is no antidote, Danny uses his special power of the "iron fist" to counteract the poison in his system. He then finds himself hunted by the police for his alleged murder of Chaka; the latter had dressed his own disapproving and decent brother, William Hao, in his clothing and sent him out, mesmerized, to attack Iron Fist. These stories were full of flashing action and strikingly rendered fight scenes that were garnering the strip many fans (if not quite enough).

Iron Fist 11 and 12 pits our hero against Thor's foe the Wrecker and his Wrecking Crew, all of whom have super-strength of supernatural origin. To save hostage Misty Knight's life, Danny has to break into Avengers mansion and disable the alarms so the Crew can get in and ambush the Wrecker's most hated foe, Thor. IM winds up having to fight a quick-judging Captain America, although they later team up to defeat the Wrecking Crew (although this battle seems much too fast and easy). A full-page panel depicting an angry Cap standing over the fallen form of Iron Fist, like the personification of righteous wrath and power, is one of the most striking drawings ever done by Byrne (inked by Dan Adkins).

Iron Fist 13 features a lively battle between Iron Fist and old Hulk enemy Boomerang, hired by terrorists to kill the martial arts hero while they take care of the "traitor" Alan Cavanaugh. The more interesting aspect of the story, however, was not the fight but Danny Rand's interplay with Misty Knight, with whom he seemed to be developing real affection -- and vice versa -- more even than he might have initially felt for Colleen Wing. Misty is appalled that Danny has befriended a known terrorist as Cavanaugh, because to her he is little different from the man who built the bomb that blew her arm off. Danny reacts negatively to her attitude -- even though she was, after all, a victim, giving her a unique viewpoint Rand can't possibly understand -- and the two temporarily end their friendship.

Misty happened to be African-American. Danny appeared to be Caucasian -- although his "true" family name turned out to be Rand-K'ai instead of Rand -- and it was never quite clear if Colleen Wing was Asian, Caucasian, or of mixed heritage. (The letters column in *Power Man* 68 made it clear that her father was Hawaiian and mostly Chinese and her mother was Japanese, but Colleen generally looked more Irish than anything else.) Some readers objected to the fact that this martial arts-oriented comic had a white hero who always bested the Asian bad guys.

The final two issues of *Iron Fist* has him first meeting the deadly mercenary Sabre-Tooth, and then encountering those merry mutants, the X-Men. Sabre-Tooth, who became a major player in the Marvel Universe and who even joined the X-Men many, many years later, made his debut appearance in IF 14. IF 15 had a riotous battle between Danny and the mutants -- Misty Knight is Jean Grey's roommate -- when Wolverine mistakes Iron Fist for a burglar. Iron Fist wonders if there might be some connection between Sabre-Tooth and Wolverine, who have a similar savagery; of course, there was.

Many characters have no life after their own books are canceled, but Iron Fist was quite a bit luckier. First he appeared with Spider-Man in *Marvel Team-Up* 31(1975). In this the duo encounter Drom, the Backwards Man, who tries to steal energy from them to save himself from chronal dissipation. Seconds after being born, as Drom explains it, "my infant form was somehow exchanged through time with my aged body" and he's been growing younger ever since. But Drom is defeated, and he fades into nothingness. Peter Parker makes a tape recording of what happened because eventually the very memory of Drom will fade as well [Conway/Mooney/Colletta]. In *Marvel Team-Up* 63 - 64, Davos, aka the Steel Serpent, who is the son of Danny's martial arts teacher in K'un-lun (and who'd been stalking him in *Iron Fist* for months), comes after him in an attempt to steal away the "iron fist" power which Davos thinks is rightfully his. Steel Serpent defeats his opponent and does steal away the force of the Iron Fist, but in a rematch Davos discovers that he can not fully control this incredible and explosive power and is destroyed. Danny and Misty Knight are also reunited and realize they are in love with one another. (Their undeniable age difference is never addressed.) Frankly, the web-spinner didn't fit too neatly into the stories, which were done by Claremont and Byrne. Next, Iron Fist wound up in *Power Man*, which -- on the cover at least -- was re-titled *Power Man Iron Fist* (like *Green Lantern Green Arrow*) with the 50th issue. Iron Fist's further adventures are detailed in the section on *Power Man* (see chapter 17).

Shang-Chi at last met Daniel Rand, Iron Fist, in *Master of Kung Fu Annual* 1 [1976], during the time when the latter is searching London for a kidnaped Colleen Wing and asks the former for help. Surprisingly the two do not pit their martial arts prowess against one another, but instead become friends, sharing a forgettable adventure in another mystical city adjacent to K'un-Lun and fighting another would-be embittered despot magician. The story was not memorable.

CHAPTER THIRTEEN: THOR AND THE ETERNALS

As the bronze age began Stan Lee and Jack Kirby were still the creators behind the adventures of Thor. After saving his once-love Jane Foster from the machinations of a morbidly obese millionaire who wants to switch bodies with the Thunder God; fending off an attack by the Ringmaster, his Circus of Crime, and the hypnotized troll Ulik; and having his power stolen by the robotic Crypto-Man, whose creator sacrifices his life to save the city and his mother, Thor becomes embroiled in a major storyline beginning with *Thor* 175, the Fall of Asgard. Thor's half-brother, Loki, takes advantage of an attack by Mountain Giants on Asgard to invade Odin's chambers as he sleeps, and steals the Ring Imperial off his finger, making him absolute ruler of Asgard. The Asgardians place more faith in whosoever wears the ring than in blunt reality and refuse to aid Thor in attacking the usurper.

Loki places Odin in a container and removes him from Asgard, but because of this the spell Odin cast over the gigantic fiery demon Surtur to restrain him is broken. Surtur awakens to attack the city and melt its buildings. Loki, of course, flees to Earth even as Thor dispatches Sif and Balder to locate Odin and battles Surtur with the Warriors Three - grim Hogun, dashing Fandral and voluminous Volstagg -- at his side. Things look desperate until Odin returns and sends Surtur back into the bowels of the earth.

Thor

The next big story arc began in *Thor* 179, which also marked the last time "King" Kirby drew the strip. Aching for revenge, Loki is able to make himself look like Thor and vice versa. As Thor tries to convince his friends that he only looks like the God of Evil, Loki goes on a rampage of destruction in his Thor disguise. Odin grabs up "Loki" from Earth and in a fury at his perfidy banishes him to Hades, wherein its ruler, Mephisto, is able to see through the disguise and realize he's actually got Thor as a new subject. Sif and the Warriors Three travel to Hades to free Thor, who manages to get Loki to discard his hammer for too long during their battle, whereupon Thor turns into Donald Blake, and then into the rightful Thor by tapping the walking stick that transforms into Mjolnir. In his right form, Loki bids a hasty retreat.

The final two segments of Stan Lee's exciting story were penciled by Neal Adams, who did a superlative job. To give the art continuity, Joe Sinnott inked over Adams' pencils to make them more Kirbyesque. (Sinnott also inked John Buscema, who soon became the main Thor artist, for the same reason.) Kirby himself had left Marvel for DC Comics by this time. An amusing aspect of this story is that gruff Odin assures his vizier that he knows everything that has transpired. "Odin need not hear. Odin hath only to know," he intones, which makes you wonder why the old blowhard didn't "know" that Loki was actually Thor when he banished him to Hades!

In *Thor* 182 - 183, with art by Buscema and Sinnott, Goldilocks learns of a plan by Dr. Doom to unleash deadly missiles on the world from a young woman whose beloved father, a rocket scientist, is being held prisoner by the monarch and has been forced to build these weapons. Thor could have easily flown to Latveria where Doom rules, or told the Fantastic Four about Doom's plot, but instead he has his alter ago announce that he has a new method for healing any disfigurement, no matter how bad. (Thor never considers that this will not only raise false hope in Doom, but in thousands of others.) True to his plan, Doom kidnaps Blake, but when he shows the doctor his face, Blake is so appalled by what he sees that he cries out that absolutely nothing can be done to help him. Naturally, Doom doesn't take well to this tactless pronouncement, but Thor puts paid to his evil plans to wipe out several cities. In an interesting twist, it turns out that the rocket scientist who designed the missiles had not been kidnapped after all, but was working for money, and couldn't care less about his daughter. After the greedy man is killed, Thor tells his daughter a more heroic story out of compassion.

A new "epic" concerning "The Worlds Beyond" began in *Thor* 184. Odin tells Thor that a dark mass that resembles grasping fingers is approaching Asgard and Earth even as it swallows up and seemingly destroys dozens of planets. The Warriors Three had gone to investigate and never returned, and Odin himself doesn't do all that well against these mysterious forces. After stopping Loki and the frost giants from yet another attack on Asgard during Odin's absence, Thor takes off after his friends and father, discovering that this powerful force -- Infinity -- is making slaves out of the inhabitants of all the worlds it's absorbed into its dark mass. What's worse, the giant Odinsword is slowly pulling itself out of its scabbard, which could signal Ragnarok, the end of the universe, and the Earth itself isn't doing too well, either, as severe storms sweep across the planet and then horrifying cataclysms begin. Infinity turns out to be a portion of Odin himself, created when Hela, the goddess of Death, came across a sleeping Odin in the container in which Loki placed him in an earlier storyline, and tried without success to steal away his life force. With Infinity, Hela hopes to bring Death to everything and usher innumerable souls to her domain.

With the aid of Thor and his companions -- even enemies like Loki and Karnilla, the Norn Queen do their best to prevent total destruction -- Odin re-absorbs his evil self and with one

wave makes everything all right in Asgard, on Earth, and presumably everywhere else. In this way Stan Lee was able to cir-
cumvent having many months of stories throughout the Marvel Universe that would have had to deal with the aftermath of
so much death and destruction. *Voila!* Everything went back to
the way it was before Infinity appeared, making Odin seem
more powerful than ever before (but not powerful enough to
sense long before who and what Infinity was and to deal with
it).

The story had an interesting postscript in *Thor* 189 - 190 in
which a furious if super-cool Hela -- who can't understand why
anyone would fear death -- decides she'll at least claim the life
of Odin's beloved son. She tracks Thor to Earth where he's hoping to avoid her while in his Don Blake guise until his father
can come up with a plan. Learning of her journey to Earth,
Odin dispatches fat Volstagg to warn Thor, and the lovable,
corpulent one, thoroughly confused by Earth ways, winds up
temporarily incarcerated in a psycho ward. Hela forces Blake to
become Thor by threatening innocents, and not even Odin's
entreaties can get her to spare his son's life. Odin finally slays
Hela in desperation -- odd that the goddess of death can die --
but Thor points out that Death is necessary for many different
reasons, and Odin brings her back to life. Only Sif's poignant
pleas for the life of her beloved finally touch Hela's heart and
Thor is spared -- for now. Meanwhile Loki has again taken advantage of Odin's absence to steal the Odinring and take over
Asgard (you'd think that Odin would have realized he should
never leave home without that damned ring).

Odin refuses Thor's entreaties to reject Loki as Asgard's ruler;
he wears the ring and that's that. Loki makes Odin take his
Odinsleep and creates a non-human powerhouse fighter
named the Demolisher to terrorize the earth and keep Thor
busy. He then announces that Sif is to be his bride, and orders
her to prepare for the wedding. Balder, who is unable to fight
for Asgard because of a vow he made to save Thor's life some
time before, calls to the heavens for help and asks the Silver

Surfer to intercede. The Surfer takes care of the Demolisher as Thor goes back to Asgard to prevent a wedding. The Warriors Three awaken Odin from his Sleep and incur his wrath, but it turns out there wasn't much to fear anyway, as if the ring is worn too long by an unworthy ruler, it begins to burn -- Loki hurls the ring away from him and is banished. Once again Odin saves the day by barely lifting a finger. John Buscema penciled these stories under a variety of inkers -- Vince Colletta probably worked best -- and his work was excellent, although not quite on the level of Kirby at the top of his game, although it was similarly dynamic and strikingly composed. Gerry Conway took over as scripter during the Demolisher epic but was probably, at first, working from Stan Lee's plot ideas.

Blackworld and Ego Prime

The next Thor epic combined the renewed menace of silver age foe Mangog [*Thor* 195 - 198], released from his prison by Loki, with further threats from the Well at the Edge of the World and a strange place called Blackworld, where Odin has the blonde warrior woman Hildegard take Sif for protection -- just as he sent Thor (and the Warriors Three) on a quest that would either help save the day or at least keep the Thunder God out of danger. (An out-of-character act for Odin who places his son in danger on a regular basis. But Odin's motives were often confused and inexplicable. The All-Father never liked to let anyone know his plans, probably because Lee, Conway etc., weren't quite certain from issue to issue exactly what those plans were!) Naturally, there turns out to be as much deadly intrigue in these places as in Asgard. On Blackworld, the environment keeps changing on an hourly basis, with a small village becoming a metropolis in barely a day. The colonizer Tana Nile, an interesting character from the silver age [131 - 133], shows up to warn Sif and Hildegarde of someone she only refers to as "Him." Meanwhile Thor, Odin and the others fight a desperate war against Mangog in Asgard.

Mangog's energy expires and he shrinks out of sight, but not without claiming the life of Odin. Both Hela and Pluto, who rule different netherworlds, come to claim Odin's soul, and wind up battling one another [*Thor* 199]. Hela finally gives Odin back his life, if only to keep him out of the hands of Pluto [201]. Meanwhile, Sif and Hildegarde discover that "Him" is actually Ego-Prime, a portion of Ego, the Living Planet, whom Thor battled in the silver age. The Colonizers had use for another Earth-like planet, but having sworn to Thor that they would leave the real globe alone, Tana Nile tried to create a new Earth by planting part of Ego in its firmament. Tana has just finished telling her tale when Blackworld, which has entered the atomic age, suddenly erupts in a nuclear explosion and is destroyed - she and her companions, including Ego-Prime, are somehow hurled to the real planet earth. Thor and his warrior friends have conveniently traveled to Earth as well, and engage Ego-Prime in battle as he explains that he basically wishes to purify the world by ridding it of its human infection.

But Heimdall has brought three young people -- an Israeli soldier, an Asian female farmer, and a Black American artist -- to the battle and they are transformed into new, young Gods by an energy blast from Ego-Prime [203], and it was this that Odin desired all along. Yes, the wise All-Father was manipulating everything behind the scenes, which absolutely infuriates Thor: "Wert thou certain that all thy precious pawns would survive thy planning and plotting," he thunders, "or didst thou not even care?" Odin is so outraged by this accusation of cruelty (actually he doesn't like it when anyone criticizes him), that he banishes Thor and even all of his companions to Earth, which he did more than once during the silver age. In the intriguing *Thor* 204 Thor and his buddies hang out at Avengers mansion and elsewhere, but one by one they all disappear in the shadows, snatched away by half-seen creatures, until they learn they've been dragged to evil Mephisto's realm. In the next issue Mephisto throws everything, including Adolf Hitler, against Thor but the Thunder God prevails.

Thor 210 - 211 brought back the hateful troll, Ulik, who had a mad-on for Thor since the silver age. Ulik taunts Thor with the suggestion that the latter only wins battles because of his mighty hammer, so Thor agrees to fight the troll without it. Base betrayal -- during the battle the hammer is spirited away by other trolls, and Ulik not only attacks Thor from behind, but uses his own weapon, a club of stone, to batter him. Thor, with only seconds before he'll revert to comparatively puny Don Blake, dives into the fiery pit into which the trolls have thrown Mjolnir. He regains his weapon, and finds an unexpected ally in the wife of the troll king, who seems to find him "fair." Although the trolls are supposed to be creatures of Asgard, they are now denizens beneath the ground of Earth (like the Moleman's) and burrow up to attack New York. With the aid of his warrior pals and even Tana Nile, who is stranded on Earth, Thor routs the invaders.

Thor and Odin eventually mend fences, after an adventure in which the denizens of Asgard are drugged and sold into slavery; when they return to Asgard they find that a slew of imposters await them, leading into a battle which pits Thor against Thor, Odin against Odin, then father against son, and so on. The imposters were created by the wizard Igron, who had been Loki's assistant until the latter banished him to the land of the trolls. A sword whack from Balder knocks out the wizard and the false gods are easily defeated in a tale with some fine art by both John and Sal Buscema [*Thor* 217].

The Black Stars

During several issues there had been references to the sinister "Black Stars" and in *Thor* 218 their menace was fully revealed when the billions of inhabitants of Rigel, Tana Nile's home planet, must flee at their approach. Three times larger than Jupiter, the black stars are reaching out to consume the galaxy, blasting Rigel to pieces with unimaginable power and using gargantuan matter scoops to suck up the debris to use for energy. Inside one of these scoops Thor and his companions meet a comparative giant named Avalon, whose race lives and dies inside the scoop and maintains the equipment. But Avalon is a pygmy compared to the race who live on the largest of the planets in the Black Stars, who are so gargantuan that Thor and his allies are microscopic in comparison. (While this leads to a striking final panel in *Thor* 219, it makes little sense for such large people to employ such tiny scoops.) Despite the disadvantage of their size, Thor, Avalon and the others manage to defeat whatever the aliens throw at them and convince them they can happily survive without decimating entire galaxies [220].

In the next few issues Thor travels to Olympus where again he battles Hercules over a misunderstanding. As he had in the silver age, Hercules hangs around for a few months, and is there to witness the first appearance of Galactus' new herald, the fiery, flying Firelord [*Thor* 225]. Although the question of whether Thor changed into Don Blake or Blake into Thor had been settled in the silver age (Odin had created the identity of Blake to teach Thor humility) Thor/Blake inexplicably develops an identity crisis, with Don wondering if he wants to stay in the guise of the gifted surgeon. Thor and Hercules' rivalry over who was stronger continued to amuse, with the Olympian making fun of the Asgardian's winged battle helmet. "Only thou would have the poor taste to wear the ugly thing," Hercules says. As for Firelord, his summoning of Galactus causes a worldwide panic, but it turns out that the big fellow only wants to team up with Thor against the living planet, Ego, who is now raging out of control.

Thor 228 revealed that Ego had once been a scientist on a planet whose sun was about to go nova. "Egros" supervised the construction of suspended animation pods deep inside the earth for the planet's entire population, but the sun exploded too soon and Egros was caught in the blast. His entire race was destroyed except for some of the consciousness and life force which merged with Ego's own; Ego has dealt with survivor guilt for centuries. Galactus, Thor and Hercules manage to subdue the living planet while Galactus attaches a rocket to the world that sends it off on a possibly eternal voyage throughout space. How this eliminates the mad planet's threat is never made quite clear.

Rich Buckler briefly took over as penciler, but his work wasn't on the same level as John Buscema's, although Joe Sinnott's inking helped. A new story arc began in which several people commit suicide by fire, muttering about how they will not die, but this plot goes nowhere, devolving into Thor and Hercules facing a fear-demon of some sort [*Thor* 229 - 230]. In a more interesting development, Odin disappears and Thor's old love Jane Foster, reappears, as one of the potential suicides influenced by Fear. She is dying due to her injuries, and Thor fully remembers the love he once felt for her; she seems to have lost the will to live. Eventually Jane makes a full recovery via Sif's noble sacrifice, transferring her life energies to Jane so that the man they both love, Thor, can be with the woman he truly loves, Jane [236]. However, Sif's spirit brings about some changes in Jane.

In the meantime Loki comes back into the picture, now armed with a portion of Dormammu's power, which he acquired during the Avengers-Defenders war. Since Odin is not in Asgard, Loki seizes the throne yet again and sends his ensorcelled troops against Thor and Earth. After Firelord and the Avengers help rout the mesmerized Asgardians, Thor and his half-brother have a furious solo battle which ends with Loki defeated; Thor sheds a tear for him, which is probably a lot more than Loki would have done. As for Odin, he has followed in his son's footsteps and created a new mortal identity for himself on Midgard, Orrin, who lives on a California commune -- he's under a spell of forgetfulness and will not come out of it for an undisclosed period. He regains his own mind after a forgettable interlude with some ancient Egyptian gods.

John Buscema's pencils, inked by Joe Sinnott, continued to impress, as we witnessed Hercules knocking aggressive seer Kamo Tharnn on his keister; Orrin brushing off an out of control car with one wave of his meaty arm; Hercules holding a collapsing ferris wheel full of people on his back; and a savage, well-detailed battle between Thor and the Absorbing Man

[*Thor* 236]. John's brother Sal Buscema took over temporarily while Sinnott remained on inks and the art remained first-rate, but Gerry Conway, who'd scripted a great many issues, went off to greener pastures. Bill Mantlo did a few issues, then Len Wein took over as scripter and editor, with John Buscema back on pencils. Wein replaced Hercules with the Warriors 3 -- Fandral, Hogan, and Volgstagg -- and had Sif eventually taking over the corporeal form of Jane Foster.

Jane and Sif

Wein's first story arc concerned Thor's old silver age foe the Tomorrow Man, who came from the future. This time he wanted Thor and his friends, the Warriors 3, to be his allies in order to prevent cosmic creatures called the Time Twisters from obliterating the 50th century. Tomorrow Man, who has made himself King of the Earth, sends ordinary citizens against the Twisters, and in an effective and sobering scene they are all reduced to dust as their age is either accelerated or devolved out of existence. Thor and his allies also have little luck against the Twisters - indeed 50th century Earth is des-troyed - until they hit upon the idea of using TM's time cube to take them back to the entities' infancy and destroying them. 50th century Earth and all of its people are restored but TM finds that he is no longer on the throne [*Thor* 242 - 245].

Despite Sif's spirit inhabiting and energizing the body of Jane Foster, Odin still objects to her relationship with Thor. The lady has become an altogether different Jane, capturing a troll king, beating off attackers, and getting into a knife-and-claw catfight with a fiery South American revolutionary named Gypsy [*Thor* 247]. Jane, however, never expresses any remorse over Sif's fate, and Thor's thoughts keep returning to Sif ... Sif herself reappears when Jane travels to Asgard, two conscious-ness's sharing the same form, the former now ascendant. Thor finds himself torn between the two women but has to set that aside when he challenges his father, who seems to have gone mad. But Odin is actually the dreaded Mangog in disguise; he is defeated after nearly unsheathing the Odinsword and bringing about the end of everything [248 - 250].

The next story arc concerned Thor's search for his missing father; Mangog was not responsible for Odin's disappearance and no one in the universe seems to know where he is. Thor's quest brings him into conflict with the troll Ulik; a huge dragon with a ruby eye in its forehead; and the badly-named but memorable albino monster Trogg, who was reminiscent of the kind of monsters Jack Kirby and Dick Ayers had created for Marvel's old horror comics. Speaking of which, Thor and his comrades also encounter the Stone Men from Saturn, who first battled the Thunder God in his very first appearance in *Journey Into Mystery* 83. Some of the most intriguing beings Thor and his pals run into are a race called the Levianon who inhabit a dilapidated star ship. After depleting their own world's resources, the Levianon do the same thing to the ship that took them off their collapsing planet, until they now live in squalor and are victimized by an enormous, tentacled monster called Sporr, who turns out to be a supposedly benevolent being [256 - 257]. John Buscema's pencils were not that well served by the inking of Tony DeZuniga, and when Walter Simonson took over from Buscema the results, while hardly terrible, were much less felicitous.

Len Wein kept turning out some memorable stories, however, as Thor and his companions continue the search for Odin and beyond. Thor's old foe the Gray Gargoyle reappeared as captain of a group of alien slave traders in *Thor* 258 - 259. The Enchantress and the Executioner menace the realm eternal but are beaten back by brave Balder and the Norn Queen, who wages a war with her fellow sorceress that results in the Enchantress being royally trounced [260]. (Four issues later voluminous Volstagg would almost defeat the Enchantress by crushing her with his belly!) Then there was the Doomsday Star, a planet that literally has a wall surrounding it, the home of a dying race who are using the kidnapped Odin's energies to stay alive [261 - 263].

Freeing the All-Father, Thor and the others return home only to discover that Loki is once more on the throne of Asgard. This culminated in an exciting story that embroils Loki, Karnilla, the Norn Queen, the Destroyer, and just about everyone else in Asgard while, as usual, Odin sleeps his Odinsleep in an underground dungeon during the battle. When it is all over Odin strips Loki of his godhood and his memory and turns him into a Midgardian bowery bum [*Thor* 264 - 266]. The work of Simsonson and DeZuniga was never on the level of Jack Kirby or John Buscema but it improved to the point where it was often quite dramatic and attractive.

Wanting to return to Midgard and take up his life as Don Blake again -- perhaps to have a respite from all the Asgardian madness of the past year or two -- Thor returns to Earth where the good doctor is offered a job at a clinic. Sif stays in Asgard, and there is absolutely no talk about Jane Foster, with whom Thor had supposedly been madly in love. Before Blake can decide whether or not to work at the clinic, he battles several foes in rapid succession: the mad Damocles; the Stiltman; Blastaar; an artificial intelligence called Faust -- only the Stiltman story [269] was memorable, along with a striking full-page portrait of our hero at the end of *Thor* 271. Roy Thomas, John Buscema and Tom Palmer became the new-old creative team with the following issue, a charming tale in which Thor tells several young boys about his boyhood adventure with a magical giant.

Once More Harris Hobbes

The next story arc featured Harris Hobbes, a reporter who had blackmailed Thor into taking him to Asgard by learning of his Blake identity back in the silver age. Hobbes has destroyed the evidence but still wants Thor to let him take a camera crew to Asgard for television's "sweeps" week. With the aid of Loki, who has regained his memory and power, Hobbes and his crew wind up in the realm eternal only to learn that it may not be so eternal: Loki claims Ragnarok, the twilight of the Gods, is coming, to be heralded by the death of Balder, who does indeed die. Odin calls all of the goddesses back to Asgard to face whatever may come with their men; among the ladies is Sigyn, the heretofore unseen wife of Loki. Odin is able to siphon off some of his power to hold Balder in suspended animation, but it extremely limits Odin's own abilities.

Thus this is a terrible time for a new deadly Thor to enter the fray -- cameraman Red Norvell, who is hot for Sif and has been aided in gaining the powers of a Thunder God via Loki. The God of Mischief defends himself at his trial by boldly stating that he was only doing what he was destined to do, and therefore should not be punished. In the meantime the New Thor is able to wrest Mjolnir away from the true Thor and defeat him, causing the death of another young crewmember, even as Hela gathers her forces, which include trolls, the giant wolf Fenris, and the gargantuan Midgard serpent, to attack Asgard [*Thor* 273 - 277].

Although it seems as if Ragnarok has truly arrived, it develops that Odin is only up to his usual tricks. He made certain prophecies only appear to have transpired to fool Hela into assaulting Asgard prematurely, even going so far as to switch the site of battle from the realm eternal to a vast empty plain. A disappointed Hela, who now may not be able to fulfill her plans for centuries, returns to her own realm as the New Thor, Red Norvell, perishes in a battle with the Midgard serpent, whom Thor manages to defeat. When Odin reveals his rather sneaky behind-the-scenes plans, Thor is furious at the deception and his father's manipulations, and especially the fact that two mortals died; Norvell, in fact, was meant to die in Thor's place. Odin, equally furious, argues that it was their decision to travel to Asgard, and orders his son to stay forever in the realm eternal. When Thor refuses, Odin banishes him from Asgard for good [*Thor* 278]. Although Odin's long-ago actions had helped instill a love of humanity and Midgard in Thor, it seems that his father does not share those particular affections.

The art for these issues was surprisingly uneven, given how the Buscema-Palmer combination had done so much excellent work in the past. The art for the climactic *Thor* 278 was substandard even given the fact that Palmer was replaced by Chic

Stone, which would not account for Buscema's uninspired penciling. In *Thor* 280 the guest artist was Wayne Boring, silver age Superman artist, who drew a story of Thor encountering two Hyperions, the evil one from the Squadron Sinister and the more or less good one from the Squadron Supreme; as Hyperion was Marvel's version of Superman, the choice of artist made perfect sense. Then Roy Thomas began a lengthy arc which focused on concepts created by Jack Kirby for *The Eternals*. It began in *Thor Annual* 7, which took place in the past, wherein Thor encounters Ikaris' father, Virako, who sacrifices his life during a battle with monstrous deviants and their creatures. Thor also learned of the menace of the Celestials.

The Celestials

During this massive and amazing storyline, Thor discovers the mountainous Arishem and his fifty-year judgment of earth and hates the idea of anything happening to his beloved Midgard. This brings him into conflict with: Kro, the Great Tode, and other deviants and mutates from *Eternals* (discussed later in this chapter); the "Forgotten One" who has been rechristened "Hero" by the Celestials and is an Eternal variation of Hercules, Samson, Atlas and others; and even the towering celestials themselves, with Thor actually engaging these giants in combat with negative results. One of the Celestials shows Thor an image of Odin kneeling before Arishem even as Odin travels to Olympus to ask Zeus and the other Greek gods to help him fight off any attempt to interfere with the Celestials. This leads to the gods of Asgard and Olympus joining together to storm Olympia (home of the Eternals, not to be confused with Olympus), where the Eternal leader Zuras battles Zeus and in an incredible development Odin fights and actually threatens to slay his own son. Odin is about to deliver the death stroke in fact when he halts and cries out that he just can't kill his only blood son again. Odin retreats, as does a perturbed Zeus, who recognizes that his main reason for fighting was his annoyance with these upstarts of "Olympia" [*Thor* 283 - 292].

The Celestial saga was interrupted as Thor determines to

find out what his father meant about killing his blood son once before. Over several more issues the reader is given a mythological tour of the destruction of the original Asgard; the birth of a new Odin (the character we're familiar with), formed from the remnants of the Aesir of legend; and Odin's first son, the mortal Seigmund, formed by a union between Odin and an earth woman. Creating two Asgards, two Odins, and two Thors was a way to reconcile all the inconsistencies over the years by separating the mythological Asgard from the Marvel version. This angered some readers, who felt that Thor should always have been and remained the mythological version, as had first been suggested, but the editorial reply was that it was always the Marvel version of Thor that had been worshiped by the (comic book) Vikings back in the day.

Meanwhile Odin's wife, Frigga, goddess of marriages, is enraged by Odin's infidelity and demands Seigmund's death. Although Odin does his best to prevent it, he is forced to kill his own son due to a vow he made because Brunnhilda, the Valkyrie he sent to slay Seigmund, fails to comply with his wishes. Siegmund's son Seigfried, who is also imbued with, shall we say, the essence of Thor (or his spirit) as his father was, battles Fafnir the Dragon for a magical golden ring. Now the comic was not just incorporating bits and pieces of the Marvel mythos and Norse legends but even Wagnerian opera, as some of the stories were based on *Siegfried* and *Gotterdammerung* from the composer's Ring cycle [293 - 299].

Seigfried is also slain, but Odin brings him back to life. (Thor's two previous human incarnations explain his bond with Midgard and its inhabitants.) Thor learns that years before Odin had every intention of taking on the Celestials, and gathered together many other deities whose fates were linked with those of earth. Unfortunately, the Celestials threatened to utterly eradicate the mystical links between these gods and the world, so Odin and the others were forced to back down. Now, however, Odin has changed his mind, takes back the power with which he recreated the Asgardian gods, and enters the form of the Destroyer, now grown to giant-size, to battle Arishem and the others. Odin fails, and is seemingly destroyed, and Thor is also unable to defeat the space giants. At the last minute Mother Earth -- who turns out to be Thor's true mother, another reason for his bond with the planet -- offers up twelve of her children, young gods, to go off with the Celestials and share knowledge with them, causing Arishem to spare the planet and depart with his companions. Unfortunately Odin and the other Asgardians, aside from Thor, are dead, their Ragnarok having finally come, albeit in a different manner than expected [*Thor* 300].

The Celestial/Origin stories took over a year and a half to tell with some readers losing interest long before the conclusion. One problem was that the admirable efforts to explain away every single inconsistency may have created more confusion than anything else, especially pertaining to Thor's maternal heritage and the fact that the second human Thor (or Seigfried) that Odin brought back to life had actually been his grandson. Some readers felt it was ridiculous to make so many changes in *Thor* just to blend the series in with another series (*The Eternals*) that hardly lasted longer than the Celestial saga. The clearing up of old inconsistencies often created new ones. For instance, Frigga objects to Seigmund, the first human incarnation of Thor, to the point where she orders his death, yet becomes a loving mother to Thor himself. This may all have been clear to the writers and editors but the readers were certainly confused. The early episodes of the story arc were incredibly suspenseful and exciting and featured one interesting revelation after another, however. While Roy Thomas conceived the whole business, the final issues were scripted by Ralph Macchio and Marc Gruenwald.

Asgardians Restored

In *Thor* 301 the Norse god is able to bring Odin and the others back to life by using a portion of the power of all the other gods to restore the Asgardians. (The only hold out is many-armed Shiva from the Hindu pantheon, but when he is defeated in battle he complies.) Then, so as not to offend religious readers -- even though these were stories of purest fantasy -- *Thor* 303 published a story by Doug Moench in which Thor aids a priest who has lost his faith, a faith he regains when he sees the power of the Thunder God. Wondering if he's been worshiping the wrong god all along, Thor assures him -- and certain readers -- that there is a "universal higher force" behind all the other gods and faiths.

Macchio and Gruenwald continued their work on *Thor* -- with Keith Pollard and Chic Stone turning in some effective art work -- with their stories often having certain sub-texts, such as the death of an elderly woman Thor briefly meets during a battle with the Wrecking Crew [304], or the heartbreak of a little boy when the robot Gabriel, who has become a substitute for his late father, is shattered by Thor's hammer [305]. Meanwhile an excellent backup story by the same creative team has Karnilla employing her usual trickery to ensnare Balder, threatening to kill another woman he loves unless he agrees to marry her. Balder does agree, to save her life, but the woman commits suicide to spare him [304 - 306].

Thor 311 presented a different and memorable story in which Dr. Donald Blake (Thor has returned to earth to work in a free clinic) tries to save the life of a black boy who has been shot by police. The youth had stolen something from a store, and one of the policemen thought he was going for a gun when he put his hand inside his jacket. The police officer is distraught, but crowds of angry black people occupy the clinic and violence threatens to break out at any moment. When Blake is through with the operation, he changes into the thunder god and does his best to calm the crowd, only to learn that in his absence the boy has died. Although the nurse insists that the boy would have died anyway, Blake's boss at the clinic removes him from duty with a review to follow. Meanwhile the boy's grieving mother screams at the crowd that there has been enough violence, and they disperse. Intelligent and well-handled, looking at all sides, the blending of Norse god with inner city conflict (and situations that are still going on today) shouldn't have worked but it worked very well [Moench/Pollard/Day].

Thor 316 - 317 brought back an antagonist who was first introduced in Thor comics in the silver age, the Superbeast, or Man-Beast, created by the High Evolutionary. The hateful creature manages to get into a spaceship with Thor in pursuit, and Mjolnir winds up inside the capsule as it hurls off into space. Thor clings to the ship as it ascends and is able to get at the hammer before sixty seconds pass and he reverts to Don Blake, who could never have survived in space. Unfortunately, many issues of Thor at this time were mediocre, far below the level of the Celestials storyline and other impressive arcs, with the nadir perhaps being the appearance of the "Zaniac" -- an actor in a mad slasher film who becomes irradiated and goes berserk -- in Thor 319. In this issue Don Blake moved to Chicago to start a new practice after renewing his acquaintanceship with Dr. Shawna Lynde, with whom he went to medical school. Along with the substandard stories was inferior artwork; Keith Pollard was replaced by Alan Kupperberg, whose pencils were unimpressive no matter who inked them.

Even when Thor came up with an intriguing story arc, it was muffed, such as what should have been an epic concerning the Midgard serpent. The first couple of installments to the story, in which Tyr and Loki team up with the Serpent to steal away the immortality-giving golden apples, forcing Odin and the others to go to earth to preserve their energy, appeared as backups. Thor 327 was the full-length climax, with Tyr and his allies attacking Odin and his troops in Asgard, while Thor attempts to stop the serpent from causing disastrous upheaval on earth. Doug Moench's script had thoroughly evil Loki regretting his actions simply because he was wrong in suspecting his father of infidelity -- why would he care either way? Loki claims that he enjoys causing mischief as the god of same, but that Tyr's plan is too evil, something Loki, who'd schemed innumerable times to destroy Thor, Odin and the Realm Eternal, would never think in a million years. One would not have hoped for Kirby or Buscema art at this point, but it certainly would have helped bring this abrupt and too-short saga to life.

At least there were interesting developments when Sif insists on staying on earth with Thor, although she hates Midgard, seems to have contempt for mortals, and isn't especially attracted to his alter ego, Donald Blake. Sif is also jealous of Shawna Lynde, who clearly has feelings for Blake and thinks of Sif, or "Sybil," as his cousin. Thor can't understand why Sif doesn't switch to Jane Foster when she's on earth. This causes a decided problem when Blake is accused of doing away with the missing Miss Foster by her one-time fiancé Keith Kincaid, but eventually those two are reunited. Alan Zelenetz scripted these good tales and also brought Thor into conflict with Dracula when the Lord of the Undead took a bite out of Sif. The vampire gives Thor a run for his money but is nearly pulverized before his rescue by Dracula cultists, who spirit him away [332- 333]. Zelenetz also wrote an interesting story in which a prospective priest is kicked out of the seminary and becomes the Crusader, who tries to kill Thor because some misguided people in Chicago have chosen to worship him.

Sif decides to go back to Asgard without Thor and drown her loneliness in combat. But a much bigger change occurs with *Thor* 337 in which an alien named Beta Ray Bill comes to earth and becomes an alternate Thor when he gains possession of his hammer; Walter Simonson was both the author and artist. Thus Thor entered the copper age without Mjolnir.

There were a number of Thor annuals during the bronze age, with the best being *Thor Annual 5*. This features an excellent story, set far in the past, detailing the first long-ago meeting between Thor and Hercules who, manipulated by crafty Loki, become enemies. Hence the armies of Asgard and Olympus engage in warfare, only to learn that neither faction can ever really best the other [Englehart/Buscema/DeZuniga]. One spectacular two-page panel shows the two armies coming together in fierce and dramatic combat. Of course, in the silver age Thor's first meeting with Hercules occurred many years later.

The Eternals

As the Eternals played a big role in a long story arc in *Thor*, the series will be discussed in this chapter. Jack Kirby, disappointed with DC's failure to promote his Fourth World comics, returned to Marvel and there worked on several series. *The Eternals* debuted in 1976. Inspired by such works as "Chariots of the Gods" about extraterrestrials, Kirby created a saga which posited that long ago celestial beings came to earth and manipulated the genes of apes. This resulted in three distinct races: humans, the largest segment; Eternals, a much smaller group of immortal and powerful super-beings; and Deviants, grotesque enemies of the Eternals, none of which resemble any other and whose atoms are unstable. One of the Eternals is Ikaris, who has taken on the identity of Ike Harris. He and his companions, archeologists Dr. Damian and his daughter Margo, explore ancient ruins in the Andes, and discover vestiges of the space gods who first visited so long ago. Ikaris has turned on a beacon to guide the Celestials back to earth, a return which the Deviant leader, Kro, has tried to prevent. The very interesting first issue ends with representatives of all three races anxiously waiting to meet the Celestial visitors and see what they look like.

In *Eternals* 2 we learn that the Deviants once overran the earth and enslaved humans. When the Celestials first returned, the Deviants, fearful of having their power usurped, fired upon the extraterrestrial ships, with the result that the aliens devastated the earth, bringing about the Great Flood and engendering Noah's ark, which Ikaris helped steer toward land. In the present day, the Eternal Ajak heads the ground crew that helps guide the gigantic Celestial Arishem, leader of the fourth host, to earth. Arishem will stand atop his pedestal for fifty years, after which it will be decided if Earth is to live or to die. During that time the entire surrounding area in the Andes will be cut off from the rest of the planet. Dr. Damian is fascinated and wants to stay, but Ikaris forces Margo to leave because her whole life will be swallowed up. Margo fights against Ikaris because she doesn't want to leave her father. Ikaris takes Margo to New York, where she is taken under the wing of the female Eternal, Sirsy, who is also the Circe of legend [3]; later her name is spelled Sersi.

In *Eternals* 4 the Deviants launch a monster attack, literally, on New York City, in the hopes that humans will blame the alien Celestials and a war between both groups will begin. Kro, growing horns, is mistaken for Satan, and the Deviants' mutates for demons. Neither the Fantastic Four nor the Avengers show up during this siege, although a mention of Ben Grimm in the following issue, and the brief introduction of three SHIELD agents in the next, makes it clear that *The Eternals* is part of the regular Marvel universe. (In a later issue it is suggested that the Marvel heroes were just comic book characters.) Deviants and Eternals enact a truce while they wait to see what the humans will do.

Eternals 5 introduces Olympia, the home of the Eternals, which like Olympus, is on top of a mountain. Other eternals include swift, frantic Makarri (Mercury); the intellectual Mobius-like Domo; mischievous Sprite, who can create things out of air by manipulating atoms; the leader of the Eternals, red-bearded Zorus; and his tough blonde warrior daughter, Thena. Haughty Sersi might be the feistiest of the bunch. When she and Margo are captured by deviants, the former says: "Oh shut up! I'm bored with the lot of you. Even Attila the Hun was more entertaining. He behaved like a slob, but at least he liked music and dancing." Sersi doesn't spare Margo, either, calling her "a silly little human who will probably be old and bent before she learns the joy of living." (In a later issue Margo calls Sersi a "featherbrain.") Ikaris comes from the "polar" eternals and is not a favorite of Sersi's. Many eternals live among men in cities around the world and have "normal" occupations.

Eternals 7 takes us back inside the area where Arishem hovers and the other Celestials go about their business. Seeing

cubes of what he is told are compressed atoms of earth creatures, Dr. Damian wonders if any of the cubes contain humans,
and the three aforementioned SHIELD agents, having been
captured, are released from their containers. The agents try to
escape their fifty-year captivity and are put back into a cube,
making one wonder what their loved ones will think of their
disappearances. In *Eternals* 8 it is revealed that Thena and Kro
had a romance centuries before, but any chance of it being
rekindled is destroyed when the compassionate Thena sees
wagons of especially hideous "rejects" being taken to cremator-
iums as if the Deviants were Nazis. Another reject, considered
ugly by some of the Deviants, is as handsome as a movie star.
This "reject" is put in an arena with the monstrous mutate
Karkas, a hulking creature with bright red skin like a boiled
lobster, a huge head, misshapen legs, and claws on his hands
and feet.

In the Deviant City of Toads lorded over by a fat green monstrosity named the Great Tode, the Reject and Karkas battle
nearly to the death, with the handsome one revealed as the
true killing machine and Karkas as a creature of more sensitivity. Thena, visiting the City of Toads with Kro by her side, takes
pity on both combatants and dematerializes with them to offer
them sanctuary in Olympia; Kro is heartbroken by her departure. By this time some of the giant Celestials have revealed
themselves all over the world, making one wonder why the
Andes had to be sealed off in the first place. The Russians fire a
missile at the Celestial at their gate which flies right back at
them to their base, but only in their minds -- which is not
enough to prevent cardiac seizures in everyone watching. In
the meantime all of the Eternals, gathered together and flying,
swirl together into a mist to form the gigantic brain-like Uni-
Mind, a red mushroom that soars into space to find out what it
can about the Celestials.

The Uni-Mind seems relatively useless, however, as a space
drama unfolds which the big brain seems rather oblivious to.
Human astronauts arrive near the Celestial mother ship -- "big-

ger than Cape Canaveral," as they put it -- even as three Deviants pilot a missile to blow it up. A third factor is the not-so-forgotten "Forgotten One," a meddling hero punished by Zuras who now flies into space to destroy said bomb while all of the other Eternals are otherwise occupied. Once the Uni-Mind returns to earth and the Eternals have once more become individuals, their mission -- even the dire situation itself -- seems to have been forgotten. Instead Sersi and the others begin a trip to New York to party, and are interrupted by a robot of the Hulk that has come to life due to its irradiation by cosmic energy given off by the Uni-Mind. Although this was not the "real" Hulk, he was clearly placed on the cover to boost the disappointing sales of the series [*Eternals* 14 - 15].

The Eternals next battle the mind-controlling Dromedan, an ancient horror that was created by the Deviants and set free by the rampage of the pseudo-Hulk. Although belittled by sexist remarks from Ikaris and the others, it is Sersi who comes up with the plan to defeat the creature [16 - 17]. Then Ikaris' cousin, Druig, desiring personal glory, learns that an internecine quarrel among Celestials led to one of the gigantic beings being destroyed eons ago by a special weapon. Ikaris tries to stop Druig from using this hidden weapon to fire upon the Celestial in the polar region, but it nearly destroys the entire area until the Celestial itself saves the day with a wave of its mammoth hand. And with that, the 19th issue, the series was over except for the first and only annual, which featured Thena, The Reject and Karkas battling a Deviant who can bring nasties back from the past. It was one of the most exciting and best-drawn stories in the series.

The Eternals was an interesting comic that should have had a longer life. While one could easily see the similarities between Eternals and the New Gods -- Ikaris being Orion, Makarri being Lightray, the Uni-Mind being a larger manifestation of the Infinity Man -- *Eternals* still had enough differences to make it a viable series. Although Kirby's prose could be as stilted as ever, he created intriguing characters, such as the progressive if occasionally bitchy Sersi, and inter-relationships, such as the abortive romance between Thena and Kro. In fact, the characterization was a strong point which only needed better scripting to bring it to life, although at times it hit the mark such as when Thena observes: "Were the Deviants to exercise their nobler qualities, they would shed the 'self-hatred' that plagues them." Kirby's art was uneven, improving when Mike Royer took over the inking, and some of their work was quite good, the Kirby magic not having completely dissipated. The art in *Eternals* 15, however, was especially mediocre, almost as if Mike Royer did more of the penciling than Kirby did. As noted, the saga of the Eternals was continued in *Thor Annual* 7 and *Thor* 283 - 292, and the characters returned years later in subsequent, albeit brief *Eternals* series from Marvel, while Sersi became a member of the Avengers. Iron Man/Jim Rhodes encountered the Eternals, all of whom had been captured by their enemies the Deviants, in the worthless, badly-drawn and written *Iron Man Annual* 6.

CHAPTER FOURTEEN:
THE AVENGERS

At the beginning of the bronze age for the Avengers, Henry Pym was still in the Yellowjacket identity he had created at the end of the silver age; and Clint Barton, better known as Hawkeye, had given up his bow and arrows and used Pym's growth formula to become the giant-sized Goliath. He wore an outfit that showed off his chest and biceps, causing two young women to giggle that he'd be more likely to catch the sniffles than a "super-baddie" [*Avengers* 74]. Hawkeye was not pleased.

Avengers 72 presented "Did You Hear the One About Scorpio?" [Thomas/S.Buscema/Grainger] which took a villain who had bedeviled Nick Fury and made him only one member of an international crime cartel called Zodiac. A striking two-page panel introduced the full membership of the group, who would return to try and make life miserable for the Avengers in the future after being driven off, if not soundly defeated, herein. In this issue, Nick Fury has supposedly been killed, but he turns out to be Scorpio in disguise, which especially infuriates Aries, the ram-headed leader of Scorpio, who vows revenge as he and his partners make a fast exit after a brief battle. Rick Jones, still bonded with Captain Marvel as he was at the end of the silver age, makes a guest appearance, as does the good captain in a flashback.

The Sons of the Serpent, a racist group that first appeared in *Avengers* 32 and turned out to be tools of the Red Chinese, reappeared in *Avengers* 73 - 74. The players in this drama include the Black Panther, who decides to relocate to his adopted country, the U.S., as well as talk show hosts Montague Hale, who is black, and Dan Dunn, who is white and racist. After being attacked by members of the Serpents, Hale loses his program because the sponsors fear controversy, which is clearly not the case for Dunn's sponsors, as Hale appears on Dunn's uncanceled program, along with a lovely black singer named Monica Lynn. Lynn has no interest in causes, black or otherwise, until she, too, is attacked by the Serpents and rescued by the Panther. (Monica would later appear in the Black Panther's own series -- see chapter 17.) Then T'challa is captured by the Serpents and a lookalike is sent out to trash businesses who support the Serpents in the hopes to discredit both the Panther and the Avengers. In the improbable ending of the story the two leaders of the Serpents are revealed to be both Dunn and Hale, who were more interested in power for themselves than in anything else. (One presumes that the two men hoped to foment race riots and a black/white civil war and take over during the chaos, but this is never made clear.) The John Buscema/ Tom Palmer art for *Avengers* 74 was particularly good and Roy Thomas' scripts were well-meaning, if unsubtle.

Avengers 75 - 76 sent Yellowjacket and the Wasp off to do research; brought back Quicksilver and his sister, the Scarlet Witch; and introduced Arkon, a butch, vituperative ruler of another war-loving dimension who decides to get the light and energy they need to keep their world alive by destroying the earth with a nuclear blast; luckily the Avengers intervene before he can blitz the planet and then they save his world as well. In *Avengers* 77 Tony Stark tells the Avengers (who at this point did not know he was Iron Man) that he needs the back rent on the mansion, a small fortune, because a power play by Cornelius Van Lunt is threatening to topple Stark Industries, which is vital for US defense. The Avengers actually go to work for Van Lunt as demolitionists, and also battle the Split-Second Squad, a group of specialty robbers with no super-powers. The squad is run by a masked character named Kronus, who turns out to be a flunky of Van Lunt's who hopes to frame him for the death of the Avengers in an unsafe tunnel they are told to repair. The cover shows Van Lunt thundering about how "even the Avengers can be bought!" but the inside story is not quite that provocative.

Avengers 77 - 78 marked the debut of the Lethal Legion, whose leader is the Grim Reaper from *Avengers* 52, who blames the Avengers for the death of his brother, Simon Williams, the one-time villain, Wonder Man. The Lethal Legion consists of such foes from the past as the Man-Ape, the Living Laser, and three-time losers the Swordsman and Power Man. The exciting battle between both groups culminates in the Avengers being thrown into a giant beaker filled with poison gas, but at the last minute the Reaper saves them -- after discovering that his brother's brain patterns had been used to form the mind of the android Vision, one of the prisoners. However, the Vision had switched places with Power Man and the Avengers have little trouble in mopping up the rest of the startled Legionnaires, the Reaper among them. It was one of the best super-heroes vs super-baddies stories in Avengers history.

Corny Van Lunt reappeared in a two-part story in *Avengers* 80 - 81, which introduced the angry Native American hero Red Wolf (Will Talltrees), and his trained wolf partner, Lobo. Van Lunt covets the property owned by Red Wolf's father, and has the old man and his wife murdered in order to get it. The Avengers are torn between going after Van Lunt; taking on drug dealers who are threatening T'challa's students (he has become a teacher in an inner city school); or going after the reborn Zodiac -- so different members take on different assignments. While this would just seem to make common sense, some members think it might signify the end of the team. It was during this storyline that the seeds were sown for the eventual romance between the Scarlet Witch and the Vision, who shows great concern for Wanda when she's captured by Van Lunt, even as she realizes that the android is much warmer and more human than she realized. Meanwhile Zodiac reappeared in *Avengers* 81, making hostages out of the inhabitants of Manhattan when they cut off the island and demand a million in ransom, a scheme which the Avengers and Daredevil defeat, an exciting tale told, surprisingly, in just one issue. It is revealed that Van Lunt had been funding the crime cartel and using land adjacent to the Talltrees' to train the army that took over New York. (The members of Zodiac also caused problems in a three-part story in *Iron Man* 35 and 36 and *Daredevil* 73.)

Avengers 83 was one of a number of bronze age "women's lib" stories in which male writers used the movement as a story point without really examining the issue in any depth. Old-time foe The Enchantress has a mad-on for all men because her partner, the Executioner, has deserted her for another woman. She disguises herself as the Valkyrie, a supposed woman scientist who was abused by male associates, and uses spells to turn the Wasp, Madame Medusa, the Scarlet Witch and the Black Widow into the "Liberators." The women go to Rutland, Vermont where the male Avengers are appearing in the annual Halloween parade, and encounter the Masters of Evil (Klaw, Radioactive Man, the Melter and Whirlwind), who are there to kidnap a scientist with a miraculous new time-invention. After helping the boys get rid of the Masters, the ladies then turn on the fellows, until the Enchantress, who wants the machine for her own ends, decides to get rid of all of them with one explosive spell that the Scarlet Witch sends right back at her, freeing her and the other women from her control. Unfortunately, the Enchantress has not been atomized, but flung into the dimension of that barbarian Arkon [*Avengers* 84], whom she takes on as an ally. Another visitor to Arkon's magical world is the Black Knight, who comes to see if he could do something about the evil force that seems to be growing inside of his mystical sword.

In *Avengers* 85 - 86 some of the heroes accidentally wind up on a parallel earth where there are no Avengers, but rather a super-group of commie busters known as the Squadron Supreme. At first Hawkeye thinks they are the Squadron Sinister that he met in the silver age because they have some similar members, such as Nighthawk, but this is a different group altogether. Other members include American Eagle, Lady Lark, another Hawkeye, Tom Thumb and other Squadron Sinister clones such as Dr. Spectrum, Whizzer and Hyperion. The Avengers have had a vision of a super-nova destroying this earth because of a special rocket about to be launched, but the Squadron members think they are saboteurs and refuse to abort. The Avengers intervene anyway, saving the world from disaster. The squadron members are variations of the Justice League of America.

The first installment in *Avengers* 85 has some excellent battle scenes and very good art from John Buscema and Frank Giacoia. Unfortunately the follow-up in the following issue is a disappointment. Instead of a major battle between the Avengers and the Squadron Supreme (which would finally happen quite a few issues later), the main antagonist is a 10-year-old boy genius with an oversized, misshapen head nicknamed Brainchild, who designed the aforementioned rocket to destroy the Earth and himself due to his bitterness at being called a freak. Worse, the art by Sal Buscema and Jim Mooney was rushed and unattractive, Mooney's inks doing nothing for Sal B.'s pencil work. Sal took over from brother John for the next few issues.

Captain Marvel and the Kree-Skrull War

Avengers 89 began a lengthy story arc concerning Captain Marvel, the alien Kree race he belonged to, and their hated space-rivals the Skrulls. The captain and Rick Jones, who had maintained a special link since the end of the silver age, are finally separated (formerly Marvel could only appear on Earth when Rick switched places with him in the Negative Zone) and Marvel's life is saved by the Vision. Ronan and the Sentry, old foes of Marvel's and the Fantastic Four, come to earth to not only destroy Marvel but to plunge the world way back down on the evolutionary scale so that the human race can never present a threat to the Kree. The Vision and the Scarlet Witch nearly kiss during this story but the former holds back at the last instant, worried about the ramifications. The two are falling in love, bringing different reactions from their teammates and themselves over the next several issues.

Things really kicked into high gear in *Avengers* 92 when news of the Kree de-evolution plot, successfully thwarted by the Avengers, gets out, as well as the news that Captain Marvel is a Kree. The Avengers are suspected of harboring a dangerous alien (instead of turning him over to the Feds), and a commission headed by a Senator H. Warren Craddock is convened to investigate. The public turns against our heroes, and finally Iron Man, Thor, and Captain America appear to tell the others -- Scarlet Witch, Hawkeye, The Vision and Goliath -- that they are permanently disbanding the Avengers due to their irresponsible actions. Iron Man and his companions turn out to be imposters, Skrulls, in *Avengers* 93, a double-sized issue penciled by Neal Adams, and the four skrulls who originally appeared in *Fantastic Four* 2 and impersonated those heroes -- and who'd been turned into grazing cows by Mr. Fantastic -- finally made a re-appearance, as did the nasty Super-Skrull. *Avengers* 94 also featured an exciting "Fantastic Voyage"-type sequence wherein the Ant-Man enters the Vision's body to find out why he's collapsed and has to deal with the android's dangerous internal defense systems.

In the next few issues the Skrulls kidnap Marvel, Quicksilver, and the Witch to the Andromeda galaxy, where the Skrull emperor threatens them with death, and his pacifist daughter, Anelle, pleads for their lives; Craddock sics Mandroids (men inside metal suits) against the Avengers; Black Bolt's storyline from *Amazing Adventures* [see volume 2] is wrapped up [*Avengers* 95]; and the Avengers help the Inhumans defeat Maximus the Mad and his Kree allies in the Great Refuge. The defeated Kree steal away and take Rick Jones captive, where he winds up on the Kree homeworld and meets up with the usurper Ronan, who wants to turn the stripling into his "body slave," as well as the freakish Kree Supreme Intelligence, who has been manipulating many things behind the scenes.

The Avengers go to the Andromeda galaxy in a spaceship to rescue their comrades even as the Supreme Intelligence awakens hidden power (which is inside every human mind) in the brain of Rick Jones, who creates three-dimensional superheroes from the past to take on the Kree even as the Avengers and Captain Marvel handle the Skrulls. Craddock is revealed to be a Skrull who took the real senator's place, and in order to save Rick Jones' life, Captain Marvel must once again bond with the boy, an idea that does not sit well with him but with which he complies. Goliath realizes he has no more of Henry Pym's growth formula and will eventually go back to being Hawkeye with a new costume and no mask. The lengthy intergalactic saga ended with *Avengers* 97, and featured some very good art by both Neal Adams and John Buscema. Adams' work could be very dynamic but sometimes it was also rushed and sloppy.

"Five Dooms to Save Tomorrow" [*Avengers* 101] was an adaptation of a 1964 Harlan Ellison story refitted to feature the Avengers. A mild-mannered clerk named Leonard Tippett is told by the Watcher that he must use his awakening power to kill off five individuals whose offspring will set in motion a series of events that will lead to nuclear annihilation. Tippett hates the idea of killing anyone but is haunted by the fact that sparing these five might bring about the deaths of millions. The Avengers think there must be a better way to deal with things than killing innocent people, so do their best to stop Tippett in his mission. After defeating the man they learn that the true threat to the world is Tippett himself, and the Watcher prepares to take him away for the earth's ultimate safety. Now the Avengers are willing to fight for Tippett, but the man decides that he would rather make this One Great Sacrifice and be a hero, although his heroism will be unknown to anyone but the Avengers.

Avengers 102 - 104 presented an entertaining three-parter pitting the Avengers against the X-Men's robotic foes the Sentinels, and functioned as a sequel to certain stories in *The X-Men.* These issues were drawn by Rich Buckler and Joe Sinnott and were the last Avengers tales told by Roy Thomas. Steve Englehart took over as scripter with *Avengers* 105 while Thomas remained as editor. First Englehart did another sequel to the silver age Thomas-Adams run on *X-Men* by bringing back the evolved mutants from the Savage Land from *X-Men* 62 - 64 with mediocre results. Then he brought back the Space Phantom, not seen since *Avengers* 2, and teamed him up with the Grim Reaper [106 - 108]. The Space Phantom could plunge anyone he chose into limbo and take their place, becoming their exact duplicate and gaining their super-powers. Although these issues were fun, the plotting was awkward and the art by a variety of artists was unmemorable.

Avengers 109 introduced an interesting foe in the form of Champion, one of the world's wealthiest men, who is fully nine feet tall and has become master of virtually every form of skill and combat known to man. Bitter, arrogant, and sociopathic, he thinks nothing of a scheme to send California hurtling into the ocean, killing millions, merely because it suits his plans, but the Avengers mop up his operation pretty quickly and he came and went in just one issue. Champion never reappeared until the third volume of *The Avengers* many years later, perhaps because he was too reminiscent of the extraterrestrial Stranger in appearance. *Avengers* 110 - 111 briefly brought back the X-Men, who almost literally had nothing to say, because old foe Magneto had figured out how to mind-control his victims by manipulating the iron in the blood in their brains. He similarly mesmerized half of the Avengers before the other half figured out a way to waylay his mad, ambitious plan to use atomic blasts to make more mutants. By this time Hawkeye, back in his original uniform, had left the group, and Black Widow, who'd been dallying with guest-star Daredevil in his own comic for several issues, left DD to rejoin the Avengers -- for one issue only, featuring the Lion-God -- but not before he and Hawkeye fought over her in *Daredevil* 99.

Wanda and the Vision reveal their love for one another to the public in *Avengers* 113 and are beset by a group of completely illogical fanatics who fear androids will take over the world, and who turn themselves into human bombs in order to kill the Vision. When their plans fail, the would-be assassins all blow themselves up, in a tale that is a chilling reminder of the lengths hate-crazed, ignorant people will go to to get rid of the things that threaten them. In the following issue we see the faces of two people who were skulking about in the two previous issues, and who turn out to be the Swordsman, an old member/enemy of the group, and his lady friend, a new character, a mystical Asian lady with martial arts skills named [preying] Mantis, who was originally conceived as a prostitute.

The Swordsman has reformed and wants to rejoin the Avengers, but Cap strenuously objects, until the others remind him that Hawkeye and Scarlet Witch also had criminal records (but the Swordsman, without giving details, admits to killing people, which should certainly have prohibited his membership). Swordsman is allowed in on probation, and Mantis is invited to accompany him, leading her to hug and kiss all of the male members, leaving lipstick prints on Thor, Cap and the Vision. She and Swordsman help the Avengers defeat a second attack by the Lion-God [*Avengers* 114].

At the end of *Avengers* 115 -- a highly forgettable issue in which our heroes tackle some under-earth troglodytes -- Loki and Dormammu forge an unholy alliance. The latter wants to secure a device called the Evil Eye (first seen in *Fantastic Four* during the silver age) which has been blown into six parts and scattered around the globe. Dormammu hopes to expand his own dimension so that it will envelop the earth, and he can then sidestep his vow never to invade the home world of Dr. Strange. He decides to enlist the members of the Defenders to get the eye for him, and thus begins the Avengers-Defenders War [see volume two]. The Avengers next big battle was a rematch with Zodiac in *Avengers* 120 - 122. The group is now led by Taurus, the bull, whose new scheme is to cause the deaths of every Gemini in Manhattan and then, having proven their power, make demands.

Zodiac

So confident are the members of Zodiac that they attack the Avengers in their own mansion with a new weapon, but leave them alive and defeated. The Avengers manage to destroy the weapon that would doom all the Geminis, but the members of Zodiac escape. The new Aries challenges Taurus' leadership, but when the two literally butt heads, the latter comes up the winner. Aries gathers his allies together and asks Cornelius Van Lunt, who finances the group, for extra money for a coup, but Van Lunt turns out to be Taurus and catches both the conspirators and the Avengers in a trap, a warehouse that is actually a rocket and blasts off into space with the combatants inside. Heroes and villains try to work together to escape the space-trap, but an interesting complication comes in the form of Thor's hammer, which he throws through a force field at the side of the "barn" only to discover that now it can't make its way back to him; he goes into hiding in the shadows as he changes back to a powerless Don Blake. Then with an assist from Wanda's hex power, Iron Man is able to escape the field and retrieve the weightless hammer, but as he uses his thrusters to push the rocket back towards earth, the hammer becomes heavy again -- it traps him as the barn begins to burn up in the atmosphere, dooming everyone inside. An unlikely savior comes in the form of Libra, who usually maintains a balance, but recues the group because he wrongly believes that Mantis is among them -- she is his daughter.

Libra claims Mantis is the daughter of a Vietnamese woman that he married, but Mantis has no memory of the childhood he describes, when she was supposedly taught special abilities by monks. Complicating matters is the fact that both Wanda and Swordsman sense a growing attraction or attachment between Mantis and the Vision, who mightily admires the Asian woman's strength of mind. The Vision has been experiencing moments when he freezes up and is afraid he is malfunctioning, while Wanda of late has been expressing hatred of ordinary humans. Wanda discovers that her brother Pietro still wants nothing to do with her because of her relationship with the android Vision, even at his wedding to Crystal of the Inhumans, which takes place at the Great Refuge. Before the ceremony can begin, Omega -- who'd attacked the Inhumans before -- reappears but turns out to be the mad robot Ultron-7, not seen since the silver age; Maximus had discovered his decapitated cranium and attached it to Omega's head. Working with the Fantastic Four, the Avengers tackle Ultron, but he is ultimately defeated by a burst of power from little Franklin Richards, an action which happily awakens him from his coma [*Avengers* 127 and *Fantastic Four* 150]. Wanda learns that her and Pietro's father is the golden age super-speedster the Whizzer of the All-Winners Squad in *Giant-Size Avengers* 1, although this later turns out to be untrue.

More mysteries about Mantis are revealed when Kang shows up in *Avengers* 129 and insists that either she, the Scarlet Witch, or aged Agatha Harkness, who is counseling Wanda in the art of witchcraft, must be a "Celestial Madonna," who will become his bride and give birth to an all-powerful heir. Kang kidnaps the ladies as well as three Avengers and uses their bodies to power some destructive robots. Swordsman and the returning Hawkeye are all that remain to stop Kang's plan, but they have an unexpected ally - Pharoah Rama-Tut, who is actually Kang in another guise. This older and wiser version of Kang (who first became Rama-Tut in an earlier period) has lived enough years to rue his empty days of conquest and vows to stop his younger self from killing the Madonna -- Mantis. Locked in battle Kang and Rama-Tut disappear after Swordsman dies protecting the formerly faithless but now repentant Mantis from being killed by Kang [*Giant-Size Avengers* 2].

In *Avengers* 130 the Avengers accompany Mantis to Saigon where she puts Swordsman's body to rest and seeks answers about her past. They encounter Titanium Man, Crimson Dynamo, and the Radioactive Man, now calling themselves the

Titanic Three and who are in charge of this communist territory, and have a brief skirmish. In the following issue Kang and Rama-Tut are rescued from time limbo by Immortus, who once fought the Avengers back in the silver age. After imprisoning Rama, Kang and Immortus join forces to attack the Avengers by summoning up a "Legion of the Unliving" consisting of Wonder Man, the original Human Torch, The Ghost, The Frankenstein Monster, Midnight, and even Baron Zemo. During their battle in the catacombs below Immortus' palace, it is discovered that the Vision's body is the same as that of the Human Torch, and Immortus reveals that he is yet another manifestation of Kang, who betrayed him, leading him to help the Avengers, although he claims that this was his plan all along [*Giant-Size Avengers* 3].

Avengers 133 - 135 (and *Giant-Size Avengers* 4) began a long investigation into the origins of both the Vision and Mantis. Vision's story was a relatively simple one, as we learn that Ultron stole the dormant robotic form of the golden age Human Torch to create the Vision. Mantis' origin, however, is a convoluted if interesting tale that encompasses such elements as the beginnings of the Kree-Skrull War, the secret behind the Watcher's ruined blue city on the moon, a sentient plant race called the Cotati who share a world with the early Kree, and such characters as the Swordsman's resuscitated corpse, Dormammu and his sister Umar, and even the Space Phantom. Bolstered by some good if verbose dialogue, Steve Englehart's script juggles, combines, and expands upon a lot of interesting plot threads from the past, although it has an especially bizarre conclusion. Wanda and the Vision finally exchange vows, and Mantis marries a tree -- one of the aforementioned Cotati -- so that they can create a race that will boast the best qualities of both human and plant life. Mantis will "bond" with the Swordsman's body (apparently infused with the spirit of the Cotati or something like that) to create offspring, and the two -- or three, if you count the tree -- soar into the heavens (as cosmic characters always do in Marvel comics) after they change into energy. Mercifully, perhaps, Mantis and her tree husband were not seen again for many, many years.

Moondragon and the Beast (fresh from his exploits in *Amazing Adventures*) join the group in *Avengers* 137, and Yellowjacket and the Wasp return, just as the Stranger attacks, only to turn out to be the Toad from the Brotherhood of Evil Mutants using the former's weaponry. The Wasp is injured during the fight and while she's hospitalized Jan and Hank's long-time foe, Whirlwind (who began life as the Human Top in silver age issues of *Tales to Astonish*), and who unbeknownst to the couple was once their chauffeur, makes an attempt upon her life and on Yellowjacket's which fails; he is finally captured [139]. Even though he is obviously upset over the fact that Jan's injuries might be fatal, Pym's anger and hysteria give hints of future developments in his neurotic life. When he also falls into a coma and grows to 150 feet, the Beast concocts a formula which the intangible Vision delivers to Pym's heart, the reverse of an earlier situation when Pym went into the Vision's body at ant-size to heal him [94].

Squadron Supreme

New penciler George Perez took over from George Tuska with *Avengers* 141. This also began a long storyline involving the Squadron Supreme from another dimension, as first seen in *Avengers* 85-86. Some of the Squadron have traveled to our earth to work for the corrupt Roxxon corporation, whose boss, Hugh Jones, has been corrupted himself by the serpent crown. As several Avengers deal with the Squadron, others travel back to 1873 to find the missing Hawkeye, who's been caught in a trap by Kang; there they encounter several of Marvel's popular Western heroes such as Two-Gun Kid and Rawhide Kid. Kang is destroyed, meaning that his future selves such as Rama-Tut and Immortus fade out of existence.

In another development, Patsy Walker, who'd appeared in *Amazing Adventures* with Hank McCoy, shows up out of the blue insisting he keep his promise to turn her into a superheroine. She goes along when the Avengers confront the Roxxon group, including her ex-husband Colonel Baxter, and in a slightly ridiculous development they come across the costume of the Cat in a storage area inside the building. Patsy puts on the uniform and is figuratively transformed into the Hellcat, even though she hasn't one whit of experience as a costumed fighter; the uniform itself seems to give her Olympic athlete-like abilities. As the Squadron Supreme advances on the group, the Roxxon chief sends them all hurtling back to the Squadron's dimension [*Avengers* 144].

The Squadron storyline was temporarily interrupted by an entertaining two-part fill-in [*Avengers* 145- 146] written by Tony Isabella and drawn by Don Heck and John Tartaglione. In this the masked Assassin is hired for one billion dollars to kill the Avengers (the clients are a group of their unnamed enemies) and uses a special weapon to put Captain America in a coma. As the other Avengers wait at the hospital and the Beast uses a special concoction to dissipate the radioactivity in Cap's system, a nurse gives them some doctored coffee. Still the Avengers are able to prevent the Assassin's cohorts from murdering them, and the Assassin, revealed to be the nurse, is gunned down by her own men, who don't recognize her.

The Squadron storyline resumed with *Avengers* 147, wherein it develops that the influence of the Serpent Crown has spread throughout their earth, even affecting President Nelson Rockefeller, who wears it on his head. After different teams of Avengers battle various groupings of Squadron members a la the Justice League of America, the Beast masquerades as the president and manages to awaken the Squadron's eyes to how their country is really being run by unseen corporate men and various conglomerates (in a dig at the situation in the U.S.) due to the insidious serpent crown. This leads to big changes in that Other World. Back in their own world, the Avengers wrap up Hugh Jones, Colonel Baxter, and Roxxon, who are defeated despite their super-weapon, which turns out to be a beefed up Sub-Mariner opponent named Orka.

Moondragon so annoys Thor with her constant remarks

about how she and he are gods and how Thor is vastly superior to the other Avengers, that when Orka knocks her unconscious Thor dreads the moment when she wakes up and begins her "overbearing" chatter again. But during his battle with Orka he realizes that on Midgard he does tend to hold back from using his full God-like power so he doesn't slaughter his opponents, who tend to be more powerful on Asgard. This led to the somewhat unlikely development of Thor quitting the Avengers because he was a "big fish in a small pond" who had stayed with the group, as he put it, only due to "vanity." Although George Perez hadn't quite developed into the artist he would become on such series as *New Teen Titans*, there was a certain something about his work from the first, even though its effectiveness at this point depended in large part on the inker: Vince Colletta seemed to work best.

The Wasp and Yellowjacket officially rejoined the team in *Avengers* 151, along with the Beast, while Moondragon took Hellcat off for some much needed training. Then who should show up but the supposedly dead Wonder Man, who has apparently been resuscitated as a "zuvembie" (zombie) by a mysterious dark god who employs a character called the Black Talon [152], but all the facts behind Wonder Man's resurrection from the dead would not be revealed for some time. New writer Gerry Conway brought in such reliable characters as Sub-Mariner and Dr. Doom, but also included the never-interesting undersea despot Attuma. Perez' pencils continued to gain dynamism although Pablo Marcos may not have been the best inking choice. (*Marvel Premiere* 55 presented a solo story of Wonder Man returning to the factory he once owned and dealing with criminals who have taken it over, including a mysterious female boss who stays in the shadows; she was apparently Iron man foe/lover Madame Masque. The nice art was by Ron Wilson and Joe Sinnott, and the story and script by Bob Layton and David Michelinie.)

Jim Shooter threw Graviton, a scientist who accidentally acquired control over gravity, against the Avengers in *Avengers*

158 - 159, then gave Hank Pym another nervous breakdown -- he forgot everything that had occurred since his early days as Ant-Man. This was engineered by Ultron, who wanted Hank as an ally so he would create a bride for him, which Pym does, using Jan's brain patterns and some of her life force [160 - 161]. The she-robot returns in *Avengers* 170 - 171 where she leads the heroes to Ultron's base inside a convent, and turns against her master; she was eventually christened Jocasta. We finally learn that Wonder Man was not dead, but dormant, all those years since being killed by Zemo, and has been reborn as a kind of energy creature out of a figurative cocoon.

The souped-up Lethal Legion -- Whirlwind, Power Man, and Living Laser -- attack in the same issue under the command of early foe Count Nefaria, who has stolen energy from the afore-mentioned trio to give himself massive power a thousand times greater or more. He attacks and easily bests the Avengers, and is even able to successfully square off with Thor, until the Vision saves the day by becoming diamond-hard and simply dropping on Nefaria from a great height [*Avengers* 164 - 166]. This three-parter was the best story to appear in the comic in a long time thanks to Shooter's scripting and the pencils of guest-artist John Byrne. An interesting sequence has the Scarlet Witch registering her annoyance at how Thor shows up and rescues everyone at the last minute when *she* is the one Nefaria should fear -- a little bit of mutant hubris -- since Thor doesn't even know what magic is being used to snatch him from Asgard to Earth whenever he is needed.

Korvac

Avengers 167 began a lengthy, memorable, and major storyline guest-starring the Guardians of the Galaxy, who have come back in time in pursuit of a foe named Korvac (who first appeared in different form in *The Defenders*). The Guardians fear that Korvac traveled to the 20th century to kill their leader, Vance Astro, who was born in that time period (before being placed in suspended animation for a thousand years and waking up to form the Guardians). The group from the future

asks the Avengers for help guarding the life of young Astro as
they suspect Korvac will try and kill him to prevent their formation. Starhawk, the most mysterious of the guardians, confronts a man named Michael, whom he deems "the Enemy," in
his home in Forest Hills, but is destroyed by Michael, who is so
powerful that he instantly recreates Starhawk but deletes his
ability to remember or even perceive his "Enemy."

In the meantime Henry Peter Gyrich, special agent of the Na-
tional Security Council, easily breaks into Avengers HQ to illus-
trate their blatant security breaches, leading him to withdraw
their priority status with the government [*Avengers* 168], while
Cap and Iron Man come to blows when the former accuses the
latter of being a poor leader, allowing his job for Stark Industries to take precedent over his duties as Avengers chairman
(this prefigures their antagonism decades later during the
"Civil War"). In a very weird development women find the
Beast sexy despite his animal-like appearance, reminding one
of how the ladies found Gorilla Grodd irresistible in a silver age
issue of *The Flash* (that at least was caused by undue influence).
In a more serious turn of events numerous heroes from Two-
Gun Kid to Quicksilver to Captain America simply began blink-
ing out of existence.

The Avengers call in virtually all of their members to try to
figure out why they are disappearing one by one, which has the
effect of making almost all of the rest of them vanish in rapid
spurts. Tracing energy readings to a spacecraft they discover
that their old foe the Collector is behind the snatchings (as well
as Thor's sudden appearances), only the Collector claims he
was merely trying to get them out of the reach of the Enemy,
who wants to reimagine the universe. The Collector sent his
daughter, Carina, to become Michael's lover so that she could
spy on him, but she fell in love with him instead. Just as the
Collector is about to say who Michael really is, he is obliterated
by him in an instant [*Avengers* 173 - 174]. Michael is revealed to
be Korvac, the very foe the Guardians of the Galaxy are on the
hunt for, who was transformed into a god-like being when he

tapped into the data banks of Galactus and was overloaded with power. He no longer has thoughts of revenge but wishes to make, in his opinion, compassionate adjustments to reality without other cosmic beings being the wiser.

The more intuitive, psychic members of the Avengers compile what information they've acquired, and realize that the person they're after is in Forest Hills. Since they can no longer use Quinjets, thanks to Gyrich, and not all of them can fly, they commandeer a city bus [!] and take it out to Queens, where they pay a call on Michael. The latter is able to fool the heroes into thinking nothing is wrong until Starhawk cries out in anger that there's no one there - the Avengers are talking to empty space. Since Starhawk can no longer perceive Korak/Michael, the Avengers realize they've got the right guy after all - and all Hell breaks loose.

Although Michael professes to have a benevolent purpose in wanting to, in essence, take over the universe, his first action is to attack the heroes for what sounds like simple revenge. He knows that such cosmic deities as Odin, Mephistofeles, and Eternity will team up to defeat him; referring to the Avengers as the vanguard of their opposition, he begins slaughtering them. However, when in his psychic distress he reaches out for Carina, her mind is confused and conflicted -- this causes Michael to lose the will to live and he dies. Carina herself lashes out at the remaining heroes with her own power, but also commits suicide by causing the energy of Thor's hammer to blast her. Moondragon sheds tears because she bonded with Michael's mind and sensed he was truly good and noble, but there's absolutely no reason to think that the world recreated by Michael would have been any better than the one before it. And nutty, pretentious Moondragon was not nearly as smart as she thinks she is [*Avengers* 176 - 177]. In any case she purges the memory of her outburst from the other heroes who are brought back to life by Michael just before his own demise.

This was followed by a weird, forgettable story showcasing the Beast, and a two-parter [Tom DeFalco/Jim Mooney] in which the Avengers tangle with a character named the Stinger, who wants to capture them and sell them to the highest bidder. This story also includes a half-deranged mutant named Bloodhawk, who sacrifices his life aiding the heroes against the Stinger after first battling them, as well as a gargantuan rock idol that comes to life. Jim Shooter having been made Marvel's editor-in-chief, a new creative team was assembled consisting of David Michelinie and John Byrne. Their first order of business was to bring back Gyrich to enforce policies required by the government in order for the Avengers to regain their priority status. There could be a core group of seven members only, with others called in when needed.

Because there must be minority members, Hawkeye discovers that he's out of the roster in favor of the Falcon, who isn't even a member but who is African-American. The Falcon isn't thrilled to be the token black on the team, although Ms. Marvel eagerly jumps into the fray when the Scarlet Witch goes off with her brother to explore their parentage. They learn that Bob Frank/Whizzer is not their real father, that they were raised by an old gypsy man, but still don't know the identity of their biological father, although enough clues were given to make most readers know who he was [*Avengers* 185 - 187].

There was a run of fair-to middling stories, such as a battle with the Absorbing Man, the aforementioned Wundagore trilogy which guest-stars a loser magician named Modred, and a dull tale featuring elemental monsters like something out of *Metal Men*. Although he was no longer a regular member, Hawkeye, who nonetheless seemed to appear in every issue, was headlined in an entertaining story in *Avengers* 189 wherein he tangles with Ms. Marvel's alien foe Death-Bird while he is guarding a warehouse she attempts to loot. *Avengers* 191 - 192 featured an excellent two-parter in which a Federal hearing is convened by Gyrich to determine once and for all if the Avengers merit priority status from the government, during which a bizarre rock-like monster stalks through the city. The heroes leave the hearing to tackle this monstrosity, only to discover that the creature is actually Thor's old foe, the Grey Gargoyle, covered up inside a lot of space debris. He initially gives them a tough time, turning many members into stone statues, until teamwork finishes him off. John Byrne seemed to have settled into the role of Avengers penciller, offering his best art job to date under the finishes of Dan Green. Unfortunately, this was Byrne's last Avengers issue for a long time.

Avengers 195 - 197 featured a three-part story in which the Avengers discover that a mental institution is a cover up for a training camp for the henchmen used by various super-villains. The head of this operation is a devilish masked man named Taskmaster whose "photographic reflexes" enable him to instantly duplicate the athletic and unusual actions of anyone, including super-heroes. Yellowjacket and the new Ant-Man (Scott Lang) work together for the first time to infiltrate this institution. (Hawkeye and Ant-Man/Scott Lang also teamed up against Taskmaster in *Avengers* 223.) Jocasta is nominated for Avengers membership due to her helpful actions in this adventure. Like Byrne before him, George Perez had also grown as an artist and offered some superlative pencils for these issues, especially for *Avengers* 197, which was embellished by Jack Abel. Perez' work on subsequent issues, however, was wildly uneven, often looking rushed and uninspired. That was not the case with Perez' work on the memorable *Avengers Annual* 8, well-scripted by Roger Slifer, which pitted the heroes against the members of the Squadron Sinister and guest-starred Thundra, who had a too-brief battle with Ms. Marvel.

The Mortification of Ms. Marvel

Although she was a character who certainly had untapped potential, Ms. Marvel was pretty much treated like the stereotype of a feminist -- humorless, always jumping to conclusions where men were concerned, and so on -- since joining the Avengers. When she discovers that she is pregnant even though there couldn't possibly be a father, none of her teammates seem to understand how violated she feels [*Avengers* 198]. Overnight she goes from being three months to six months pregnant and finally gives birth in the double-sized *Avengers* 200. The child, who calls himself Marcus, grows both physically and intellectually at an astounding rate until he is full-grown and rather handsome.

Marcus turns out to be the son of Immortus, who knew that his living on earth instead of in limbo (to end his loneliness after his father's death) would cause havoc with the time stream, so Marcus contrives to have Carol Danvers fall in love with him ("with a subtle assist from my father's machines") and pours his essence into her so that she can "give birth" to him on earth. He begins to build a machine to stop the alarming time displacements that are happening around Avengers mansion due to his presence -- a tyrannosaur appears in their backyard, for instance -- but the heroes think the machine is the cause of the problem and destroy it. Now Marcus has no choice but to go back to limbo and his lonely life, except that Ms. Marvel decides to go with him. Iron Man raises a slight objection, but even though Marcus mentions that "subtle assist" in making Carol love him they do nothing to prevent her departure (essentially the woman was kidnaped and raped). It was almost as if David Michelinie and his co-plotters (including Jim Shooter and Perez) had figured that all the feisty feminist needed was a good lay and a good man and she could live happily ever after. Taken on its own fantasy terms -- a baby that develops to adulthood in a couple of days, and so on -- the story wasn't a bad one, but it certainly was a nasty, insensitive joke as far as Ms. Marvel was concerned; it would have repercussions.

It was left to Christopher Claremont to give Ms. Marvel back her dignity in a sequel to *Avengers* 200. In the excellent *Avengers Annual* 10 (drawn by Michael Golden and Armando Gil) the heroes learn that Carol has been out of limbo and living in San Francisco for months after she is attacked by Rogue and virtually left for dead. Professor X helps her get her memories back as the Avengers deal with Rogue, who wants to siphon off their abilities to help Mystique break the other members of the Brotherhood of Evil Mutants (Blob, Pyro, Avalanche, and Destiny) out of Riker's Island. A major battle develops between the two groups, with the Avengers barely winning.

At the end they go to see Carol in Westchester and she tells them that Marcus died shortly after arriving in limbo due to miscalculations he'd made; she was able to escape limbo using Immortus' machines. She never contacted them because of her hatred and sense of betrayal. "There I was, pregnant by an unknown source..." she tells the assemblage. "Confused, terrified, shaken to the core of my being, as a hero, a person, a woman. I turned to you for help and I got jokes ... your concerns were for the baby, not for how it came to be -- nor of the cost to me of that conception. You took everything Marcus said at face value. You didn't question, you didn't doubt. You simply let me go with a smile and a wave and a bouncy bon voyage. That was your mistake, for which I paid the price."

After this the monthly series entered a period of stagnation. There were acceptable stories with Ultron and the Yellow Claw (who wants to sterilize the world), but other issues were not as memorable. Gene Colan was again put on pencils as he had been at the very end of the silver age, but his style was never suitable for *The Avengers*. *Avengers* 209 reintroduced Beast's old-time girlfriend, Vera, from silver age issues of *The X-Men* and *Amazing Adventures*. Hank and Vera have reconnected and fallen in love just when a Skrull poisons her and tells Hank he'll bring her back to life if he turns over certain powerful objects to him. But Hank realizes the tremendous devastation and loss of life that may occur, so in anguish he destroys the objects, dooming Vera. At the end Reed Richards discovers that Vera is only in suspended animation, that there's still hope, but it might be some time before Vera can be brought back to life, which happens in later issues of *Dr. Strange* and *The Defenders*.

Jim Shooter returned as scripter for *Avengers* 211 and the "old order changeth" again. Captain America decides to trim the group to six members for greater efficiency but before he can do so former member Moondragon, acting more like her "Madame Macabre" self of old, uses her mind-control powers to gather all of the members old and new and make the choices herself. She eventually decides to leave, as do the Beast, the Vision, Scarlet Witch, and Wonder Man. The new line-up consists of Cap, Iron Man, Thor, Yellowjacket, the Wasp, and ... Tigra. Lonely Jocasta was supposed to be a reserve member, but thinking she's excluded she goes off on her own. [She was not seen again until *Marvel Two-In-One* 92 - 93, in which she seeks help from the FF when Ultron begins messing with her cybernetic systems and she makes the ultimate sacrifice to stop him. There was a funeral for her in *Avengers* 231.] Moondragon returned in 219 - 220 wherein she takes over an entire planet for "its own good," sleeps with Thor after manipulating his mind, kills her father Drax when he attacks her, and gets a good sock in the jaw from the Wasp, after which she is taken to Odin for final judgment.

Henry Pym

Henry Pym rejoins the team because his research work has gone nowhere, and frustration has taken its toll. He resents his wife Jan's success as a hero as well as her wealth, and takes it out on her in front of the others. In *Avengers* 212 Pym fires on a grieving, angry woman known as the Elf-Queen even though she had ceased her attack on the heroes. In the following issue a court-martial is convened (which seems a mite drastic) and Tigra thinks that Pym "gives me the creeps." (Many years later they became lovers in Avengers Academy after Jan's death.) Hank goes so far as to give his wife a black eye. At the court-martial Captain America acts as prosecutor, even though he remembers an incident in his own past that could have turned into a disaster, but, oddly, no one is appointed to defend Hank. Instead Hank blames Cap for everything in an almost manic way, then has a robot he built attack the group so he can play hero. Instead the Wasp has to shut down the robot when Pym fails to stop it, furthering Hank's humiliation. Don Blake tells

Tony Stark that Hank's actions are due to a nervous breakdown caused by extreme stress. Whatever the case, Jan has had enough and decides to get a divorce [213 - 214].

Tigra seemed like a foolish and unnecessary addition to the ranks of the group until *Avengers* 215 - 216, a harrowing tale wherein the heroes and the world are at the mercy of the child-like, half-insane Owen Reece, the Miracle Man who'd first battled the Fantastic Four (who briefly appear as guest-stars although Silver Surfer has a bigger role). Tigra, who underneath her flippant attitude (like a lower-case Wasp) is plagued with doubts as to her worthiness as a hero, is an important part of the story. Thinking her companions have been killed by Reece, Tigra determines to slay him but can't bring herself to kill him, something which Iron Man later feels is necessary. But instead of slaying him, Tigra is able to use logic and understanding to make Reece give himself up (although the thought of him still existing with all that power is frightening). Still, Tigra resigns from the group just as she's getting interesting. In this story Iron Man and Thor reveal their secret identities to the other members for the first time.

Meanwhile Hank has more problems in *Avengers* 217, in which his old adversary Egghead, who caused his niece Trish Starr to lose an arm in an issue of *The Defenders*, tells him that he wants to make amends. He gives Hank an artificial arm for Trish to wear. Finding no booby traps, Hank attaches the arm, only to be told by Egghead that it will blow up if he doesn't help commit a robbery. Hank is forced to fight Jan and his former comrades to prevent Trish's death, but when he is defeated, Egghead turns off the signals controlling the arm, and it develops that there was never a bomb inside; thanks to her psychotic uncle, Trish has no memory of his involvement. Hank is arrested and jailed.

Avengers 218 featured an unusual story scripted by J. M. De-Matteis and co-plotted with Jim Shooter. In this a small boy who comes to Avengers mansion insists that he isn't actually a child and desperately needs their help. To prove what he's saying he shoots himself in the head and dies, his body disintegrating until it reforms into a fetus and then into the boy again. The "child" has lived over and over again down through the centuries, always reconstituting after death, and he is sick and tired of living. Because of a recent incident he now remembers all of his past lives and all of the pain he has endured. He wants the Avengers to help him die but Thor argues that immortality is a blessing; the child replies that he is not a God and none of his past lives were especially wonderful or god-like. The boy contrives to enter a space shuttle and fly into the sun, but instead of destroying him it only turns him into a huge, deadly fire being (similar to Surtur) who is a menace to the entire planet. The Avengers manage to kill him -- but again he comes back as the boy. This time, however, he has no memory of his past lives, and can start anew with a fresh slate. But Iron Man wonders if the boy is only faking his amnesia ... Perhaps the strangest sequence has two hobos who resemble Laurel and Hardy seeking money, food and perhaps sexual favors from the boy in a railway car he is hitching a ride in.

Hawkeye returned to the team and She-Hulk [see volume 2] joined in *Avengers* 221. In the following issue Egghead resurfaces with a new Masters of Evil consisting of Whirlwind, who was in prison with Pym, Moonstone, the Scorpion, and Namor's foe, Tiger Shark. By now Jan had become the chairperson of the Avengers, part of her maturation process, although writer Jim Shooter still had her saying things like "icky" and "oh pooh!" She and Anthony Stark have an affair, but she calls it quits when she learns he is also Iron Man, a friend of Hank's, in an especially well-written story by Alan Zelenetz in *Avengers* 224. In *Avengers* 228 - 230 Egghead reassembles his Masters of Evil and adds members Shocker, Radioactive Man, and the Beetle. They break into the courtroom where Hank is on trial and kidnap him, making it seem as if it was something he had planned all along. During the battle the Radioactive Man sucks away the gamma energy that created She-Hulk and leaves her a quivering and helpless Jennifer Walter, until

Hawkeye goads and teases her into converting back into her big green and powerful self. In Egghead's suburban HQ he forces Hank to work on a project for him, but Pym fools him by building a weapon that he uses against the Masters of Evil. Egghead is killed during the battle. The charges against Hank are dropped, it is suggested he could be a reserve Avenger, but Pym wants no part of super-hero-ing. Henry and Jan go their separate ways and in the moving conclusion a stalwart Jan finally breaks down into tears.

The Avenger's next and newest member, the female Captain Marvel, a black woman named Monica Rambeau from New Orleans, first appeared in *Amazing Spider-Man Annual* 16, which was drawn very nicely by both John Romita Sr. and Jr.. Monica gained her powers accidentally by helping an elderly professor stop a Roxxon Oil scientist who wants to use a destructive new device to wipe out a city as a test. The device explodes, and Monica is imbued with energy powers that can transform her, and have her zipping around at super-sonic speed, as light waves, x-rays, micro waves, and the like. Unfortunately, if she can't control the energy build-up of extradimensional forces in her body she could explode like a megaton bomb. Spider-Man mistakes her for a villain, but Iron Man is able to siphon off her excess energy. She joined the Avengers in 227 about the time that Mark Gruenwald took over as editor and Roger Stern, who wrote the Spider-Man annual, came on board as scripter. Bob Hall and Dan Green, whose artwork had never been very inspired, were replaced by Al Milgrom and Joe Sinnott and there was a distinct and immediate improvement.

Thanos' brother, Eros, codenamed Starfox, comes to earth looking for adventure and becomes a member-in-training of the Avengers, while Iron Man quits because Tony Stark has developed a drinking problem and his replacement as the armored bodyguard is too inexperienced. She-Hulk and the rather silly-looking Eros have the bad taste to sleep together in *Avengers* 234. Nova foe Blackout, Moonstone, Electro and the Rhino almost cause a meltdown at Project Pegasus in *Avengers*

237, the same issue in which Spider-Man is offered a spot as a Avenger-in-training (he wants the $1000 a week stipend) but is nixed by the government because they know so little about him. Spidey muses that they rejected him but accepted an alien, Starfox! This issue also had a particularly good art job by Milgrom and Sinnott.

The bronze age of The Avengers ended with the Vision, who'd been damaged, restored by technology from Eros' home world and developing new powers that make his teammates wonder if he's getting an ego problem. Eros was a dipstick, She-Hulk a bully, and some of the members of the group were completely unable to see things from the p.o.v. of ordinary people without super-powers, although this aspect of their characters was not explored or even alluded to in the scripts. In other words, the often arrogant Avengers were not a completely likable bunch of people, but the series was quite entertaining in spite of it.

CHAPTER FIFTEEN:
THE FLASH

As the Scarlet Speedster entered the bronze age, his Rogue's Gallery of super-powered adversaries were nowhere to be seen for several issues. Instead the comic offered human interest stories in which the Flash played a pivotal role and Barry Allen's character was highlighted a little more than usual: he "marries" a woman possessed by the spirit of a bride who disappeared on her wedding day in order to exorcise her; recues a dog that saved his life but might be put to death for allegedly killing his master; and overcomes his childhood fear of roller coasters to save everyone's life when the track busts a rail. In *The Flash* 197 Barry joins an amateur acting society, but when everyone calls in sick on opening night due to the flu, he enacts every single part in the play at super-speed, and even has everyone show up on stage for a curtain call at the same time. In the same issue he zooms to a dying planet by racing across the beam of light from a telescope, then after saving the planet jumps back into the light beam by running across some grains of sand he's thrown into the air. The stories were contributed by such writers as Robert Kanigher and Mike Friedrich while Gil Kane contributed some impressive artwork.

A dastardly villain finally reared her head in *Flash* 200, which featured the one and only appearance in the series of sexy Asian scientist, Dr. Lu. Dr. Lu has brain-washed Flash so that he thinks she's Iris, and when she asks him to get her hair spray is actually sending him a signal to assassinate the U.S. president with a laser pistol. Dr. Lu's plan fails, however, because she gives Flash a good-bye kiss, but her lipstick tastes of spice whereas Iris' has a honey flavor. Before Flash can doom the president, it hits him that something's wrong and he comes out of his trance. The new Flash penciller beginning with this issue was Irv Novick, with Murphy Anderson on inks. This began a long association for Novick with the "Modern Mercury."

In *Flash* 203 Iris Allen learns that she was actually born one thousand years in the future, and that the absent-minded Professor West is not her real father. During a period of disaster in the future, Iris' parents shot her back in time (in an incident similar to the origin of Superman) so that she would survive a nuclear attack on the city where she was born. Now she goes back to the future and discovers that twenty-five years have passed since her "expulsion," and her real parents are still alive. Flash follows and takes care of the bad guys in the future and returns to his own time with his wife. The otherwise forgettable story by Robert Kanigher would have many repercussions years later. More interesting was Kanigher's tale in *Flash* 206 in which two people killed in accidents are brought back to life by haughty aliens after their loved ones -- a husband in one case, and a mother in another -- agree to give up their own lives in return after 24 hours, during which they are impervious to death or injury. Flash's intervention insures a happy ending, but the story was not developed as well as it could have been, and at least one reader noted the over-use of sci fi cliches.

Rogues Gallery

In trying to be more relevant or "earthbound" as in *Green Lantern* of the early seventies, *The Flash* suffered because his stories and art weren't intense or graphic like, say, in the two-part heroin storyline in GL (see volume two). Long-time readers clamored for a return of Flash's costumed foes; the Mirror Master had appeared in an Elongated Man back-up in *Flash* 206 but otherwise the Rogue's Gallery was tragically absent.

Finally in *Flash* 209 new scripter Cary Bates, beginning a very long run on the title, hit one out of the ballpark and came up with the first truly memorable bronze-age issue of the series.

In "Beyond the Speed of Life" the Trickster and Captain Boomerang, unknowingly manipulated by super-ape Gorilla Grodd, who is smarter than both of them, think they have finally finished off the Flash. They don't realize that at the very moment of their attack, Flash's psychic aura was snatched out of his body at nearly impossible speed by a being known as the Sentinel. The Sentinel needs the Flash to help him destroy a creature on the rim of the universe known as the Devourer, who is literally threatening to eat away the solar system. Flash does the job, and is put back in his body in time to "come back from the dead" and take care of the three rogues before they have a chance to react to his seeming resurrection. The story is fun, and makes good use not only of the colorful cast of villains created in the series, but of Flash's unique and unusual abilities. Irv Novick's pencils had an especially polished look under Dick Giordano's inks. There was nothing remotely "relevant" about it and the fans couldn't care less.

Bates brought back the mad magician from the future, Abra Kadabra, in *Flash* 212, wherein the villain uses his wizardry to trap the Flash and a boy he's babysitting in a bizarre cartoon show inside a TV set, a trap that the speedster has to struggle to escape before the cartoon world implodes and he and the boy are killed. Len Wein scripted a zany but entertaining tale in *Flash* 217 in which the speedster develops four arguing duplicates due to the machinations of a computer built by his father-in-law, Professor West. In *Flash* 219 the Flash winds up temporarily joining forces with the Top inside the latter's maximum security prison cell after being maneuvered there by the Mirror Master, who was the Top's roommate before breaking out, stealing his roomie's cash out of a Top-style satellite, and turning his former cell into a death trap for the scarlet speedster; this was another winner from Bates.

Bates continued to use the members of the Rogue's Gallery,

but some of the stories were like bad imitations of silver age tales without the art of premiere Flash artist Carmine Infantino to at least make them look good. Bates' nadir, however, was a more unusual story in *Flash* 228 in which he gave himself a co-starring role as he accidentally enters a dimension where the Flash and Central City actually exist and helps Flash battle the Trickster. Bates introduced college student Stacey Conwell as a border in the Allen home in *Flash* 232. Stacey was the daughter of Barry's old friend, Charlie Conwell, who was assassinated while running for office in a previous issue. Although it will cause problems for him in maintaining his secret identity, Barry knows that Charlie would have wanted Stacey to live with them, so they ask her to move in while she attends school. She added nothing to the series.

The Reverse-Flash, Professor Zoom, figured in a three parter in *Flash* 235 - 237, although he only worked behind the scenes in the first two issues. The evil speedster imbues Iris with a special energy that will interact with her husband's speed force and cause world-wide destruction if the two merely touch. Professor Zoom promises to keep the earth safe in every time period if she marries him, as her marriage to Barry, a thousand years in the past, is no longer legal. Jay Garrick, the original Flash from Earth-2 and golden age hero Dr. Fate spirit Iris away from Earth-1 and try to cure her while a frantic Barry scours his own planet looking for his missing wife. Finally he decides to see if Iris is back in the future world she comes from, although Jay and Fate try to prevent him from doing so. Fate uses a mystic bolt to cross the dimensional and time barriers and fill Barry in on what's going on, and the speedster is able to figure out a way to remove the deadly energy from Iris. The story illustrates both the strengths and weaknesses in Bates' scripting. On one hand, the stories are entertaining and suspenseful, unfolding as a mystery (where did Iris go? Why did Jay Garrrick snatch her from her home? etc.), but the plot is full of illogic. There's no reason why Barry couldn't have been told what was going on from the first so he wouldn't have worried about his wife and wondered if she were alive or dead, and it would hardly have taken him two weeks to get around to seeing if Iris was with her real parents in the future. And so on.

Bates (with an assist from Bob Rozakis) offered up an unusual villain in *Flash* 238: Barry Allen's hair stylist! When Barry gets a new haircut at Rasmussen's House of Hair he has no idea that the trip will help him capture a crook who has the baffling ability to switch places with other men after he commits a crime, getting away scot free. Barry learns that the startled men who inexplicably wind up at the scene of assorted thefts and burglaries were all customers of Rasmussen's, and figures out that the hair stylist somehow has the ability to zero in on them and switch places with them via swatches of their hair. In one exciting sequence Flash races after his foe, who has switched places with someone on an airliner, and creates a whirlpool via which he can climb miles upward into the sky and board the plane in mid-air.

In *Flash* 239, Paul Gambi, the master tailor introduced in the silver age who made all the costumes for the Rogue's Gallery, gets out of jail and makes Flash a new uniform which makes him run off and hide the loot he takes away from criminals. But Gambi, who has genuinely gone straight after a stay in prison, isn't behind this -- it's the Mirror Master at fault. In the same issue Barry loses his temper and tells Iris, who is constantly after him about being late even though she knows a super-hero has unexpected emergencies, to stop nagging him. One reader commented that he would have found it hard to live with Iris' "constant complaining" himself.

In *Flash* 243 - 244 the members of the Rogue's Gallery learn that one of their number, The Top (Roscoe Dillon), has just died and sent them a message with the grim details. Spinning at great speed for years awakened some of the Top's dormant brain power, and he was able to use his mind to make inanimate objects whirl like tops as well. Unfortunately for Dillon, Flash's super-speed vibrations create a fatal illness in his brain that eventually kills him. Dillon has left a nasty surprise for everyone -- during his last half-dozen robberies, he planted bombs which have to be collected and put together to prevent them from exploding: just one missing part and Central City will go boom. Since the city is their stomping grounds, the Rogues find themselves in the bizarre position of having to save it, as they fear Flash will never believe their story. So Captain Cold, Captain Boomerang, the Trickster, the Weather Wizard, Heatwave, and Mirror Master all set out to "steal" the bombs before they can go off. Flash learns of the plan and in an even more bizarre development helps them in their robberies, working behind the scenes to prevent the police from stopping them. Mirror Master spots the Flash and zaps him, but when MM arrives at the Rogues' HQ with the last piece of the bomb, he and the others learn there are 720 possible combinations to unlock and disarm the bombs. Fortunately, Flash revives and uses his powers to get the right combination before the city gets blown to smithereens. The story was one of Bates' all-time best, with a great premise and excellent use of the Rogues Gallery -- one of the very best Flash stories of the bronze age, in fact.

Golden Glider

Flash 250 - 251 introduced a persistent and diabolical foe -- Flash's first and only major female antagonist -- in the Golden Glider, who was the younger sister of Captain Cold. Lisa Snart is a world-famous figure skater, who has been taught many of her famous spinning moves by her lover, Roscoe Dillon, the Top. Shattered by Dillon's death, she has become a villainess whose sole preoccupation is the destruction of the man she thinks is responsible for her lover's demise -- the Flash. Wearing an outfit similar to her skating costume, and gliding through the air on skates that can produce their own ice and were built by her brother, GG prevents Cold from killing the Flash only because she wants the speedster to suffer first. Coming to the conclusion that the Flash and Iris Allen are "involved," she tries to freeze-dry Iris but is stymied in her efforts and captured by the Flash.

In *Flash* 257 GG, having figured out the Flash's real identity, tries to kill off both Iris and Barry's parents. She plants deadly jewels in the latter's home that places them in a coma and erects a force field that prevents them from leaving or medical personnel from getting through. Four issues later she tries a psychological approach by hypnotizing a handsome writer into becoming the new hero, the Ringmaster, who is able to (temporarily) capture the Gilder -- only because she lets him -- when the Flash has always failed to do so. Escaping from jail the Glider mesmerizes Iris into falling for the Ringmaster and leaving Barry, whose reactions of jealousy over this new hero are at first rather petty (before Iris' actions) but quite realistic. In a snit over the public's adulation of the Ringmaster, a TV host's sneering at him, and Iris' alleged betrayal, he quits being the Flash -- but bounces back, exposes GG's plot, and soon has Iris back in his arms.

Flash 254 - 256, in addition to featuring the Rogues Gallery, brought back a villain who hadn't been seen since *Showcase* 4 in 1956: Mazdan, another evildoer from the future. Mazdan, who wants revenge on Flash for getting him imprisoned in his own time period, creates such realistic illusions in the Flash's head that the speedster doesn't know what's real and what isn't. At their convention the Rogues give the Flash a "Roscoe" award for keeping them on their toes before abruptly disappearing, thanks to the Mirror Master. The Roscoe award, which only the Flash can see, creates a "flashback" effect which has the hero automatically and unwillingly running away in reverse every time he tries to capture one of the rogues. In spite of this, Flash is able to round up the criminals, but Mazdan uses his science to make Barry think he's living several years in the past, that he and Iris aren't yet married, and that the Top is still alive. Flash manages to see through his foe's tricks, but he defeats him a bit too easily considering Mazdan's abilities to make Flash have such realistic hallucinations.

Flash 258 - 259 brought Green Lantern's foe Black Hand to Central City, where the villain steals away Flash's protective aura and reduces him to ashes when he runs after him without it, leaving only his smoldering boots on the burning roadway. But Flash manages to save himself by compressing his atoms inside his ring along with his costume, although his ability to go after his enemy is severely compromised by his having to reduce his speed to again keep from bursting into flames. Flash maneuvers his foe into an airless representation of the moon where his missing aura won't be such a problem and trounces him. Black Hand had combined the stolen aura with GL's power ring energy to create a nearly invulnerable force field around him, but it proves no match for his flashy opponent. Flash's next opponent in the following issue, the Viper, turns out to be a private eye with a split personality -- and an ancestor of Iris Allen's -- who seemingly dies in the morning, attacks the Flash in the afternoon, and gets married in the evening after his psychological problems have been ironed out by Barry's father-in-law from the future. Joe Giella's inks over Novick's pencils gave the comic a more attractive look but Frank McLaughlin was used more often.

Flash 266 - 267 brought back Mick Rory, Heat Wave, a rival of fellow rogue Captain Cold as well as his opposite number. Writer Cary Bates didn't just come up with a new weapon or death trap for the villain; he explored Rory's psyche as the bad guy's shrink gets to the bottom of his mania for heat and his terror of frigid temperatures. Rory does, however, come up with a diabolical way of getting rid of his nemesis, replacing a millionaire's frozen form in a cryogenic unit with the Flash's unconscious body, hoping he won't be discovered until the 21st century. Rory takes a peek at Flash's face under his mask, thinks it seems familiar, but just can't place it. In *Flash* 268 comic book collector Barry Allen and his young neighbor get caught up in a tug of war for a golden age Flash comic that has been saturated with an element that causes the comic to instantly teleport to anyone who concentrates on it, consciously or not. By gaining the formula, the crooks hope to be able to steal anything they want to by simply willing the loot to come to them.

The Death of Iris

Flash 270 - 272 introduced a new, unusual menace in the form of the Clown, another bad guy with a revenge motive. Despite his amusing appearance, the Clown made a formidable opponent for the Flash, whom he hates because the speedster hadn't made a planned appearance at a circus due to a Justice League emergency. On that very day, Lyle Corley, the Clown's true identity, was performing a high-wire act with three other members of his family. When a black-out occurs due to red tape at City Hall, the Corley family plummets to the ground, with only Lyle surviving. As the Clown, he kidnaps three officials he holds responsible for the black-out, and places them in the same high-wire position that his family was in, along with the Flash, whom he freezes with sonics.

An important sub-plot involves a scientist named Nephron who is hoping to use brain stimulation to convert a murderous volunteer convict, Clive Yorkin, into a docile and productive member of society, an experiment that Barry has his doubts about. There is also a young lady named Melanie, a Flash groupie, who develops mind-control powers that force Flash to come to her side whenever she wishes it. Meanwhile some drug dealers hide a supply of heroin stolen from police HQ in Barry's lab and Iris is feeling so neglected that she thinks her marriage is in trouble. Ross Andru replaced Julius Schwartz as editor beginning with *Flash* 271 and Alex Saviuk became the new penciller. His cartoonish work may not have seemed like the best fit considering some of the grim events coming up in the series, but it was often quite lively and effective.

The aforementioned sub-plots came to a head in the next few issues. Yorkin escapes after placing Nephron in the experimental chair and frying his brain. Melanie forces Flash to come to a motel room and unmask, finds his looks ordinary, and walks out of the room muttering about her disappointment. "I always thought I was kind of sexy," thinks Barry. Iris, seeing the woman and her husband inside, comes to the wrong conclusion and nearly wrecks her car and herself until Flash's timely intervention, after which they talk, make up, renew their commitment to one another, and decide to have a baby. And then Yorkin breaks into a party the Allens' are attending -- and murders Iris [275]. The fact that Iris seemed to be bothered by Barry's frequent fade-outs during dinner and the like more than ever before, and seemed to no longer have any kind of career that might help her occupy her time, indicated that the powers-that-be thought a single hero who could concentrate on foes and battles would be better than a married one.

Barry has been slipped some drugs by the dealers who left the heroin in his lab, which affects his actions over the next few days. He thinks he's killed Yorkin when he didn't, thinks Iris is still alive, and is hospitalized, where he's told the terrible truth about his wife. He goes to the Justice League satellite and begs Superman, Wonder Woman and Green Lantern to do everything they can to bring Iris back to life, but when they tell him they are unable to do so he becomes enraged and tries to trash the place [276]. The JLA are able to get him under control despite the drugs that are still in his system, and he is able to remain calm for Iris' funeral. Coming to terms with his wife's death (apparently Bates didn't want to drag out the grief too long, but Barry did seem to get over the tragedy in a comparative "flash"), he searches for Yorkin, who is not only completely insane but has developed the ability to suck the life out of anyone he touches. The Flash comes across the stark white, drained and dead bodies of cops, derelicts and young movie patrons alike even as Melanie uses her powers to hone in on the maniac, who is eventually destroyed in a sinkhole [280].

Looking at videotapes of Iris' death -- which brings all of the pain and loss back to Barry -- Flash realizes that Clive Yorkin was not her murderer. The Reverse-Flash shows up to send Flash on what's meant to be a one-way trip to the molten center of the earth via special boots that lock onto his feet, and taunts him that he knows who really killed Iris; a trip to the future tells Flash that Iris' murder is marked unsolved. Barry's boss, Chief of Police Paulsen, turns out to be a member of the heroin gang, and the person who put a hit out on Barry and an undercover detective that he's working with. Paulsen, who takes orders from a mysterious voice whose identity he does not know, flees to South America, but the Flash catches up to him and takes him into custody, showing little compassion for the man's perplexed and frightened wife and little boy.

No wonder -- this Flash is actually "Professor Zoom," the Reverse-Flash, in disguise, checking to make sure how much Paulsen knows about Iris' death [*Flash* 281 - 282]. Not only is Professor Zoom the mysterious man behind the heroin racket (there is so little crime in his 25th century that he's come back to the 20th for a little excitement), but he's also Iris' murderer, killing her because she spurned his grotesque and psychotic protestations of love. Flash learns the truth in *Flash* 283, but when he tries to take his miserable opponent back to the future in the latter's time bubble, they get lost in the time stream. Flash jumps out, but the last we see of Professor Zoom, at least in this story arc, he's on a one-way path to the beginning of time and virtual non-existence.

Al Desmond and William Dawson

The new penciller for The Flash was Don Heck, a talented artist whose style wasn't really appropriate for the scarlet speedster. Len Wein took over as editor beginning with *Flash* 284 (he was eventually succeeded by Mike Barr and Ernie Colon). The following issue introduced Barry's new boss, Captain Darryl Frye, who was obsessed with punctuality, as well as Barry's new neighbors (after he moves from the house he shared with Iris to an apartment building): the beautiful if icy Fiona, and the friendly African-American scientist Mack, who works at STAR Labs, and his very likable son, Troy. *Flash* 286 introduced a brand new rogue for the speedster to play with, the Rainbow Raider, who is a bitter man named Roy G. Bivolo. Bivolo's color blindness has prevented him from attaining success as an artist, despite his talent, so he steals paintings he can't fully appreciate so that nobody else can enjoy them, either. Wearing a special headpiece whose rays enable him to manipulate the full spectrum of colors and speed across an artificial rainbow, he bleaches the Flash white (causing considerable secret identity problems), and is clearly the victor of their first battle, but not of their second. Bivolo's gimmick and motives made him unique among Flash's "colorful" foes.

Long-time reformed foe Al Desmond, who had fought the Flash both as Dr. Alchemy and Mr. Element in the silver age, came back in a three-part story in *Flash* 287 - 289. Al has a "psychic" twin with the same name, who goes on a looting spree as Dr. Alchemy and frames the real Desmond for his crimes. Al fights back by donning the guise of Mr. Element again, and defeats his foe with the aid of the Flash. In one exciting sequence Alchemy turns a building's infrastructure to rubber, causing it to bend over and wobble, heading towards complete destruction along with everyone inside it, until Flash sets things right; then Dr. A transforms the Flash into water vapor and the speedster reconstitutes himself by forming a cloud and *raining* himself back into solidity. In *Flash* 290 - 291 the speedster discovers what's ailing Fiona when it turns out she was in the witness protection program. She innocently worked for a mob boss who is the spitting image of Barry Allen, and has been targeted for a hit by a hired killer and master of disguise known as Sabre-Tooth. Once Flash has taken care of the bad guys, Barry takes Fiona out to dinner, apparently not caring about any emotional backlash the woman might experience while dating a man who looks just like her would-be murderer.

The Flash had entertaining battles with old foes the Mirror Master (292 and 306), the Pied Piper (293 and 307, which reveals both his past and psychological underpinnings), and Captain Cold (297); then there was a two-part set-to with Gorilla Grodd in *Flash* 294 - 295. Some years before, Solovar, the leader of the hidden African city of super-intelligent apes, had revealed their existence to the human world. But Solovar is appalled that his delegates to the UN have discovered "leisure" time and are watching television and the like, so with the

Flash's permission he decides to blanket the world with rays that will wipe away mankind's knowledge of the super-simians. (How this will prevent the apes from wanting to watch "Gilligan's Island" is never explained.) Grodd escapes prison by transforming back into the body of William Desmond, into whose form he had placed his consciousness in the silver age (having then transformed Desmond's human body into an ape's).

Turning back into a gorilla, Grodd further manipulates things by erasing all knowledge of himself from humans and apes alike, then tries to get Solovar and the Flash to destroy one another, a plot that fails. In the meantime Solovar's obnoxious remarks about his race's superiority to humans never seem to get on Barry's nerves (especially considering how often he has to save the ingrates from Grodd's attacks) and poor William Dawson, chosen at random to house Grodd's mind, remains dead and unmourned. Later, however, the disembodied mind of Dawson battles Grodd in *Flash* 313 and finally gets his human body back, while Grodd's mind winds up in a derelict whose brain has nearly been eaten away by alcohol, which opens a whole new can of worms; the writer was Mike Barr.

Carmine Infantino

Long-time Flash artist Carmine Infantino, who had drawn most of the silver age adventures of the Flash as well as many of the golden age's, and was considered the premiere Flash artist, returned with *Flash* 296 and stayed for the remainder of the run. Infantino was especially adept at creating an always stylish sensation of lightning-fast, dizzying and often dazzling movement for the character. A variety of inkers worked on Infantino's pencils until Dennis Jensen took over with *Flash* 307, giving Infantino's work a new luster and richness. Rodin Rodriguez' inks also worked well with Infantino's pencils, if not quite as well as Jensen's.

In *Flash* 297 Barry's parents finally decide to see their son *after a year has gone by* because they believed he needed to deal with his crushing grief over Iris' death on his own [great parents, eh?] They get into a car accident, Barry's mother falls into a coma, and Dr. Allen moves in with his son while she recuperates, whereupon he begins to act very strangely. The senior citizen starts spending his time with a woman half his age, who turns out to be Lisa Snart, the Golden Glider. In one of the most bizarre developments in the series, Dr. Allen is now harboring the consciousness of the long-dead Roscoe Dillon, whose astral self entered the good doctor's body during a period when his heart stopped and he was technically dead; this occurred immediately after the car accident. The plan is for the twosome to kill the Flash, and for Dillon to depart the elder Allen's body and enter his handsome young son's, a plan that Flash jettisons with his usual combination of luck and adeptness [303].

The Flash 300 -- a celebration of the 25th year of publication of the silver age Flash -- was a double-size special which reviewed the speedster's life, career, and antagonists in an intriguing and suspenseful framework. As the story opens, Barry Allen is swathed in bandages and has been in a sanitarium for many years. No one believes his story that he is the Flash, and he is told that the accident that supposedly made him superfast actually created multiple serious burns and left him paralyzed. Because of the depressing state of his reality, he has created a fake super-heroic identity from the old comic books he used to read. Iris shows up alive, but tells Barry she is married to another man and has children. But Barry is convinced that one of his foes has engineered this entire scenario and goes back over the past to see if he can figure out who has done this to him. The psychiatrist who is treating him makes the mistake of bringing Professor Zoom to see Barry to prove that his murder of Iris is no more than a fantasy. But, Barry thinks, if there's no Flash, how can there be a Reverse-Flash? Barry goes along with his captor's devious plot to make him think he's an ordinary Joe only so that he can get past his illusions and get back into his uniform -- and then sends Abra Kadabra, the architect of the plot, back to prison in the future era he comes from. All of Barry's visitors were "magically" created by Abra Kadabra, who gives himself away by making them applaud him. (One does have to wonder why these unreal creations spoke to one another even at times when Barry couldn't possibly hear or see them?)

The Flash 304 introduced one of the speedster's most memorable and fascinating villains, Colonel Computron. W. W. Wiggins, the penny-pinching tycoon who owns the Wiggins toy company has just brought out a new toy called Captain Computron. The toy was created because of the micro-technic genius of mild-mannered employee Basil Nurblin, who is given a lousy bonus of 99 dollars for a toy that will net the company millions. This doesn't sit well with his sourpuss of a wife, Francine, who is a bit of an electronics genius herself. Then Colonel Computron shows up in a bulky high-tech computer-like outfit that hides both his face and form and tries to kill Wiggins. When Flash interferes, the Colonel turns him into a computer image and then a blip in a video game (there's an in-joke harkening back to the classic silver age cover in which the Flash is turned into a living puppet). Flash survives and saves Wiggins while the Colonel escapes and Basil and Francine each query the other as to their whereabouts that night.

Colonel Computron returned in *The Flash* 310 - 311 and now there is a new suspect for his secret identity, Basil and Francine Nurblin's obese daughter, Lena/Luna, who hates how her parents are always fighting over money and everything else. When Computron launches a new attack on Wiggins, who forces all of his employees to attend his son's birthday party, he discovers the man has a unique bodyguard, Captain Boomerang. (Wiggins inadvertently created the villain when he hired boomerang expert Digger Harkness to dress up as a Captain Boomerang and help advertise his new boomerang-based toy; this occurred in one of the best Flash stories of the silver age.) Now Harkness is grateful for his long-ago "help" and offers to protect him from Computron -- for a price. But the Colonel tells the Captain that he'll help him finally get rid of his nemesis the

Flash if he steps aside and lets him have his way with Wiggins. The two men cook up a "Boom Boom Boomerang" that snaps Flash on a one-way trip back into the past, but Harkness goes with him when the Colonel betrays him. Flash is able to save himself and Digger from a band of bloodthirsty pirates and get back to the 20th century, where he is just in time to save Wiggins from another attack and capture Captain Boomerang, while the Colonel again escapes, his identity still unknown. (He or she was never to appear again, at least not in the pages of *The Flash*, although in other series it was suggested that Basil had been the Colonel in the Flash stories and Lena took over afterward.)

The Eradicator

Flash 314 began a new story arc that introduced the take-no-prisoners vigilante, the Eradicator. Dressed in an imposing dark outfit and mask, the Eradicator uses a special weapon to wipe out criminals in Central City. Employing the principle of molecular distortion, the weapon mutates human bodies into something resembling bicarbonate of soda, leaving behind only his opponent's clothing and a lot of bubbly foam. Meanwhile, Fiona has started dating her boss, who is Senator Creed Phillips, as he runs for a new term on a law and order platform. Old Green Lantern foe Goldface, who wears a rock solid gold costume, has prodigious strength, and is both ruthless and fearless, arrives in Central City to take over the mobs, and pretty much trounces Flash during their first encounter. Mick Rory, who has gotten parole and given up his Heat Wave identity to go straight, is threatened and nearly killed by Golden Glider and her brother Captain Cold, who see him as a traitor to the Rogues, and he's then kidnapped by Goldface, who's heard rumors that Rory knows Flash's secret identity [315]. Goldface kills a cop to force Flash to stay off the streets, threatening to kill more officers if he dares to appear. An amusing sub-plot concerns Chief Frye's decision to become a ludicrous costumed hero named Captain Invincible and taking an appalled Barry into his confidence.

Flash has an exciting, brutal and frankly ferocious fight with Goldface -- one of the most exciting to ever appear in the comic -- that he nearly loses before he is finally able to corral the crook, one of the few, if only, villains who seems utterly immune to Flash's various super-speed tricks (although one has to wonder why Flash didn't expend most of his efforts in getting the guy out of his armor). Flash stops the Eradicator from reducing Goldface to soap bubbles, but the former escapes, only to reappear when Fiona and Creed Phillips are attacked in the park by muggers. Creed and the Eradicator are revealed to be one and the same person with a split personality [*Flash* 316 - 317]. The Eradicator not only murders criminals, but also kills off anyone who might know or suspect his identity, including his doctor and his loyal butler of 20 years, "for the greater good," as he puts it, as well as a security guard who tries to stop him from kidnapping Fiona after Creed converts to his evil alter ego in the middle of a television interview. The Eradicator nearly succeeds into turning the scarlet speedster into fizz, but Phillips' mind takes over and he obliterates himself instead [318 - 320].

Flash still had plenty of problems despite the death of the Eradicator as revealed in *Flash* 321. Hitman Sabre-Tooth busts out of prison and accepts a contract on Barry Allen from a man whose brother was incarcerated due to Barry's evidence as a police scientist. In the following issue, the hired killer turns out to be a protege of Sabre-Tooth's, carrying on in his stead, and is also revealed to be female. Barry admits to himself that he's fallen in love with Fiona, but still feels like he's being unfaithful to dead Iris. And the Reverse-Flash finally finds his way out of the time-limbo he'd been lost in and decides to make the Flash's life miserable again, but first he kills off the lady Sabre-Tooth before she can murder Barry -- he reserves that pleasure for himself. Barry gets an enthusiastic "yes" from Fiona in response to his marriage proposal, but on the wedding day finds he has to absent himself to take care of the threat of Professor Zoom. The two battle it out across the seas and con-

tinents until the Reverse Flash heads toward the chapel --
where Fiona, feeling jilted, waits anxiously -- fully intending to
murder her just as he murdered Iris. Fortunately Barry stops
him from doing so, breaking his neck and killing him in the
process [323 - 325]. Thus Eobard Thawne dies several centuries
before he was even born.

In events that are perhaps not as unrealistic as one might imagine, Flash is indicted for manslaughter in the death of Professor Zoom. In the meantime, poor Fiona has a nervous breakdown, and it isn't helped when doctors tell her that she
couldn't possibly have seen Barry Allen in her room as she
thought she did; they are of course unaware that Barry zipped
past hospital security as the Flash. Barry is so distraught over
how things have turned out that he trashes his own apartment, fully aware that his life as Barry Allen and his aborted
relationship with poor Fiona must come to an end, especially if
he is convicted as the Flash. The Justice League decides on
whether or not to oust Flash, with six for and six against, until
Superman casts the deciding vote and with compassion and
good judgment allows Flash to remain [*Flash* 329]. (Wonder
Woman voted against Flash in cold, moralistic fashion even
though she herself killed someone in WW 251.) Flash himself
isn't certain if he wanted to kill Thawne or not. (Although this
storyline continued into the copper age, as the Flash series
ended in less than two years its final issues will be covered in
this volume).

Flash was torn with love for, and despair over, Fiona, who is
put in a strait-jacket and locked in a padded cell, and his anguish is well-delineated in a scene in *Flash* 330. (Some readers
pointed out that Flash could have told Fiona his secret identity
so at least she'd know she'd actually seen Barry in the hospital
and understand why he seemed to walk out on their wedding.)
Barry chooses an old friend of his, a small-town lawyer, to defend the Flash, but the man is nearly killed by a bomb in his
office. His partner, Cecile Horton, takes over, even though she
has a secret grudge against the Flash. Frankly, the minute she

tells Flash that she hates the ground he runs on, he should have fired her, and it's a little ridiculous that he doesn't. Fiona recovers and says that she thinks less and less about Barry. While Flash has to contend with attacks from Gorilla Grodd and the Rainbow Raider, not to mention a hypnotic hate campaign orchestrated by the Pied Piper behind the scenes, there is an attempt on Cecile's life as well [*Flash* 335 - 336]. A famous defense lawyer with money troubles who hoped to take over Flash's case turns out to be the culprit.

After the Flash uncovers the Piper's manipulations and escapes his latest doom trap, he captures him, but his foe's mind, not tightly-wrapped in the best of times, has begun unraveling. The other members of the Rogues Gallery blame the Flash for the Piper's condition, and vow to destroy him, using as a dupe a super-strong, mentally deficient giant known as "Dufus," but whom they dress in a costume and re-christen "Big Sir." By this time writer Cary Bates was also editing the magazine, hence there was no one to pull him up short on one of his more tasteless ideas, the exploitation of a clearly "retarded" individual by Flash's enemies (although Dufus does get the last laugh). Considering how well Bates kept throwing twists and turns at the reader he was entitled to an occasional misstep. More problematic, perhaps, was the fact that the art often seemed rushed and unattractive, as if Infantino was being given too much of a work load. Inker Dennis Jensen was unable to work on every issue, and judging from some of his sloppy, uninspired panels, Infantino had trouble keeping up as well. His modern work could often be excellent but it lacked the simple elegance of his silver age pencils.

The Trial

Flash's trial finally began in *Flash* 340. Although some readers complained that the story was being dragged out for way too many months, most appreciated Bates' often clever plotting and how he worked the Rogues and other menaces into each issue. The DA announces that the charges against Flash have been upped from manslaughter to second degree murder due to new evidence. He then demonstrates how none of the eyewitnesses could possibly testify to what happened as the two speedsters were moving at such high velocity that their actions could not possibly have been visible. Meanwhile the Rogues sic Big Sir on the Flash by convincing him that the speedster was responsible for the death of his beloved pet mouse; eventually the big guy smashes Flash in the face with a futuristic battle mace. But Flash gets his face - and Dufus' mind - repaired by his super-gorilla friends and the two of them mop up the Rogues in record time [341 - 342].

In *Flash* 343 it is finally revealed why Cecile Horton hates Flash and it goes back to his battle with Goldface many issues earlier. As noted, Goldface killed a cop in *Flash* 316, who turns out to be Cecile's father, Jack O'Malley, and threatened to kill more if Flash showed his face on the streets of Central City. *Flash* 343 revises this sequence a bit and has it that Goldface claims that he issued his edict to the Flash before killing O'Malley, which is why Cecile blames the Flash for her father's death. Frankly, even if the Flash had known beforehand of Goldface's plans, which he didn't, what about the conviction among many that you simply can't give into terrorists? And why should Cecile hate Flash more than she does her father's true murderer, Goldface? Visiting Goldface in prison and nearly being killed by him during his escape attempt, she learns the truth and asks Flash for his forgiveness.

Cecile figures out the Flash's secret identity and decides to unmask him in court, figuring everyone will agree that he had a right to use deadly force when the Reverse-Flash had already murdered his first wife (but also giving him a stronger motive to commit murder, which doesn't occur to her or Bates). But she gets a big shock -- Barry now has a completely different face due to the surgery he received in Gorilla City. When Captain Frye tells Cecile that the Reverse-Flash is alive and well and back in Central City, she doesn't believe him, even as someone who looks and sounds exactly like Professor Zoom runs about in super-speed attacking and capturing the other

Rogues, and then tries to crush them to death in a nasty doom-trap. Despite the efforts of juror Nathan Newbury, who has been occupied by the mind of a certain someone from the future, to convince the other jurors to acquit the Flash, the speed-ster is found guilty -- due to the interference of the Reverse-Flash.

Most of the answers were found in *Flash* 350, the final issue of the series, in which the Reverse-Flash is revealed to actually be Abra Kadabra, who has cooked up a scheme that will convince everyone he is the greatest magician of all time. His manipulations have actually been to save the Flash's life, in essence doing the impossible, as Barry Allen is fated to die and presumably nothing can be done about it. Flash and the Rogues team up to defeat Abra in the 64th century, spoiling his plans, then Barry goes to the 30th century to be reunited with -- his "late" wife, Iris. Apparently Iris' parents, who already knew when she was supposed to die in the past, arranged to have her consciousness withdrawn at the proper time and inserted into the body of a young woman who had died in their own time period. Iris' mind then went back in time to inhabit one of the jurors, the aforementioned Nathan Newbury. The revelations in *Flash* 350 were a bit spoiled by sequences in an early issue of the *Crisis on Infinite Earths* maxi-series; in a later issue Barry was actually killed off. (Kid Flash became the Flash, but Barry Allen was eventually re-introduced many years later.) Readers were left with many questions about the whole business with Iris but as it was the final issue, these questions were never resolved.

Despite its contrivances and dumb moments and occasional rushed artwork, *The Flash* of the bronze age was a remarkably entertaining and memorable series, one that successfully combined a certain decided grimness with the "fantastic," almost campy edge of the Rogues, Big Sir, and all the rest. There was no other series quite like it.

The Flash had several appearances with Batman in *The Brave and the Bold* during the bronze age. In the best of these, B&B

125, the two team up in an excellent story involving: an Asian drug lord; a deal he has with the US government to destroy his heroin crops; a missing aviatrix whom the drug lord keeps captive; and a lady criminal and lookalike of the aviatrix who escapes from prison via trampoline, all the elements perfectly blended together in a tale by Bob Haney with many surprises and fine art by Jim Aparo. There was also a good story in which Flash and Batman team up to tackle the Rainbow Raider.

The 62-page *Flash Spectacular* in 1978 used Grodd, the super-Gorilla with mind-control powers, to link stories of Flash and his other speedy compatriots before a final chapter in which everyone appears for a climactic battle. In their chapters, Kid Flash (Wally West) and the Flash of Earth-2 (Jay Garrick) reveal their secret identities, the former to his parents, the latter to the press. Jay Garrick's chapter also features the first-ever meeting of the original Flash with fellow golden age speedster, Johnny Quick, who have a skirmish due to Grodd's machinations.

CHAPTER SIXTEEN: UNDERSEA ACTION

-- *AQUAMAN, SUB-MARINER, ASTON-ISHING TALES, SUPER-VILLAIN TEAM-UP*

D C's Aquaman and Marvel's Prince Namor, the Sub-Mariner had both begun life in the golden age, had relative success in the silver age, and continued to be a part of their respective universes in the bronze age and afterward. Aquaman, created by Paul Norris and Mort Weisinger, made his debut in *More Fun Comics* 73 in 1941. Sub-Mariner, created by Bill Everett, beat out his main competitor by two years, debuting in *Marvel Comics* 1 in 1939.

Aquaman

Aquaman had already published nearly fifty issues in the silver age. As the bronze age began the evil Ocean Master comes to warn Aquaman of an alliance he has made with some malevolent aliens. OM remembers that Arthur Curry (Aquaman) is his brother and tells him and wife Mera that he regrets what he's done. One of the aliens zaps Aquaman into a weird dimension where people are only allowed to "talk" - via telepathy - in areas similar to houses of worship. Meanwhile in a back-up strip beginning with *Aquaman* 50, Deadman -- the murdered hero from the silver age *Strange Adventures* who is able to enter the bodies of anyone he chooses in order to interact with the living -- tries to save Aquaman's life and helps him behind-the-scenes in stories closely tied to the sea king's continuity. It turns out that Aquaman has been shrunken into a world inside Meras's ring, while Deadman foils the dastardly plot of the aliens. The main Aquaman tales were written by Steve Skeates and drawn by Jim Aparo, while the Deadman back-ups were both written and drawn by Neal Adams. Despite Aparo's excellent artwork, the stories in *Aquaman* 50 - 52 were instantly forgettable; Aquaman did not work well in weird dimensions.

Aquaman 53 could only be an improvement, but not by much. This story reintroduced -- and also got rid of -- the evil organization O.G.R.E., which had plagued Aquaman and Mera a few minor times in the silver age. Agents from OGRE tell a dumb California millionaire that Atlantis is going to rise and when it does California will sink, plunging his beautiful estate beneath the ocean waves. The idiot -- unaware that the underwater city is inhabited -- then consents to buy an A-bomb OGRE will drop on Atlantis. They also employ long-time Aquaman foe Black Manta to distract the sea king while they go about their business. Aquaman sicced a large squid on the OGRE submarine in one of the story's best -- and best-drawn -- sequences.

Aquaman 54 continued the downward trend in a frankly awful story seemingly mixing the supernatural with the western genre, with Aquaman even having a showdown in an underwater city inspired by the old west. The fact that it all turned out to be a fantasy Aquaman was having as he was tied up in a mind-control machine didn't make the slightest difference. At one point the understandably confused Aquaman shouts out" "No self-respecting author would write trash like this!" -- probably echoing the sentiments of most of the readers. It was as if editor Dick Giordano and writer Skeates had absolutely no idea of what to do with the character. Jim Aparo's fine art was consistently wasted. Aquaman returned to the universe inside Mera's ring for *Aquaman* 55, making it two trips too many to that silly dimension.

Then came *Aquaman* 56, which was a quantum leap forward

-- which came too late. In "The Creature that Devoured Detroit" Aquaman learns that Don Powers, an ex-cop friend of his, has put up a satellite that will continuously beam sunlight onto the city, reducing the crime rate by eliminating darkness. Unfortunately a side effect of the ever-present sunshine is that algae in the lake is growing at such an advanced rate that green gunk is spilling out everywhere and the city may soon have to be evacuated. Oddly, Powers refuses to shut down the satellite, accusing Aquaman of being a "leftist environmentalist." What Powers doesn't tell Aquaman is that he is Detroit's resident super-hero, the Crusader, and his eyesight is failing, making him unable to work in the night-time hours. He hopes to catch the organizers of a crime ring, and go out in one final burst of glory, before the city can be too affected by the multiplying algae. Adding to the story's strength are such interesting touches as the squabbling married couple who open the story, and the fact that Aquaman -- who's supposed to appear on the *Tonight Show* (or a variation thereof) -- doesn't make his entrance on cue because he's learned of the desperate situation in Detroit, leaving the host nonplussed. The Crusader, who dies in this issue, could not have known that in the copper age the Justice League of America would make their HQ in his city. Jim Aparo turned in one of his finest art jobs.

Wouldn't you know that just when Skeates gets on the beam, *Aquaman* is canceled with that issue, although that wasn't the end for the character or for his comic. Aquaman next appeared in *Adventure* 435 [1974], as a back-up for the Spectre, with Skeates and Paul Levitz on scripts and Mike Grell on art. Skeates brought the Black Manta back as a major villain, but didn't explain why Aquaman turned the insidious creep over to his henchmen in issue 435 instead of imprisoning the man -- a major, continuing threat to his kingdom -- in Atlantis. The story ideas were good but the pages allotted to them too short to make very effective adventures. Aquaman took over *Adventure* beginning with 441 with Levitz as writer and Jim Aparo back as artist. Foes included a pirate who wants to turn Atlantis into a haven for land criminals, and a group of terrorists who are threatening acres of kelp beds that provide food for Aquaman's people. In 444 he has a memorable rematch with silver age foe the Fisherman, who is using dolphins to smuggle heroin into France.

In *Adventure* 445 Aquaman faced two threats at once: His brother, Orm, the Ocean Master, who is inexplicably back to hating him again, and Karshon, the new King of Atlantis, who ousted the "absentee" king by popular consent during one of Aquaman's frequent absences from the city. In truth, Aquaman's role as a super-hero left him little time to act as a head of state, but Karshon went so far as to frame him for theft. In succeeding issues, the exiled-from-Atlantis Aquaman retreats to a vacation home with Mera and Aquababy, and discovers that the Black Manta is funneling weapons to Karshon. In *Adventure* 448 Karshon is revealed to be Green Lantern's old silver age foe, the Shark, a mutated shark given human intelligence by radiation; as Karshon he appeared fully human. Reverting to his hybrid appearance, the bloodthirsty Shark hunts Aquaman, but the sea king figures out how to change his opponent back into an ordinary fish. Aquaman decides to let his friend Vulko become the new King of Atlantis while he concentrates on being a super-hero.

Aquaman vs. Aqualad

From *Adventure* 449 - 451 Aquaman faced such foes as the Marine Marauder, who could also control sea creatures via artificial means; Flash's foe the Weather Wizard; and the JLA's very first opponent, the alien starfish, Starro. In *Adventure* 452, writer David Micheline shook things up a bit. First we learn that Black Manta really *is* black, and plans to use other African-Americans to take over the sea. To this end Black Manta captures Aquababy (Arthur Curry Jr.), puts both Aquaman and Aqualad in an arena, and tells them that if one of them isn't dead in five minutes, Aquababy will suffocate from lack of water.

Certainly an untenable situation, but Micheline asks us to believe that Aquaman would immediately try to kill Aqualad. "He's my son!" he screams of Aquababy -- but Aqualad, whom Aquaman has raised from childhood and still affectionately calls "minnow," is also like a son to him -- or is he? The two manage to figure out a way to get out of the arena without anyone dying, but discover that Aquababy is dead. Although Aqualad says that he understands intellectually why Aquaman did what he did -- tried to kill him -- he is still shattered emotionally and tells Aquaman he will not help him pursue Black Manta, that for now they need to go their separate ways. Aquaman, still reeling from the death of Arthur Jr, essentially calls Aqualad an ingrate. Dramatic stuff, certainly, but not entirely credible.

With this Aquaman got his own title back while Aqualad got a brief back-up series in *Adventure* 453 - 455. It had already been revealed that Aqualad came from a hitherto unsuspected race of purple-eyed undersea pacifists known as the Idyllists. Now, after what happened with his mentor and father surrogate Aquaman, Aqualad sets out on a search for his real parents. He discovers that his father and mother were actually the King and Queen of the Idyllists, only his father went mad and tried to embroil his peace-loving people into conquest and warfare, whereupon they, regretfully, killed him (an odd action for pacifists, who could have simply imprisoned him or sent him into exile). Paul Kupperberg, Carl Potts, and Dick Giordano were the creative team for these forgettable stories.

In *Aquaman* 57 Aquaman catches up with Black Manta and captures him with the aid of one of Manta's men, Carl Durham. Not only is Durham disillusioned when he learns that Manta has no political motives and couldn't care less about other black people, but he can't see any point in murdering Aquaman. Durham is given the ability to breath underwater by the Manta, and learns that he can no longer breath air. "All I wanted was a place where my people could belong," he says, "and now I don't belong anywhere." In the following issues Aquaman fights against the Fisherman, the Scavenger, and, the mastermind behind them both, Kobra (see chapter eleven), all the while trying to keep out painful thoughts of Arthur Jr.'s death and his wife's apparent desertion.

In back-up stories in *Aquaman* 58 - 60 we learn that Aquababy still has a spark of life in him, and Vulko dispatches Mera to the dimension she originally came from to bring back a device that might save him. Unfortunately, she comes back too late and her child is dead. In *Aquaman* 62 the sea hero is finally reunited with his wife, but discovers she is furious at him, blaming him for the death of their son because he took off after Black Manta -- and several other opponents -- instead of aiding her in saving Arthur Jr. (Of course Aquaman thought his son was dead and didn't know about the device in Mera's dimension). Mera decides to forgive him after she aids him in a battle against a lame new villain named Seaquake.

In the final issue, *Aquaman* 63, Aqualad returns and so does crazy Orm, the Ocean Master, Aquaman's insanely jealous sibling. The two have a no-holds-barred battle, but Aquaman and Aqualad once more become a team. Unfortunately, the main problem between the two men -- Aquaman's all too ready willingness to kill a young man who was supposed to be like a son to him -- is never addressed, the problem left unspoken and unresolved, although the narration makes it clear that there are things the two need to say to one another at some point in time. At the end of the story Aqualad even asks Aquaman and Mera how Arthur Jr. is (!), although in *Adventure* 452 he is, like Aquaman, clearly present at the baby's supposed death, a goof of major proportions. One problem may have been the change in writer -- Paul Kupperberg did the scripts for the final two issues. Don Newton took over the art from Jim Aparo beginning with *Aquaman* 60 and it was not an improvement.

But that was not the end of the sea king. When *Adventure* expanded to a dollar comic Aquaman was given one of the slots from 460 - 466, with Kupperberg and Newton remaining the creative team. The main story arc of these tales has Aquaman coming into conflict with Vulko and Atlantis because of a group called Universal Food Products or UFP. UFP has entered into a deal with Atlantis for the latter to produce food stuffs on the sea bottom which the former will distribute to the starving masses on the land. But during his own investigation Aquaman discovers that there will be serious consequences to using the atomic generator and fertilizer supplied by UFP. Knowing of Aquaman's distrust for and prejudice against land dwellers, Vulko stubbornly chooses not to listen to him, and even Aqualad and Mera turn against him, until Aqualad overhears a conversation between his mentor and the head of UFP. Vulko's own tests prove that Aquaman was right, and the whole business is resolved rather quickly after that.

Aquaman's Further Adventures

In *Adventure* 465 - 466 Aquaman is trying to rescue a stricken submarine when he encounters Helga, the head of a secret Nazi cult under the Antarctic who try to infiltrate Atlantis for nefarious purposes in an entertaining two-part tale by Bob Rozakis. In this story Aquaman acquires a new pet named Siggy, a mutant seahorse experimented on by the Nazis and deemed a failure, but who helps save the day at the sea king's command.

Aquaman next made his way over to the dollar-sized *World's Finest*, where he lasted three issues, with Bob Rozakis still scripting. In WF 262 he discovers the secret of the Sargasso Sea, which actually leads to another dimension, and tries to free the people trapped there. In the next issue he decides to make his home and HQ in the city of New Venice, whose assistance he had come to after it was flooded. Now the first floors of all of the buildings are underwater, and he, Mera and Siggy move into the first sunken floor of the police department. Dr. Light, still on a mission begun in the silver age to wipe out all JLA members, tries to kill Aquaman but is, predictably, defeated.

Next it was back to *Adventure* for four issues beginning with 475 [1980] with J. M. DeMatteis as writer and Dick Giordano on art. The first story got off to a bang, with Aquaman running to fetch Vulko (the king of Atlantis is also a doctor) when Mera develops a raging fever so hot it makes the water around her actually boil. Along the way he encounters old foe the Scavenger, who is trying to steal some equipment Aquaman desperately needs to rescue the people still trapped in the Sargasso Sea dimension. DeMatteis gives Aquaman - who's been around since the golden age - a speech as he battles the villain that expresses how his fans had always felt about him: "I was in the world-saving game when people like Firestorm and Black Lightning were still in diapers. I've worked hard to earn the respect and trust of every living creature beneath the waves, and I take my job very seriously. So get this through your head, punk - I'm Aquaman, King of the Seven Seas - and I'm the best!"

In *Adventure* 476 Aquaman not only has to deal with his wife's mysterious disappearance, but the emergence of a powerful megalomaniac pretending to be Poseidon. This character tries to smash New Venice with an army of hypnotized sea creatures. Aquaman commands a dolphin to snatch away Poseidon's trident, from whence his power comes, and the animal drops dead from the stress of successfully struggling against Poseidon. Aquaman, who had felt like a puppet while under Poseidon's control, wonders if the sea creatures he commands feel the same way he did when carrying out his orders. But the denizens of the deep parade past a brooding Aquaman to let him know that there actually is a special bond and a unique love between them and the king of the sea. (Well, maybe ...) In the next two issues of *Adventure* Aquaman battles Black Manta again, who not only tries to attack Atlantis but also sends missiles hurtling towards New Venice.

After that the Aquaman strip moved once again, this time to *Action Comics,* where the story was continued in issue 517. Black Manta turns out to be a robot -- the real one is still in prison -- and Ocean Master is pulling the strings. More incredibly, Poseidon turns out to be Aquaman's long-dead father -- or at least the essence of him -- placed in an android form by Aquaman's immortal mother, come back to life and now insane. Poseidon regains his memory and teams up with his son to take on his "dead" wife and other son, Ocean Master, who refers to her as "mother" even though his mother was a different woman entirely (Orm and Arthur are half-brothers). De-Matteis' increasingly absurd and convoluted plotting -- the writer seemed not so much to be tying up loose ends as throwing in every ridiculous thing he could think of -- came to a climax in *Action* 520, where Aquaman's parents expire not a moment too soon. Aquaman had several more decidedly minor-league adventures in *Action* back-ups, sometimes teaming with Airwave or the Atom; these tales by Bob Rozakis and Alex Saviuk, geared for younger readers, seemed to exist in a vacuum and were not remotely memorable.

One of the best Aquaman stories ever published was not in *Aquaman*, *Adventure* or *Action* but in *The Brave and the Bold* 114 [1974]: "Last Jet to Gotham." A plane carrying a wanted Mafioso is flying into Gotham when it suddenly goes down due to a gigantic water spout. Batman contacts Aquaman to see if he has any information, and the sea king tells a startled Batman that he was responsible for bringing the plane down. Batman goes to the area where the plane was last seen and finds the aircraft underwater, the passengers slowly running out of air. Aquaman informs Batman that he had to make a difficult decision. He learned that there is a hydrogen bomb on board the plane that will detonate the minute it lands at Gotham airport, which is below sea level; the barometric pressure will trigger the bomb, not only destroying everyone on board but all of Gotham City. In this harrowing story the two heroes must not only save the passengers, outwit hit men determined to kill the Mafioso before he can be arrested and squeal, avoid attacks by the Navy, who see Aquaman as a criminal, but also prevent the plane from ever arriving at Gotham airport with the bomb still aboard. They succeed, of course, and Commissioner Gordon says of Aquaman: "He's a strange being -- so proud, cold-blooded and hard to figure. He scares me --!" To which Batman replies : "Me, too, sometimes ... But take him all in all, he's ...

beautiful!" The tense, excellent script was by Bob Haney, and the fine art by Jim Aparo.

Prince Namor

Meanwhile *Marvel's* sub-sea adventurer was having troubles of his own. At the end of the silver age, Sub-Mariner was on the run, temporarily stripped of his ability to survive in the ocean, after the human authorities mistakenly believe he is allied with invading aliens. Namor is able to prevent war with the Atlanteans, as well as the destruction of New York via saurian monstrosities who have been summoned by an over-anxious Lord Seth [*Sub-Mariner* 21]. Dr. Dorcas resurfaced in *Sub-Mariner* 23 where Namor first encounters the mighty whale-man, Orca, whose existence comes about due to the machinations of Dorcas and his ally, Warlord Krang, who still covets Lady Dorma. Krang orders Orca, who can mentally command killer whales, to attack Atlantis, while the equally evil hybrid Tiger Shark tells Dorma that he will help defend the city in Namor's absence if she agrees to marry him. Fortunately she is spared that fate when both Orca and Tiger Shark seem to die as they battle each other. Dorma becomes very jealous of Diane Arliss, the late Tiger Shark's sister, even though Namor doesn't return her feelings for him.

The tension between Atlantis and the surface world builds in *Sub-Mariner* 25, in which Namor is furious when deadly gas has been accidentally dumped near the city, killing many. Namor decides to forbid any ships from sailing in the waters over Atlantis, then goes to New York to address the United Nations. Namor wants Atlantis to join the U.N., but dignitaries argue that it is too war-like a nation to ever be admitted. Namor points out that the despoiling of the oceans and the threat to the environment, indeed to all life human or Atlantean, is much worse than anything his people could do. Tension increases when Namor is blamed for attacks on ships by a monstrous squid, which turns out to be a mechanical contraption run by Captain Kraken. Kraken and his men meet their fate at the bottom of the ocean as the fake monster is grabbed and crushed by a real octopus of much, much larger size.

In rapid succession Namor is embroiled in fights with Hercules; Captain Marvel and Rick Jones; and Stingray and Triton of the Inhumans. In most of these battles Namor is a puppet forced to fight by others or is only fighting as a subterfuge. That was not the case when Namor encounters the new ruler of Lemuria, Llyra, who claims to be a half-human hybrid like Sub-Mariner. This dangerous female foe has the ability to make all sea creatures do her bidding, and when Namor refuses her request to join her as a conqueror of both sea and land, she orders a multitude of oceanic inhabitants to destroy him. Instead Llyra destroys herself. She had told Namor that she had a fully-human twin named Laura, but Namor discovers that Llyra and Laura are actually one person with a split personality. Llyra was too good a character to stay dead, however, and she didn't. Then with his allies, the Hulk and the Silver Surfer, Namor finds he must battle the Avengers due to a misunderstanding over an experimental weather station that Namor is convinced will explode. The art in these issues, by Sal Buscema and Jim Mooney, was particularly attractive [S-M 34 - 35].

Namor at last proposes to Lady Dorma in *Sub-Mariner* 33. Three issues later the two are married -- or are they? Not only does Attuma attack on their wedding day, but after Namor has kissed his bride, she transforms into the new "Queen of All Atlantis" -- Llyra, whose mother used technology to bring her daughter back from the dead. When Llyra discovers that her marriage to Namor will not be accepted by the Atlanteans, she rushes to kill the kidnapped Lady Dorma, who dies in his arms. Although Namor, frankly, had not treated Dorma all that well, he still seems anguished by her passing [36 - 37]. Reviewing his past life, and blaming only himself for problems with the surface world (which began decades before when he killed two deep sea divers he mistook for invading robots), Namor decides to abdicate and leaves Atlantis [38].

Namor tries to take up residence on an abandoned island near Manhattan, and the authorities are so unnerved by his peaceful presence that they bomb the island to pieces to get rid of him. Diane Arliss, whose heart was broken due to the news of Namor's wedding, is now sorry for the death of Dorma. Knowing Namor feels cut off from both Atlanteans and surface dwellers, she uncovers a bit of news that suggests his father, Leonard McKenzie, may still be alive. Gerry Conway took over as scripter with Ross Andru and others on art, and the series plummeted in quality. Conway detoured from Subby's quest for his father, and instead introduced terrible sub-plots and awful characters such as Tuval, the Mind-Master, and the living rock-man, Rock, whose mother turns half a town into monsters; and even dragged in Mr. Kline, the mysterious master villain from Conway's other Marvel comics. George Tuska's art was similarly rushed and lousy. At one point Captain McKenzie turns out to be in a crowd not far from Namor, but the two don't meet until later [43].

Things improved dramatically with *Sub-Mariner* 44, in which an angry Namor battles the Human Torch in Boston even as the duo of Tiger Shark and Llyra attack their enemy with the monstrous fish, Krago. This issue has a strange scene wherein the Human Torch goes into a clothing shop to look for hipper duds and the clerk makes a flippant but inoffensive remark which causes Johnny Storm to burn the guy's beard off his face! (Ironically Storm brought the amnesiac Namor back into the modern world by doing the same thing to him.) Marie Severin returned to the series as the new penciller, and her work, combined with Jim Mooney's inks, was a winning combination, but she didn't stay long with the strip.

Diane Arliss and Walter Newell have located Namor's aged father, but he is spirited away by Llyra. Namor and his father are reunited on Llyra's ship, where some of Namor's strength is siphoned off to reenergize Tiger Shark. Walter Newell becomes Stingray and enters the fray, but Tiger Shark, before he escapes, lobs a metal rod at Mackenzie that kills him [46]. Colan and Esposito did the art for this issue, while Gerry Conway's script, a vast improvement over his initial Sub-Mariner work, contains some good character delineation. For instance, watching Namor raging, the Torch realizes how his teammates and others have felt about his acting like a hot-head on numerous occasions, and how often it must be a trial to them.

Namor goes into shock because of his father's sudden demise -- the two had no real time to get to know each other -- and develops amnesia. Most readers were anxious for Subby to track down Llyra and Tiger Shark for the murders of his loved ones, but instead he winds up allying himself with Dr. Doom against the monstrous Modok, who has a cosmic cube in his possession. Dr. Doom seems to feel some sort of kinship with Namor, even though he tried to betray him during their first "alliance" way back in *Fantastic Four* 6 and afterwards. The Cosmic Cube explodes at the end of the story, but it would be seen again - and again [47 - 49].

Bill Everett

In the special 50th issue of *Sub-Mariner*, which was both written and drawn by Namor's creator, Bill Everett, Namor learns that his cousin and childhood friend, Namora, is dead, and may even have been killed by hated Llyra, who reappears (and whose back story has been tinkered with quite a bit). Namor also encounters a young woman he thinks is drowning, but she accuses him of being a "masher." Apparently she didn't notice Namor's unique ears or she would have realized he was the very man she was looking for, Prince Namor. The girl turns out to be Namora's daughter, Namorita or Nita. Llyra winds up plunging head first into an oil spring, and gets stuck there, apparently dying. Nita develops a crush on her cousin, and isn't too happy when he insists she stay with an aged Betty Dean.

Everett stayed with the strip, fashioning a tale that embroils Sub-Mariner and the fiery Japanese mutant (and former X-Men foe) Sunfire in a conflict due to the machinations of another Japanese megalomaniac named the Dragon-Lord, who wants to bring Japan back to glory then take over the world [52 - 54]. The story in *Sub-Mariner* 55, about a mutant King-Kong-sized monster who captures ships and sailors, isn't memorable but for the fact that it focuses almost as much on the kidnaped men as it does on the hero and villain of the piece. In the next issue, the Atlanteans accidentally slaughter a group of mermen from outer space, and a woman named Tamara, one of their race, seeks vengeance. Tamara is no match for Namor, but after she is defeated Namor decides to make her a citizen of Atlantis. Tamara wanders off, gets lost, and is picked up by a Russian trawler, and eventually is taken to the U.N.

Learning she is a captive, Namor tries to free her but in a somewhat contrived development, battles Thor, who is standing guard over the red-skinned wench; Namor loses. Namor than launches a raid on New York to rescue Tamara -- who is not even a true Atlantean -- and makes the mistake of allowing a brute named Lorvex, who tried to force himself on the pretty alien, to lead the party. On his own Lorvex carries out a full-scale attack on Manhattan. "Yankee stadium -- City Hall -- the Met all fall into flame and ruin before the savage Atlantean onslaught," reads the caption. (The Avengers, Fantastic Four and other heroes are conveniently out of town.)

Namor is able to halt the attack, but gives a sharp warning to the assemblage at the United Nations. Namor then learns that the surface people do not intend to retaliate and Namor is made Prince of Atlantis once more. It not only seems strange that Namor is still a "prince" instead of a king, but it is completely improbable that there would have been no loss of life and no retaliation considering the "flame and ruin" that envelops the whole city, and the reactions of the inhabitants are never shown. One had the sense that neither new writer Steve Gerber nor editor Roy Thomas had subjected these scripts to careful scrutiny.

The next story arc focused on Dr. Hydro, who is green and scaly and lives on an island-like floating base that can be moved around over the oceans at will. Hydro kidnaps plane loads of people (including Betty Dean), transforms them into green, gilled men and women like himself, and forms them into an army to attack Atlantis. Namor and his young cousin, along with Tamara, who is, unfortunately, still around, defeat Hydro and his forces, but then discover that these kidnapped green gill people cannot be changed back to their normal selves [61 - 63]. Namor, who essentially sentences Hydro to death, is appalled to see that the Amphibians, as they are called, have been herded behind barbed wire as "the enemy," but Namor also suspects blatant racism among his own people. The Amphibians, who once had normal human lives, are numb from shock.

Bill Everett passed away and was replaced by a number of fill-in artists until Don Heck took over from him. Everett's art wasn't as polished as that of other artists, especially when he employed his own inks, and it wasn't always pretty, but each issue had its share of striking panels and boasted some very effective drawing. Heck's first story introduced Virago, an undersea she-monster who has cruelly and violently taken over the undersea people of another dimension. Namor returns with several emissaries to this dimension, is captured, and must fight Virago in a duel to the death. She transforms into a truly hideous "she-beast," as strong as the Hulk, as Namor puts it, and wins the first battle. She goes to attack Atlantis and winds up joining forces with Orca. Escaping from a group of maddened killer sharks, Namor smashes into a wreck filled with a deadly gas and undergoes a metamorphosis. He can no longer function outside of water, so Reed Richards fashions the sea prince a spiffy new blue suit to enable him to survive on land. The same gas that altered Namor's chemistry floats over to and pollutes the waters of Atlantis, instantly striking down all of the inhabitants, as well as Virago and Orca [64 - 67].

Namor returns to Atlantis to find all of its inhabitants seemingly dead, but before he can rage against the surface world once more Nita appears and tells him that most of his people are only in suspended animation. The Amphibians are still alive, and among them is a scientist, Dr. Croft, who tells Namor he can revive the Atlanteans but requires a device created by one of his colleagues, Dr. Walthers. Namor takes off to the same university where Spider-Man is a student, and discovers that Walther's evil lab assistant has transformed into a villain named Force. After a minor skirmish with Spider-Man, Namor defeats Force, and uses the device to place a protective shield over Atlantis until its residents can revive, while Namor makes Hydrobase, the floating island built by Dr. Hydro, his new home, bringing along with him Tamara, Nita, and the Amphibians [68 - 69]. Although Betty Dean is one of the amphibians, she is not seen or mentioned throughout the storyline until one panel in *Sub-Mariner* 70. Much space was wasted on the struggles of peace-loving revolutionaries against the remaining forces of Virago in the dimension known as Zephryland, a sub-plot that was probably meant to be relevant to the real world but was only tedious and page-consuming.

Marv Wolfman and George Tuska were the creative team on *Sub-Mariner* 70 - 71 in which Namor battles a lame villain called the Piranha. The final issue, 72, was drawn by Dan Adkins and written by Steve Skeates, who, as noted, had done many scripts for *Aquaman*. This poorly-plotted story of Namor's tussle with an alien slime beast from the stars was a very inauspicious wind-up to the series. Namor was not quite done, however. He became co-star, along with Dr. Doom, of *Super-Villain Team-Up*, beginning with two giant-size issues in 1975.

Super-Villain Team-Up

By now Namor had become so embittered over events in his kingdom, whose subjects were still in suspended animation despite the best efforts of Dr. Croft and various stratagems, that his hatred and need for revenge against the surface people took precedence over everything. Namor often seemed demented, as it never occurred to him to seek help from Reed Richards, Henry Pym, or others who would have been sympathetic to his cause and his people. *Giant-Size Super-Villain Team-Up* 1 consisted mostly of reprints but there was a framing story in which Namor proposes an alliance with Dr. Doom.

After reviewing their testy relationship over the years, Doom rejects the offer and the two briefly battle [Thomas/J.Buscema/Sinnott].

But first a word about Doctor Doom and what he had been up to in the interim. Like *Amazing Adventures*, *Astonishing Tales* was another split book featuring two separate strips, in this case, Ka-Zar, hero of the lost Savage Land, and Dr. Doom, archenemy of the Fantastic Four. Roy Thomas (later Larry Lieber) and Wally Wood were the creative team behind the misadventures of the scarred, sociopathic ruler of Latveria. In the first installment Doom puts a copy of his own mind into a bandaged artificial "Doomsman" that he hopes to use in one of his schemes, but the pseudo-mummy runs away during an attack on Doom's castle by Prince Rudolpho, who is the rightful heir to the throne. Rudolpho and his ally, a weird man in a featureless helmet known only as the "Faceless One," get the Doomsman to fight on their side, but only temporarily, as Doom regains mental control and banishes his creation, who's developed free will, to another dimension. The Faceless One turns out to be a multi-legged, alien spheroid that sits atop a dummy human body. Doom destroys his own castle rather than give it up to Rudolpho and the alien, who disappears while Rudolpho vows to fight another day [AT 3].

In *Astonishing Tales* 4 - 5 Doom vacations on the Riveria, causing his usual havoc amongst the locals, while his petrified subjects hastily rebuild the palace. During his absence the Red Skull and his Exiles (last seen in Captain America in the silver age) attack and take over Latveria from the already subjugated villagers, hoping to use it as a launching pad for a new Third Reich. When Doom returns he is defeated with gas and put on display in the public square, but the sun recharges his armor and he fights back to a decisive victory, convincing the Skull and the Exiles that he has shrunk them in size when it is only an illusion. In the following two issues Doom comes into conflict with the Black Panther when he travels to the hero's homeland of Wakanda in search of the metal vibranium. In Doom's final appearance in AT 8 he fights a demon in an attempt to wrest his dead mother's soul away from the Dark Beyond, and fails, as he apparently does each year. The last few issues of the strip were written by Gerry Conway, while George Tuska and Gene Colan handled the art chores.

The next issue of *Giant-Size Super-Villain Team-Up* was an all-new story in which Dr. Doom approaches Namor this time and decides to take him up on his offer. He advises Namor that he will be at the surface world's mercy if they learn that all of his subjects and armies are comatose, and will need his help. For his end, Doom wishes to create a new energy crisis and approves of Namor's habit of destroying oil tankers. The pair travel to Doom's castle in Latveria where a revolution of android workers led by Doom's creation and counterpart, the Doomsman (from *Astonishing Tales)*, is defeated, whereupon the Doomsman escapes [Thomas/Sekowsky/Grianger].

Giant-Size Super Villain Team-Up was reduced to a regular-sized comic and lost the words "giant-sized" in the title even as it came out with a new first issue. Continuing from the GSS-VTU 2, Subby decides to reject Doom's offer of an alliance even as Doom reviews his past history and realizes too many "lesser beings" have trumped him time and again -- he needs an ally if he is to rule the world. Namor returns to Hydrobase to discover the amphibians have been attacked by the unholy alliance of Attuma, Dr. Dorcas, and Tiger Shark, who get the better of him. In the next issue Doom, who has been monitoring events, shows up at Hydrobase to assist a captured Namor, but no one is able to prevent Betty Dean's death at the hands of Dr. Dorcas.

An absolutely enraged Namor breaks free, but Doom spirits him away, telling him to forget such petty matters and that he is in no condition to fight anyone. However, Doom realizes that Namor can not concentrate on anything else until there has been justice for Betty and the others, so the duo return to Hydrobase where Dorcas is killed and Attuma and Tiger Shark are roundly trounced. But Doom makes the mistake of murdering Attuma's harmless court jester, who dared to make fun of the

King of Latveria, an action which will have repercussions [SVTU 1 - 3]. The writers for this entertaining trilogy included Tony Isabella and Jim Shooter, and there were a number of artists, including George Tuska and Sal Buscema and the combination of George Evans and Jack Abel, which probably worked the best. After one issue written by Bill Mantlo, Steve Englehart took over as scripter while Herb Trimpe did the art.

Namor decides that he wants no part of an alliance with Doom, seeing him as a soulless creature who murders helpless innocents, such as the dead jester. Eventually Doom manages to dissipate the efficacy of the special uniform that Reed Richards made for Namor. Doom attacks Atlantis, whose citizens remain in their coma, and causes much destruction until Namor agrees to be Doom's slave if he stops the bombardment. Doom has an antidote that can keep Namor alive while out of water, and he challenges Richards to create his own formula, to no avail. Impatient as ever, Namor decides to honor his vow and reports to Latveria, another case of a hero honoring a vow that was only forced upon him to save others. "Namor's word is his bond," Namor thinks as he attacks the Fantastic Four at Doom's direction, yet it is not really credible that the arrogant Prince Namor would obey anyone's orders, especially someone he despises as much as Doom. Namor even tries to commit suicide by trying to fly when he's still weak, which would indicate that his working with Doom has nothing to do with the antidote. In an even more improbable development, after defeating Subby the FF advance on Doom's castle only to encounter Secretary of State Henry Kissinger, who tells him that the U.S. has signed a non-aggression pact with Latveria and the FF cannot engage him. Meanwhile a shadowy character named the Shroud enters Latveria with the goal of murdering Doom [4- 6].

The FF fight amongst themselves as regards Kissinger's decision, with Reed refusing to buck the government and assuring the others that the secretary's aim is to neutralize Doom. The Torch reminds Reed that Doom is bent on world conquest and is little more than a modern-day Hitler. The masked Shroud appears to Namor and tells him his origin, which seems cobbled together from Batman, Dr. Strange, and Daredevil. The Shroud and Doom battle, and it seems as if the former has claimed victory when some maddened hounds enter the fray -- Doom falls into a river where he is found by Nita and Tamara, who have journeyed to Latveria to help Namor. Doom lies to them and claims that he and Namor are still allies, and he travels to Hydrobase to supposedly effect a cure for the Amphibians. Namor and the Shroud go on the run from angry Latverians and encounter the Ringmaster and his Circus of Crime. A second Dr. Doom appears which turns out to be Prince Rudolpho in disguise [7 - 8].

The Red Skull

Super-Villain Team-Up 9 throws together Namor, Doom, the Shroud, the Avengers and Attuma; this issue was drawn by Jim Shooter, who proved much less effective as artist than writer. Namorita was referred to as Namor's "younger sister" in this issue, but was back to being his cousin thereafter. The battle with Attuma was stretched out to include three issues of *The Avengers* [154 - 156]. Namor then learns that Doom has hired a man named Orbiter to bring undersea miners to strip all of the ore from Atlantis. Still disguised as Doom, Rudolpho makes his way to the throne room only to find it already occupied by the Red Skull (SVTU 10). Dr. Doom returns from Hydrobase and winds up becoming allies with Captain America against the Skull, who plans to use one of Doom's weapons to enslave the earth.

Doom vows to help revive the Atlanteans if Namor will immediately aid him against the Skull, and the prince complies. As Namor feels that he and his people will not be affected by the weapon, he refuses to help further, but Doom manages to defeat his Nazi rival on the moon anyway. Doom does honor his vow and brings Namor's people out of their comas just in time to fight off an invasion by Warlord Krang. Once again Namor is on the throne and happily reunited with his loyal subjects, but he doesn't thank Doom as he knows he only did what he did because of his vow. All talk of Namor continuing to serve as Doom's slave is forgotten [11 - 12]. Bill Mantlo and Keith Giffen worked on these issues, which had plenty of twists and turns. Other artists for SVTU included George Evans, Sal Buscema and George Tuska, while Jim Shooter also contributed a couple of scripts.

Namor was given a one issue try-out in *Marvel Spotlight* 27 in 1976. This completely undistinguished tale of the sea king battling an undersea cyborg was hardly likely to lead into a new series, and it didn't. Namor also appeared with the Thing in *Marvel Two-in-One* 28 and 81. In the first story the two men battle a race of piranha-men, and in the second their opponent is big-headed Modok. Tom DeFalco's script for the latter has an interesting if somewhat suspect sub-text, as Namor decides to come to the hated surface world for a stroll down the Bowery where he was discovered years before by the Human Torch. While it might be credible that the "half-breed" Namor doesn't feel at home in either Atlantis or on the surface, it's a bit hard to swallow that he was happiest when he was a homeless, starving, amnesiac bum in the Bowery; being homeless is hardly better than being a well-fed prince, even one without a kingdom. Namor hopes to reunite with a woman who was kind to him, a bag lady named Mary, but she recoils in anger when she sees him, thinking he's a freak, and is angry that he was never really one of her beloved Bowery people to begin with.

Namor is a fascinating but often infuriating character, his legitimate grievances not making up for the sheer obnoxiousness he often exhibits. The sea prince doesn't seem willing to understand that the entire human race does not consist of madmen who create deadly weapons or pollute the seas, nor are they all nitwit politicians and criminals. No one ever mentions great statesmen and humanitarians, or great writers, composers, and other artists, people who have made miraculous advances in science and medicine that have helped thousands. There are surface people Namor likes and admires, but most of them he discriminates against as badly as any other bigot.

Enter Magneto

This concluded Namor's adventures in the bronze age, aside from guest appearances, as he did not appear in the final issues of *Super-Villain Team-Up*. SVTU 14 was the first part of a two-part tale continued in *Champions* 16. Magneto comes to Latveria to offer an alliance with Doom, who tells him that he has already conquered the world due to a hypno gas (which is basically the weapon the Skull wanted to use) and proves to Magneto that he, and everyone else, are under his control. Doom frees Magneto from his dominance just to add a little excitement to the game, and the Master of Magnetism winds up battling first the Avengers, and then the Champions, most of whom are in thrall to Doom. Working with the Beast and Ghost Rider, Magneto is able to triumph over the Latverian king. Even with two installments, the story seemed too short to do it justice, and, as noted, didn't quite seem like a part of normal Marvel continuity.

As for the last two issues of *Super Villain Team-Up*, they were devoted to the exploits of the Red Skull and his partner, the Hate Monger, whose men rescue the Skull from the moon after his battle with Doom. The Skull has his HQ on the Isle of Exiles, where he keeps chained prisoners in cages with glass see-through tops, upon which he sits and has a good dinner with the Hatemonger while the prisoners, whom he observes for his sadistic delight, starve below -- a disturbing image indeed. The goal of this gruesome twosome is to build a new cosmic cube with which to take over the world. Not wanting to share the power, the Skull tries to force Jewish prisoner Yousuf Tov to slay the Hate Monger via a pain-causing implant in his neck. The Hatemonger reveals himself to be the real Adolf Hitler (as was implied in the silver age), only with a cloned brain that can transfer from body to body. The Skull has mixed emotions about murdering his Fuhrer, but Hitler also plans to betray the Skull by entering the cube and becoming one with its power.

Unfortunately for Adolf, the cube is imperfect, and only becomes Hitler's eternal prison. Peter Gillis turned in some good scripts for these entertaining issues, while the art was handled by Carmine Infantino and the team of Arvell Jones and Bruce Patterson.

CHAPTER SEVENTEEN: BLACK IS BEAUTIFUL

-- BLACK PANTHER, BLACK LIGHTNING, BLACK GOLIATH, HERO FOR HIRE, POWER MAN

I t took a long time for black characters to emerge as stars in their own books, but it finally began happening in the bronze age. The Black Panther was given two series that were very different in approach, but it was Luke Cage, or Power Man, of *Hero for Hire*, who had more staying power, at least in his own book. Black Goliath, also known as the new Giant-Man, did not stick around for long. DC contributed Black Lightning, whose series was short-lived but who became part of general DCU continuity.

The Black Panther

T'challa, King of the African nation of Wakanda, aka the Black Panther, was first introduced in *Fantastic Four* 52 in the silver age, eventually becoming a member of the Avengers, but he didn't get his own series until *Jungle Action* 5 in 1973. The creative team was Roy Thomas and John Buscema, and the Avengers were guest-stars. The Panther returns to Wakanda and discovers that his second-in-command, M'Baku, has turned himself into the Man-Ape and needs to dethrone T'challa because he wants the nation to return to its primitive ways. For the next issue the creative team became writer Don McGregor and artist Rich Buckler (with Klaus Janson on inks) both of whom invigorated the strip by bringing the Panther back to basics in Wakanda. Some of T'challa's advisers feel he has stayed away too long and is unaware of what is happening in the land he rules, and T'challa admits to himself that he doesn't feel the same natural connection to the land that he did before his foray with the Avengers. Erik Killmonger, a native even more evil than M'Baku, wants to take over from T'challa and tries to kill him.

In *Jungle Action* 7 the Panther encounters Killmonger's lieutenant, a scarred white man rechristened Venomm because he works with and is immune to snakes. Killmonger also has a black female lieutenant named Malice, who turns up in JA 8. Another member of the cast is former singer, Monica Lynn, introduced in *The Avengers*, who has come to Wakanda to rediscover herself but is treated horribly as an "out-worlder." T'challa tells her, "Too many people warp the word 'heritage,' Monica. They use it to mean superiority, when it is only meant to give one identity." In JA 9 T'challa has to deal with an attack by Baron Macabre and his zombies but even worse, Monica is accused of using a spear to murder one of the Panther's advisers, Zatama. Gil Kane did the pencils for this issue, and Jansen's inks helped keep the look of the book fairly consistent, which was also true when Billy Graham took over as penciller with JA 10.

Marvel had high hopes for the Panther series -- they even went so far as to include synopses and panel reprints from the first few stories in the back of *Jungle Action* 9 to get new readers up to speed -- a good idea, as due to a glitch there were four months between JA 9 and 10. A reader pointed out that in this supposedly modern nation there was a huge discrepancy between the Panther's technologically-rich and opulent palace and the huts in which many villagers made their homes in the outlying areas -- not that such a situation was necessarily unrealistic. The series made the point that Wakanda had experienced culture shock due to the changes made when the nation became rich (for some at least) due to its huge and valuable mound of vibranium, and some felt that T'challa was not sensitive enough to these issues.

Baron Macabre's zombies turn out not to be as dead as they seemed, but the baron is in the service of the hideous King Cadaver, a man with a grotesque, misshapen, alien-like head; both of them work for Killmonger. It develops that a jealous serving woman, Tanzika, framed Monica for the murder of Zatama, her former lover. In a cavern deep inside the Land of the Chilling Mist, a comet that fell to earth casts rays that mutate men for Killmonger, who once more battles the Panther and leaves him for dead in a frozen wasteland with a wolf pack in the vicinity [JA 12]. T'challa survives, of course, only to face 12-foot white gorillas set upon him by Sombre, another one of Killmonger's weirdies. In *Jungle Action* 14 T'challa enters Serpent Valley on the trail of Killmonger (who for an arch-enemy seemed to make only occasional appearances in the book), and runs into living dinosaurs, including a tyrannosaurus rex that tries to make a meal out of him. This scene was depicted on the impressive cover, but alas the story inside was not on the same level. Pablo Marcos took over as inker over Graham's pencils but the results were not as good. Dan Green was a worse choice yet. Bob McLeod and Graham himself also did inks with variable results.

Jungle Action 15 introduced yet another lieutenant in Killmonger's army, a nasty character with the almost laughable name of Salamander K'ruel. Near death, the Panther still manages to tame a pterodactyl that is trying to eat him, and for unaccountable reasons drags a defeated K'ruel back to his palace when he himself can barely stand. In this T'challa seems less noble than stupid. Don McGregor's captions got wordier than ever, the thoughts and dialogue of the characters even more verbose and pretentious. Every reader knew that there was a difference between bloodless TV and comic book violence and real violence, but it seemed as if McGregor needed to state it in every issue. The proverbs coming out of the mouths of many characters were on the level of Charlie Chan, yet one reader compared the comic to "Hamlet!" Too many pages were devoted to supporting characters who were not that important to the strip, although McGregor's attempts to flesh out these people were admirable.

Jungle Action 17 wrapped up the 12-part arc of "Panther's Rage" with brachiosaurs directed by Killmonger storming the palace, and T'challa and Killmonger having their final battle where they had their first -- the Panther is the victor, aided by a little boy, Kantu, whose father was murdered by Killmonger. In the epilogue in the next issue, Killmonger's apparent lover, Madame Slay, has T'challa tied to two leopards who nearly drag him to a horrible death, but he survives while she does not. Apparently even dinosaurs on the cover couldn't increase sales because with the very next issue the series was no longer set in Wakanda and all of the supporting cast was gone with the exception of Monica Lynn.

Jungle Action 19 begins in Georgia where Monica has come because of the death of her sister, Angela. She meets white reporter, Kevin Trublood, as well as violent members of a group called the Dragon's Circle, which in many ways resembles the Ku Klux Klan except some of its members are black. Members of both groups -- the Circle and the Clan -- attack the house of Monica's parents, but T'challa sends them scurrying back into the night. There are varying stories about what happened to Angela, with the sheriff thinking she committed suicide and a man she dated feeling it was murder. The answers never come because *Jungle Action* ended with its 24th issue due to low sales and we never learned at this time who murdered Angela or exactly who the Dragon's Circle was, although it seemed to be linked to an unseen preacher. A black flying character named Wind Eagle appeared in the final issue, and seemed to be working with the Dragon's Circle, whose motives remained unrevealed. (Some of the answers were revealed in *Marvel Premiere* 51 - 53, which were published after Jack Kirby's *Black Panther* series wound up its run.)

The series began well and had an intriguing, if unresolved wind-up, but it began to deteriorate. McGregor's writing and characterizations were good, but the strip was badly and often unnecessarily over-narrated. As well, Graham's artwork began to look too rushed and unattractive. Still, it had several good issues and interesting stories.

Enter Jack Kirby

It wasn't long before T'challa was given his own series again -- with co-creator Jack Kirby at the helm as editor, writer, and artist (with an inking assist by Mike Royer and editorial guidance from Archie Goodwin, who undoubtedly cleaned up Kirby's formerly awkward dialogue) -- and *Black Panther* debuted in 1977. The series could not have been more different than the one in *Jungle Action*, as it got things off to a bang with the death of a collector who is murdered over a brass artifact shaped like a toad. T'challa has agreed to help a suspicious character named Mr. Little, because the latter invoked the name of the Panther's grandfather and claims the brass toad was once in the old man's possession. The toad is an ancient time machine and through the ages it has brought forth creatures from the past and created many legends. The latest possessor of the toad was slaughtered by a warrior out of time, while Mr. Little is himself almost killed by an African woman named Princess Zanda. During a melee between her men and the Panther, the toad brings forth a hideous creature from the future ...

This being from "Hatch-22" in a far-flung future has great destructive powers, so the Panther decides to find the toad's twin, the only object that can send things back to their own time period. Mr. Little takes them to the legendary treasure of King Solomon, where they locate the frog, defeat the gargantuan cavern's guardian, put the two brass pieces together, and send the "Hatch-22" beast back to the future just before he can destroy them. T'challa learns that the princess and Little are but two members of a group of fanatical Collectors, a group that includes Colonel Pigman and the decrepit -- and delightfully named -- Silas Mourner. Princess Zanda, herself a ruler of a nation rich in diamonds and oil, then threatens nuclear extinction for Wakanda if the Panther doesn't go find an immortality formula in a lost land for her.

T'challa manages to outwit Zanda and the other collectors and tries to make his way back to Wakanda. In his absence N'Gassi has become ruler, but he is confronted by the problem of the Panther's half-brother, General Jakaara, who exposes himself to raw vibranium and turns into a monster. Four of T'challa's relatives band together to become the costumed "Black Musketeers" and temporarily defeat Jakaara. N'Gassi is still unimpressed by these Musketeers, deeming the quartet "an aging financier ... a female grown too fat ... a racing driver (Khanata) and a doctor, barely into manhood (Joshua Itobo)."

T'challa's race to Wakanda is delayed by the interference of the Sudanese authorities, who try to arrest him. Strangely, he never tells anyone that he belongs to the famous Avengers, nor that he is the king of an African nation. A worse problem is that Jakaara mutates further, and his power is now capable of cracking the world wide open, but the Panther manages to destroy him [BP 7 - 10]. The incident in the Vibranium mine with Jakaara gives T'challa psychic power, putting him in touch with Khanata, who was been kidnapped by Kiber, a scientist who transforms captive humans into energy that he subsequently absorbs [BP 11- 12].

Kirby left the series with the 13th issue, just before the conclusion of the Kiber story. Some readers felt that Kirby had gone too far in the other direction from *Jungle Action*, which, even in a sometimes pretentious way, could be considered far more "relevant" than Kirby's tales of alien frogs and time travel. One correspondent suggested that Kirby's somewhat regressive approach to heroes like the Panther and Captain

America could lead into a new book called "Marvel's Muscle-bound Mindless Minions." In truth, Kirby was stuck back in a simpler and more childish era that was at odds with the more modern approach of the bronze age, especially its later years, and his artwork, while still exciting and dynamic, seemed at times rather light and cartoonish in contrast to other artists' work of the period. At the same time Kirby's undeniable skill insured that the strip's art was almost always of a high order in spite of this. Unfortunately, in the Kirby series, T'challa was no longer a dimensional human being but a "super black" who was both king and super-hero.

Jim Shooter and Ed Hannigan took over as writers, with Jerry Bingham and Gene Day on art. Kiber turns out to be a mere lifeless projection of the villain, whose actual body has become a huge blob attached to the floor of his laboratory. *Black Panther* 14 brought an entirely new direction, as T'challa decides to end Wakanda's isolation and moves into the nation's beautiful new embassy in New York City. Monica Lynn and Kevin Trublood from *Jungle Action* were briefly reintroduced, as was Wind Eagle. In the final and 15th issue the Avengers help the Panther defeat his long-tine nemesis, Klaw, Master of Sound.

Panther in *Premiere*

In a few months the story was continued in *Marvel Premiere* 51 - 53 with the same creative team. T'challa doesn't even remember his former lover, Monica Lynn, who reminds him of the events in *Jungle Action* concerning her murdered sister, the Klan and the Dragon's Circle. Wind Eagle, who was black in *Jungle Action*, but is now Hispanic, attacks the Panther, and is killed by a sniper's bullet. T'challa and the others travel back to Georgia, where it develops that the Dragon's Circle tried to brainwash the Panther over to their side but only succeeded in wiping out his memory. T'challa forgot all about Monica, but she and Kevin have begun a relationship in the meantime. In the bayou T'challa battles a cloaked being on horseback, a personification of hate, called the Soul Strangler, and briefly encounters the spirits of oppressed black men who live in the swamp. The Dragon cult was behind the murder of Monica's sister, apparently employing her supposed boyfriend as a hit-man for the cult's enemies, including, inexplicably, Wind Eagle. Wordy and a touch ridiculous, these issues were not nearly as much fun as Kirby's. The Black Panther would have more series in the copper and modern age.

One of the letter col writers for *Marvel Premiere* 52 was James Owsley (aka Christopher Priest), who complained that some of the black people seen in a previous issue starring the Falcon were Harlem stereotypes, an opinion with which whoever wrote the reply disagreed. Owsley later wrote his own Black Panther series years later after he went to work for Marvel.

The Panther had several appearances in Marvel's team-up comics. In *Marvel Team-Up* 20 (1974), he teamed up with Spider-Man to take on the maniacal Stegron, who brought a mass of dinosaurs to Manhattan. This featured an excellent double-page spread depicting the creatures on the rampage in Times Square [Wein/Bescema/Giacoia/Esposito]. In *Team-Up* 87 (1979), the Panther is impersonated by the villainous Hell-razor, whose employer, Roxxon Oil, wants Wakanda's vi-branium. *Marvel Two-in-One* 40 - 41 makes better use of the Panther in a tale in which he and the Thing investigate the dis-appearances of several prominent black people. The Panther is using his "Luke Charles" teacher's identity in these stories, which feature the villainy of Dr. Opatu, aka Dr. Spectrum, as well as a vampire-like monster, and even Idi Amin of Uganda [Slifer/DeFalco/Kraft/Wilson/Marcos]!

Black Lightning

"Justice, like lightning, should ever appear, to some men hope, to other men fear" were words penned by Jefferson Pierce, aka Black Lightning, at age 21. *Black Lightning* debuted in 1977 under the creative team of writer/creator Tony Isabella and 17-year-old artist Trevor von Eeden. Inker Vince Colletta was brought in to put some professional gloss over the neo-phyte von Eeden's not-bad pencils. Young African-American

Jefferson Pierce got out of his dangerous gang-infested Metropolis neighborhood to become an Olympic decathlon champion and then returned to his old neighborhood to teach in the high school. When he takes on some pushers who are trying to sell dope in the school, they retaliate by killing one of his most promising students. With the help of Peter Gambi, who runs a tailor shop above which Pierce grew to manhood, Pierce dresses in a sharp blue and yellow outfit with a white mask and becomes Black Lightning. He also wears an electromagnetic bolt that can repel bullets and give him added strength. His first adversaries are the gang known as the 100, run by the portly albino Tobias Whale. Whale was basically a more grotesque version of Spider-Man foe the Kingpin in that his face with its shark-like maw seemed barely human.

Black Lightning 2 - 3 added some elements of intrigue to the series. Peter Gambi somehow is acquainted with Talia, daughter of Batman's enemy, Ra's Al Ghul, who comes to Suicide Slum to assassinate Merlyn, a hired gun who once worked for the League of Assassins -- and tried to take on the Justice League -- and now is a hit man for The 100. Merlyn escapes, but in a free-for-all in the High School gym, a 100 employee named Joey Toledo is killed -- by Merlyn -- and Black Lightning is unfairly accused of the crime. As he has no official status with the Metropolis police as Superman does, he is hunted by both the law and The 100. Another member of the cast was Inspector Henderson, who was featured on the old "Adventures of Superman" TV series of the 60's and rarely seen in the comics. And there was also a new teacher named Lynn, who is obviously someone from Pierce's past with whom he has no great desire to become reacquainted.

In *Black Lightning* 4 - 5, our hero not only battles the Cyclotronic Man (who'd originally appeared in *Batman* as "Bag 'O Bones" but now has souped-up powers) but has a brief slugfest with Superman when the latter mistakenly thinks he's attacked and killed Jimmy Olsen. We also learn that Inspector Henderson's own son is working for The 100 and was instrumental in bringing BL into conflict with Olsen. *Black Lightning* 6 - 7 brings Jefferson into conflict with supposed hired gun Syonide, who kidnaps Peter Gambi to discover BL's weaknesses. An interesting development emerges when Syonide, who captures BL and brings him to Whale, tells the latter that while he did hunt people he never, ever killed them; Syonide winds up dying himself, as does Peter Gambi, throwing himself in front of a death beam meant for Black Lightning.

Apparently Gambi had shot Jefferson's father during a robbery years before and had been trying to atone for it ever since. The real story behind this was never told; Gambi left Jefferson a letter to read in case of his death, but Pierce tears it up and throws it into the man's grave. (It is uncertain if Peter was related to Paul Gambi, who tailored uniforms for the Flash's Rogue's Gallery.) The mysterious Lynn turns out to be Pierce's ex-wife, who gets wise to his secret. "Do you honestly think a mask and a wig can fool a woman who's seen you in your birthday suit?" she tells him.

Signaling a change in direction for the book, Black Lightning manages to wipe up the Metropolis branch of The 100 and give Tobias Whale a well-deserved trouncing in *Black Lightning* 7 - 8. He decides to stay in Suicide Slum where there are ample enough guys to deal with, such as the hostage-taking Annihilator in BL 9 and Flash-foe the Trickster in BL 10. Then the series was canceled with the 11th issue due to low sales, although there was certainly a lot of potential both in the character and in the comic.

Black Lightning Redux

Black Lightning got a slot in *World's Finest* beginning with 257. The initial creative team was Gerry Conway and George Tuska, and the villain was BL's first major foe, Tobias Whale. Whale is now on the outs with The 100, and suggests that he and Lightning team up to destroy them. In the next issue, with O'Neill and Buckler at the creative helm, the unlikely partners take off after a woman, Tabby, who has run off with all the information on The 100 that Whale has amassed. Whale tries to crack Lightning's skull at the first opportunity, of course. In WF 260 BL appears in the heretofore unpublished final issue of his own comic battling Green Lantern's silver age foe Dr. Polaris, master of magnetism, wherein one of Jefferson Pierce's students turns out to be the bad guy's troubled nephew.

The Black Lightning strip was then moved to *Detective*, where he appeared in back-ups by Martin Pasko and Pat Broderick beginning in *Detective* 490 - 491, which brings him into conflict with drug dealers and a voodoo cult; during this story he loses his electrical powers. He continued his career as a super-hero using his athletic abilities in *Detective* 494 in an excellent story by J. M. de Matteis. Pierce tries to help a gifted student who seems defeated by grim life in the ghetto, including the deaths of his sister and mother. A vigilante named Slime Killer who is tracking down and murdering drug dealers and muggers turns out to be the boy's deeply disturbed and angry father.

The follow-up story, in which some black youths kidnap frightened young women for ransom, was provocative but much less successful. Black Lightning doesn't agree with a white cop that the young men are "animals," feeling that they were shaped by the violence of their lives and surroundings, but even he nearly loses it when one of the youths brutally murders one of the terrified girls -- still he's determined not to think of even him as an "animal." If there was any problem with the story it's that the point was never made that not everyone raised in the crime-infested streets of a ghetto becomes a violent sociopath, and there's never any excuse for brutalizing and murdering young women.

Readers argued that Jefferson Pierce had been an English teacher in his own series, and the switch to physical education teacher made him seem like a stereotype, while others opined that the differences between Black Lightning and his alter ego (in terms of appearance and speech patterns) had been minimized if not erased altogether. Black Lightning not only worked with the Justice League but later on joined the team of Batman and the Outsiders.

Black Goliath

Black Goliath, initially written by Tony Isabella and drawn by George Tuska, made its debut in early 1976. Bill Foster, the big guy in the costume, had been around at least since *Avengers 32*, when Henry Pym/Giant-Man asks for his assistance after Pym gets stuck at about 12 feet in height. Foster not only helps Pym but eventually irons out all of the kinks in Pym's formula; unfortunately, he, too, supposedly becomes trapped at giant-size. In *Power Man* 24 - 25 Foster hires himself out to a circus to raise money to find a cure for his condition, but the circus is run by the evil Ringmaster. This alone might have brought him into conflict with Luke Cage, but there was also the fact that Cage is now dating Foster's ex-wife.

In *Black Goliath* 1 we learn that Foster had only pretended to be trapped at giant-size and to be strapped for cash as a ploy for winning back the affection and love of his ex-wife, a ploy that doesn't work. Foster is now working for Stark industries in L.A. -- making him one of the few super-heroes on the west coast -- and has three genius colleagues on his staff. He is uncertain about a future as a super-hero but figures he'll give it a try. To distinguish himself from the previous heroes named Goliath -- Henry Pym and Clint Barton aka Hawkeye -- he calls himself Black Goliath; Foster also happens to be African-American.

Black Goliath's foes included Atom-Smasher, Vulcan, and the Stilt-Man, who uses his Z-gun to send BG spiraling out of the universe and onto another planet, where he encounters a deadly out-sized robot. The writers for the short-lived series were, as noted, Tony Isabella (who came up with the concept) and Chris Claremont, and the pencillers included, in addition to George Tuska, Don Heck, Rich Buckler and Keith Pollard. Despite some good scripts, an interesting supporting cast, a likable hero, more than serviceable art, and a lot of possibility, *Black Goliath* proved to have less staying power than the original Giant-Man in *Tales to Astonish*, being canceled after only five issues due to poor sales. Black Goliath guest-starred in the unmemorable *Marvel Two-in-One* 24 in which he and the Thing take on the menace of the Hijacker, an old Ant-Man foe who hadn't been seen since *Tales to Astonish* 40 in the silver age. Black Goliath also appeared in issues of *The Champions*.

The Really New Giant-Man

Black Goliath played an important part in "The Pegasus Project" arc, which began in *Marvel Two-in-One* 53 and continued over several issues, embroiling such characters as Quasar, who runs security for the project; the cyborg Deathlok from the future; Thundra from *Fantastic Four*; Wundarr from *Man-Thing*, who has an origin similar to Superman's but who has the mind of an infant; and others. The project's main purpose is to investigate new sources of energy, and some powerful individuals are either patients or prisoners in the complex. In MTIO 55 Bill Foster comes to the project for some experiments and changes into Black Goliath when the big child-like mutant Nuklo is released from containment. Seeing that Foster has put on a brand new super-hero costume, the Thing suggests Bill change his name as well: 'Everybody knows you're black, and Goliath was a bad guy - so why not Giant-Man?" So Giant-Man it is.

Thundra, fooled into working for the bad guys, breaks into the project with the help of the "Grabblers" -- Titania, Screamin' Mimi, Letha and Poundcakes -- a group of female wrestlers/villainesses that are clearly modeled on Jack Kirby's "Female Furies" from Apokalips. When Giant-Man engages Titania and Poundcakes, the ladies seem to be winning until he literally knocks both their heads together. No one realizes that the Grabblers entered the project so they could leave equipment there to be used by the sinister Dr. Tom Lightner, formerly a villain named Black Sun. Thundra has a major battle with the Thing, even as she again confesses her love for him; the Thing is triumphant after getting angry at her remarks about Alicia.

Solarr and Klaw break free of confinement and engage the Thing, Giant-Man and the others in battle, even as Lightner completes his machine and Wundarr, who can absorb energy, wakes up and approaches the cosmic cube. Wundarr gains intelligence and the new costumed identity of Aquarian, and is soon brimming over with peace and love, especially for his "Uncle Ben." Lightner attempts to use his machine to shift the entire complex into a different dimension where the Roxxon Corporation can plunder it of its scientific resources, but instead he finds himself transformed into the quasi-cosmic Nth Man. When Quasar is unable to stop the Nth Man from expanding into our universe, Giant-Man, who discovered he is dying from radiation poisoning after battling Atom-Smasher, tries to stop Lightner by throwing himself into his body, but this ploy fails. Aquarian then enters the Nth Man's form, and anchored to our world by the Thing, Thundra, and others, he rescues Giant-Man, and manages to destroy the threat of Dr. Lightner. George Perez did the pencils for most of these issues, and his work was especially good for the climax in MTIO 58, though he would get even better over the next few years.

Giant-Man had one more appearance in *Marvel Two-in-One*, guest-starring with the Thing and Iceman in MTIO 76. Bill accompanies Ben and Alicia on a trip to the circus where they not only run into Bobby Drake, but the Ringmaster and his Circus of Crime. Many years later Foster died during the "Civil War" storyline that crossed over into all of Marvel's super-hero comics.

Hero for Hire

An African-American man named Lucas is in prison for drug charges, where he is bedeviled by sinister Warden Rackham and his sadistic guard Quint, both of whom are fired by a new reformer warden. Lucas admits that he had a sleazy and criminal early life, but insists he got out of the gangs and was framed by a former friend named Willis Stryker after they had a falling out over a woman named Reva; Reva, who was going to marry Lucas, was killed when Stryker used her as a shield to protect him from a rival gang's bullets. Lucas is given a chance for parole by Noah Burstein, who wants to use him to test a chemical solution that may be able to cure diseases and even halt the aging process. While bathing in the solution after being deliberately and willingly infected by Burstein, Lucas gets more than he bargained for when Rackham, who blames Lucas for his dismissal, turns up the power on the electro-chemical bath and it explodes. Lucas discovers that he now has the strength to literally shatter the walls of the prison, so he impulsively escapes. The guards fire at him and assume that he died in the hail of bullets, but he actually makes his way across the country to New York City and a new life. Putting on a cos-tume and printing business cards a year later, he advertises himself as a "Hero for Hire" and gives himself the new name of Luke Cage. The first issue of *Hero for Hire* debuted in 1972. It was written by Archie Goodwin and drawn by George Tuska and Billy Graham.

In the second issue Cage meets Dr. Claire Temple, who works at a clinic with, of all people, Noah Burstein. Cage also rents an office above a movie theater in Times Square and meets the owner's nephew, David Griffith or "D.W." Most significantly, Luke has a final battle with Stryker, who now calls himself Dia-mondback and has a trick set of deadly knives. Trying to off Cage, Stryker instead gets blown up by one of his explosive stil-ettos. Burstein is put off by Cage's mercenary use of his powers, but agrees not to turn him in to the police. (Oddly, he shows no interest in examining Luke or learning the extent of his abil-ities.)

In HFH 3 Luke gets his first client, who's murdered in his office after he blurts out news of a plot by Colonel Gideon Mace to use embittered vets to take over the city - but only as a ploy to rob Manhattan's bank vaults. Mace has a real mace on the end of his arm to replace the hand he lost, which proves no help when he tries to swim away late in the story and presum-ably drowns. (Mace would return more than once, however.) In HFH 4 Cage uncovers the secret of "The Phantom of 42nd Street," a hulking monstrosity who's invading movie theaters once owned by a silent movie star who died in a fire. HFH 5, written by new scripe Steve Englehart, introduced one of Cage's most interesting foes, the morbidly obese Black Mariah. She is a 400 pound female who leads a gang that uses a phony ambulance to drag off the bodies of wealthy citizens who die in public places. They steal everything from the dead people's wallets, and use their keys to loot their homes and offices before anyone gets wise. Black Mariah tries to use her bulk to smash Cage, but he is too quick for the voluminous viper.

Hero for Hire 8 - 9 brought Luke Cage much closer to the regular Marvel universe when he is hired by no less than Doctor Doom to go after some renegade robots hiding out in Bedford-Stuyvesant. Cage completes his task but gets stiffed by Doom, so he invades the HQ of the Fantastic Four and asks for a special plane to fly him to Latveria. Once there he gets involved in a war between Doom and some revolutionaries but winds up not only holding his own in battle with Doom but actually saving the dictator's life. The stories were pretty silly, however, and at odds with the more realistic tone that the series had maintained beforehand. A bigger problem was Englehart's ignorant use in an earlier story of a yiddish word that was an insulting term for black people, for which he apologized. (Oddly, in describing a chase scene in another issue he referred to Simon Legree and Little Eva from *Uncle Tom's Cabin!*)

In *Hero for Hire* 10 - 11 Cage meets a man who is known as Senor Suerte (Luck) when he is in his illegal gambling casinos, and Senor Muerte (Death) when he puts on his special red costume. This uniform is rigged up to give one of Muerte's hands a high-powered charge that will sizzle and literally turn anyone who grasps it to ash, only Muerte never knows beforehand which hand will get the current. Cage, of course, is only knocked unconscious by the voltage. In the second part of the story he finds himself chained to a tunnel which is rapidly filling with water. In a very harrowing sequence, he uses all of his strength to break free, but finds it difficult to stay afloat due to his weight and the chains of his costume. The Tuska/Graham art brought home all the intensity of this sequence. Suerte/

Muerte was a great foe for Cage, but he wound up in ashes himself at the end of the story. Chemistro, another interesting foe who appeared in issue 12, was alive but out of commission when the dust cleared after he tries using a special alchemy gun to get even with the firm that fired him. Lionfang from HFH 13, who exchanged powers with big felines while giving them some of his smarts, also bit the dust.

Luke's past caught up with him in a trilogy in *Hero for Hire* 14 - 16, in which old warden Rackham teams up with a columnist who discovered the truth about Cage's origins and his stay in Seagate prison. Claire winds up being arrested for the columnist's murder, even though he was actually shot by Rackham, and also learns the truth. Two old cell mates of Cage come to town looking for trouble, as well as a nasty vigilante known as Stiletto. But the cell mates keep silent about Cage's past after he saves their lives. The entertaining stories were written by Steve Englehart and Tony Isabella and drawn by Billy Graham, with an inking assist in one issue from Frank McLaughlin.

Beginning with issue 17, the title of the series was switched to *Power Man*. Cage was furious to see that his activities barely rate a mention in the paper while heroes such as Iron Man and Captain America get pages and pages of publicity. He decides to come up with a new heroic identity to solve the problem. A better reason for Cage to take on a new name was to increase the flagging sales for the comic, which it did. Len Wein took over the scripting chores, with George Tuska back on pencils and Billy Graham still on inks, although Vince Colletta took over with the following issue. Cage stopped calling everyone, including his opponents, "darling" and "honey." "Christmas" -- presumably a cleaned-up version of "Christ!" -- was Cage's oath of choice as it was for other African-American characters even from other companies.

In *Power Man* 18 Cage takes on Steeplejack, a high-rise maniac who explodes at the finish. PM 19 - 20 brings Cage into conflict with mob boss Cornell Cottonmouth, the source of the drugs with which Stryker framed Cage. Unfortunately, Cage can't find any records that might clear him. In PM 21 the original Power Man, a silver age villain who tackled the Avengers with the help of the Enchantress, objects to Cage's use of "his" name and challenges him to a battle - which the bad guy loses. If nothing else this helped confirm the fact that Luke's power levels were almost in a class with the Thing and other heavy hitters. The creative team for this issue was Tony Isabella and artist Ron Wilson. Stiletto reappeared in issue 22, along with his brother, Discus, and they turned out to be the sons of the reform warden Tyler, who had not been seen since HFH 1. The exact motives for their violent actions were not well-delineated at that time.

Power Man 27 brought writer Bill Mantlo to the strip for one issue and featured early art by future fan favorite George Perez. The story is a fairly interesting character study of a washed-up boxer who temporarily gets great strength, and his manager, a father surrogate, who has to helplessly watch as the younger man's mind deteriorates due to a blood clot. Don MacGregor became the new writer -- with George Tuska temporarily back on pencils -- with the next issue, beginning a story arc concerning the bug-like hit man Cockroach Hamilton, his boss, Piranha Jones, who has pointy, sharpened, stainless steel teeth, and a chemical company president named Charlton Grundge who's planning to move a convoy of a dangerous substance through the streets of Manhattan [PM 28 - 31]. Cage winds up bolted to either side of a toll bridge by Cockroach just as a boat is coming down the river, but manages to break free before he can be snapped in half. PM 31 has an especially vivid cover showing Piranha Jones, teeth poised to bite, forcing Cage down into a tank filled with hungry, man-eating fish. Cockroach and Piranha were two of the more colorful and interesting of Cage's rogue's gallery. (A fill-in issue during this arc also introduced a grotesque mutated villain called Mr. Fish.)

Despite some stilted moments *Power Man* 32 is a powerful story wherein Cage tries to protect a black family who have moved into a white neighborhood and are being terrorized by a flame-wielding racist who calls himself Wildfire. The villain is a neighbor who can't deal with all the social progress of the period and is therefore threatened and intimidated by it. While some of Cage's foes were at least casual racists, or at least made ugly remarks because he was their opponent, Wildfire was the first opponent whose very motivation was hatred of blacks or indeed of anyone different. Wildfire's actions result in the death of a child and PM 33 has a beautifully handled funeral sequence. MacGregor followed this up with a three-part story in which two brothers named Spear and the Mangler try to kill Noah Burstein because they blame him for the death of a third sibling during an experiment in prison.

During and after MacGregor's well-received run on the book there were a variety of writers and artists on the series, including Frank Robbins, Marie Severin, Bill Mantlo, Bob Brown, and Marv Wolfman. There was also a *Power Man Annual* 1, by the creative team of writer Chris Claremont and golden age artist Lee Elias, who eventually worked on the regular book. This exciting James Bond-type story has Cage in Japan playing bodyguard for a pretty volcanologist who is targeted for assassination by some unknown group, and at the same time is kidnaped by Moses Magnum AKA Magnum Force, whose manic desire to tap the earth's core for its wealth may bring about world-wide catastrophe. At one point Magnum throws Luke out of a plane and only his super-strong body prevents his death as he rolls down snow-covered mountain tops and eventually splashes into the ocean.

Power Man 41 - 42 introduced a new black super-hero/vigilante called Thunderbolt, who has super-speed powers due to a freak lightning accident (and other complications) a la Flash. In real life he is an assistant D.A. whose younger brother was killed by a hit man. Tbolt and Power Man battle a greedy baddie named the Goldbug who flies around in a specially-designed ship like DC's Blue Beetle. But a bigger menace to Luke is a man named Sneagle from the IRS, who wants to know why he hasn't paid any taxes for years. Luke has managed to evade the

questions of a cop named Quentin Chase as to his social security number, but he knew if the IRS did a major investigation the
jig was up about his past.

Luke decides to go on the lam and leave New York -- and
Claire and Noah -- and head for Chicago, where he takes the
name Marc Lucas and once again encounters Colonel Gideon
Mace. Mace holds the city hostage with a cobalt bomb, and his
battle with Luke was stretched over four issues. *Power Man* 46
was an exciting, nail-biting story in which he has to deal with
a crazy, jealous sniper and a conflagration in an apartment
house that threatens a sweet old lady along with the threat of
the bomb. Luke becomes friends with Burgundy, a woman who
had once worked with Mace because she wrongly believes he
had tried to save her late husband's life in Viet Nam.

And then the martial arts hero Iron Fist (see chapter 12) entered Luke's life in a big way .

Power Man and Iron Fist

Iron Fist first entered the strip in *Power Man* 48, when John
Bushmaster kidnaps Claire Temple and Noah Burstein to force
Cage to go after Misty Knight, who had gotten close to Bushmaster -- and betrayed him -- as part of an undercover operation. After battling Iron Fist to a standstill, Cage tells him and
Misty the desperate situation he's in, and they all go to free
Bushmaster's prisoners. Bushmaster has forced Burstein to
turn him into a second Power Man, but an explosion - which
only Luke seems to survive - cuts short their battle. Better still,
one of Bushmaster's confederates gives Luke evidence that he
had been framed.

In *Power Man* 50 Luke agrees to join Misty and Colleen in
their investigating group Nightwing Restorations, and Claire
Temple bids him farewell; she just can't deal with her boyfriend's violent lifestyle and the constant danger he is in -- as if
to prove her point, Stiletto and Discus invade the celebration
over Luke's exoneration. It doesn't take Cage too long to find a
new honey, a self-absorbed beauty named Harmony Young.

John Byrne had been drawing the series but he left to concentrate on *The X-Men*; the strip had a number of other artists, including Mike Zeck and Sal Buscema. Then Claremont left and was replaced by Ed Hannigan. The first story arc involved the Teenage Black Genius Villainess, Nightshade, who has put together a group of super-androids in an attempt to take over the rackets. Danny and Joy Meachum come to an understanding, with Danny giving her full control of his share of Rand-Meachum until he feels he has earned it (but only a couple of issues later he still has a sizable fortune). Then he and Luke go into business together as "Heroes for Hire;" Luke resigns from Nightwing Restorations while Misty and Colleen become supporting players in *The X-Men*.

The new creative team of Ed Hannigan and Lee Elias only lasted two issues, then it was announced that the series would have another new team and yet another new direction. Mary Jo Duffy became the new writer while Trevon von Eeden did the pencils beginning with *Power Man 56*. There were no major concept changes, although Duffy did focus more than before on the financial disparity between struggling Luke and wealthy Danny. The first two-parter had our boys guarding Egyptian treasures in a museum and encountering silver age X-Men foe, Professor Abdul, The Living Monolith, who can grow into a giant. In an unintentionally amusing sequence the boys go to Abdul's apartment and find him waiting inside, already grown into the gargantuan monolith -- his apartment had to have the highest ceilings in all of New York City! The X-Men help deal with their old antagonist, who seems more silly than threatening this time out even if he grows nearly as big as a skyscraper.

Power Man 59 - 60 brought back ex-terrorist Alan Cavanaugh, who became chief suspect when an exclusive rooftop restaurant is fire-bombed. When Danny, who is dining with Colleen and Misty, sees Alan, he stupidly invites him to their table in spite of the fact that he and Misty already broke up once over his friendship with the former I.R.A. man; Alan wisely declines. When Alan risks his life to save Iron Fist and others,

Misty saves his life as well. The series never really dealt in an intelligent way with Cavanaugh. When he first appears he claims that he never set bombs to actually kill anyone (sure!) and that one of his bombs "misfired," killing twelve people -- mostly women and children (and forever altering the lives of their loved ones). He spent some time in jail but the "British could never prove anything and they had to let me go." The question that he, Iron Fist, and the writers of the series never answer is that if Cavanaugh is so sorry for his actions, yearning for atonement, why didn't he just confess and serve out his sentence? Instead at the end of PM 60 he goes off to see the world, something his 12 dead victims could never do. As some readers of the series complained, terrorists of any stripe rarely feel sorry for their victims. Cavanaugh was nothing but a cartoon terrorist who could only exist in a comic book.

Kerry Gammill became regular artist for *Power Man* beginning with issue 61, and while his work had a certain flair to it, it also left much to be desired at first. Luke's film-loving pal, D.W., was hurt in an explosion, but as the character never seemed like a real, dimensional person the incident had little impact. Jeryn Howarth and his employee Jennie Royce - executive secretary for Heroes for Hire - were much more interesting. In PM 65 Howarth discovers that half of his all-babe security force are criminals out to steal him blind, and Jennie -- "the only woman you've ever hired who isn't at least an 8," as she puts it -- saves his life by clobbering one of the women with a valuable piece of art. The guest-star for the issue was El Aguila, the Zorro-like good guy/bad guy who gives the breathless Ms. Royce a big smooch at the end. The amusing story was a far cry from the more intense tales that had once appeared in both *Power Man* and *Iron Fist*.

Both writer Duffy and artist Gammill seemed to start hitting their stride with *Power Man* 67 - 68, in which the boys deal with John Bushmaster, who's kidnaped Noah Burstein's new wife to force the doctor to remove Luke's powers. That he succeeds in doing just as Arthur Nagan, the "headman" Luke had battled in

The Defenders, comes looking for revenge. Luckily the power loss is only temporary, and both Nagan and Bushmaster are dealt with; Bushmaster turns to metal and falls to pieces. In a very entertaining story in PM 71, the boys come into conflict with a ultra-confident character named Montenegro, who is completely unimpressed by them and almost defeats them on his lonesome. Montenegro is after a coin which contains an electronics damper that instantly shuts off any kind of machinery. His associates resemble Peter Lorre, Sidney Greenstreet, and Humphrey Bogart from the film "The Maltese Falcon," not the only time these characters were re-interpreted for comics.

Power Man 75 brought Iron Fist -- with Luke along for the ride -- back to the city of K'un-Lun, where they come afoul not only of Master Khan and his Ninja, but "Uncle" Yu-Ti, who, it turns out, has always been working for Khan. Danny learns that his father accidentally stumbled upon K'un-Lun and he was adopted by jealous Yu-Ti's father as repayment for saving their lives. Danny also discovers that he had a sister who was killed by the plant people and who are enemies of the residents of K'un-Lun. In this special double-sized issue, our heroes participate in a war against the plant people, but are sickened by the fact that the K'un-Lun warriors even kill helpless children and old people of the vegetable race, known as the Hylthri. K'un-Lun is also an incredibly misogynous city where woman are considered less than nothing. At the story's end, Danny turns his back on the city forever and returns with Luke to New York and his true friends (although it wasn't until the copper age and after the end of the series that readers learned this wasn't the real Danny).

Power Man 77 had a crazy, comical tale set in the ballet milieu in which our boys -- aided by Daredevil -- must protect a couple of Russian dancers from a duo known as Boris and Ninotchka. An on-stage battle naturally turns the new ballet into a hit with the startled audience. This whimsical approach didn't always work, however, such as a Doctor Who-inspired tale in PM

79 which has other-dimensional robots causing havoc back-stage at a play. PM 84, in which the fellows have a rematch with Sabretooth and his partner, the Constrictor, after the former attacks Cage's girlfriend Harmony (thinking she's Misty Knight), was an improvement, but oddly not as entertaining as the following issue in which the boys tackle Marvel's oldest villain, the Moleman. This story, written by Denny O'Neill, was well-served by Keith Pollard's pencils.

Denny O'Neill and Denys Cowan became the regular creative team with *Power Man* 86, an exciting story in which the guys are hired to protect a drugged-up rock star as he travels cross country in a train, only it turns out that there's a lot more going on than the heroes realize. This story had a few good twists even though the villain, Goldeneye, wasn't that memorable. O'Neill's script underlined the difference between wealthy Danny's bleeding heart liberalism and hard-luck Cage's more practical and realistic -- if unsympathetic -- attitude.

O'Neill in general brought the series back down to Earth, eschewing the whimsy and humor for stories with a harder edge. There was no sign of insouciant Bob Diamond, a one-dimensional supporting character, Oscar-winning movie star, and martial arts champion who'd never seemed remotely like a real person. O'Neill also brought back old villains Scimitar and Black Mariah -- the latter not seen since *Hero for Hire* 5 -- as they teamed up to deal a deadly recreational drug that was killing its young users in *Power Man* 88. Cage finally had another major slug-fest with the massive Mariah. In that same issue his pal "D.W." -- depressed at his aimless life and stalled ambitions -- came more to life as a character than he had in the previous 87 issues!

Kurt Busiek then replaced O'Neill, and Ernie Chan took over from Cowan. Busiek's first story was a good one in which the heroes, working together, manage to come up with a way to outwit and defeat silver age X-Men foe Unus, the Untouchable, whose powerful force field ostensibly protects him from being touched by anyone, let alone punched [PM 90]. Then there was an entertaining two-parter which introduced a new, nervous but dangerous Chemistro who temporarily changes Colleen Wing and Bob Diamond -- whom Busiek brought back, unfortunately -- to glass.

Busiek gave Danny a suspect, late-in-coming identity crisis over learning that Master Kahn controlled K'un-Lun. A more realistic development was the way street people in Times Square turn against Cage because they see him as some kind of super-cop. This leads to Cage leaving 42nd street in anger until he sees an elderly woman about to be mugged and realizes he is still needed by good people in the area. In the meantime, Iron Fist has his hands full with a mysterious, bloodthirsty wolf-woman from K'un-Lun named Fera, while D. W. follows the boys around for a documentary he is making on Heroes for Hire, Inc. Ward Meachum gets back into the action as a stooge for Master Kahn, whose manipulations are all directed at bringing him to Earth's dimension for the special double-sized 100th issue. Alas, Kahn remained an utterly one-dimensional and lackluster villain and the story, although not without action, was a disappointment because of it. *Power Man* 100 was the last issue of the bronze age.

Power Man and Iron Fist also appeared in other Marvel comics, sometimes together, sometimes not. *Marvel Team-Up* 75 presents a creditable tale in which Power Man and Spider-Man tackle a gang who set fire to buildings, a story which was also a tribute to "New York's Bravest," the city's firefighters [Claremont/Macchio/Byrne/Gordon]. Spider-Man feels an affection and kinship with Luke because he thinks the two men are both loners; ironically, it was around this time that Cage teamed up with Iron Fist. Power Man teamed with the Thing for *Marvel Two-in-One* 13, in which the two tackle "Braggadoom, the Mountain That Walked Like a Man." This homage to the monster comics of the fifties and sixties could have been a disaster, but thanks to an excellent script by Roger Slifer and Len Wein, it was exciting and even had some humanistic touches. The art, by Ron Wilson and Vince Colletta, features a great two-page spread depicting the 300-foot Braggadoom tearing apart a suspension bridge. Power Man also appeared in a team-up with the Son of Satan in MTU 126 in an interesting tale in which Luke tries to help an old friend who's fallen on hard times but doesn't reckon on the man's susceptibility to desperation and evil. [DeMatteis/Hall/Esposito].

Power Man and Iron Fist teamed up with the Hulk in the vastly entertaining *Marvel Team-Up Annual* 3 [Stren/Trimpe]. In this the wily young villainess Nightshade actually manages to convince the Hulk to steal a computer circuit from the Rand-Meachum corporation, a circuit that is being transported in a train guarded by Luke and Danny; Machine Man also gets into the action. A subsequent team up with the Hulk in MTU 105 was less successful. PM and IF also guest-starred with the Thing in *Marvel Two-in-One* 94. In this Luke and Danny are hired to find a disillusioned millionaire who only wants to be left alone and get away from the "advisers" who have corrupted his life and work, but when they try to take him to these people, their employers, the Thing mightily objects and a battle royale ensues [Kraft/Wilson/Villamonte]. Lastly PM and IF were featured - along with extra guest-stars Daredevil and Moonknight—in MTU Annual 4, in which the Kingpin tries to kill off our heroes using the power of the Purple Man. The plot was clever even if Frank Miller's script could have used a little work.

AFTERWORD

AUTHOR'S NOTE

NOTE: VOLUME TWO of this book, entitled **SUPERHEROIC: THE BRONZE AGE OF COMICS VOLUME TWO**, is now available in both kindle and trade paperback formats. This new volume covers Superman; Jack Kirby's Fourth World (*New Gods, Forever People, Mr. Miracle*); the Fantastic Four; She-Hulk, Spider-Woman; Captain America, Daredevil ; Iron Man; Green Lantern; the Defenders; Firestorm; Nova, Ka-Zar; and many, many others from Marvel, DC and other publishers.

ABOUT THE AUTHOR

William Schoell

WILLIAM SCHOELL is the author of several horror-suspense novels in addition to biographies and books on the performing arts and popular culture.

BOOKS IN THIS SERIES

THE BRONZE AGE OF COMICS

A look back at super-hero comics books published approximately from 1970 to 1983 published in two volumes.

Superhuman: The Bronze Age Of Comics Volume One

Superheroic: The Bronze Age Of Comics Volume Two

The author examines such titles as Captain America, Fantastic Four, Superman, World's Finest, DC Comics Presents, The Defenders, Green Lantern, Iron Man, Incredible Hulk and many, many others.

BOOKS BY THIS AUTHOR

The Horror Comics: Fiends, Freaks And Fantastic Creatures

From the Golden Age of the 1940s, through the Silver Age of the '60s, up until the early '80s--the end of the Bronze Age. Included are the earliest series, like American Comics Group's Adventures into the Unknown and Prize Comics' Frankenstein, and the controversial and gory comics of the '40s, such as EC's infamous and influential Tales from the Crypt. The resurgence of monster-horror titles during the '60s is explored, along with the return of horror anthologies like Dell Comics' Ghost Stories and Charlton's Ghostly Tales from the Haunted House. The explosion of horror titles following the relaxation of the comics code in the '70s is fully documented with chapters on Marvel's prodigious output--The Tomb of Dracula, Werewolf by Night and others--DC's anthologies--Witching Hour and Ghosts--and titles such as Swamp Thing, as well as the notable contributions of firms like Gold Key and Atlas. This book examines how horror comics exploited everyday terrors, and often reflected societal attitudes toward women and people who were different.

The Silver Age Of Comics

A colorful, in-depth look at comic books published during the silver age from 1956 - 1969, looking at Batman, Superman, Justice League, Avengers, X-Men, Doom Patrol, Green Lantern, the Hulk, Iron Man, and many many others.

Made in the USA
Middletown, DE
23 February 2022

61710124R00215